"**The appearance of this exceptional new book** is something of an historical event. It is undoubtedly one of the most exciting books on Chinese medicine yet to appear in English."
— *The Journal of Chinese Medicine*

"A true American book on traditional Chinese medicine has finally been written. Dr. Kaptchuk's concluding chapter is extremely thought-provoking and deserves careful attention from practitioners of both medicines, Eastern and Western."
— *American Journal of Acupuncture*

"Ted Kaptchuk's book [has] something for practically everyone. . . . Kaptchuk, himself an extraordinary combination of elements, is a thinker whose writing is more accessible than that of Joseph Needham or Manfred Porkert with no less scholarship. There is more here to think about, chew over, ponder or reflect upon than you are liable to find elsewhere. . . . This may sound like a rave review: it is."
— *Journal of Traditional Acupuncture*

"THE WEB THAT HAS NO WEAVER is an encyclopedia of how to tell from the Eastern perspective 'what is wrong.'"
— Larry Dossey, author of *Space, Time, and Medicine*

"Valuable as a compendium of traditional Chinese medical doctrine."
— Joseph Needham, author of *Science and Civilization in China*

"The only approximation for authenticity is *The Barefoot Doctor's Manual*, and this will take readers much further." — *The Kirkus Reviews*

"A very ambitious and singular undertaking. . . . Although the work is explicitly detailed, it is readable and does not require previous knowledge of Chinese thought or language." — *Library Journal*

"Dr. Kaptchuk has become a lyricist for the art of healing. And the more he tells us about traditional Chinese medicine, the more clearly we see the link between philosophy, art, and the physician's craft."
— *Houston Chronicle*

MD Magazine interviews the author of "a book that goes beyond acupuncture to reveal the mysteries of Chinese medicine and the civilization that gave it birth":

Why did you write *The Web That Has No Weaver*?
There is a tendency in the West either to overvalue traditional Chinese medicine because it is holistic and spiritual or to dismiss it as mere hocus-pocus. Both views are barriers to a genuine understanding, barriers I hope this book will break down.

How would you describe Chinese medicine?
Chinese medicine is a prescientific system of thought and practice developed over thousands of years. It is a form of logical, rational thinking alien to the West because it is deeply rooted in a philosophy that has developed its own perception of the body, health, and disease.

For example, Chinese theory does not include the concept of the nervous system, yet it treats neurologic disorders. Nor does it recognize *Streptococcus pneumoniae* as a pathologic cause of pneumonia, yet it can effectively treat the disease....Although Western medicine does not recognize what the Chinese describe as "dampness of the spleen" as a specific disease, it does treat similar disorders of the spleen. In other words, the vocabulary of the two traditions reflects two different worlds, but both can heal the same patient.

TED J. KAPTCHUK earned his Bachelor of Arts degree from Columbia University and his doctorate in Oriental Medicine from the Macau Institute of Chinese Medicine in 1975. Now director of the Pain and Stress Relief Clinic of the Lemuel Shattuck Hospital in Boston, he also lectures around the world.

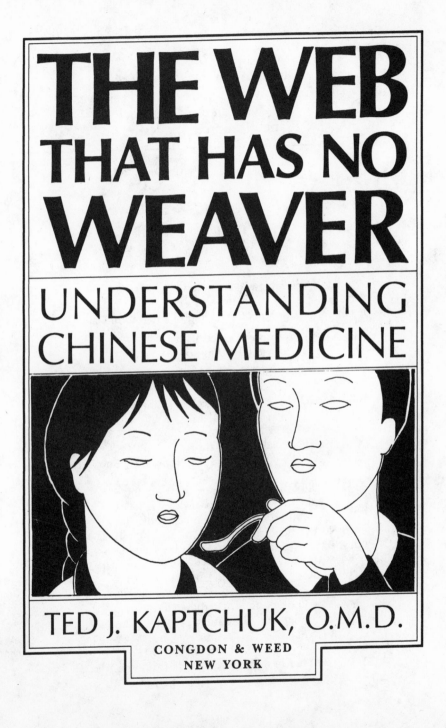

THE WEB THAT HAS NO WEAVER

UNDERSTANDING CHINESE MEDICINE

TED J. KAPTCHUK, O.M.D.

CONGDON & WEED
NEW YORK

Dedicated to the memory of
Ted Gold, my grandparents, and relatives
who died for the
Sanctification of the Name

Copyright © 1983 by Ted J. Kaptchuk

Library of Congress Cataloging in Publication Data

Kaptchuk, Ted J., 1947–
The web that has no weaver.

Bibliography: p. 366
Includes Index.
1. Medicine, Chinese. 2. Medicine, Chinese—Philosophy.
I. Title.
R601.K36   610'.951   82-2511
ISBN 0-86553-109-9 (pbk.)   AACR2
ISBN 0-8092-2933-1Z (Contemporary Books, Inc.: pbk.)

Published by Congdon & Weed, Inc.
298 Fifth Avenue, New York, N.Y. 10001
Distributed by Contemporary Books, Inc.
180 North Michigan Avenue, Chicago, Illinois 60601
Published simultaneously in Canada by Beaverbooks, Ltd.
195 Allstate Parkway, Valleywood Business Park
Markham, Ontario L3R 4T8 Canada

Book design by Barbara Huntley
Cover design and illustration by Jackie Schuman

Acknowledgments

MICHAEL STEINLAUF, my oldest friend, who took a series of garbled lectures and made them intelligible. Without Michael's literary help this manuscript might just as well have stayed in Chinese. ✢ HARVEY BLUME, my oldest comrade, whose poetic and philosophic illuminations are scattered throughout this book. His imprint is especially evident in the remarks on Hegel and Aristotle. ✢ DAN BENSKY, my classmate in Macao, who shared my studies and contributed invaluable ideas, writing, and criticism to this manuscript. ✢ STEVE J. BENNETT, freelance scholar and writer, who helped to clarify the ideas and prose of this manuscript. ✢ MARGARET CAUDILL, my constant medical mentor and collaborator, who provided criticism and stability. ✢ GRETCHEN SALISBURY, for being my editor, and for the enormous work she did to get this book into shape. ✢ RANDY BAROLET, my teaching colleague, who helped with the writing. ✢ LIZ COFFIN, JUNE NUSSER, and KENDRA CROSSEN for patient editing and rewriting. ✢ BARBARA HUNTLEY, who, by her design, transformed an unconventional manuscript into a book. ✢ SATYA AMBROSE for the illustrations. ✢ NATALIA MUINA for editorial assistance, and the Jing that helped me to get through the writing of this volume. ✢ FRANCESCA LOPORTO for criticism and the gift of Spirit. ✢ KIIKO MATSUMOTO for scholarly archeology in pre-Tang-dynasty texts. ✢ ANDY GAMBLE, MARIA TADD, and JON

ACKNOWLEDGMENTS

KORITZ for help with idea development. ✢ PAUL and ANDY EPSTEIN for help with writing. ✢ PAUL PARKER and MARK EPSTEIN for criticism and writing. ✢ NOAH WEINBERG for help in getting down to basics and lighting fires. ✢ JONATHAN LIEFF for spiritual and medical advice. ✢ WENDY POMERANTZ for editorial assistance. ✢ FRED KLARER and KEN DEWOSKIN for translation suggestions. ✢ NANCY TRICHTER for being my literary agent and a source of constant encouragement. ✢ CODY for being Cody. ✢ LIEB SCHEINER, E. V. WALTER, and STEVEN KLARER for research assistance. ✢ MARSHA WOOLF, JOYCE SINGER, SAVITRI CLARK, PAUL SHULMAN, RICHARD MICHAEL ZUCKER, WALTER TORDA, CHOU MAN-XING, SEKYO NAM, MARTHA KATZ, LIU YUN-HUA, GIOVANNI MACIOCIA, ELLEN PEARLMAN, JANET GENERALLI, and SUSAN ZIMELIS for support. ✢ The FRIENDS, ACUPUNCTURISTS, MEDICAL DOCTORS, OSTEOPATHS, THERAPISTS, HEALERS, and STUDENTS who attended my lectures in England and Australia and asked the many questions that helped to focus this volume. ✢ The STUDENTS, FACULTY, and ADMINISTRATION of the New England School of Acupuncture, who provided an environment for writing and teaching. ✢ MY TEACHERS of the traditional medicine of China, who gave so unselfishly, especially YU JIN-NIANG, XIE ZHANG-CAI, LING LING-XIAN, CHEN YI-QING, and YUAN BAIN-HONG. ✢ MY PATIENTS, who taught me so much, especially that the effort of writing this volume was more than literary or scholarly. ✢ My adoptive godmother, LAM PUI-YIN, whose pureness kept me going physically and spiritually during hard times in medical school. ✢ MY PARENTS and SISTER, whose love is always with me.

Foreword

Early in the 1970s, in the wake of a new politically sanctioned exchange of information between China and the United States, there appeared in the press a number of anecdotal descriptions of surgery without anesthesia being performed in China. A technique called acupuncture was used, whereby slender needles pierced the skin at predetermined foci on the body, the patient being fully awake during the procedure but not feeling the scalpel. Over the next several years this ancient technique of acupuncture enjoyed a brief surge of popularity in the United States, where it was touted by some as a new method to induce analgesia, indeed, as the long-awaited panacea from the Orient. This sudden enthusiasm was quickly followed by a backlash within the medical establishment, which, unable to obtain "scientific proof" of claims made by acupuncture proponents, was ready to abandon it and to forbid its practice in the United States. This attempt was unsuccessful, however, and investigations of the possible application of acupuncture to Western medicine have continued. The evidence now indicates that acupuncture can induce analgesia and that its use is associated with measurable physiological changes (see Chapter 4, note 11). Recent medical reviews show that acupuncture is slowly beginning to be integrated into certain areas of Western medicine (*Annals of Internal Medicine* 93 [1980]:588; *Psychology Today* 14 [1980]:81).

Although acupuncture itself has gained some acceptance, the Western medical and scientific community has never considered seriously the medical tradition and culture from which this technique sprang. As if a full understanding of acupuncture were encompassed by knowing where to stick the needles! This absurdity is compounded by the fact that the idea of isolating a part from its natural environment for investigation is antithetical to the philosophy and culture of the Chinese medical tradition. There may well be inaccuracies, biases, and misrepresentations that have grown up around the acupuncture tradition over the centuries. But any meaningful discussion of acupuncture and its applicability requires more information than has heretofore been presented.

The problem does not lie entirely with the medical and scientific establishment. Almost none of the traditional Chinese medical texts are available in English, and those that are available make little or no attempt to present the cultural medical tradition *in toto*. Even translated works pose the problem of a completely unfamiliar approach to disease and a foreign terminology. Only someone familiar with the Chinese language, naturalist and Taoist philosophy, and with Chinese culture as it has been influenced by these philosophies, would be able to comprehend the Chinese medical tradition.

The chapters to follow begin an important exposition of the ancient art of Chinese medicine in terms that can be understood by a Western audience. The author has deftly avoided, as much as possible, the pitfall of interpreting Chinese theory through Western terminology, thereby leaving the central Chinese concept of medical patterns and disharmonies undisturbed.

A word of caution to those who would judge the images and vocabulary as inconsequential or as the babblings of a primitive society because of their own lack of familiarity with the terms: For thousands of years the Chinese have observed life processes and relationships between man and his environment. From this observation, the art of Chinese medicine has developed vocabulary to describe myriad subtle body patterns, a method of description not available to Western medicine because of its emphasis on disease states. The Chinese approach is a more holistic consideration of health and disease and of the delicate interplay between these opposing forces.

In a time of increased awareness of environment, health, and the personal responsibility of mankind, it seems that an integration of East and West should be mutually beneficial. Dr. Kaptchuk has attempted a most difficult job, to begin bridging the gap by making available this critical and timely exposition to those who wish to understand the art of medicine from a different viewpoint. Indeed, the web may have found its weaver.

MARGARET A. CAUDILL, M.D., Ph.D.
Research Fellow in Medicine,
Harvard Medical School, Division
of Behavioral Medicine, Beth
Israel Hospital, Boston

Contents

Author's Note

Certain translated terms that I use in this book have connotations for Chinese medicine that are quite different from what is ordinarily expected in English. For example, the Spleen of Chinese medicine is different from the spleen recognized in the West. I have capitalized such English words to account for the special meaning rather than overwhelm the reader with Chinese terminology. Only a few terms for which there are no adequate English equivalents are regularly referred to in romanized Chinese.

Romanization generally follows the Pinyin system used in the People's Republic of China and now being accepted throughout the world. (A pronunciation guide appears on page xvii.) However, the more conventional spellings are retained for a few familiar terms and names.

Chinese characters are sometimes given in addition to romanized or translated terms, for two reasons. First, Chinese words can often be romanized and translated in so many different ways that ultimately only the character form remains a reliable means of identification. Second, the pronunciation of many characters is identical; for example, the character *shen* that means Spirit is different from the *shen* that means Kidney. Presenting the character serves to make such distinctions clear.

Consideration for those uninitiated into the Chinese language has especially guided the preparation of the notes and the Chinese bibliography. To make the reference notes appear less forbidding, I have cited each Chinese work in short form, with its title in English translation (set in Roman type). In the case of book citations, a bracketed number corresponds to a numbered entry in the Selected Bibliography.

The Chinese sources in the Selected Bibliography are arranged as a kind of catalogue of medical literature that may interest readers even if they are unlikely ever to consult a publication in Chinese. They are divided into eight sections: *Nei Jing* and *Nan Jing* and commentaries; other classical sources; reference books; contemporary introductory texts used to train traditional physicians; contemporary writings; miscellaneous sources (including specialty titles); sources on the history of Chinese medicine; and journals. Titles are given first in English translation, then in Chinese (the same is true of the annotated Historical Bibliography in Appendix I).

The reader is encouraged to browse through the rather extensive notes to each chapter, which contain some interesting digressions from the main text.

The Pinyin Phonetic Alphabet

The following table shows pronunciations with approximate English equivalents. In parentheses are the corresponding letters in the Wade-Giles system.

a (a) as in *far*
b (p) as in *be*
c (ts', tz') like *ts* in *its*
ch (ch) as in *church*, strongly aspirated
d (t) as in *door*
e (e) as in *her*
f (f) as in *fit*
g (k) as in *go*
h (h) as in *her*, strongly aspirated
i (i) like the vowel sound in *eat* or the *i* in *sir*
j (ch) as in *jeep*
k (k') as in *kite*, strongly aspirated
l (l) as in *last*
m (m) as in *me*
n (n) as in *no*
o (o) like the vowel sound in *paw*
p (p') as in *park*, strongly aspirated
q (ch') like the *ch* in *cheat*
r (j) as in *red* or like the *z* in *azure*

s (s, ss, sz) as in *sister*

sh (sh) as in *shine*

t (t') as in *ton*, strongly aspirated

u (u) as in *too*; also in the French *tu*

v (v) used only to produce foreign words, national minority words, and local dialects

w (w) semi-vowel in syllables beginning with *u* when not preceded by consonants, pronounced as in *want*

x (hs) like *sh* in *sheet*

y semi-vowel in syllables beginning with *i* or *u* when not preceded by consonants, pronounced as in *yes*

z (ts, tz) as in *zone*

zh (ch) like the first consonant in *jump*

ai like *ie* in *tie*

ao like *ow* in *how*

ei like *ay* in *bay*

ie like *ie* in *experience*

ou like *oe* in *toe*

Introduction

The vast conceptual gulf separating Chinese and Western medicine first struck me ten years ago when I was a student of traditional Chinese medicine in Macao. I was in a dermatology class. One of my Chinese teachers was discussing the disease known in the West as herpes zoster or shingles, a painful and acute viral infection characterized by vesicular eruptions along the nerves on the trunk of the body or the face. Dr. Yu began to describe how an eruption on the face indicated a different disease process than did an eruption on the trunk. I raised my hand and asked incredulously how two identical eruptions (identical from the Western viewpoint and hence my own) could signify different disease processes simply because of their location. My teacher, amused by my confusion, smiled and explained that an eruption appearing on the face was different from an eruption on the lower trunk because its relationship to the entire body was different. From my Western view, the two manifestations of shingles were the same in and of themselves; but the Chinese view demanded another perspective—*seeing the relationship of the symptom to the whole body.* That day in class posed a basic dilemma for me: How could both systems of medicine be clinically effective, claim to be rational, and yet be so different?

When I returned to the United States, I thought at first that the system of medicine I had learned in China was so foreign, so inexplicable, that I should abandon it and study at an American medical school. But I soon discovered that there was a need for the information I had brought back, a demand for greater knowledge about the Chinese system of healing. Despite its strangeness—or perhaps because of its aura of mystery—people were willing to try it, most often as a last resort, but sometimes even as a first alternative. I also knew my training itself was valuable—it worked; I could help Westerners with it. And so I began to teach and to operate a private practice. I later encountered mainstream medical interest in the Chinese healing art and was invited to work in various hospitals. I now find myself director of a pain clinic in the Boston area's largest chronic-disease hospital.

I had also planned to do a series of translations of traditional Chinese medical texts, directed to the professional community. But as a result of my teaching experience, I gradually gave up that notion. It was not enough to present the Chinese words in English. To make them intelligible to a Westerner I had to try to present the whole Chinese medical system in its cultural context—to translate not just the words, but the ideas behind the words, so that the words could be interpreted properly and understood. I realized that the material I had intended to translate for my first volume was more than just the groundwork of a medical corpus. It presented a frame of reference entirely different from our own, an approach to health and disease, to reality and the altering of reality, completely foreign to the West. The material itself raised larger questions for a wider audience, and I determined to write a book addressed to that audience as well—general readers who would like to understand and learn from the ancient traditions of the Orient.

Although it is so little known in the West, the Chinese system of healing is a vital medical approach. It is not likely to be overthrown by Western medicine, and it has its own strong claim on the future. Yet because Chinese and Western medicine exist simultaneously, and because their philosophies and methods are so different, they provide implicit criticism of each other.

I have found the very existence of these two distinct and incompatible paradigms in the world of medicine both exciting and disturbing. As a result of this tension, I have come to believe that an introductory work on Chinese medicine must grapple with the questions a Westerner is likely to ask when he or she encounters the Chinese medical world-view. Simply translating texts into English would have avoided this dialogue; I have chosen instead to engage in it. And so this book is both a presentation of Chinese medicine and a commentary on it, by a Westerner committed to a Western perspective who also knows China and is a practitioner of China's medicine.

I should note that at times it was a very great problem to explain Chinese concepts with a Western vocabulary. I have tried, but there are still some difficult sections. Where the reader encounters such difficulties, in most cases it's best just to read on; greater familiarity with the material and hence with the thought process behind it will bring the reward of greater clarity.

As the first systematic exposition in English of the principles of Chinese medicine, this book should be of value to all students of medicine and healing. And because it also examines the medical and scientific thought of another culture, I hope it will interest many others in the Chinese way of healing.

One more personal note. One reason I had for leaving the States at the end of the sixties was a desire to reject what I thought was ordinary and to search for the miraculous. I was part of the twentieth century's "journey to the East." One of the important lessons I learned was that much of what we think is extraordinary in another place is just the ordinary not understood or experienced. I hope that besides making Chinese medicine more accessible to the West, this book will contribute to a deeper understanding and acceptance of the Western point of departure—that it will help reawaken respect for and awe of our own extraordinariness. In many ways my personal journey to the East brought me back to the West.

THE WEB THAT HAS NO WEAVER

A story is told in China about a peasant who had worked as a maintenance man in a newly established Western missionary hospital. When he retired to his remote home village, he took with him some hypodermic needles and lots of antibiotics. He put up a shingle, and whenever someone came to him with a fever, he injected the patient with the wonder drugs. A remarkable percentage of these people got well, despite the fact that this practitioner of Western medicine knew next to nothing about what he was doing. In the West today, much of what passes for Chinese medicine is not very different from the so-called Western medicine practiced by this Chinese peasant. Out of a complex medical system, only the bare essentials of acupuncture technique have reached the West. Patients often get well from such treatment because acupuncture, like Western antibiotics, is strong medicine. But the theoretical depth and full clinical potential of Chinese medicine remain virtually unknown.

As a result, many Westerners have strange notions about Chinese medicine. Some of them see it as hocus-pocus—the product of primitive or magical thinking. If a patient is cured by means of herbs or acupuncture, they see only two possible explanations: Either the cure was psychosomatic, or it was an accident, the happy result of hit-or-miss pin-sticking which the practitioner did not understand. They assume that current Western science and medicine have a unique handle on Truth—all else is superstition.

Other Westerners have a more favorable but equally erroneous view of Chinese medicine. Deeply and often justifiably disturbed by many of the products of Western science and culture, they assume that the Chinese system, because it is felt to be more ancient, more spiritual, or more holistic, is also more "true" than Western medicine. This attitude threatens to turn Chinese medicine from a rational body of knowledge into a religious faith system. Both attitudes mystify the subject—one by arrogantly undervaluing it, the other by setting it on a pedestal. Both are barriers to understanding.

Actually, Chinese medicine is a coherent and independent system of thought and practice that has been developed over two millennia. Based on ancient texts, it is the result of a continuous process of critical thinking, as well as extensive clinical observation and testing. It represents a thorough formulation and reformulation of material by respected clinicians and theoreticians. It is also, however, rooted in the philosophy, logic, sensibility, and habits of a civilization entirely foreign to our own. It has therefore developed its own perception of the body and of health and disease.

Chinese medicine considers important certain aspects of the human body that are not significant to Western medicine. At the same time, Western medicine observes and can describe aspects of the human body that are insignificant or not perceptible to Chinese medicine. For instance, Chinese medical theory does not have the concept of a nervous system. Nevertheless, it has been demonstrated that Chinese medicine can be used to treat neurological disorders.[1] Similarly, Chinese medicine does not perceive an endocrine system, yet it treats what Western medicine calls endocrine disorders.[2] Nor does traditional Chinese medicine recognize *Streptococcus pneumoniae* as a pathological cause of pneumonia, yet often it effectively treats the disease.[3]

Chinese medicine also uses terminology that is strange to the Western ear. For example, the Chinese refer to certain diseases as being generated by "Dampness," "Heat," or "Wind." Modern Western medicine does not recognize Dampness, yet can treat what Chinese medicine describes as Dampness of the Spleen. Modern Western medicine does not speak of Fire, but can, from a Chinese perspective, stoke the Fire of the Kidney or extinguish excess Fire raging out of control in the Lungs. In Western medicine, Wind is not considered a disease factor; yet Western medicine is able to prevent Liver Wind from going to the head, or to extinguish rampaging Wind in the skin. The perceptions of the two traditions reflect two different worlds, but both can heal the same body.

The difference between the two medicines, however, is greater than that between their descriptive language. The actual logical structure underlying the methodology, the habitual mental operations that guide the physician's clinical insight and critical judgment, differs radically in the two traditions. What Michel Foucault says about medical perception in different historical periods could apply as well to these different cultural traditions: "Not only the names of diseases, not only the grouping of systems were not the same; but the fundamental perceptual codes that were applied to patients' bodies, the field of objects to which observation addressed itself, the surfaces and depths traversed by the doctor's gaze, the whole system of orientation of his gaze also varied."[4]

The two different logical structures have pointed the two medicines in different directions. Western medicine is concerned mainly with isolable disease categories or agents of disease, which it zeroes in on, isolates, and tries to change, control, or destroy. The Western physician starts with a symptom, then searches for the underlying mechanism—a precise *cause* for a specific *disease*.[5] The disease may affect various parts of the body, but it is a relatively well-defined, self-contained phenomenon. Precise diagnosis frames an exact, quantifiable description of a narrow area. The physician's logic is analytic—cutting through the accumulation of bodily phenomena like a surgeon's scalpel to isolate one single entity or cause.

The Chinese physician, in contrast, directs his or her attention to the complete physiological and psychological individual. All relevant information, including the symptom as well as the patient's other general characteristics, is gathered and woven together until it forms what Chinese medicine calls a "pattern of disharmony." This pattern of disharmony describes a situation of "imbalance" in a patient's body. Oriental diagnostic technique does not turn up a specific disease entity or a precise cause, but renders an almost poetic, yet workable, description of a whole person. The question of cause and effect is always secondary to the overall pattern. One does not ask, "What X is causing Y?" but rather, "What is the relationship between X and Y?" The Chinese are interested in discerning the relationships among bodily events occurring at the same time. The logic of Chinese medicine is organismic or synthetic, attempting to organize symptoms and signs into understandable configurations. The total configurations, the patterns of disharmony, provide the framework for treatment. The therapy then attempts to bring the configuration into balance, to restore harmony to the individual.

This difference between Western and Eastern perception can be illustrated by portions of recent clinical studies done in hospitals in China.[6] In a typical study a Western physician, using upper-gastrointestinal X-rays or endoscopy by means of a fiberscope, diagnoses six patients with stomach pain as having peptic ulcer disease. From the Western doctor's perspective, based on the analytic tendency to narrow diagnosis to an underlying entity, all these patients suffer from the same disorder. The physician then sends the patients to a Chinese doctor for examination. The following results are found.

Upon questioning and examining the first patient, the Chinese physician finds pain that increases at touch (by palpation) but diminishes with the application of cold compresses. The patient has a robust constitution, a reddish complexion, and a full, deep voice. He seems assertive and even aggressive. He is constipated and has dark yellow urine. His tongue has a greasy yellow coating; his pulse is "full" and "wiry." The Oriental physician characterizes this patient as having the pattern of disharmony called "Damp Heat Affecting the Spleen."

When the Chinese physician examines the second patient, he finds a different set of signs, which comprise another overall pattern. The patient is thin. Her complexion is ashen, though her cheeks are ruddy. She is constantly thirsty, her palms are sweaty, and she has a tendency toward constipation, insomnia, and night sweats. She seems nervous and fidgety. Her tongue is dry and slightly red, with no "moss"; her pulse is "thin" and also a bit "fast." This patient is said to have the pattern of "Deficient Yin Affecting the Stomach," a disharmony very different from that of the first patient. Accordingly, a different treatment would be prescribed.

The third patient reports that massage and heat somewhat alleviate his pain, which is experienced as a minor but persistent discomfort. He is temporarily relieved by eating. The patient fears cold, has a pale face, sweats spontaneously in the daytime, and wants to sleep a lot. His urine is clear and his urination frequent; sometimes he has to get up in the middle of the night to empty his bladder. He appears timid, almost afraid. His tongue is moist and pale, his pulse "empty." The patient's condition is diagnosed as the pattern of "Exhausted Fire of the Middle Burner," sometimes called "Deficient Cold Affecting the Spleen."

The fourth patient complains of very severe cramping pain; his movement and affect is ponderous and heavy. Hot-water bottles relieve the pain, but massaging the abdomen makes it worse. The patient has a bright white face and a tendency toward loose stools. His tongue has an especially thick, white, moist coating; his pulse is "tight" and "slippery." These signs lead to a diagnosis of the pattern of "Excess Cold Dampness Affecting the Spleen and Stomach."

The fifth patient experiences much sour belching and has headaches. Her pain is sharp, and although massaging the abdomen makes it diminish, heat and cold have no effect. She is very moody. Emotional distress, especially anger or melancholy, seems to precipitate attacks of pain; the pain is also worse during menses. Strangely enough, the patient's tongue is normal, but her pulse is particularly "wiry." The physician concludes that she is affected by the pattern of "disharmony of the Liver invading the Spleen."

The sixth patient has an extremely severe stabbing pain in the stomach that sometimes goes around to his back. The pain is much worse after eating and is aggravated by the slightest touch. He has had episodes of vomiting blood, and produces blackish stools. The patient is very thin and has a rather dark complexion. His tongue is a darkish purple and has markedly red eruptions on the sides. His pulse is "choppy." The Chinese physician describes the patient's problem as a "disharmony of Congealed Blood in the Stomach."

So the Chinese doctor, searching for and organizing signs and symptoms that a Western doctor might never heed, distinguishes six patterns of disharmony where Western medicine perceives only one disease. The patterns of disharmony are similar to what the West calls diseases in that their discovery tells the physician how to prescribe treatment. But they are different from diseases because they cannot be isolated from the patient in whom they occur. To Western medicine, understanding an illness means uncovering a distinct entity that is separate from the patient's being; to Chinese medicine, understanding means perceiving the relationships between all the patient's signs and symptoms. When confronted by a patient with stomach pain, the Western physician must look beyond the screen of symptoms for an underlying pathological mechanism—a peptic ulcer in this case, but it could have been an infection or a tumor or a nervous disorder. A Chinese physician examining the same patient must discern a pattern of disharmony made up of the entire accumulation of symptoms and signs.*

The Chinese method is thus holistic, based on the idea that no single part can be understood except in its relation to the whole. A symptom, therefore, is not traced back to a cause, but is looked at as a part of a totality. If a person has a symptom, Chinese medicine wants to know how the symptom fits into the patient's entire bodily pattern. A person who is well, or "in harmony," has no distressing symptoms and expresses mental, physical, and spiritual balance. When that person is ill, the symptom is only one part of a complete bodily imbalance that can be seen in other aspects of his or her life and behavior. Understanding that overall pattern, with the symptom as part of it, is the challenge of Chinese medicine. The Chinese system is not less logical than the Western, just less analytical.[7]

Yin (陰) and Yang (陽) Theory†

The logic underlying Chinese medical theory—a logic which assumes that a part can be understood only in its relation to the whole—can also be called synthetic or dialectical. In Chinese early naturalist and Taoist thought, this dialectical logic that explains relationships, patterns, and change is called Yin-Yang theory.††

---

*From a Western medical viewpoint, the Chinese physician is assessing the patient's specific and general physiological and psychological response to a disease entity.

†The Chinese characters for Yin and Yang are written here in the old style. Other characters in this book are simplified modern characters.

††Although the Chinese identify the relationships between phenomena primarily by the patterns of Yin and Yang, another system of categorization, known as the Five Phases, was also in use in early China. In this system, Wood, Fire, Earth, Metal, and Water were seen as a set of emblems by which all things and events in the universe could be organized. Although the Five Phases categories permeate virtually every aspect of traditional Chinese thought, leaving a significant impression on Chinese medical theory, this influence is for the most part formal and linguistic in nature. The Five Phases proved too mechanical, while Yin-Yang theory, because of its greater flexibility, was much more practical for the Chinese physician. It accommodated clinical changes and theoretical developments that the tradition required in order to grow. (For a detailed discussion of the Five Phases in Chinese medicine, see Appendix H.)

Yin-Yang theory is based on the philosophical construct of two polar complements, called Yin and Yang. These complementary opposites are neither forces nor material entities. Nor are they mythical concepts that transcend rationality. Rather, they are convenient labels used to describe how things function in relation to each other and to the universe. They are used to explain the continuous process of natural change. But Yin and Yang are not only a set of correspondences; they also represent a way of thinking. In this system of thought, all things are seen as parts of a whole. No entity can ever be isolated from its relationship to other entities; no thing can exist in and of itself. There are no absolutes. Yin and Yang must, necessarily, contain within themselves the possibility of opposition and change.

The character for Yin originally meant the shady side of a slope. It is associated with such qualities as cold, rest, responsiveness, passivity, darkness, interiority, downwardness, inwardness, and decrease.

The original meaning of Yang was the sunny side of a slope. The term implies brightness and is part of one common Chinese expression for the sun. Yang is associated with qualities such as heat, stimulation, movement, activity, excitement, vigor, light, exteriority, upwardness, outwardness, and increase.

Working with these ideas, Chinese thought and Chinese medical tradition have developed five principles of Yin and Yang.[8]

All things have two aspects: a Yin aspect and a Yang aspect.

Thus, time can be divided into night and day, place into earth and heaven, season into inactive periods (fall and winter) and active periods (spring and summer), species into female and male, temperature into cold and hot, weight into light and heavy, and so on. Inside and outside, down and up, passive and active, empty and full are all examples of Yin-Yang categories. These qualities are opposites, yet they describe relative aspects of the same phenomena. Yin and Yang qualities exist in relation to each other.

In terms of the body, the front is considered Yin and the back Yang. The upper part of the body is considered more Yang than the lower part; the outer parts of the body (skin, hair, etc.) are more Yang than the inner Organs. The Yin and Yang of the body are often described metaphorically as the body's Water and Fire. Illnesses that are characterized by weakness, slowness, coldness, and underactivity are Yin; illnesses that manifest strength, forceful movements, heat, and overactivity are Yang.

The philosopher Zou Yen (c. 305–240 B.C.E.) describes this idea this way: "Heaven is high, the earth is low, and thus [Heaven and Earth] are fixed. As the high and low are thus made clear, the honorable and humble have their place accordingly. As activity and tranquillity have their constancy, the strong and the weak are thus differentiated. . . . Cold and hot season take their turn. . . . [Heaven] knows the great beginning, and [Earth] acts to bring things to completion. . . . [Heaven] is Yang and [Earth] is Yin."[9]

Any Yin or Yang aspect can be further
divided into Yin and Yang.

This means that within each Yin and Yang category, another Yin and Yang category can be distinguished. It is an extension of the logic that divides all phenomena into Yin and Yang aspects, allowing further division within aspects *ad infinitum*. For example, temperature can be divided into cold (Yin) and hot (Yang), but cold can be divided further into icy cold (Yin) and moderately cold (Yang). In the body, the front of the trunk is Yin compared with the back, but the front can be divided further so that the abdomen is Yin in relation to the chest. Within a Yin illness characterized by Coldness there may be aspects of Yang such as sharp, forceful contractions. Within a Yang illness of Heat and hyperactivity there may be weakness and loss of weight, both Yin qualities.

Chuang Tzu (Zhuang Zi), the Taoist philosopher, (fl. probably between 400 and 300 B.C.E.) describes the unfolding of Yin and Yang, and the notion of the unity of opposites, in a radical paradoxical way: "There is nothing in the world greater than the tip of a hair that grows in the autumn, while Mount Tai is small. No one lives a longer life than a child who dies in infancy, but Peng Zu (who lived many hundred years) died prematurely."[10]

Yin and Yang mutually create each other.

Although Yin and Yang can be distinguished, they cannot be separated. They depend on each other for definition. And the things in which Yin and Yang are distinguished could not be defined without the existence of Yin and Yang qualities. For instance, one cannot speak of temperature apart from its Yin and Yang aspects, cold and heat. Similarly, one could not speak of height unless there were both tallness and shortness. Such opposite aspects depend on and define each other.

Another example might be the relationship between a couple in which one partner can be (relatively) passive only if the other partner is (relatively) aggressive, and vice versa. Passivity and aggression can be measured only in comparison with each other. The activity (Yang) of the body is nourished by its physical form (Yin), and the physical form is created and maintained by the activity of the body. In illness, overactivity has meaning only in relation to a condition of underactivity, and vice versa.

Lao Tzu (Lao Zi), the reputed founder of Taoism, declares in the *Tao-te Ching* (or *Dao-de Jing*—the Classic of the Tao and Its Virtue):

> *Being and non-being produce each other;*
> *Difficult and easy complete each other;*
> *Long and short contrast each other;*
> *High and low distinguish each other;*
> *Sound and voice harmonize each other;*
> *Front and back follow each other.*[11]

Yin and Yang control each other.

If Yin is excessive, then Yang will be too weak, and vice versa. If the temperature is neither too cold nor too hot, then both cold and hot aspects are mutually controlled and held in check.

If it is too cold, then there is not enough heat, and vice versa. Yin and Yang balance each other.

In our example of the couple, the extent to which one partner can be aggressive depends on the extent to which the other is passive, and vice versa. They exert mutual control over each other. An illness of Fire in the body may be due to insufficient Water; an illness of Water may be due to insufficient Fire.

Lao Tzu alludes to this concept when he says:

> *He who stands on tiptoe is not steady.*
> *He who strides forward does not go.*
> *He who shows himself is not luminous.*
> *He who justifies himself is not prominent.*
> *He who boasts of himself is not given credit.*
> *He who brags does not endure for long.*[12]

Yin and Yang transform into each other.

This principle is a formula for the nature of organic process. It suggests two types of transformations: changes that occur harmoniously, in the normal course of events, and the sudden ruptures and transformations characteristic of extremely disharmonious situations.

Because Yin and Yang create each other in even the most stable relationships, Yin and Yang are always subtly transforming into each other. This constant transformation is the source of all change. It is a give-and-take relationship that is life activity itself. In the dynamics of the body, the nature of transformation can be illustrated by the manner in which inhalation is followed by exhalation, or periods of activity and exertion must be succeeded by nourishment and rest. In normal life such regular transformations occur smoothly, maintaining a proper, healthy balance of Yin and Yang in the body.

In a relationship in which Yin and Yang are unbalanced for prolonged periods of time or in an extreme manner, the resulting transformations may be quite drastic. Harmony means that the proportions of Yin and Yang are relatively balanced; disharmony means that the proportions are unequal and there is imbalance. A deficiency of one aspect implies an excess of the other. Extreme disharmony means that the deficiency of one aspect cannot continue to support the excess of another aspect. The resulting change may be rebalancing or, if that is not possible, either the transformation into opposites or the cessation of existence.

To return to the couple, let's assume a disharmonious relationship in which one partner is excessively aggressive and the other excessively passive. This situation can have three possible outcomes: Either they sit down and talk it out, agreeing to a rearrangement of attitudes (i.e., they rebalance their relationship); or one day the passive partner gets fed up and waits for the other with an ax (i.e., a radical transformation of Yin into Yang occurs); or they separate, putting an end to the relationship.

In clinical practice, one of these three kinds of transformation is always possible. For example, when a patient has a pattern with very high fever and much sweating (considered an excess of Yang, or Fire), the patient may be in danger of suddenly going into shock (an extreme Yin, or Cold, condition). This is because Yang cannot continue to exist in such extreme relation to Yin without some transformation occurring. Either a gradual transformation, a rebalancing, must take place—medication and healing; or a radical transformation will occur— shock; or Yin and Yang will separate and existence will cease—death.

Lao Tzu describes the transformation process poetically:

> *In order to contract,*
> *It is necessary first to expand.*
> *In order to weaken,*
> *It is necessary first to strengthen.*
> *In order to destroy,*
> *It is necessary first to promote.*
> *In order to grasp,*
> *It is necessary first to give.*[13]

And also:

> *People hate to be orphaned, the lonely ones, and*
> *the unworthy.*
> *And yet kings and lords call themselves by these*
> *names.*
> *Therefore it is often the case that things gain*
> *by losing and lose by gaining.*[14]

Yin-Yang theory is well illustrated by the traditional Chinese Taoist symbol (Figure 1). The circle representing the whole is divided into Yin (black) and Yang (white).

The small circles of opposite shading illustrate that within the Yin there is Yang and vice versa. The dynamic curve dividing them indicates that Yin and Yang are continuously merging. Thus Yin and Yang create each other, control each other, and transform into each other.

FIGURE 1

Traditional Yin-Yang Symbol

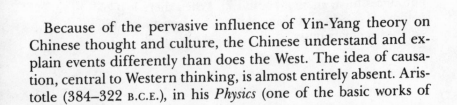

Because of the pervasive influence of Yin-Yang theory on Chinese thought and culture, the Chinese understand and explain events differently than does the West. The idea of causation, central to Western thinking, is almost entirely absent. Aristotle (384–322 B.C.E.), in his *Physics* (one of the basic works of

Western philosophy), pens the archetypal formulation of this Western notion: "Men do not think they know a thing till they have grasped the 'why' of it (which is to grasp its primary cause)."[15] For the Chinese however, phenomena occur independently of an external act of creation, and there is no great need to search for a cause.

> Tao produced the One.
> The One produced the two.
> The two produced the three.
> And the three produced the ten thousand things.
> The ten thousand things carry the Yin and
>   embrace the Yang and through the blending
>   of the Qi* they achieve harmony.[16]

In Chinese thought, events and phenomena unfold through a kind of spontaneous cooperation, an inner dynamic in the nature of things. Wang Cong (c. 27–100 C.E.), the great Taoist scientist, philosopher, and skeptic, describes the inner working of the universe as follows:

The way to Heaven is to take no action. Therefore in the spring it does not act to start life, in summer it does not act to help grow, in autumn it does not act to bring maturity, and in winter it does not act to store up. When the . . . Yang comes forth itself, things naturally come to life and grow. When the . . . Yin arises of itself, things naturally mature and are stored up. . . . Originally no result is sought, and yet results are achieved. . . .

Since Heaven takes no action, it does not speak. When the time comes for calamities and strange transformations, the [Qi] produces them spontaneously. . . . When there is [Cold] in the Stomach, it aches. It is not that man causes it. Rather, the [Qi] does it spontaneously. . . .[17]

Joseph Needham, the great historian of Chinese science,

---

*Qi, often spelled ch'i (or ki in Japanese), is discussed in Chapter 2.

summarizes the Chinese view of causation this way: "Conceptions are not subsumed under one another but placed side by side in a *pattern*, and things influence one another not by acts of mechanical causation, but by a kind of 'inductance'. . . . The key-word in Chinese thought is *Order* and above all *Pattern*. . . . Things behave in particular ways not necessarily because of prior actions or impulsions of other things, but because their position in the ever-moving cyclical universe was such that they were endowed with intrinsic natures which made that behavior inevitable for them. . . . They were thus parts in existential dependence upon the whole world-organism."[18]

The Chinese assume that the universe is continuously changing. Its movement is the result not of a first cause or creator, but of an inner dynamic of cyclical patterns. Just as the sun maps out four distinct seasons in its yearly round, so all biological organisms go through four seasons in a lifetime: birth, maturation, decline, and death. The constancy of the cosmos is in these patterns of change, which are regular. The cosmos itself is an integral whole, a web of interrelated things and events. Within this web of relationships and change, any entity can be defined only by its function, and has significance only as part of the whole pattern.

This metaphysics that emphasizes the perception of patterns is basic to Chinese thinking. It results in part from Taoism, which altogether lacks the idea of a creator, and whose concern is insight into the web of phenomena, not the weaver. For the Chinese, that web has no weaver, no creator; in the West the final concern is always the creator or cause and the phenomenon is merely its reflection. The Western mind seeks to discover and encounter what is beyond, behind, or the cause of phenomena. In the Chinese view, the truth of things is immanent; in the Western, truth is transcendent. Knowledge, within the Chinese framework, consists in the accurate perception of the inner movement of the web of phenomena. The desire for knowledge is the desire to understand the interrelationships or patterns within that web, and to become attuned to the unseen dynamic.

Of Chinese Painters and Chinese Physicians

The arts in China were nourished by the same naturalist and Taoist thought that fed Chinese philosophy and medicine. All Chinese art attempts to express the ideas of balance, harmony, and change that are contained in Yin-Yang theory. In landscape painting, the harmonious spirit of nature is revealed through the depiction of a scene that depends on proportion and measure to create beauty.

Wang Yun's *Mountain Landscape* (Figure 2) is a traditional Chinese landscape painting. In it, the artist has captured the essence of nature as he sees it, in balance and in flux. The painting is like the Taoist symbol (Figure 1), containing Yin and Yang in their proper proportions but constantly interacting and transforming into each other.

The scene depicts a vast range of elements, from the towering mountain to the little trickling stream. Nature is shown as a balance of the yielding Yin (foliage, water) and the unyielding Yang (rock, trees). There are the dynamic (water, people) and the quiescent (mountains, houses); the slow (trees) and the fast (mist); the dark and the light; the solid and the liquid. All things contain both Yin and Yang. The water, for instance, is both yielding (Yin) and dynamic (Yang).

The picture is a totality, and each detail takes on meaning only insofar as it participates in the whole. The mountain is immense by virtue of its smaller foothills; the people are small by virtue of the vastness of nature. All things are shown in their proper relationships to the things around them.

Through a kind of poetic logic, the Chinese also think of the landscape painting as a microcosm of the universe. In it are contained all the elements of nature, and it serves as a model of the cosmic process. The landscape painter sees in a particular scene a unique configuration of the natural elements. His composition includes those elements, or signs, that are specific to a certain scene, but it also participates in the larger reality. The elements within the microcosm correspond to elements within the macrocosm. For example, winter is death, a budding tree is

FIGURE 2

Mountain Landscape by Wang Yun (Qing dynasty)
Courtesy Museum of Fine Arts, Boston;
purchased in China, received December 1913.

spring, a lake is all water, a person is humankind. The painting depicts a time and place that through their correspondence with the universe become timeless and placeless.

In a similar way, the Chinese think of each person as a cosmos in miniature. A person manifests the same patterns as does the painting or the universe. The Yang or Fire aspects of the body are the dynamic and transforming, while the Yin or Water aspects are the more yielding and nourishing. One person projects the heat and quickness of summer Fire; another person resembles the quiescence and coolness of winter Cold; a third replicates heaviness and moisture of Dampness; a fourth has the shriveled appearance of a Dry Chinese autumn; and many people display some aspects of the various seasons simultaneously. Harmony and health are the balanced interplay of these tendencies.

In each person, as in every landscape, there are signs that, when balanced, define health or beauty. If the signs are out of balance, the person is ill or the painting is ugly. So the Chinese physician looks at a patient the way a painter looks at a landscape—as a particular arrangement of signs in which the essence of the whole can be seen. The body's signs, of course, are somewhat different from nature's signs—including color of face, expression of emotions, sensations of comfort or pain, quality of pulse—but they express the essence of the bodily landscape.

Is Chinese medicine an art? Is it a science? If we mean by science the relatively recent intellectual and technological development in the West, Chinese medicine is not scientific. It is instead a prescientific tradition that has survived into the modern age and remains another way of doing things. But it does resemble science in that it is grounded in conscientious observation of phenomena, guided by a rational, logically consistent, and communicable thought process. It has a body of knowledge with standards of measurement that allow practitioners systematically to describe, diagnose, and treat illness. Its measurements, however, are not the linear yardsticks of weight, number, time, and volume used by modern science but rather images of the macrocosm. Yet it also demands the artistic sensitivity of synthetic logic—always aware that the whole defines the parts and that the pattern may transform the significance of any one measurement within it: What is Yin in one person may be Yang in another. Because it deals with images, Chinese medicine allows and demands a recognition and assessment of quality.

This artistic sensitivity allows the physician to stay in touch with subtle refinements of meaning, to discern shades of significance in bodily signs; but most important, it allows awareness of the process that exists around and between linear measurements. Chinese medicine is not primarily quantitative. It recognizes that each person's pattern has a unique texture; each image has an essential quality.

The Chinese doctor's effort to recognize patterns within the characteristic signs of a particular individual is a creative one. But it is here that the concerns of the artist and the doctor begin to diverge. The artist uses his vision and skill to portray an ideal of balance and harmony on a paper scroll. The physician, however, uses his perception to recognize *dis*harmony, and must then apply his specialized skill to try to restore health—to achieve balance and harmony within a living organism.

Hallowed Tradition and Modern Research: It May Be Beautiful, but Does It Work?

Traditional medicine can be considered an art, and it can claim to be a science. But the important question to ask about a medical practice is: Does it work? Is Chinese medicine just an interesting philosophical curiosity or is it a viable system of healing? Can it treat what the West defines as real diseases? And can Western science measure its results and appreciate its value?

Because of the unique history of modern China, traditional medicine has been the subject of comprehensive study and testing over the past thirty years.

After the victory of the Chinese Revolution in 1949, the Chinese decided to take a fresh look at their traditional medical system. Many of China's new leaders were tempted to discard their prescientific medical inheritance, along with other old-fashioned practices and remnants of underdevelopment. Their overall desire was to emulate the developed countries—to industrialize, electrify, and modernize. Another faction of the leadership, however, saw that although China did need to accept modern medicine, there might also be some practical and theoretical usefulness in the traditional medicine. The issue was whether or not it would prove efficacious from a modern perspective.[19] To answer that question, the Chinese performed thousands of experiments and clinical studies during the fifties.[20] The result was that in 1958 the Central Committee decided to give traditional and modern medicine equal respect and place in China.

The medical reports are still produced incessantly, and include such titles as the following.

Clinical Analysis of 290 Cases of Chronic Glomerular Nephritis Treated with Traditional Herbs.[21]

Observations of the Efficacy of Subcutaneous Acupuncture in Treating 121 Cases of Bronchial Asthma.[22]

Study of Treatment of Early Stage Cervical Carcinoma with Traditional Chinese Herbs, Including Analysis of Treatment Effect on Twenty-four Cases and a Preliminary Investigation of the Treatment Mechanism.[23]

Traditional Chinese Medical Treatment of Angina Pectoris—Report of 112 Cases.[24]

The pages of such studies fill entire libraries, yet it is not their quantity that is important, but rather their conclusions: that traditional Chinese medicine can hold its own, that it does work clinically.[25]

It is now evident that Chinese medicine is an effective healing method. Sometimes, traditional Chinese medicine can alleviate or treat illnesses that modern medicine is incapable of dealing with; at other times, the opposite is true, especially in those cases that require surgery or intervention with high-technology equipment.[26]

The efficacy of traditional Chinese medicine can be illustrated by means of the previously mentioned study of ulcer patients. In that study, there were actually sixty-five patients, all of whom were observed by Western-trained physicians while being treated with traditional Chinese methods.[27] Every patient received a complete Western medical examination and was diagnosed as having peptic ulcer disease. The patients were then sent to traditional physicians, whose diagnoses roughly corresponded to the six different patterns described earlier.

The Chinese doctors gave each patient a unique herbal treatment based on his or her particular diagnosis. No Western treatment was administered, nor were any dietary restrictions imposed. The average length of treatment was two months, and modern Western techniques were used to evaluate the treatment's utility. The results were complete recovery in fifty-three patients (81.5 percent), significant improvement in seven patients (10.8 percent), some improvement in two patients (3.1 percent), no change in two patients, and a worsening of the condition in one patient due to complications unrelated to the treatment.

Another example is the angina study listed above. For that study 112 patients with angina pectoris were treated and observed for six months to two and a half years. All the patients were first given complete Western medical examinations and then diagnosed by traditional Chinese methods. In general, one of five distinct patterns was found in each case, and different herbs were prescribed for each pattern. Assessment of the therapy, based on subjective patient findings, was as follows: 34.8 percent of the patients improved markedly, 56.2 percent showed general improvement, and 9 percent remained unchanged. The overall percentage of subjective improvement was 91 percent. There were 91 patients who had abnormal electrocardiograph reports before treatment. Of these, 15.4 percent showed marked improvement after treatment, 23.1 percent showed moderate improvement, 10.9 percent showed an increase to abnormal reports, and 50.6 percent showed no change. The most interesting results, however, were seen when the patients' blood was examined. The serum cholesterol and triglyceride levels had dropped markedly in all cases after treatment. Western medicine considers low levels of these substances beneficial in reducing the threat of atherosclerotic heart disease. These changes occurred without dietary restrictions and without the use of modern drugs to lower the level of blood lipids before or after treatment.[28]

Research has also been done to isolate the effective components of particular Chinese medical treatments in dealing with diseases recognized by the West. For example, experiments have discovered the active ingredients of herbs and have tried to develop efficient anesthesia using acupuncture. Many studies have attempted to extract from Chinese medicine new, Western-style cures for malaria, hypertension, viral infections, cancer, and other diseases. Common types of studies include "Use of the Traditional Herb *Desmodium rubrum* (Lour) D.C. to treat Epidemic B. Encephalitis"; "Traditional Herb, *Siegesbeckia orientalis*, in Treatment of Hypertension"; and "Antibiotic Properties of Fourteen Herbs on Diphtheria Bacillus and Their Action on Diphtheria Toxin."

Such studies are aimed at separating out the effective components of Chinese medicine and introducing them into the framework of modern Western medicine. Much of value has indeed been incorporated into the Western medicine that is practiced in China today. Someday, these components may well appear in Western medicine as practiced in the Occident. Yet, although this knowledge, with its use of traditional herbs and acupuncture, has the veneer of Chinese medicine, the actual application and methodology are clearly Western in orientation. The theory of Yin and Yang and other traditional concepts are left behind. And while new and valuable techniques are learned, the extraction of the practice from its theory calls into question the need for the traditional framework.

Fortunately for its future, however, the results of the studies generally demonstrate that traditional Chinese medicine does work best when left in the context of Chinese logic.[29] In most cases, pattern weaving based on Yin-Yang theory produced better clinical results than the mechanical application of Chinese remedies within a Western context.[30] The traditional medicine works not only because it has an effective arsenal of therapeutic devices, but also because it knows best how to use them. Western observation also confirms that the medicine is especially effective in the clinic. This is because the Chinese view of health and disease as inseparable from a specific person means that the treatment will be well tailored to that person. Such personal shaping seems to maximize the effectiveness of the therapies.

Western clinical studies of traditional Chinese medicine, by proving its practical efficacy, have helped it win its battle for survival in the twentieth century, and promise it a place in the future of medicine.

Ancient but Still Alive

Chinese medicine is more than two thousand years old. Yet over all that time, it has retained an aesthetic and pragmatic relevance for humankind today. Of course, any tradition remains vital only insofar as it allows itself to grow and develop. The Chinese tradition is no different. Based on ancient and revered texts, it has continued to discover itself anew.

The *Huang-di Nei-jing* or Inner Classic of the Yellow Emperor (hereafter referred to as the *Nei Jing*) is the source of all Chinese medical theory, the Chinese equivalent of the Hippocratic corpus. Compiled by unknown authors between 300 and 100 B.C.E., it is the oldest of the Chinese medical texts. The knowledge and theoretical formulations it contains are the basic medical ideas developed and elaborated by later thinkers.

The *Nei Jing* has been called the bible of Chinese medicine, and the rest of Chinese medicine can be compared to rabbinical exegesis or interpretation of doctrine by church fathers. Just as, in the Jewish tradition, later authorities needed to explain theoretical issues raised by the Torah, so Chinese commentators added glosses on the *Nei Jing* that elucidated or even amended its seminal ideas. The Chinese medical tradition thus brings together folk remedies and the therapeutics of China's physician-literati who served the Imperial Court.[31] It synthesized the medicine of one dynasty and another, one place and another, one thinker and another. Every dynasty has produced practitioners equal in stature to Galen, Avicenna, or Paracelsus, and all of them have made important additions and revisions to the tradition.[32]

In China today, the primary textbooks used to train traditional doctors are contemporary interpretations and clarifications of Qing dynasty (1644–1911) formulas and commentaries. These books are, in turn, clarifications of Ming dynasty (1368–1644) reworkings, which are also reworkings of earlier material. This process goes all the way back to the Han dynasty (202 B.C.E.–220 C.E.). Such transmission through the dynastic pathway not only preserved and encapsulated the original sources, but also elucidated and reformed them. (See Appendix I: Historical Bibliography.)

It is for this reason that the *Nei Jing*, although it is the source of the tradition, is usually one of the last texts to be studied in contemporary schools of Chinese medicine. The *Nei Jing*, written in archaic language, is often unclear and inconsistent, and can only be understood after much preparation.[33] Without the commentaries and modifications of later eras, the *Nei Jing* would be almost completely unintelligible.[34] So the source requires the tradition to explain it, but both are necessary to guide Chinese theory and practice.

Within Chinese medicine, as in all traditional systems, there is a tension between that which is tacitly recognized as no longer useful and that which continues to be accepted as profound. This book attempts to bring Chinese medicine to a Western audience, and because it does so within the ancient tradition, it is, finally, another commentary on the commentaries.

Notes

1. See, for example, Treatment with Traditional Chinese Medicine of Five Types of Nervous System Disorders, Shanghai Journal of Traditional Chinese Medicine, SJTCM, January 1980, pp. 14–16.

2. See references to the uses of traditional medicine for treating endocrine disorders in Shanghai Second Medical Hospital, Handbook of Internal Medicine [88], pp. 579–650.

3. See three articles on treating lobar pneumonia caused by *Streptococcus pneumoniae* with traditional herbal medicines in Journal of Traditional Chinese Medicine, JTCM, February 1959, pp. 31–41. For an interesting nontechnical English-language discussion of treating pneumonia in children with traditional herbal methods, see "Combining Chinese and Western Medicine to Treat Pneumonia in Children," *China Reconstructs*, November 1972, pp. 19–21.

4. Michel Foucault, *The Birth of the Clinic* (New York: Vintage Books, 1973) p. 54.

5. Obviously, this statement is an oversimplification which is necessary in order to make some distinctions between Eastern and Western medical tendencies. It represents an ideal methodology (especially applicable to biochemical situations), not necessarily applicable to all disciplines or all concerns of Western medicine. For example:

In traditional fields of medical science, the goal of a thorough clinical analysis is accurate diagnosis, that is, establishing the "disease" which underlies the overt clinical symptoms. This diagnostic model is ill-suited to the problems of psychopathology, with but few exceptions, since mental disorders rarely can be ascribed to a single or clearly delineated cause or "disease." Of course, certain events may have played a central role in the development of a disorder, but these initial influences interweave with new influences and reactions which then become an integral part of the disorder. A pervasive network of secondary factors emerge to add fresh momentum to the initial influences and to extend them in ways that are far removed from the original circumstances. Given the complexity of this sequence, any effort to diagnose *the* disease or *the* cause will be futile indeed. [Theodore Millon, *Modern Psychopathology: A Biosocial Approach to Maladaptive Learning and Functioning* (Philadelphia: W. B. Saunders, 1969), pp. 74–75]

Some statements in this volume that concern Western medicine have been simplified to the point of being polemical. In order to dramatize a dichotomy they ignore the very important evolution in the last few decades toward interdisciplinary and integrative medicine, and the even more recent development of "holistic" medicine. A modern hospital's medical team employs a wide variety of approaches that go far beyond the late nineteenth century biochemical models. For example, a pain unit may include rehabilitation, occupational, and physical therapists, a nurse, a psychiatrist, a social worker, art, movement, or music therapists, a relaxation counselor, and a nutritionist, as well as the pathologist, internist, radiologist, anesthesiologist, and surgeon. The newer concepts of holistic health are an extension of the current Western concern to go beyond a reductionist model. Indeed, this book itself can be viewed as part of the growing holistic interest.

6. See Clinical Observations of Traditional Chinese Medical Approaches to 65 Cases of Ulcers, JTCM, June 1959, pp. 30–33. See also Typing of Peptic Ulcer Disease According to Traditional Chinese Medicine and Preliminary Exploration of Its Pathological Basis, JTCM, February 1980, pp. 17–21. The research report Analysis of Effectiveness of Traditional Chinese Medicine in Treating 126 Cases of Gastrointestinal Ulcers in JTCM, February 1960, distinguishes twelve distinct traditional medical patterns in its study group.

7. Manfred Porkert states this idea this way: "We should always keep in mind that Western science is not more rational than Chinese science, merely more analytical" (Porkert, *The Theoretical Foundations of Chinese Medicine*, p. 46).

8. I have translated these five principles from the discussion appearing in Shanghai Institute, Foundations of Traditional Chinese Medicine [53], pp. 22–25. It should be noted that the presentation of material in this volume follows the sequence and general content of this standard textbook.

9. Quoted in Wing-tsit Chan, *A Source Book in Chinese Philosophy*, p. 248.

10. Ibid., p. 186. Some minor changes in romanization have been made in this quotation.

11. From chap. 2 of the *Tao-te Ching*. Ibid., p. 140. There is considerable scholarly debate over who should be assigned the title or nickname Lao Tzu. Some scholars place Lao Tzu in the seventh century B.C.E., some in the sixth as an elder contemporary of Confucius, and some in the fourth as the teacher of Chuang Tzu. Still other scholars say Lao Tzu is merely a legendary figure. Even if he was a historical personage, it may be that the *Tao-te Ching* in its present form was compiled by several authors after his time. In any case, the *Tao-te Ching* is the classical formulation of Taoist philosophy.

12. From chap. 24 of the *Tao-te Ching*. Ibid., p. 152.

13. From chap. 36 of the *Tao-te Ching*. Ibid., p. 157.

14. From chap. 42 of the *Tao-te Ching*. Ibid., p. 161. During the Warring States period (475–221 B.C.E.) Chinese kings referred to themselves as solitary or lonely ones.

15. *Physics* 194.18–20. In R. McKeon, *The Basic Works of Aristotle*, p. 240.

16. From chap. 42 of the *Tao-te Ching*, in Chan, *Chinese Philosophy*, p. 160.

17. From the Balanced Inquiries by Wang Cong (Wang Ch'ung). Ibid., pp. 298–299.

18. J. Needham, *Science and Civilization in China*, vol. 2, pp. 280–281. Again it must be said that the emphasis of this chapter is the contrast of Far East and West, and in order to make distinctions, some simplification is necessary. The synthetic proclivity of Chinese thought is the main tendency but not its exclusive method. Needham writes:

> Chinese scientific thought saw related phenomena as synchronous or emblematically paired rather than caused or causing. . . . But it would, I think, be most unfortunate if one were to assume that there were never any elements of temporal causal succession in their world-outlook. . . . Simultaneous appearance of widely separated events was surely, for the ancient Chinese, the manifestation of an underlying cosmic pattern. . . . But we never maintained that this exhausted the Chinese way of looking at Nature, and it is possible to find many passages and descriptions of natural events which indicate conceptions of causes and effects in time.
> [*Annals of Science* 32 (1975): 491]

19. For a discussion of the political, economic, and social influences (i.e., extramedical forces) at work in establishing traditional Chinese medicine on an equal footing with modern medicine, see "The Ideology of Medical Revivalism in Modern China" by Ralph C. Croizier in *Asian Medical Systems*, ed. by Charles Leslie (Berkeley: University of California Press, 1976).

20. Clinical experiments performed in China often do not meet the criteria of the biomedical communities of the industrial nations. The biggest problem with research done in China is that almost none of the studies are double-blind, in which neither the physician nor the patient knows who is getting a treatment and who a placebo. The Chinese believe that in human clinical experiments the use of double-blind studies is unethical as it deprives deserving people of treatment. (Many studies lack any controls whatsoever.)

Most of the clinical studies are diverse random selections of large numbers of patients with a specific Western disease who are then treated with traditional methods. The evaluation of the treatment is by Western-style measurement and examination. These studies document measured improvement presumed to occur because of the traditional medical intervention. (The animal research, usually performed with more controls, also provides enormous data on physiologic changes effected by traditional medicine.)

All these clinical trials and experiments lack the absolute criteria of modern scientific standards. Many of the studies are poorly constructed and use imprecise assessment methods. They would most properly be called clinical observations. They do, however, point to the need for further research in the West. Chinese scientists feel they are valuable in themselves and can determine with some significance the efficacy of treatment. See Chapter 4, note 12.

21. Chinese Journal of Internal Medicine, CJIM, January 1965.

22. Ibid., October 1963.

23. See JTCM, June 1965.

24. *Chinese Medical Journal* (English edition), Beijing, May 1977.

25. To get a further idea of the scope of these titles it is worth glancing at John E. Fogarty International Center for Advanced Study in the Health Sciences, *A Bibliography of Chinese Sources on Medicine and Public Health in the People's Republic of China: 1960–1970.* (Washington, D.C.: U.S. Dept. of HEW, NIH, 1973). Many of the titles listed concern studies on traditional Chinese medicine.

26. For all the research on the traditional medicine in China by Western-style scientists and medical workers, a survey of the extensive literature uncovers little or no generalized discussion of which illnesses call for one medical approach rather than the other. The thrust is to examine the efficacy of the traditional medicine and not to compare it with Western medicine. My observation in clinical situations in

China and in reading the literature points to a rough tendency to use Western medicine in acute and emergency situations and Chinese medicine in chronic situations. Often, however, the choice is left to patients, and also commonly both systems are used simultaneously. From my own experience, Western medicine is often more effective when it has a definite and clear idea of the disease etiology (e.g., bacterial infections). When a precise etiology evades Western medicine (e.g., in cases of chronic low back pain), Chinese medicine seems more effective. Also it seems that Chinese medicine is preferred for functional disorders, while Western medicine has an edge in organic disorders. Generalizations sometimes can be heard in discussion with doctors in China; for example, for chronic bronchial asthma or arthritis, Chinese medicine is often said to be better, while in bacterial infections and in cases needing surgery, Western medicine is better. But with a stubborn persistence these generalizations are unable to predict any particular patient's response to treatment. Many times I have seen clinical cases in which Western medicine worked better in treating arthritis or Chinese medicine eliminated the need for an operation or cleared up a persistent infection.

Western medical scientists often suspect that much of Chinese medicine's effectiveness is due to the power of suggestion. While to some extent (as in any medicine) this may be true, it should be noted that in China, Western medicine is more likely to enjoy this advantage. To Chinese patients, Western medicine has prestige and an aura of the mysterious and foreign, whereas their own country's medicine is more ordinary and common.

27. See Clinical Observations of Traditional Chinese Medical Approach to 65 Cases of Ulcers, JTCM, June 1959, pp. 30–33.

28. It has been noted that many Chinese herbs dramatically reduce blood cholesterol even though the traditional system does not recognize cholesterol. For an interesting discussion combining Western and Chinese methodologies, see Eight Methods of Lowering Lipidemia by Traditional Chinese Medicine, SJTCM, November 1979.

29. See Qin Bo-wei's discussion in the chapter on Suitability of Using Traditional Chinese Medical Theory and Methods to Treat Western Diagnosed Disease in his famous Medical Lecture Notes of Qian Zhai [64], pp. 168–192.

30. A common opinion in modern China is that acupuncture, as opposed to herbal medicine, works almost as well in a high proportion of cases even when isolated and disentangled from the traditional Chinese medical view. This has allowed it to be easily incorporated into modern medicine in China and is one factor that makes it more easily transmitted to the West. This ability to isolate from the traditional theory probably is related to the fact that acupuncture often induces the body toward homeostasis, so an incorrect selection of points (from the traditional view) does little harm and only somewhat reduces the treatment's positive effect. The herbs seem to have more harmful effects if improperly used (because their actions seem to be through complex biochemistry), and the traditional theory prevents such misuse. Also, the precise use of herbs seems to maximize the positive effect of the treatment more than the precise use of the acupuncture point. A discussion of the single-directional effects of herbs as compared with the homeostatic effects of acupuncture is presented by Wei Jia in his theoretical essay On the Applicability of Moxibustion in Heat Patterns, JTCM, November 1980, p. 48. An opposite approach to acupuncture, suggesting the continued need for a traditional framework, underlies Yang Ming-yuan's Concise Acupuncture (*Jian-ming Zhen-jiu Xue*) (Harbin: Heilongjiang People's Press, 1981).

31. In general one ought to distinguish traditional Chinese medicine, which is the subject of this volume, from Chinese folk medicine. Folk medicine is largely empirical, involving relatively simple remedies applied by nonprofessional, informally educated practitioners. The traditional medicine, however, is, as Ralph Croizier defines it, "a theoretically articulated body of ideas about disease causation and treatment contained in a written tradition and practiced by men whose knowledge of that tradition causes their society to recognize them as medical specialists." "Traditional Medicine as a Basis for Chinese Medical Practices" by Ralph Croizier in *Medicine and Public Health in the People's Republic of China*, ed. by J. R. Quinn (Washington, D.C.: John E. Fogarty International Center, U.S. Dept. of HEW, NIH, 1973), p. 5.

32. While the point of the discussion is that Chinese medicine is progressive in a qualitative sense, it should be noted that this is true also in quantitative ways. Joseph Needham makes the point, perhaps even too emphatically, in *The Grand Titration: Science and Society in East and West* (p. 277): "It would be quite a mistake to imagine that Chinese culture never generated this conception [of a progressive development of knowledge], for one can find textual evidence in every period showing that in spite of their veneration for the sages, Chinese scholars and scientific men believed that there had been progress beyond the knowledge of their distant ancestor. . . ." Needham goes on to plot a curve on a graph demonstrating the tremendous increase in the number of entries in pharmacopoeias through the centuries. Also see note 6 for Chapter 4 for a discussion of the increased number of acupuncture points recognized in various historical periods.

33. Many translators prefer not to deal with this problem. Translating ancient Chinese scientific texts into comprehensible language is an extraordinarily difficult task. First, determining that the text in hand is actually what it is purported to be is a laborious job for the scholar. Through the millennia, original texts have gone through series of emendations and alterations so that what actually comes down to us must be thoroughly compared with other editions and traced in the literary documents left by each dynasty.

Second, and much more troublesome, is the problem of creating an accurate vocabulary for translating Chinese technical terms. Chinese is a pictographic language, and once it passed its formative stages, people simply did not invent a new character to express a narrow technical concept, as is done with an alphabetic language when a new word is needed. Old characters were simply given new meanings—which must be ferreted out by translators separated from the original material by a vast gulf of time and space. To translate Chinese medical texts directly, using the everyday meanings of such characters, would result in inscrutable gibberish. At the other extreme, to arbitrarily introduce Western technical terms would be to turn the Chinese text into a projection of the Western mind. Unfortunately, most translations of the *Nei Jing* in whole or in part reflect little sensitivity to either of these considerations and should be read with considerable caution.

34. The compilation of various "disparate texts [into the *Nei Jing*] has brought about repetitions, uncertainties, contradictions even, which a full commentary cannot always manage to clarify or reconcile." Huard and Wong, *Chinese Medicine*, p. 39.

Reading the collection of some seventy Greek medical writings of about 400 B.C.E. attributed to Hippocrates, one is struck by a similarity in structure. The doctrine of humors is used in terminology and outlook but nowhere does a systematic or clear presentation appear. Contradictory ideas are frequent, but at the same time there is a sense of a rational perspective not bound by fixed rules but based on empirical observation. Only later do codifiers provide systematization and consistency.

Also, both Hippocrates and the *Nei Jing* represent the same monumental break from earlier supernatural and magical healing systems (e.g., Babylonian or Siberian shamanistic). Hippocrates explicitly rejects magico-religious notions of disease and speaks of illness as a knowable, natural phenomenon subject to investigation and observation:

> My own view is that those who first attributed a sacred character to this malady were like the magicians, purifiers, charlatans and quacks of our own day. . . . This disease styled sacred comes from the same causes as others, from the things that come from the changing restlessness of winds. These things are divine. So that there is no need to put the disease in a special class and to consider it more divine than the others; they are all divine and all human. Each has a nature and power of its own; none is hopeless or incapable of treatment. . . . So the physician [can give] . . . useful treatment, without having recourse to purifications and magic. [*The Sacred Disease*, Jones, trans., *Hippocrates*, vol. 2, p. 139, p. 183.]

The *Nei Jing* speaks in the same terms: "In treating illness, it is necessary to examine the entire context, scrutinize the symptoms, observe the emotions and attitudes. If one insists on the presence of ghosts and spirits one cannot speak of therapeutics." (Inner Classic of the Yellow Emperor: Simple Questions [1], sec. 3, chap. 11, p. 78. Later cited as *Su Wen*. This is the first half of the *Nei Jing*.)

Elsewhere in the *Nei Jing* the Yellow Emperor asks:

> What if there has been no encounter with a Pernicious Influence nor any emotional disturbance and suddenly one falls ill? Is this not the result of the supernatural?

And Qi Bo (his minister and teacher) replies:

> This also has its reason. A Pernicious Influence lies dormant and waits to manifest; the will has its loathings and yearnings; the Blood and Qi are thrown into turbulence and the two Qis clash. The origin is subtle, neither visible nor audible, and *it only seems* to be the supernatural. [Classic of the Spiritual Axis [2], sec. 9, chap. 58, p. 397. Later cited as *Ling Shu*. This is the second half of the *Nei Jing*.]

While these rational notions clearly dominated both medical traditions, the problem of grave diseases unaffected by human endeavor, and of fate in general, could not be banished altogether—just moved to the periphery. The Imperial Medical Academy (tai-yi-shu) of the Tang dynasty (618–907 C.E.) had an incantation-taboo department, and one of the thirteen departments of the Yuan dynasty (1271–1368 C.E.) Academy was spirit-healing. Likewise, the Greek physicians often relied on the temples of Asclepius as a friendly ally, just as a chaplain is sometimes called into the intensive care unit in a modern hospital.

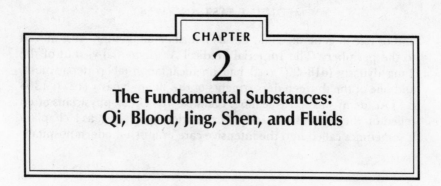

The highly developed constructs of chemistry, biochemistry, anatomy, and physiology that form the groundwork for modern Western medicine are of little importance to the Chinese. What concerns them is diagnosis—organizing signs and symptoms to arrive at an accurate perception of "what is going on." Chinese medicine therefore has a very limited theory of the human organism itself. Where Western medicine, seeking a pathological mechanism behind the veil of symptoms, needs a theory that also goes beyond the meeting of doctor and patient to an auxiliary body of knowledge,[1] Chinese medicine rarely looks further than the patient himself. Theory is necessary only to guide the physician's perceptions.

The essential ideas of Chinese medicine are not elaborate; they are not even strictly the province of the physician. Most of them are the views about health and disease that are shared by the ordinary members of Chinese society. These ideas include axioms and formulas, modes of perception, and definitions of function. It is only in their application by the physician that they become clinically useful.

These ideas are cultural and speculative constructs that provide orientation and direction for the practical patient situation. There are few secrets of Oriental wisdom buried here. When presented outside the context of Chinese civilization, or of practical diagnosis and therapeutics, these ideas are fragmented and without great significance. The "truth" of these ideas lies in the way the physician can use them to treat real people with real complaints. They are valuable because they comprise a medical paradigm that makes possible the substantive discussion of "what is going on," thereby allowing the physician to diagnose patterns of disharmony. Through diagnosis and treatment the ideas are pragmatically tested and examined for validity, consistency, and truth.

Because this is a book on fundamental principles, it is mainly about diagnosis. (Its counterpart in the West would be about chemistry and biology, or anatomy and physiology.) This chapter begins with descriptions of the basic Yin and Yang substances of the body and their relationships. It will introduce ideas and vocabulary that will lead, later on, into a fuller exposition of the "stuff" of the bodily landscape and what is going on within it.

It is important to remember that Chinese medical theory does not move in a linear way from proposition to proposition. Instead, learning Chinese medicine is like going from simple drawings to fine paintings. The whole is always present; the Yin and Yang can only be refined, never abandoned.

Qi (氣)

The idea of Qi is fundamental to Chinese medical thinking, yet no one English word or phrase can adequately capture its meaning. We can say that everything in the universe, organic and inorganic, is composed of and defined by its Qi. But Qi is not some primordial, immutable material, nor is it merely vital energy, although the word is occasionally so translated. Chinese thought does not distinguish between matter and energy, but we can perhaps think of Qi as matter on the verge of becoming energy, or energy at the point of materializing.[2] To Chinese thought, however, such discussion of what a concept means in itself—a discussion that the Western mind expects in any systematic exposition—is completely foreign. Neither the classical nor modern Chinese texts speculate on the nature of Qi, nor do they attempt to conceptualize it. Rather, Qi is perceived functionally—by what it does.

Origins of Qi

All the Qi in the body is referred to in general terms as Normal or Upright Qi (*zheng-qi*) or as True Qi (*zhen-qi*). Normal Qi is Qi before it is differentiated into specific forms or is associated with specific functions.

The Chinese conceive of three sources of Normal Qi. The first of these is Original Qi (*yuan-qi*), also called Prenatal Qi, which is transmitted by parents to their children at conception. This Qi is partly responsible for an individual's inherited constitution. It is stored in the Kidneys. The second source is Grain Qi (*gu-qi*), which is derived from the digestion of food. The third is Natural Air Qi (*kong-qi*), which is extracted by the Lungs from the air we breathe.

These three forms of Qi intermingle to produce the Normal Qi that permeates the entire body. There is "no place that does not have it, and no place it does not penetrate."[3]

Functions of Qi

Normal Qi, once formed, can be divided into many different specific types of Qi which have specific functions. One Sinologist has identified thirty-two distinct categories in the literature of the past 2,500 years, and has posed a useful analogy between Qi and electrical energy. Just as Westerners recognize electricity as a general phenomenon displayed in specific forms (high and low voltage, high and low amperage), the Chinese recognize Qi as a general phenomenon with many variant aspects and functions.[4]

Within the body, Normal Qi (usually just called Qi) has five major functions.[5] Through these activities, Qi is responsible for the physical integrity of any entity, and for the changes that entity undergoes.

Qi is the source of all movement in the body
and accompanies all movement.

This function includes movement in its broadest sense: Gross
physical activity (walking, dancing), involuntary movement
(breathing, heartbeat), willed action (eating, speaking), mental
action (thinking, rejoicing, dreaming), and development,
growth, and life-process (birth, maturation, and aging) are all
movements that depend on the Qi.

Qi is *not* the cause of movement, because Qi is inseparable
from movement. For example, Qi is the source of growth in the
body, but also grows with the body. For the Chinese, Qi is not a
metaphor; it is a real phenomenon that makes possible integrative descriptions of bodily changes. Diagnostic methods exist
for determining its strength and motion, and there are specific
treatments for supplementing its deficiency, draining its excess,
and regulating its flow.

In the body, Qi is in constant motion and has four primary
directions: ascending, descending, entering, and leaving. The
Nei Jing states: "Without entering and leaving there is no development, without ascending and descending no transformation, absorption, and storing."[6] Normal physiological activity is
Qi moving harmoniously in these various directions. If there is
insufficient Qi, if the Qi is obstructed or moves in "rebellion" or
moves "recklessly," or if any of the Qi directions lose their "regulation," disharmony will result.

Qi protects the body.

It resists the entry into the body of pathological environmental agents, called External Pernicious Influences (discussed in
Chapter 5), and combats them if they do manage to penetrate.
The *Nei Jing* says: "If Pernicious Influences abide, the Qi must
be deficient."[7]

Qi is the source of harmonious transformation in the body.

When food is ingested it is transformed into other substances
such as Blood, Qi itself, tears, sweat, and urine. These changes
depend on the transformative function of Qi.

Qi governs retention of the body's Substances and Organs.

In other words, Qi "keeps everything in"—it holds Organs in their proper place, keeps the Blood in the Blood pathways, and prevents excessive loss of the various bodily fluids, such as sweat and saliva.

Qi warms the body.

Maintenance of normal heat in the body as a whole, or in any part of the body (e.g., the limbs) depends on the warming function of the Qi.

Types of Qi

Each of the five functions of Qi is apparent in all the specific types of Qi, of which there are many. Five of them, however, are especially important. These types of Qi are associated with particular actions or particular parts of the body, and most Chinese medical discussions of Qi center on one of the five primary types.

Organ Qi (zang-fu-zhi-qi)

The major functions of any Organ are referred to in terms of that Organ's Qi. Every Organ is conceived of as having its own Qi, whose activity is characterized by the Organ to which it is attached. When the Chinese speak of Heart Qi or Lung Qi, the substance Qi is the same, but its activity when related to the Heart is different from its activity when related to the Lungs; and the Heart and Lungs operate differently depending on the nature of their Qi. (Details of the particular Organ Qis are discussed in Chapter 3.)

Meridian Qi (jing-luo-zhi-qi)

Meridians are a unique and crucial part of Chinese medical theory. They are the channels or pathways through which Qi flows among the Organs and various bodily parts, adjusting and harmonizing their activity. Normal Qi flowing in this comprehensive network is called Meridian Qi.

Nutritive Qi (*ying-qi*)

This is the Qi most intimately associated with the Blood. It manifests itself in the Blood and moves with the Blood through the Blood Vessels. Its activity helps transform the purest nutrients derived from food into Blood. Nutritive Qi is an essential factor in bodily nourishment.

Protective Qi (*wei-qi*)

This is the Qi responsible for resisting and combating External Pernicious Influences when they invade the body. Considered the most Yang manifestation of Qi in the body, Protective Qi is "fierce and bold."[8] It moves within the chest and abdominal cavities, and travels between the skin and muscles. This Qi regulates the sweat glands and pores, and moistens and protects the skin and hair.

Qi of the Chest or Ancestral Qi (*zong-qi*)

This Qi gathers in the chest, where it forms a "sea of Qi."[9] The *Nei Jing* states that this Qi "collects in the chest, goes out the throat, connects with the Heart and Vessels, and moves respiration."[10] Its main function is to aid and regulate the rhythmic movement of respiration and heartbeat, and so it is intimately connected with the Lungs and Heart. The relative strength and evenness of respiration, of the voice, the heartbeat, and the movement of Blood are all related to the Qi of the Chest.[11]

Disharmonies of Qi

There are two major patterns of disharmony associated with Qi. Such patterns are generally called Qi disharmonies. The details and intricacies of Qi and other disharmonies will be discussed in later chapters.

Deficient Qi (*qi-xu*)

This is the general designation for patterns of disharmony in the body, in which the Qi is insufficient to perform any of the five Qi functions. If Deficient Qi affects the whole body, symptoms might include lethargy and lack of desire to move. Deficient Qi may also describe a particular Organ unable to perform its functions. For example, in the pattern of Deficient Kidney Qi, the Kidneys may be incapable of harmoniously regulating water, and the individual may develop such symptoms as incontinence or edema. Deficient Qi can also apply to any of the various types of Qi. Deficient Protective Qi, for instance, may lead to frequent colds and spontaneous sweating.

Collapsed Qi (*qi-xian*)

A subcategory of Deficient Qi, this implies that the Qi is so insufficient that it can no longer hold Organs in place. When there is Collapsed Qi, such disorders as prolapse of the uterus or piles may occur.

Stagnant Qi (*qi-zhi*)

This is the second broad category of Qi disharmonies. In this disharmony, the normal movement of Qi is impaired—the Qi does not flow through the body in a smooth and orderly fashion. Stagnant Qi in the limbs and Meridians may be the origin of pain and aches in the body. Stagnant Qi can also lead to impairment of an Organ. Stagnant Qi in the Lungs means the Qi is not "entering and leaving" properly. Coughing and dyspnea may be the result. Distention in the ribs and abdomen occurs with Stagnant Qi in the Liver.

Rebellious Qi (*qi-ni*)

This is a particular form of Stagnant Qi. It implies that the Qi is going in the wrong direction. For example, Chinese medicine says that Stomach Qi should go downward; if it rebels and goes upward, there may be vomiting and nausea.

All the Substances can be defined as either mostly Yin or mostly Yang. They embody the five Yin-Yang principles, and so contain both Yin and Yang aspects, but one aspect is dominant.

All patterns of disharmony (or disharmonies) can be considered either Yin conditions or Yang conditions.

Within the group of Substances, Qi is a Yang Substance. Deficient Qi is a Yin condition, a condition of depletion, in which a person exhibits the underactivity characteristic of Yin. Relative to Deficient Qi, Stagnant Qi is a Yang condition, a condition of surfeit, associated with the Yang characteristics of excessive and inappropriate movement.

Blood (xue 血)

The Blood of Chinese medical terminology is not the same as what the West calls blood. Although it is sometimes identifiable with the red fluid of Western medicine, its characteristics and functions are not so identifiable.[12]

The major activity of the Blood is to circulate continuously through the body, nourishing, maintaining, and to some extent moistening its various parts. Blood moves primarily through the Blood Vessels, but also through the Meridians (see Appendix F). Chinese medicine does not make a strict distinction between Blood Vessels and Meridians. The Chinese rarely concern themselves about precise inner physical locations—the Stomach Qi "goes upward," or the Blood "circulates," but it is seldom entirely clear what internal paths they travel or where, precisely, they go. The physical pathway is less important than the function. This tendency not to fix sites for things is contrary to the Western approach, but it is necessary to Chinese medical theorizing.

Blood, a liquid, is considered a Yin Substance.

Origins of Blood

Blood originates through the transformation of food. After the Stomach receives and "ripens" the food, the Spleen distills from it an extremely fine and purified essence. The Spleen Qi then transports this essence upward to the Lungs. During the upward movement, Nutritive Qi begins to turn the essence into

Blood. The change is completed when the essence reaches the Lungs, where the now-transformed food combines with the portion of air described as "clear." This combination finally produces Blood. The Blood is then propelled through the body by the Heart Qi in coordination with the Qi of the Chest.

Relationships of Blood

Three Organs in the body have special relationships with the Blood: the Heart, Liver, and Spleen. Blood depends on the Heart for its harmonious, smooth, and continuous circulation throughout the body. It is therefore said that "the Heart rules the Blood." The body needs less Blood when it is inactive, and then the Liver regulates the quiescent Blood. Therefore, "the Liver stores the Blood." Finally, the Blood depends on the retentive properties of Spleen Qi to keep it within the Blood Vessels and, therefore, "the Spleen governs the Blood."

Blood and Qi, though generally distinct from one another, have a mutually dependent and indissoluble relationship. Qi creates and moves the Blood and also holds it in place. Blood in turn nourishes the Organs that produce and regulate the Qi. This relationship exemplifies the principles of Yin (Blood) and Yang (Qi). A traditional saying summarizes this relationship in two principles: "Qi is the commander of the Blood . . . Blood is the mother of Qi."[13]

Disharmonies of Blood

The two major categories of Blood disharmony are Deficient Blood (*xue-xu*) and Congealed Blood (*xue-yu*). A pattern of Deficient Blood exists when the entire body, or a particular Organ or other part of the body, is insufficiently nourished by the Blood. If this condition affects the entire body, signs such as a pale and lusterless face, dizziness, and dry skin may appear. When a particular Organ is affected, there will be different signs. Deficient Qi of the Heart, for example, may lead to palpitations.

Congealed Blood means the Blood has become obstructed and is not flowing smoothly. This condition is often characterized by sharp, stabbing pains accompanied by tumors, cysts, or swelling of the Organs (most commonly the Liver).

Jing (精)

Jing, best translated as Essence, is the Substance that underlies all organic life. It is the source of organic change. Generally thought of as fluidlike, Jing is supportive and nutritive, and is the basis of reproduction and development.

Origins of Jing

Jing has two sources, which are also its characteristic aspects. Prenatal Jing (*xian-tian-zhi-jing*), also translated as Congenital Essence, is inherited from the parents. In fact, the fusion of this parental Jing is conception. Each person's Prenatal Jing is unique and will determine his or her particular growth patterns. The quantity and quality of the Prenatal Jing is fixed at birth and, together with Original Qi, determines an individual's basic makeup and constitution.

Postnatal Jing (*hou-tian-zhi-jing*) is the second source and aspect of Jing. It is derived from the purified parts of ingested food. The Postnatal Jing constantly adds vitality to the Prenatal Jing. Together, they comprise the overall Jing of the body.

Functions of Jing

An individual's development is accompanied by corresponding changes in his or her Jing. The *Nei Jing* speaks of women's development in seven-year stages:

At seven years the Kidney [Jing][14] is ascendant: The teeth change and the hair grows. At fourteen years the Dew of Heaven [Jing] arrives: The Conception Meridian flows, the Penetrating Extra Meridian is full, the menses come regularly, and the woman can conceive. At twenty-one years the Kidney [Jing] plateaus: The wisdom teeth come in and growth is at its peak. At twenty-eight years the tendons and bones are strong, the hair is at its growing peak, and the body is strong; at thirty-five years the Yang Brightness Meridian weakens, the face begins to darken, and hair falls out. At forty-two the three Yang Meridians are weak above [in the face], the face is dark, and the hair begins to turn white. At forty-nine the Conception Meridian is Deficient, the Penetrating Extra Meridian is exhausted, the Water of Heaven is dried up; the Earth Road [the menses] is not open, so weakness and infertility set in.[15]

A similar process of eight-year transitions is described for men:

At eight years the Kidney [Jing] is full: The hair is grown, and the teeth change. At sixteen years the Kidney [Jing] is abundant: The Water of Heaven [Jing] arrives, the Jing Qi is able to flow, the Yin and Yang are in harmony, and the man is fertile. At twenty-four the Kidney [Jing] plateaus: The tendons and bones are strong, the wisdom teeth come in, and growth is at its peak. At thirty-two the tendons and bones are at their strongest and the flesh is full and strong. At forty the Kidney [Jing] is weakened, the hair falls out, and the teeth are loose. At forty-eight the Yang Qi is exhausted above, the face darkens, and the hair whitens. At fifty-six the Liver [Jing] is weak, the tendons cannot move, the Dew of Heaven is used up, there is little semen, the Kidney is weak, and the appearance and body are at their end. At sixty-four the hair and teeth are gone.[16]

Thus, Jing is the material that imbues an organism with the possibility of development, from conception to death.

Disharmonies of Jing might involve improper maturation, sexual dysfunction, inability to reproduce, and premature aging. What the West calls congenital defects often are considered Jing irregularities.

Qi is the energy associated with movement (any movement—a wave in the ocean may be said to have Qi); Jing is the substance associated with the slow movement of organic change. Qi flows with the "external" aspects of movement; Jing—dark, quiescent, moist, warm—is the inner essence of growth and decline. An individual's Qi and Jing are mutually dependent. Qi emerges out of Jing, since Prenatal Jing is the root of life. But Qi helps transform food into Postnatal Jing, thereby maintaining and expanding that life. In relation to each other, Jing is Yin and Qi is Yang.

When compared with Blood, however, Jing is the more active, or Yang, phenomenon. Blood is associated with the everyday cyclical process of maintenance, nourishment, and repair. Jing is tied to ongoing, long-range development. Blood may be conceived as remaining static in time, presiding over repetitive cycles; Jing is the fluid which moves forward through time and history—the basis of reproduction, growth, ripening, withering. Therefore, in relation to Blood, Jing is Yang; in relation to Jing, Blood is Yin.

Shen (神)

Shen is best translated as Spirit. It is an elusive concept, perhaps because, in the medical tradition, it is the Substance unique to human life. If Jing is the source of life, and Qi the ability to activate and move, then Shen is the vitality behind Jing and Qi in the human body. While animate and inanimate movement are indicative of Qi, and instinctual organic processes reflect Jing, human consciousness indicates the presence of Shen.

Shen is associated with the force of human personality, the ability to think, discriminate, and choose appropriately, or, as is commonly said: "Shen is the awareness that shines out of our eyes when we are truly awake."

The origin of Shen is analogous to the origin of Jing: Each parent contributes to the creation of the offspring's Shen, yet the Shen is also continuously and materially nourished after birth. Although the English word *Spirit* may be used to translate *Shen*, Shen does have a material aspect. It is a Fundamental Substance of the human body and has no importance to medicine independent of the body.[17] It is as much a part of the body as the intestines. The Western post-Descartes spiritual-versus-material dichotomy is not relevant to Chinese medical thought.

In a healthy person, Shen is the capacity of the mind to form ideas and is the desire of the personality to live life. When Shen loses its harmony, the individual's eyes may lack luster and his or her thinking may be muddled. A person so affected may be slow and forgetful, or perhaps suffer from insomnia. Certain Shen disharmonies are marked by unreasonable responses to the environment, such as incoherent speech. Extreme Shen disharmony can lead to unconsciousness or violent madness. Because of its power to activate, Shen is considered a Yang Substance. The Chinese medical tradition speaks of Qi, Jing, and Shen as "the three treasures."

Fluids (jin-ye 津液)

Fluids are bodily liquids other than Blood—including sweat, saliva, gastric juices, and urine. The term *jin* refers to lighter and clearer fluids, while *ye* connotes fluids with a heavier, thicker nature.

The function of the Fluids is to moisten and partly to nourish the hair, skin, membranes, orifices, flesh, muscles, Inner Organs, joints, brain, marrow, and bones. Although the Fluids are considered Fundamental Substances, they are perceived as being less refined, less essential, or less "deep" than Qi, Blood, Jing, and Shen.

The Fluids are derived from ingested food and are absorbed and regulated by the Qi of various Organs, particularly the Kidneys. Therefore, the Fluids depend on the Qi, and the Qi, to some extent, depends on the Fluids to moisten and nourish the Organs that regulate Qi.

Blood and Fluids are part of a continuum of liquids in the body. Their basic natures are much the same, but they differ in the degree of their ability to nourish. The Blood is stronger, "deeper," and more potent. In Chinese theory, the cleanest or clearest part of the Fluids enters the developing Blood and unites with purified food as part of the process that creates

Blood. This relationship between Fluids and Blood is seen clinically when a severe hemorrhage causes insufficient Fluids or, conversely, when damage to the Fluids causes Deficient Blood.

Fluids, as liquids, are Yin Substances. Disharmonies of Fluids generally include dryness—of the lips, skin, eyes, etc. Most Fluid disharmonies, however, blend into the more general category of Yin or Water disharmonies, which will be discussed later.

These five fundamental Substances of the human body are basics of the Chinese system. But any aspect of Chinese medical knowledge is meaningful only in relation to the signs, symptoms, and patterns displayed by people. The concrete natures of Qi, Blood, Jing, Shen, and Fluids become clear in the myriad patterns of their disharmonies.

Notes

1. Other tendencies in Western medicine do exist that are closer to, though still different from, the Chinese style of primary reliance on clinical observation. These tendencies are often recognizably distant from the Aristotelian-Galenic-modern medical conception of searching for proximate causes. Identifiable in this tradition are authors of parts of the Hippocratic corpus and such early physicians as Herophilus of Chalcedon (fl. c. 265 B.C.E.) and Philinos of Cos (fl. c. 250 B.C.E.) and such later physicians as Thomas Sydenham (1624–1629), Georg Ernst Stahl (1660–1734), Samuel Hahnemann (1755–1843), René Laennec (1781–1826), and Armand Trousseau (1801–1867). Their primary concern was to recognize configurations of symptoms and a correct clinical response. Though I do not intend to discount this other tradition in the West, I am using the term *Western medicine* in this text to mean the orthodox nineteenth- and twentieth-century medicine that generally accepts the causative and analytic thesis of Rudolf Virchow (published in his monumental *Cellular Pathology*, 1858) and Claude Bernard *(Experimental Medicine*, 1865) that disruption of cellular function is the basis of disease and medicine must be based on an understanding of physical and chemical laws. An excellent discussion of the differing tendencies in Western medicine and the nature of "causative" medical thought is Harris Coulter, *Divided Legacy: A History of the Schism in Medical Thought*, vols. 1–3.

Remnants remain of the tendency to rely mainly on symptomology and deemphasize causation in modern medicine, especially in psychiatry. For example, the *Diagnostic and Statistical Manual of Mental Disorders* (DSM-III) (3rd ed., 1980) of the American Psychiatric Association generally eschews etiology and relies on patterns of symptoms. See Chapter 1, note 5.

2. For an excellent discussion in English on the traditional Chinese concept of Qi, see Nathan Sivin, "Chinese Alchemy and the Manipulation of Time," *Isis* 67, no. 239 (1976):513–525, and S. Bennett, "Chinese Science: Theory and Practice," *Philosophy East and West* 28, no. 4 (1978):439–453.

3. Shanghai Institute, Foundations [53], p. 38.

4. See discussion in Porkert, *Theoretical Foundations*, pp. 166–196.

5. Based on discussions appearing in Shanghai Institute, Foundations [53], pp. 23–24.

6. Inner Classic of the Yellow Emperor: Simple Questions [1], sec. 19, chap. 68, pp. 399–400. Cited as *Nei Jing* or *Su Wen*. (The *Su Wen*, or Simple Questions, is the first half of the *Nei Jing*.)

7. Ibid., sec. 9, chap. 33, p. 197.

8. Ibid., sec. 12, chap. 43, p. 245.

9. Classic of the Spiritual Axis with Vernacular Explanation [2], sec. 11, chap. 75, p. 519. This text, hereafter referred to as the *Ling Shu*, is the second half of the *Nei Jing*.

10. Ibid., sec. 10, chap. 71, p. 468.

11. The Qi of the Chest, unlike the other kinds of Qi, has only two of the three constituents of Normal Qi. It lacks Original Qi.

12. The identification of red fluid with Blood is clearly stated thus: "The Middle Burner receives Qi [here meaning pure essences of food], obtaining a sap that is transformed into a red color and is called Blood" (*Ling Shu*, sec. 6, chap. 30, p. 267). Blood is a fluid, but it also has aspects of Qi and is especially involved in activating the sense Organs. "Blood and Qi are different in name but are of the same category" (*Ling Shu*, sec. 4, chap. 18, p. 198).

13. Shanghai Institute, Foundations [53], p. 42. The quotation derives from Tang Zong-hai's Discussion of Blood Patterns (1885) [20], p. 17. Tang, however, uses the word *protector* (*shou*) instead of *mother*. At this point Tang is very reminiscent of Gong Ting-xian's discussion of Qi and Blood in Preserving Vitality in Life (*Shou-shi Bao-yuan*). In fact, the first half of the saying ("the Qi is the commander of the Blood") is taken from Gong's text (Taipei: Whirlwind Press, 1974), sec. 1, chap. 20, p. 24. Gong's book originally appeared in 1615 C.E.

14. At this point in the *Nei Jing*, the word *Qi* is often used to mean Jing.

15. *Su Wen*, sec. 1, chap. 1, pp. 4–5.

16. Ibid., sec. 1, chap. 1, pp. 5–6.

17. Note that this discussion of Shen is derived from the medical tradition, which is not necessarily congruent with some of the Taoist and other esoteric traditions in China.

Needham writes concerning this entire question: "In accord with the character of all Chinese thought, the human organism was an organism, neither purely spiritual in nature nor purely material. It was not a *machina* with a single *deus* in it, which could go off and survive somewhere else; and for any recognisable continuance of identity its parts were not separable. . . . Taoist immortality inescapably involved elements of materiality, and it had to be a continuance within this world . . . since no other, purely 'spiritual,' was conceivable. . . . The line drawn between spirit and matter in all characteristic Chinese thinking was extremely vague." Joseph Needham, *Science and Civilization in China*, vol. 5, part 2 (Cambridge: At the University Press, 1974), p. 92. This quote is part of an interesting discussion of the *hun* and *po* aspects of Shen which also play a role in Chinese medical thinking.

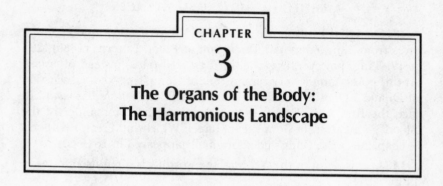

Another major feature of the bodily landscape is the Organs. Chinese medical theory recognizes a number of important Organs, which work in unison with each other and with the Fundamental Substances. This network of Organs and Substances sustains the body activities of storing and spreading, preserving and transforming, absorbing and eliminating, ascending and descending, activating and quieting. When all these activities take place harmoniously, the body is healthy and in balance.

This concept of health is very simple. The Chinese cannot measure health as is customarily done in the West. Health is not a composite of quantifiable entities, such as chemical levels in the blood and urine. In the West, health is analyzable independent of illness; it is an elaborate edifice upon which a practice of medicine is built. Health for the Chinese, however, is a theoretical state in which none of the bodily signs are abnormal. The image is balanced. The important Taoist notion—that the Tao (or Dao, the balanced and harmonious Way) that can be talked about and described is not the Tao—pervades medicine. Harmony must be simply and effortlessly stated. It is enough to say, for instance, "The Lungs in harmony administer respiration." No elaboration is needed.*

The detail and precision of Chinese medicine lie instead in its perception of *disharmony*, in its ability to recognize in signs and symptoms a pattern that becomes the basis for treatment. This theory of health is an attempt to make sense out of the practice of treating illness. For instance, in the process of finding a treatment for the symptom of edema (excessive accumulation of fluid in tissues), the Chinese formulated their theory of harmonious movement of Fluids in the body. They did not study healthy people first; they moved from perceiving and treating a *dis*harmony to the understanding of harmony.

The tendency of Chinese thought is to seek out dynamic functional activity rather than to look for the fixed somatic structures that perform the activities. Because of this, the Chinese have no system of anatomy comparable to that of the West. Thus, for example, the Organ known as the Liver is for the Chinese very different from the Western liver. The Chinese Liver is defined first by the functions associated with it, the Western liver by its physical structure. This divergence of conceptual approach makes it possible for Chinese medicine to identify Organs not recognized in the West—such as the Triple Burner—and for it not to recognize organs and glands clearly identified by Western medicine—such as the pancreas and the adrenal glands.

It is impossible to read into the Chinese system the classifications of the West. One Western authority on Chinese medicine states, erroneously: "The endocrine glands were not known to the ancient Chinese and were therefore not considered. . . . I

---

*The wider Chinese cultural notion of health as a feeling of well-being and attunement with the Tao of nature, of society, family, and inner self goes beyond the narrow confines of medicine. Rather, we would have to discuss the complex realm of Chinese religious values, philosophic perception of purpose, and personal relationships, as well as questions of economic and social status.

think the thyroid should be classified as belonging to the heart in the system of classification under twelve organs (likewise . . . the adrenal belongs to the kidney)."[1] This sort of attempt to impose parallelism on the two systems is inappropriate and leads to misunderstanding. The Chinese system must be approached and dealt with on its own terms.

Chinese medicine is a coherent system of thought that does not require validation by the West as an intellectual construct. Intellectually, the way to approach Chinese concepts is to see whether they are internally logical and consistent, not to disguise them as Western concepts or dismiss them because they do not conform to Western notions. And the system *is* internally consistent—it is an organization of all the observable manifestations of the body into an integrated set of functions and relationships. Understanding of these functions and relationships enables the practitioner to identify and treat a disharmony in them.

As a clinical construct, the Chinese concepts can be evaluated more easily. Western techniques can be used to see whether the practice derived from the theory really works. This has been done, and the results have shown that Chinese medicine can be very effective, as noted in Chapter 1. But the treatment is achieved through the use of a non-Western theoretical framework. Chinese medicine can, for instance, treat the disharmonies that Western medicine would associate with a thyroid condition. The Western doctor would treat the thyroid itself, in most cases either biochemically or surgically. The Chinese physician, however, might effect a cure through treatment of the Heart or, depending on the total configuration of signs, through treatment of the Liver, Spleen, Kidneys, or some combination of these Organs.[2] The two paradigms embrace the body differently; there is no simple correspondence.

China's lack of an anatomical theory like the West's does not mean its system is unscientific; it means only that there exist alternate systems of thought, one Eastern, one Western. In the West, even the early Greeks developed sophisticated anatomies based on the dissection of humans and apes.[3] These anatomies were often incorrect, but they grew out of the same emphasis on a causal analysis of disease that motivates modern medicine. The description of Organs that follows, however, is "not a Chinese version of anatomy, but its very antithesis."[4]

In the Chinese system, the Organs are discussed always with reference to their functions and to their relationships with the Fundamental Substances, other Organs, and other parts of the body. Indeed, it is only through these relationships that an organ can be defined. (The source of this discussion is the *Nei Jing*, from which come most of the quotations.) The relationships discussed herein are those that the Chinese medical tradition considers most important in the clinical perception of patterns.

Chinese medicine recognizes five Yin Organs (*wu-zang*) and six Yang Organs (*liu-fu*). The Yin Organs are the Heart, Lungs, Spleen, Liver, and Kidneys. The Pericardium is sometimes considered a sixth Yin Organ.[5] The function of the Yin Organs is to produce, transform, regulate, and store the Fundamental Substances—Qi, Blood, Jing, Shen (Spirit), and Fluids.

The six Yang Organs are the Gall Bladder, Stomach, Small Intestine, Large Intestine, Bladder, and Triple Burner. The Yang Organs receive, break down, and absorb that part of the food that will be transformed into Fundamental Substances, and transport and excrete the unused portion.

The Yin Organs are thought of as being deeper inside the body, and are therefore Yin in relation to the Yang Organs, which are more external. The Yin Organs are generally more important in medical theory and practice.

There are also six miscellaneous or Curious Organs (*qi-heng-zhi-fu*) mentioned in the classical literature. They are the Brain, Marrow, Bone, Blood Vessels, Uterus, and Gall Bladder.[6] The Gall Bladder is considered both a Yang Organ and a Curious Organ—Yang because it is involved in the breakdown of impure food; Curious because it alone among the Yang Organs contains a pure substance: bile. (The Curious Organs are discussed in Appendix F.)

Yin Organs (*wu-zang* 五脏)

Heart (*xin* 心)

"The Heart rules the Blood and Blood Vessels."[7] The Heart regulates the flow of Blood; when the Heart is functioning properly, the Blood flows smoothly. Thus, the Heart, the Blood, and the Blood Vessels are united by their common activity. If the Heart Blood and Heart Qi (which are mutually dependent on each other) are abundant and normal, then the pulse will be even and regular.

"The Heart stores the Shen [Spirit]."[8] It is also said that the Heart rules the Shen. When the Heart's Blood and Qi are harmonious, Shen is nourished, and the individual responds appropriately to the environment. When the Shen-storing of the Heart is impaired, the individual may show symptoms associated with the Shen, such as insomnia, excessive dreaming, or forgetfulness. More serious disorders of this type are hysteria, irrational behavior, insanity, and delirium.

"The Heart opens into the tongue."[9] "The Heart's brilliance manifests in the face."[10] The tradition also says that "the tongue is the sprout of the Heart."[11] The tongue is closely related to the Heart Qi and Heart Blood. This means that if disharmonies occur in the Heart, they are sometimes discernible in the tongue. A pale tongue might indicate Deficient Blood in the Heart; or a purplish (cyanotic) tongue might indicate Stagnant Heart Blood. The connection between Heart and tongue also means that pathological changes of the tongue such as inflammations or ulcerations can often be treated by acupuncture or herbal therapy directed at the Heart.

If the Heart Blood is abundant, the face will have a normal reddish complexion and will be moist and bright. If the Heart Blood is insufficient, the face will be pale and without luster. If it is stagnant, the face may be purplish.

Pericardium (xin-bao 心 包)

The Pericardium is the outer protective shield of the Heart. For clinical purposes it is considered a sixth Yin Organ. But in general theory, the Pericardium is not distinguished from the Heart, except by virtue of its being the first line of defense against External Pernicious Influences attacking the Heart. In acupuncture it has a separate Meridian. The role of the Pericardium is developed in Appendix A.

CLINICAL SKETCH:* A man is suffering from insomnia. He goes to a Western doctor, who finds nothing wrong but offers him sleeping pills. Later, the patient decides to try an Oriental physician. An examination confirms the doctor's suspicion that the Heart is not storing the Spirit properly, and a series of treatments is prescribed. The doctor will use acupuncture points such as Heart 7 (*Shen-men*, Spirit Door) and herbs such as Dragon Eye Fruit (longan, the fruit of *Euphoria longana*), which alleviate the condition, as they strengthen that aspect of the Heart that stores the Spirit. These treatments have no sedating side effects and, from a Western viewpoint, they appear to strengthen the nervous system.[12]

Lungs (fei 肺)

The *Nei Jing* calls the Lungs "the Lid of the Yin Organs,"[13] because they form a cap or lid on top of the thoracic cavity. Tradition also calls the Lungs the "tender organ,"[14] because they are the Yin Organ most easily affected by External Pernicious Influences.[15] The Lungs can direct movement in two directions, "descending and liquefying" (*su-jiang*) and "disseminating" (*xuan*) or circulating.

"The Lungs rule Qi."[16] This means that the Lungs administer respiration and that, in a sense, they regulate the Qi of the entire body. The Lungs are the arena in which the Qi outside

---

*This illustration and the ones that follow throughout the book are intended only as sketches to clarify the workings of Chinese medicine. They are not meant to prove or explain theoretical details.

the body meets the Qi inside the body. The Lungs take in the Natural Air Qi, propelling it downward by their descending property. This is inhalation. The disseminating property, which "makes things go 'round," allows for exhalation, the expulsion of "impure" air. When the Lungs are healthy, the Qi enters and leaves smoothly, and respiration is even and regular. When an imbalance or obstruction interferes with the Lungs, impairing either the descending or the disseminating functions, symptoms such as cough, dyspnea, asthma, or chest distention may result.

The disseminating, or circulating, function of the Lungs is very closely allied with the Qi of the Chest. Because the Qi of the Chest is involved with the movement of all the Qi and Blood in the body, a disharmony of the Lungs can produce Deficient Qi or Stagnant Qi anywhere in the body.

"The Lungs move and adjust the Water Channels."[17] The Lungs have a role in the movement and the transformation of water in the body. The Lungs move water in the same two directions that they move Qi. The descending function of the Lungs liquifies water vapor and moves it down to the Kidneys. The disseminating function circulates and scatters water vapor throughout the body, particularly through the skin and pores. Chinese medicine postulates that Water in liquid form descends while in vapor form it circulates or ascends. The movement of water by the Lungs is summarized thus: "The Lungs are the upper origin of water."[18]

Disharmonies of the Lungs' Water descending function are likely to result in problems of urination or in edema, particularly edema in the upper part of the body. Disturbances involving the disseminating function may produce perspiratory problems.

"The Lungs rule the exterior of the body."[19] "The brilliance of the Lungs is manifested in the body hair."[20] The word *exterior*, in relation to the Lungs, is a standard usage referring to the skin, sweat glands, and body hair.[21] In other words, the Lungs regulate the secretion of sweat, the moistening of the skin, and resistance to External Pernicious Influences. These functions also depend on the Protective Qi, which in turn depends on the Lungs' disseminating function. This particular relationship is considered another example of the Lungs ruling Qi. If the Lung Qi is weak, there may be too much or too little sweat, and the resistance of the Protective Qi will be poor.

"The brilliance of the Lungs is manifested in the body hair" means that the quality of the body hair indicates the condition of the Lung Qi.

> CLINICAL SKETCH: A person whose Lungs or Lung Qi is not functioning well may constantly get colds. Every time something is going around, he or she catches it. An Oriental physician may determine that the Protective Qi of such a person is weak. A series of herbal treatments, such as one called the Jade Screen, which includes *Astragalus*, and the use of acupuncture points such as Lung 9 (*Tai-yuan*, Great Abyss) and Bladder 38 (*Gao-huang-shu*, Vital's Hollow), will greatly improve the situation, as they strengthen both the Lung and the Protective Qi.[22]

"The Lungs open into the nose."[23] The nose is the "thoroughfare for respiration" and is intimately connected to the function of the Lungs. The throat is said to be the "door" of the Lungs and the "home" of the vocal cords, so both the throat and the vocal cords are also related to the Lungs. Many common nose and throat disorders are therefore treated through the Lungs.

Spleen (*pi* 脾)

"The Spleen rules transformation and transportation."[24] The Spleen is the crucial link in the process by which food is transformed into Qi and Blood. For the Chinese, it is the primary organ of digestion. The Spleen extracts the pure nutritive essences of ingested food and fluids, and transforms them into what will become Qi and Blood. Because the Spleen is the source of sufficient Blood and Qi in the body, it is traditionally referred to as the "foundation of postnatal existence" (*hou-tian-zhi-ben*).[25] The Spleen or Spleen Qi is also responsible for sending Grain Qi, derived from food and "pure essences" that will become Blood, upward to the Lungs, where finally the synthesis of Blood and Qi takes place. The Spleen directs "ascending" movement. It is also involved in the movement and transformation of Water in the body. A modern text summarizes these aspects of the Spleen by saying that it "rules the raising of the pure."[26]

If the transformative and transporting functions of the Spleen are harmonious, the Qi and Blood can be abundant and the digestive powers strong. If the Spleen is in disharmony, then the whole body, or some part of it, may develop Deficient Qi or Deficient Blood. If digestion is affected, such symptoms as abdominal distention or pain, diarrhea, or anorexia may appear.

"The Spleen governs the Blood."[27] Not only does the Spleen help to create the Blood, it also governs the Blood in the sense that it keeps the Blood flowing in its proper paths. In general, the Qi commands the blood and the particular aspect of Qi that holds the Blood in place is the Spleen Qi. If the Spleen Qi is weak, the Spleen's governing function loses its harmony, and the Blood can escape its pathways and "move recklessly." This leads to symptoms such as vomiting blood, blood in the stool, blood under the skin, menorrhagia, or uterine bleeding. Many chronic bleeding diseases are treated through the Spleen.

CLINICAL SKETCH: A woman suffers from what Western medicine calls chronic functional uterine bleeding. The Western physician wants to use a hormonal treatment but cannot, because the patient develops severe side effects. The woman goes to an Oriental physician, who diagnoses the pattern of Deficient Spleen Qi not governing the Blood. A series of treatments to strengthen the Spleen, using herbs such as atractylodes and acupuncture points such as Spleen 1 (*Yin-bai*, Hidden White), effects a radical improvement in her condition. Obviously, these treatments affect the reproductive hormones, but within the Chinese paradigm they are thought to improve the Spleen's ability to govern the Blood.[28]

"The Spleen rules the muscles, flesh,"[29] and the four limbs.[30] Not only is the Spleen the origin of Qi and Blood, but the

Spleen also transports these substances to the muscles and flesh. The movement of the muscles, flesh, and, consequently, the four limbs, depends on the power of the Spleen. Muscle tone or the appearance of the limbs often indicates the relative strength or weakness of the Spleen.

"The Spleen opens into the mouth."[31] "The Spleen's brilliance is manifested in the lips."[32] The mouth and lips are closely related to the Spleen. If the Spleen is harmonious, the mouth will be able to distinguish the five tastes,[33] and the lips will be red and moist. If the Spleen is weak, the mouth will be insensitive to taste and the lips will be pale.

Liver (gan 肝)

"The Liver rules flowing and spreading (shu-xie)."[34] The Liver or Liver Qi is responsible for the smooth movement of bodily Substances and for the regularity of body activities. It moves the Qi and Blood in all directions, sending them to every part of the body. The Nei Jing metaphorically calls the Liver "the general of an army"[35] because it maintains evenness and harmony of movement throughout the body.

Words such as soft, subtle, light, and gentle begin to characterize the desirable state of the Liver. A modern Chinese text uses the word sprinkle to describe its activity.[36] One classic herbal treatment to restore Liver harmony is called the Free and Easy Wanderer. Creating this ambience can be thought of as the function of the Liver, as well as a basic need of the Liver itself. A Liver disharmony, then, would be the converse of smoothness, and so the Liver is the Organ most sensitive to stagnation, or "stuckness."

There are three functional aspects to the Liver activity of "flowing and spreading." The first of these is that the Liver "adjusts and makes smooth." The smooth movement of Qi throughout the body is dependent on the "flowing and spreading" action of the Liver. And all activity that depends on Qi—the movement of Qi itself, of Blood, of Meridian Qi, and the activity of all the Organs—depends also on the Liver. Any impairment of Liver function can influence the circulation of Qi and Blood, leading to either Stagnant Qi or Congealed Blood. The Liver Qi can even become stagnant in its own pathways, and will then manifest symptoms like pain or distention in the flanks, swollen or painful breasts and genitals, or lower-abdominal pain.

The Liver's adjusting activity is especially important in digestion. If the Liver loses its harmonious movement it can move in the wrong direction and "invade" the Stomach and Spleen. This may be accompanied by such digestive problems as abdominal pain, nausea, belching, intestinal rumbling, or diarrhea.

The second aspect of Liver function is that it controls bile secretion. Bile is necessary for the digestion of foods and fluids. If the Liver cannot perform its spreading and flowing activities, bile production may be disrupted, causing symptoms such as jaundice, bitter taste in the mouth, vomiting of yellow fluid, distention of the flanks, or loss of appetite.

In its third aspect, the Liver harmonizes the emotions. Its gentle "sprinkling" movement is responsible for creating a relaxed, easygoing internal environment—an even disposition.[37] Any sudden change in the normal pattern of emotions can affect the flowing and dispersing function of the Liver, and, conversely, a disharmony of the Liver will directly affect the emotional state of the individual. Anger and emotional frustration are especially intertwined with the Liver. Chinese practitioners will often diagnose repeated instances of "flying off the handle" as due to a Liver disharmony.

These three aspects of Liver activity have been separated only for the purposes of discussion; in the human body, they are interrelated. Disharmony of the Liver's flowing function can affect the bile or the emotions, and vice versa. In this interconnectedness lies one of the basic principles of Chinese medicine—the medical theory never departs from the physical body, but its definition of that body includes what the West would call psychology.

"The Liver stores the Blood."[38] This statement refers to both the storage and the regulation of the Blood. It is traditionally thought that "when a person moves, the Blood moves to the Meridians" and that "when a person rests, the Blood returns to the Liver."[39] During periods of physical activity, when the body needs more Blood for nourishment, the Liver allows the Blood to move freely outward. When the body is inactive, this Blood returns to and is stored in the Liver. There are two types of storage disharmonies. One is insufficient Blood for storing. A common affliction of this disharmony is insufficient Blood to nourish the eyes, making them rough and dry. The second kind of disharmony is loss of the ability to store properly, and it manifests itself as an unusually heavy menstrual flow.

CLINICAL SKETCH: If a patient complains of dry eyes, an examination will often reveal that the blood of the Liver is deficient. Herbs like *Lycium*, which nourishes the Liver Blood, and acupuncture points such as Liver 3 (*Tai-chong*, Great Pouring) and Gall Bladder 37 (*Guang-ming*, Bright Light), will, after a number of treatments, alleviate the condition.[46]

"The Liver rules the tendons and is manifest in the nails."[41] The proper movement of all the tendons in the body is closely related to the Liver. To Chinese medicine, "tendons" is a broader category than it is in Western anatomy, for it includes ligaments and, to some extent, muscles.[42] If the Liver Blood is insufficient and incapable of nourishing the tendons, symptoms such as spasms, numbness of the limbs, and difficulty in bending or stretching may result. Liver disharmonies may also cause the nails to be thin, brittle, and pale. When the Liver Blood is plentiful, however, the tendons are supple and the nails appear pink and moist.

"The Liver opens into the eyes."[43] All of the Yin and Yang Organs contribute the purest part of their energy to the eyes, creating the brightness or awareness that characterizes harmonious Spirit. The Liver, however, has a special relationship to the function of the eyes. The *Nei Jing* says, "When the Liver is harmonized, the eyes can distinguish the five colors,"[44] and "When the Liver receives Blood, the eyes can see."[45] Therefore, many disorders of the eyes and of vision are taken to be Liver-related.

Kidneys (shen 肾)

"The Kidneys store the Jing"[46] and rule birth, development, and maturation. Jing is the Substance most closely associated with life itself; it is the source of life and of individual development. Although it is undifferentiated material, it is the Substance that gives organic life its specific character. It contains the possibility of birth, maturation, decay, and death. Jing is the potential for differentiation into Yin and Yang, which is to say it produces life, for life is the process of continual differentiation into Yin and Yang. The entire body and all the Organs of the body need Jing in order to thrive. The Kidneys, because they store Jing, bestow this potential for life activity. They have, therefore, a special relationship with the other Organs in that they hold the underlying material of each Organ's existence and are the foundation of each Organ's Yin and Yang. In other words, the Yin and Yang, or life activity, of each Organ ultimately depends on the Yin and Yang of the Kidneys. Thus, the Kidneys are the "root of life." As the medical tradition states, "The Kidneys are the mansion of Fire and Water, the residence of Yin and Yang . . . the channel of death and life."[47]

All the Organs can be characterized as either Yin or Yang. But every Organ has both a supportive, nourishing Yin aspect and an active Yang aspect. For example, the Heart's storing of Shen is a Yin function, while ruling Blood is a Yang function. The Liver's storing of Blood is Yin, while its spreading of Qi is Yang. As the primal organic material, Jing can be thought of as coming "before" Yin and Yang; but because of its undifferentiated, primordial character, it is Yin as well. It is characteristic of the dialectical movement of classical Chinese thought that Jing *can* be both before Yin and Yang and be Yin as well, and that within that Yin there is another Yin and Yang differentiation.

The Kidneys, like all organs, have both Yin and Yang aspects. Its storing activity is Yin, but some of its other activities are

Yang. The Yin of the Kidneys, depending on context, is called either Jing or Water (if Jing is before Yin and Yang). The Yang of the Kidneys has a special name. It is called *Ming-men huo*, or Life Gate Fire.[48]

The Kidneys are also called the "root of life" because Jing is the source of reproduction, development, and maturation. Conception is made possible by the power of Jing; growth to maturity is the blossoming of Jing; and the decline into old age reflects the weakening of Jing. As time passes, the Jing decreases in both vitality and quantity. Because the Kidneys store Jing, all these processes are governed by the Kidneys. Therefore, reproductive problems such as sterility or impotence and developmental disorders like retarded growth or lack of sexual maturation are seen as dysfunctions of the Kidneys' storing of Jing. Aging is considered a normal process, and when it proceeds gracefully it is not seen as an illness or a problem. If aging is premature, or if it lacks the dignity of a sense of completion, it may be the result of Kidney Jing irregularities.

"The Kidneys rule Water."[49] While the Lungs "move and adjust the Water Channels" and "liquefy vapor," and the Spleen "raises the pure," including pure fluids, the Kidneys are the foundation upon which this entire process of Water movement and transformation is built.

The words *Water* and *Fluids* are often used interchangeably, but sometimes one or the other is preferred. *Water* has a more general connotation than *Fluids*. While *Fluids* refers to Water in its particular aspects (perspiration, urine, etc.), *Water* refers to all the moisture in the body. Water is also thought of as the opposing principle to Fire, the Yin to Fire's Yang. Since Water and Fire are two of the basic forces at work both in the body and in the universe, Water is the broader, more metaphorical term.

The Kidneys rule Water through their Yang aspect, the Life Gate Fire. This Fire, or Heat, transforms Water into a "mist," a necessary first step before Fluids can ascend or circulate. All the circulation of Water in the body depends on the vaporizing power of the Kidneys. The Spleen also vaporizes pure Fluids as it raises the pure essences of food and Fluids, but its vaporization power—its Fire—is ultimately dependent on the Kidney Fire, which acts as a kind of "pilot light."

The system of Water movement may be summarized as follows. Fluids are received by the Stomach, which begins a process of separation, by which the unusable portions of food are sent to the intestines as waste and the pure Water is extracted. This process is continued by the Spleen, which then sends the pure Fluids in a vaporized state upward to the Lungs. The Lungs circulate the clear part of the Fluids throughout the body, but liquefy whatever has become impure through use and send it downward to the Kidneys. In the Kidneys, the impure part is further separated into relatively "clean" and "turbid" parts. The clear part is transformed into a mist and sent upward to the Lungs, where it rejoins the cycle. The final impure portion goes into the Bladder, where it is stored and subsequently excreted.

CLINICAL SKETCH: A patient is diagnosed by a Western physician as right-sided heart failure. The patient's chief complaint is serious edema of the entire body (anasarca). An Oriental physician gives the man a complete examination and decides that he has the pattern of Deficient Kidney Fire, unable to rule Water. The physician prescribes very warming herbs, including aconite, and the use of moxibustion (burning substances such as mugwort to stimulate an acupuncture point) at such points as Kidney 7 (*Fu-liu*, Returning Current) and Conception Vessel 4 (*Guan-yuan*, Hinge Source). After a course of treatment, the patient's symptoms are visibly alleviated. Examination by a Western physician confirms great improvement in the heart. A partial explanation of these results in Western terms could be that modern pharmacological studies have demonstrated that aconite is a potent cardiotonic. Chinese medicine, however, describes it as a warmer of the Kidney.[50]

"The Kidneys rule the bones."[51] "The Kidneys produce the marrow."[52] These two functions are an aspect of control by the Kidney Jing of birth, development, and maturation. The Kidneys store the Jing, and it is said that the Jing produces marrow. The marrow, in turn, is responsible for creating and supporting bones. Therefore, the bones' development and repair depend on the nourishment of the Kidney Jing. In a child, insufficient Kidney Jing may result in soft bones or incomplete closure of the bones of the skull. In an adult, insufficient Kidney Jing can produce weak legs and knees, brittle bones, or stiffness of the spine.

The teeth are considered the surplus of the bones, and so they too are ruled by the Kidneys. When a child's teeth develop poorly or fall out, or an adult's teeth are a constant problem, a Chinese physician will suspect an insufficient Kidney Jing.

"The Kidneys open into the ear."[53] The Kidneys manifest in the head hair.[54] There is a close relationship between the Kidneys and the ears. As the *Nei Jing* says, "The Kidney Qi goes through the ear; if the Kidney is harmonized, the ear can hear the five tones."[55] Many hearing problems are treated through the Kidneys. The poor hearing common in the elderly, for example, is a consequence of weakened Kidney Jing.

The relative moistness and vitality of head hair are also related to the Kidney Jing, and the loss of hair that accompanies aging is another manifestation of weakness of the Kidney Jing. The head hair also depends on the Blood for nourishment, which is why the tradition calls head hair "the surplus of the Blood."[56]

"The Kidneys rule the grasping of Qi."[57] While the Lungs administer respiration, normal breathing also requires assistance from the Kidneys. The Kidneys enable the Natural Air Qi to penetrate deeply, completing the inhalation process by what is called "grasping the Qi." The Kidneys are thus the "root of Qi," while the Lungs are the "foundation of Qi." Proper breathing thus depends on the Kidneys; and Kidney disharmonies may result in respiratory problems, especially chronic asthma.

Yang Organs (*liu-fu* 六腑)

The main function of the Yang Organs is to receive food, absorb the usable portions, and transmit and excrete waste.

The Yang Organs are less directly involved with the Fundamental Substances than are the Yin Organs. They are also considered more exterior than the Yin Organs. The word *exterior* (*biao*) has more to do with the ultimate life significance of an organ than with its physical location. Thus, the important Yin Organs are thought to be more interior than the less important Yang Organs.

Each Yang Organ is coupled with a Yin Organ in what is called an interior-exterior relationship. (See Table 1.)

TABLE 1

Coupled Yin and Yang Organs

Yin Organ	Yang Organ
Heart	Small Intestine
Lungs	Large Intestine
Spleen	Stomach
Liver	Gall Bladder
Kidneys	Bladder
(Pericardium)	Triple Burner

This means that the Meridian pathways (discussed in Chapter 4) of coupled Organs are connected. Sometimes this coupling has clinical significance and at other times it mainly completes a hypothetical symmetry. (See Appendix B.)

Gall Bladder (*dan* 胆)

The Gall Bladder stores and secretes bile. Bile is a bitter yellow fluid continuously produced by the surplus Qi of the Liver. The Gall Bladder sends bile downward, where it pours into the Intestines and aids the digestive process.

The Liver that produces bile and the Gall Bladder that secretes it are very dependent on each other. Any disruption of the Liver's flowing and spreading activity will affect the Gall Bladder's bile secretion. Disharmonies of the Gall Bladder will affect the Liver, possibly resulting in such symptoms as vomiting bitter fluid and jaundice generated by the "brimming over" of bile.

The *Nei Jing* says that the Gall Bladder rules decisions.[58] That is, behavior characterized by anger and rash decisions may be due to an excess of Gall Bladder Qi. Indecision and timidity may be a sign of Gall Bladder disharmony and weakness.

Stomach (*wei* 胃)

The Stomach is responsible for "receiving" and "ripening" ingested food and fluids. It is therefore called "the sea of food and fluid."[59] Food begins its decomposition in the Stomach. The "pure" part is then sent to the Spleen, which transforms it into the raw material for Qi and Blood. The "turbid" part is sent to the Small Intestine for further digestion. The Stomach and Spleen activities are closely related. While the Spleen rules "ascending," the Stomach rules "descending"; that is, it makes things move downward. Thus, the directions of their Qi activity complement each other. If the Stomach's receiving and descending functions are impaired, symptoms such as nausea, stomachache, distention, belching, or vomiting may ensue.

Small Intestine (*xiao-chang* 小肠)

The Small Intestine rules the separation of the "pure" from the "turbid." It receives what the Stomach has not completely decomposed and continues the process of separation and absorption. The "clear" part is extracted by the Small Intestine and sent to the Spleen, and the "turbid" part continues downward to the Large Intestine. Some impure ingested fluid is also sent directly to the Kidneys and Bladder. Disharmonies involving the Small Intestine may produce abdominal pain, intestinal rumblings, diarrhea, or constipation.

Large Intestine (*da-chang* 大肠)

The Large Intestine continues to move the turbid parts of the food and fluids downward, while at the same time absorbing water from this waste material. At the end of this process, the feces are formed and eliminated under the control of the Large Intestine. If the Large Intestine loses its harmony, abdominal pain, intestinal rumblings, diarrhea, or constipation may result.

Bladder (pang-guang 膀 胱)

The function of the Bladder is to receive and excrete the urine. Urine is produced in the Kidneys, out of the final portion of the turbid fluids transmitted from the Lungs, Small Intestine, and Large Intestine. Disharmonies of the Bladder may lead to urinary problems such as incontinence, burning urination, or difficulty in urinating. The coupling of the Bladder and the Kidneys reflects a clinical importance based on their complementary functions.

Triple Burner (san-jiao 三 焦)

The Chinese word for this Organ can be translated as Triple Burner, Triple Warmer, or Triple Heater. Literally, it means "three that burn" or "three that scorch." The Triple Burner is the sixth Yang Organ, although its exact Organ nature is not clear from the classical texts. Ambiguity and dispute surround this Organ.[60]

The majority of Chinese physicians agree that the Triple Burner "has a name but no shape."[61] It is best understood as the functional relationship between various Organs that regulate Water. These are mainly the Lungs, Spleen, and Kidneys, but they also include the Small Intestine and the Bladder. The Triple Burner does not exist as an entity outside of these other Organs, but rather it is the pathway that makes these Organs a complete system.

In Chinese medical thought, Fire is necessary to control Water. The name Triple Burner implies Fire, and the *Nei Jing* emphasizes the Triple Burner's control of the body's Water. In the *Nei Jing*, the Triple Burner is called the "Official of the Bursting Water Dam" and is referred to as "where the Water Channel arises."[62] The *Nei Jing* implies, so tradition has it, that those aspects of the Spleen, Kidney, Stomach, Large Intestine, Small Intestine, and Bladder that are involved in Water movement are all regulated by the Qi of the Triple Burner.

The *Nei Jing* says further that "the Upper Burner is a mist."[63] A mist is pervasive, and traditionally this would correspond to the vaporized Water in the Lungs that is later disseminated throughout the body. "The Middle Burner is a foam."[64] This is traditionally interpreted as referring to the digestive churnings of the Stomach and Spleen. "The lower Burner is a swamp."[65] It is in charge of excreting impure substances. The reference here is primarily to the Kidneys, Large and Small Intestines, and the Bladder.

There is also general agreement on another definition of the Triple Burner. This concept considers the Triple Burner a demarcation of three areas of the body. The Upper Burner is the head and chest, including the Heart and Lungs. The Middle Burner is the area below the chest but above the navel, and includes the Spleen and Stomach. The Lower Burner corresponds to the abdominal area below the navel and especially encompasses the Liver and Kidney. (The location of the Liver is related to its Meridian pathway in the lower groin.)[66]

The Organs of the body, defined as they are by their functions and relationships, are another part of the bodily web. They cannot be discussed out of context. The Chinese notions about Organs (or about anything else) are not meant to be hard pieces of a theory that can be proved or disproved. They are part of an organizing network to be used when convenient. The Chinese would be indifferent to proof in our accustomed scientific sense. In the Song dynasty (960–1279 C.E.) introduction to the Systematic Classic of Acupuncture (282 C.E.), the Imperial Medical Scholars are explicitly aware that the Meridians and much of the rest of the system are not to be found when one dissects and physically investigates. They are not troubled. They say it does not matter. The verification is the classics, the wisdom of the ancients, and the fact that the system works.[67]

In the West, since the scientific revolution, a theory must rest on a provable physical substratum of repeatable events and measurable facts. Each fact holds up the next level. William Harvey helped usher in this scientific revolution when on April 17, 1616, in a public lecture, he overthrew the classic Greek notion of blood movement and replaced it with the modern concept of circulation. The entire Greek medical edifice crumbled. Early speculations and imaginative constructs were found to be insufficient. Hard and substantial facts were to be the basis of the new knowledge. Qualities had to be reduced to quantities, images to lines, speculation to experimentation. The Chinese theories, however, resemble those of Greek antiquity. This type of fact is a speculative interpretation. For the Chinese, it is a sensory image, a poetic exploration of what is going on. The value of the Chinese theories is in aiding the organization of observation, discerning patterns, capturing interconnectedness and qualities of being. Can one prove a poetic image? It can be shared. It can be used. One can decide if it's worth listening to. . . .

Notes

1. F. Mann, *The Meridians of Acupuncture* (London: Heinemann Medical Books, 1964), p. 57.

2. See the discussion of thyroid problems and their relationship to traditional Chinese patterns of disharmony in Chengdu Institute, Internal Medicine and Pediatrics [40], pp. 538–544. Also see Introduction to Experience of Using Chinese Herbal Medicine in Hyperthyroidism, JTCM, March 1960, pp. 22–30.

3. While it is unlikely that Hippocrates of Cos (460–377 B.C.E.) performed dissection, many schools did. Erasistratus of Julis (c. 304 B.C.E.) was noted for his anatomical studies and rigorous seeking of causal explanations of diseases. For example, he described the valves of the heart, distinguished sensory and motor nerves, and accurately described the movement of food in the body. The other noted early anatomist was Herophilus of Chalcedon, who may have per-

formed vivisection on criminals, but whose interest was not in finding causal explanations. Aristotle's anatomy was quite advanced, and Galen of Pergamum (c. 129–200 C.E.) made a very sophisticated anatomy and physiology the cornerstone of his medicine. For a description of Greek anatomy, see "The History of Anatomy in Antiquity" in *Ancient Medicine: Selected Papers of Ludwig Edelstein*, ed. by Temkin and Temkin (Baltimore: Johns Hopkins Press, 1967), pp. 247–303; and Charles Singer, *A Short History of Anatomy and Physiology from the Greeks to Harvey* (New York: Dover, 1957), pp. 9–62.

In China, internal anatomy is generally irrelevant to clinical practice. The *Nei Jing* mentions dissection (*Ling Shu*, sec. 3, chap. 12, p. 156) and has records of anatomical investigation (e.g., *Ling Shu*, sec. 6, chap. 31, p. 270), but these descriptions are incidental and crude. China also had Confucian religious and ethical prohibitions against dissection, which were first written in legal code form in 653 C.E. Despite the general lack of interest and the religious barriers, sporadic instances of dissection occurred in Chinese history—e.g., the famous Song-dynasty dissection of forty-six rebels in 1045 C.E. But such occasional episodes were of no consequence in medical practice. For a discussion of the lack of a Chinese anatomy, see Jia De-dao, Concise History of China's Medicine [95], pp. 220–222.

4. Manfred Porkert, "Chinese Medicine: A Traditional Healing Science," in *Ways of Health*, ed. by David S. Sobel (New York: Harcourt Brace Jovanovich, 1979), p. 158. Also see Porkert, *Theoretical Foundations*, pp. 107–108.

5. The *Nei Jing* speaks mainly of five Yin and six Yang Organs. There are several implicit references to the Pericardium as a sixth Yin Organ, but the first explicit statement is in "Difficulty 25" of the second-century *Nan Jing* or Classic of Difficulties [3], p. 66. This book is a series of eighty-one questions and answers concerning the *Nei Jing*.

6. *Su Wen* [1], sec. 3, chap. 11, p. 77.

7. Ibid., sec. 20, chap. 44, p. 246, and sec. 3, chap. 10, p. 72.

8. *Ling Shu* [2], sec. 10, chap. 71, p. 475.

9. *Su Wen*, sec. 3, chap. 9, p. 67.

10. *Ling Shu*, sec. 4, chap. 17, p. 189.

11. Shanghai Institute, Foundations [53], p. 80.

12. For an interesting discussion of the comparative effects of Western and Chinese methods of treating insomnia, see Tianjin Institute,

Practical Clinical Handbook of Traditional Chinese Medicine [56], p. 149.

13. *Su Wen*, sec. 13, chap. 46, p. 256.

14. Ma Ruo-shui, Theoretical Foundations of Traditional Chinese Medicine [62], p. 35.

15. The Yang Organs are, in general, more susceptible to External Pernicious Influences. The Lungs are an exception. See Appendix B.

16. *Su Wen*, sec. 3, chap. 10, p. 72.

17. Ibid., sec. 7, chap. 21, p. 140.

18. Shanghai Institute, Foundations [53], p. 83.

19. *Su Wen*, sec. 3, chap. 10, p. 70.

20. Ibid.

21. The Chinese have two distinct terms for "hair": *fa*, or "head hair," and *mao*, which may be translated as "body hair" or "surface hair."

22. The effectiveness of the Chinese medical treatment may be partially related, from a Western medical perspective, to the fact that Astragulus can excite the central nervous system and stimulate human sexual hormones. (Zhongshan Institute, Clinical Use of Chinese Medicines [92], p. 330) Modern research has also verified the effect of Astragulus on the common cold, both by itself and especially in combination in the "Jade Screen," in such studies as Effect of *Radix astragali* on the Para-influenza I (Sendai) Virus Infection in Mice and on its Epidemiological Efficacy in the Prophylaxis of the Common Cold, JTCM, January 1980.

23. *Ling Shu*, sec. 4, chap. 17, p. 189.

24. This is a traditional saying that combines the meaning of several references in the *Nei Jing*, e.g., *Su Wen*, sec. 7, chap. 21, p. 139, and *Ling Shu*, sec. 4, chap. 18, p. 139.

25. Essential Readings in Medicine (*Yi-zong Bi-du*) by Li Zhong-zi, 1637 (Taipei: Wenguang, 1977), p. 6. The Kidneys in the same sentence are called "the foundation of prenatal existence" (xian-tian-zhi-ben).

26. Beijing Institute, Foundations [38], p. 12.

27. This aspect of the Spleen is not directly mentioned in the *Nei Jing* but is spoken of in "Difficulty 42" of the *Nan Jing* [3]: "The

Spleen binds [or wraps] the Blood" (p. 99). The word *govern* in relation to Spleen and Blood seems to have been used first by Tang Zong-hai in his medical classic Discussion of Blood Patterns (first published 1885) to distinguish the functions mentioned in the *Nei Jing* of the various Organs in relation to the Blood. See p. 10 of the 1977 edition [20].

28. Journals of traditional Chinese medicine in the People's Republic have frequent articles on functional uterine bleeding which report excellent results with Chinese methods. For example, see Summary of Treatment of Seventy Cases of Uterine Bleeding, JTCM, January 1959, and Discussion of Several Questions Concerning Uterine Bleeding, JTCM, August 1978.

29. *Su Wen*, sec. 12, chap. 44, p. 246.

30. Paraphrase of *Su Wen*, sec. 8, chap. 29, p. 180.

31. *Ling Shu*, sec. 4, chap. 17, p. 189.

32. *Su Wen*, sec. 3, chap. 10, p. 70.

33. *Ling Shu*, sec. 4, chap. 17, p. 189. The five tastes are bitter, sour, sweet, salty, and acrid.

34. Various aspects of the Liver's activity are mentioned in the *Nei Jing* and other early texts. Tang Zong-hai seems to have been the first to use the expression "flowing and spreading" to summarize these functions. See his Discussion of Blood Patterns [20], p. 8. This expression is now standard in all modern texts.

The *Nei Jing*'s summary of these functions is understood to be implied in the phrase "The Liver is the foundation of curtailing extremeness" (*Gan-zhe ba-ji-zhi-ben*; *Su Wen*, sec. 3, chap. 9, p. 68).

35. *Su Wen*, sec. 3, chap. 8, p. 58.

36. Beijing Institute, Foundations [38], p. 13.

37. The Liver's link to the emotions is said to be partially related to an aspect of Shen known as Hun or "Soul," which is stored in the Liver. *Ling Shu*, sec. 2, chap. 8, p. 86.

38. Ibid.

39. The second half of this statement is from *Su Wen*, sec. 3, chap. 10, p. 73. The first half of the statement is an explanation by the commentator and his compiler, Wang Bing-ci, whose edition of the *Nei-jing Su-wen* was submitted to the throne in 762 C.E. and is now the standard edition [1].

40. Chinese medicine can be used to treat a wide range of eye illnesses. For example, see the series of articles in the Zhejiang Journal of Traditional Chinese Medicine, February 1980, or such texts as Guangdong Provincial Traditional Chinese Medicine Hospital, Traditional Chinese Ophthalmology [74].

The herb *Lycium* by itself, from a Western perspective, has no obvious effect on the eyes that has been noted, but in combination with various other herbs it has a marked effect on diseases characterized by dry eyes. See Shanghai Institute, Study of Prescriptions [87], p. 236.

41. *Su Wen*, sec. 3, chap. 10, p. 70.

42. The Chinese word *jin* is here translated as tendon. The word in its traditional clinical use does not have a precise physical correlate and can refer to any (Western-defined) tendon, ligament, or muscle that is involved in a disharmony of the Liver. The muscle of the Spleen-muscle connection can be any tendon or ligament that is involved in a Spleen disharmony. This is an example of how function and relationship are more important than precise physical substrata in Chinese medicine.

43. *Ling Shu*, sec. 4, chap. 17, p. 189.

44. Ibid. The five colors are white, yellow, red, blue-green, and black.

45. *Su Wen*, sec. 3, chap. 10, p. 73.

46. Ibid., sec. 1, chap. 1, p. 6.

47. Zhang Jie-bing, Illustrated Wing to the Classic of Categories [30]. This quotation is in the Additions to Wings (*Lei-jing Fu-yi*), sec. 3, chap. 17, p. 439. The quotation is actually about the Life Gate Fire, which Zhang Jie-bing here uses as a general expression for the Kidneys. (See note 48.) The *Nan Jing* too says, "The Kidney area is the origin of the five Yin and five Yang Organs, the root of the twelve Meridians . . . and the origin of the three Burners" ("Difficulty 8," p. 17).

48. The *Nei Jing* uses the term *ming-men* to denote the shine of eyes. Later, in "Difficulty 36" of the *Nan Jing*, the term is used to designate Kidney Yang and is identified with the right Kidney. Later medical authorities disagree as to whether the Life Gate Fire is the right Kidney only, or the Yang of both Kidneys, or just a general name for the Kidney. An interesting summary of this historical debate is included in Li Tiao-hua, Patterns and Treatment of the Kidneys and Kidney Illnesses [60], pp. 2–4.

49. *Su Wen*, sec. 1, chap. 1, p. 6.

50. Zhongshan Institute, Clinical Use of Chinese Medicines [92], p. 192.

51. *Su Wen*, sec. 7, chap. 23, p. 154.

52. Ibid., sec. 2, chap. 5, p. 41.

53. *Ling Shu*, sec. 4, chap. 17, p. 189.

54. *Su Wen*, sec. 3, chap. 9, p. 68.

55. *Ling Shu*, sec. 4, chap. 17, p. 189. The five tones or musical notes are called *jiao, zhi, guan, shang,* and *yu.*

56. Traditional Chinese Medical Research Institute and Guangzhou Institute, Concise Dictionary of Traditional Chinese Medicine [34], p. 280.

57. This phrase is standard in most recent introductory or pathology texts on traditional medicine. The earliest statement of this sort is from the *Nan Jing*: "The Kidney area is . . . the door of respiration" ("Difficulty 8," p. 17). The *Nei Jing* mentions asthma as a possible Kidney or Kidney Meridian symptom (*Su Wen*, sec. 7, chap. 22, p. 148; *Ling Shu*, sec. 3, chap. 10, p. 125). Around 280 c.e., Wang Shu-he linked asthma to a possible Kidney or Kidney Meridian disharmony in his Classic of the Pulse (*Mai Jing* [22]), p. 19. Chao Yuan-fang continued this tradition in his Discussion on the Origins of Symptoms in Illness [13] of 610 c.e., sec. 15, chap. 6, p. 89. By the time of the Ming dynasty this connection between the Kidneys and breathing was firmly and formally stated by various scholars. The quotation in the text, "The Kidneys rule the grasping of Qi," now commonly used by traditional doctors, is from Ordering of Patterns and Deciding Treatments (*Lei-zheng Zhi-cai*) by Lin Pei-qin. This volume first appeared in 1839 and the quotation appears in sec. 2, p. 113 (Taipei: Whirlwind Press, 1978).

58. *Su Wen*, sec. 13, chap. 47, p. 262.

59. Ibid., sec. 3, chap. 11, p. 78.

60. For some of the flavor of these debates, see such articles as Tentative Discussion on the Triple Burner by Cheng Jia-zhang, SJTCM, October 1958; Concerning the Triple Burner Dispute,

JTCM, January 1959; and Clarification of Unsolved Problems Concerning the Triple Burner, JTCM, July 1980.

61. This statement was first made in relation to the Triple Burner in "Difficulty 38" of the *Nan Jing*. Sun Si-miao, the great Tang-dynasty physician, repeated this statement and emphasized this explanation in his Thousand Ducat Prescriptions [19] (first published 652 C.E.), sec. 20, chap. 4, p. 362. All sorts of interpretations and disagreements with this idea exist in the medical literature.

62. *Su Wen*, sec. 3, chap. 8, p. 59.

63. *Ling Shu*, sec. 4, chap. 18, p. 199.

64. Ibid.

65. Ibid.

66. In the medical tradition, only secondary mention is made of the Triple Burner's digestive and Qi function. In the *Nan Jing* ("Difficulty 31"), the Triple Burner is called the "road for nutrition" and is referred to as "the beginning and end of Qi." Zhang Jie-bing, in his Ming-dynasty commentary on the *Nei Jing*, called the *Lei Jing* or Classic of Categories, says that the Triple Burner is "the commander-in-chief of all the Qi of the various Organs, the Protective Qi, Nutritive Qi, and the Meridian Qi of the Interior and Exterior, right and left, upper and lower regions" and that it "is responsible for communication among the different parts of the body" (Zhang, Illustrated Wing [30], sec. 3, chap. 23, p. 121). Again in the *Nan Jing* ("Difficulty 66"), the Triple Burner is called the "sixth Yang Organ, responsible for supporting all the various types of Qi of the body." But the Qi and digestive functions of the Triple Burner are usually considered secondary to its Water-metabolism functions. The tradition concerning Qi is based on an unexplained, out-of-place phrase in the *Nei Jing* (*Ling Shu*, sec. 3, chap. 10, p. 131), but a comprehensive examination of the symptomology of the Triple Burner Organ (as opposed to the Meridian) in the *Nei Jing* shows it to be primarily related to Water movement (e.g., *Ling Shu*, sec. 1, chap. 2, p. 20), again confirming the central interpretation of this Organ.

67. This classic introduction was written by Lin Yi, Gao Bao-heng, and Sun Qi-guang, who were Song dynasty Imperial Medical Scholars and Librarians of the Hall of Records. This discussion appears on page 11 of Huangfu Mi's Systematic Classic of Acupuncture [15]. This text is the earliest acupuncture manual in existence.

The word *Meridian* as used in Chinese medicine came into the English language through a French translation of the Chinese term *jing-luo*.[1] *Jing** means "to go through" or "a thread in a fabric"; *luo* means "something that connects or attaches," or "a net." Meridians are the channels or pathways that carry Qi and Blood through the body. They are not Blood Vessels. Rather, they comprise an invisible network that links together all the Fundamental Substances and Organs. In Chinese Meridian theory, these channels are unseen but are thought to embody a physical reality—the Substances Qi and Blood move along them, carrying nourishment and strength. Because the Meridian system unifies all the parts of the body, it is essential for the maintenance of harmonious balance. The *Nei Jing* says: "The Meridians move the Qi and Blood, regulate Yin and Yang, moisten the tendons and bones, benefit the joints."[2]

The Meridians connect the interior of the body with the exterior. (As has been said earlier, the distinction between inner and outer has more to do with significance than with place—the interior is more important than the exterior.) This is the basis of acupuncture theory, that working with points on the surface of the body will affect what goes on inside the body, because it

*The character *jing* for Meridian is different from the term *Jing* that means Essence.

affects the activity of the Substances that are traveling through the Meridians. Every Chinese physician must have a complete grasp of the Meridian system. Most acupuncture points relate to the Meridians and most herbs a doctor prescribes will enter one or more of the Meridian pathways.

The Meridian system is made up of twelve regular Meridians that correspond to each of the five Yin and six Yang Organs, and to the Pericardium (which for the purposes of Meridian theory is an independent Organ).[3] These are sometimes called Jing Meridians. There are also eight Extra Meridians, only two of which, the Governing Vessel and the Conception Vessel[4] are considered major Meridians. This is because they have independent points—points that are not also on any of the twelve regular Meridians. The paths of the other six Extra Meridians all intersect with these twelve Meridians and have no independent points of their own. There are also many small, finer, netlike minor Meridians, called Luo Meridians. The twelve regular Meridians along with the Governing and Conception Meridians are the fourteen major Meridians: They and the minor Meridians are the warp and woof of the body.[5]

A number of books on Meridian theory have been published recently in English as a result of the Western interest in acupuncture. This chapter, therefore, will deal with Meridian theory only as it pertains to Chinese medical knowledge as a whole—for its use in explaining patterns of disharmony.

Meridian theory assumes that disorder within a Meridian generates derangement in the pathway and creates disharmony along that Meridian, or that such derangement is a result of a disharmony of the Meridian's connecting Organ. A disorder in the Stomach Meridian, for example, may cause upper toothache because the Meridian passes through the upper gums, while lower toothache may be the result of a disorder of the Large Intestine Meridian. Pain in the groin may as easily result from a Liver Meridian disorder as from a disorder of the Liver itself.

Disharmonies in an Organ may manifest themselves in the corresponding Meridians. For instance, pain along the Heart

Meridian may reflect Congealed Blood or Stagnant Qi in the Heart. Excess Fire in the Liver may follow the Meridian and generate redness in the eyes.

An understanding of the interconnections between Substances, Organs, and Meridians informs the practices of acupuncture and herbology. These are the two main forms of treatment used in Chinese medicine, and Meridian theory allows the physician to apply them to particular patients. The goal of all treatment methods in Chinese medicine is to rebalance those aspects of the body's Yin and Yang whose harmonious proportion and movement have become disordered. Agitated activity, for instance, as in the case of inappropriate anger such as that characterized by excessive Liver Qi, must be calmed. Insufficient activity, say of the Kidney Yang, must be tonified to avoid lack of sexual energy. Substances that accumulate inappropriately must be drained—as is done to correct an excess of Fluids in the abdomen. If there is not enough Qi in the Lungs, it must be replenished so that the patient does not continually catch cold. Movement must also go in the proper direction. If the Qi of the Spleen descends, causing chronic diarrhea, it must be lifted; if the Qi of the Stomach ascends, causing nausea, it must be sent down. Stagnant Qi must be moved; reckless movement of the Blood must be stabilized. Too much Cold in the Kidneys must be warmed; extra Fire in the Lungs must be cooled. Whatever is out of balance must be rebalanced. The complementary aspects of Yin and Yang must be harmonious.

The basic idea behind acupuncture (considered a Yang treatment because it moves from the exterior to the interior) is that the insertion of very fine needles into points along the Meridians can rebalance bodily disharmonies. A related technique, moxibustion, entails the application of heat from certain burning substances at the acupuncture points. The primary *moxa*, or heating substance, is mugwort—(*Artemisia vulgaris*). The action of the needles or of moxibustion affects the Qi and Blood in the Meridians, thus affecting all the Substances and Organs. The needles can reduce what is excessive, increase what is deficient, warm what is cold, cool what is hot, circulate what is stagnant, move what is congealed, stabilize what is reckless, raise what is falling, and lower what is rising.

Classical theory recognizes about 365 acupuncture points on the surface Meridians of the body.[6] With the inclusion of miscellaneous points and new points used in ear acupuncture and other recent methods, the total universe has risen to at least 2,000 points for possible use.[7] In practice, however, a typical doctor's repertoire would be only 150 points.

In contemporary texts, point location is generally based on modern anatomy. For example, a manual produced by the Academy of Traditional Chinese Medicine in 1975 describes the location of a common point as "at the lateral side . . . above the transverse popliteal crease between the *musculus vastus laterali* and the *musculus biceps femoris*."[8] Classical texts, which do not reflect an interest in detailed anatomy, refer to that same point as the place where the tip of the middle finger naturally touches the thigh when the patient is standing.[9] The classical literature locates other points by means of easily defined, yet precise, bodily landmarks such as creases, bony prominences, hairlines, and places where the skin changes in color and textural quality.

Each acupuncture point has a defined therapeutic action. The physician chooses to work on those points that are most appropriate for treating a particular individual's pattern of disharmony. Rarely are acupuncture points used singly; a combination of points is usually chosen. A typical treatment entails the insertion of five to fifteen needles. Acupuncture needles were originally made of bronze or possibly copper, tin, gold, or silver. In earlier periods, they may have been bone, horn, or slivers of bamboo, gold, or silver. They are now made of stainless steel, are of hairlike thinness, and produce relatively little pain when inserted. The depth to which a needle penetrates depends on the particular point; needles are inserted only a millimeter or two at the finger points, but they may be placed up to three or four inches deep at the buttocks' points.

Acupuncture as an anesthetic technique was given much sensationalistic coverage in the early 1970s. There were headline-making reports of major operations performed without other anesthesia, many of them witnessed by Western surgical specialists. It is true that acupuncture can be used to deaden pain. As a result, Western interest has been aimed mostly at applying the anesthetic effects of acupuncture to Western-style surgery and general pain control. A number of theories have been developed to explain the mechanisms of anesthesia through acupuncture.

The gate theory, for example, suggests that stimulation from the needles jams the lower nerve bundles in the central nervous system so that other pain signals—those from an incision—cannot reach the brain. This can be envisioned by imagining a telephone system in a major city: If too many individual lines are in use it is very difficult for an outside caller to get into the trunk lines and make a connection.[10]

Another theory of acupuncture anesthesia suggests that the insertion of the acupuncture needles may stimulate the release of endorphins, a class of opiates naturally produced within the brain. These substances are remarkably potent painkillers and could be responsible for dulling the pain impulses caused by surgical procedures.[11]

These preliminary findings and theories will generate further important research into the physiological mechanisms of acupuncture and its possible place in Western medicine. But these tentative theories are only of partial value because they isolate one of acupuncture's uses and ignore its many other clinical applications.[12] Acupuncture as part of a comprehensive system of medicine has failed to capture the interest of Western media, and so it unfortunately remains a mystery of the Far East.

If acupuncture is little known, Chinese herbology—considered a Yin treatment—is almost unknown in the West. This has led to the widespread misconception that acupuncture constitutes all of Chinese medicine. In fact, the science of herbs is central to Chinese medicine. During the last two millennia, many more books have been devoted to herbology than to acupuncture. And while Chinese physicians tend to practice both medical techniques, physicians who practice only with herbs are more numerous than those who practice only with acupuncture.[13]

The body of knowledge of Chinese herbology has been preserved in a great succession of pharmacopoeias and clinical manuals, a tradition that began during the early Han dynasty (the third century B.C.E.). The pharmacopoeias are vast catalogues of medicinal substances with therapeutic value. For example, a pharmacopoeia produced by the famous physician Li Shi-zhen, posthumously printed in 1596 C.E., included 1,892 entries. Of these, 1,173 were botanical ingredients, 444 were zoological ingredients, and 275 were derived from minerals. The most recent pharmacopoeia is a massive compilation of 5,767 entries.[14] Even the substances commonly used in the Chinese materia medica span a great range of materials, from well-known herbs and minerals such as *Ephedra* and gypsum to strange animal products such as the gallstones of a cow or secretions from the parotid gland of a particular toad.[15]

Traditional pharmacopoeias usually define each entry in terms of how the various herbs and their combinations affect imbalances of the body. The twentieth-century pharmacopoeias also describe how the substances are understood in terms of modern pharmacology, citing active compounds, and detectable biochemical effects on microorganisms, animals, and humans.

After distinguishing a particular pattern of disharmony in a patient, the practitioner of traditional Chinese medicine usually chooses a prescription from a repertoire of some 500 common classical prescriptions that can rebalance various disharmonies. These prescriptions are learned from the great clinical manuals that exist alongside the pharmacopoeias. Thus, the physician is armed with knowledge that has been tested over the past centuries of Chinese medical history. Herbs are seldom used singly; they are usually combined in prescriptions containing five to fifteen substances. The dosages average three to fifteen grams per herb. Most commonly, herbs are decocted into a drink, but pills, powders, tinctures, and poultices are also widely used. Because every patient's body is unique, the physician begins with a general prescription as delineated in the classical texts, and then adjusts the mixture to the patient by adding or deleting various herbs or by manipulating the dosages of the compounds to fit the precise disharmony.

Together, acupuncture and herbology constitute the basic therapeutic devices the Chinese physician uses to restore balance in the body. Both techniques have therapeutic access to the body through the Meridians. The pathways of these Meridians are illustrated in Figures 3 through 16,[16] which depict both the channels within the body and the external pathways along which the acupuncture points are located.

KEY TO MERIDIAN DIAGRAMS

Solid lines are Meridians on the surface of the body.

Broken lines are Meridians inside the body.

Dots are acupuncture points on the surface of the body belonging to the Meridian.

Triangles are acupuncture points on the surface of the body belonging to other Meridians that the primary Meridian is passing through.

Numbers correspond to numbers within the caption text. (These numbers should not be confused with those in references elsewhere in the text such as "Liver 2.")

All the Meridians, except the Governing and Conception Vessels, are assumed to have bilateral symmetry, even though only one side of the body is shown.

Representation of the internal organs is for the convenience of the modern reader. In the traditional system the Chinese would not be concerned with this type of anatomy.

FIGURE 3

The Lung Meridian
(*Shou-tai-yin fei-jing* 手 太 阴 肺 经)

The Lung Meridian originates in the middle portion of the body cavity (1) and runs downward, internally, to connect with the Large Intestine (2). Turning back, it passes upward through the diaphragm (3) to enter its pertaining Organ, the Lungs (4). From the internal zone between the Lungs and the throat (5), it emerges to the surface of the body under the clavicle. Descending, the Lung Meridian then runs along the medial aspect of the upper arm (6) to reach the elbow crease. From there, it runs along the anterior portion of the forearm (7), passes above the major artery of the wrist, and emerges at the radial side of the tip of the thumb (8). Another section of the Lung Meridian branches off just above the wrist and runs directly to the radial side of the tip of the index finger (9) to connect with the Large Intestine Meridian.

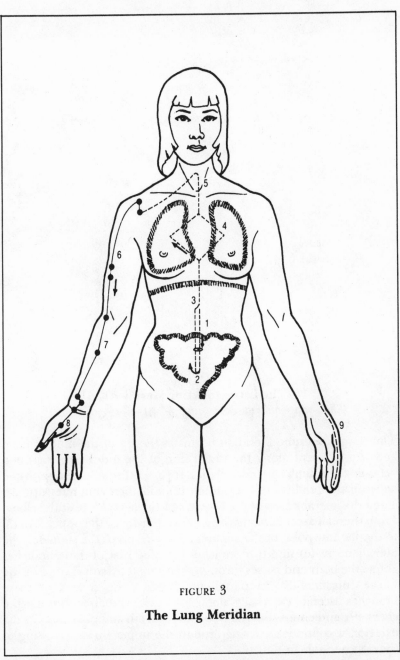

FIGURE 3

The Lung Meridian

FIGURE 4

The Large Intestine Meridian
(*Shou-yang-ming da-chang-jing* 手 阳 明 大 肠 经)

The Large Intestine Meridian begins at the tip of the index finger, and runs upward along the radial side of the index finger (1) and between the thumb and index finger. It passes through the depression between the tendons of the thumb (2) and then continues upward along the lateral aspect of the forearm to the lateral side of the elbow. From there, it ascends along the anterior border of the upper arm (3) to the highest point of the shoulder (4). On top of the shoulder, the Meridian divides into two branches (5). The first of these branches enters the body and passes through the Lung (6), diaphragm, and the Large Intestine (7), its pertaining Organ. The second of these branches ascends externally along the neck (8), passes through the cheek (9), and enters, internally, the lower teeth and gum (10). On the exterior, it continues, curving around the upper lip and crossing to the opposite side of the nose.

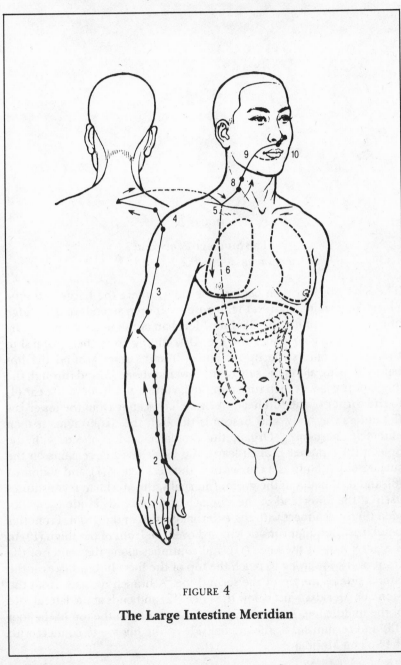

FIGURE 4

The Large Intestine Meridian

FIGURE 5

The Stomach Meridian
(*Zu-yang-ming wei-jing* 足 阳 明 胃 经)

The Stomach Meridian begins, internally, where the Large Intestine Meridian terminates, next to the nose (1). It then ascends to the bridge of the nose, meeting the Bladder Meridian at the inner corner of the eye, and emerging under the eye. Descending from there, lateral to the nose, it enters the upper gum (2) and curves around the lips before passing along the side of the lower jawbone (3) and through the angle of the jaw. It then turns upward, running in front of the ear (4) to the corner of the forehead. A branch descends from the lower jaw (5), enters the body, and descends through the diaphragm. It then enters its pertaining Organ, the Stomach, and connects with the Spleen (6). Another branch leaves the lower jaw, but remains on the surface of the body as it crosses over the neck, chest (7), and abdomen (8), and terminates in the groin. Internally, the Meridian reconstitutes itself at the lower end of the stomach and descends inside the abdomen (9) to reconnect with the external branch in the groin. From this point, the Meridian runs downward over the front of the thigh (10) to the outer side of the knee (11), and continues along the center of the front of the lower leg to reach the top of the foot. It terminates at the lateral side of the tip of the second toe. A branch deviates from the Stomach Meridian just below the knee (12) and ends at the lateral side of the middle toe. A short branch also leaves from the top of the foot (13) and terminates at the medial side of the big toe to connect with the Spleen Meridian.

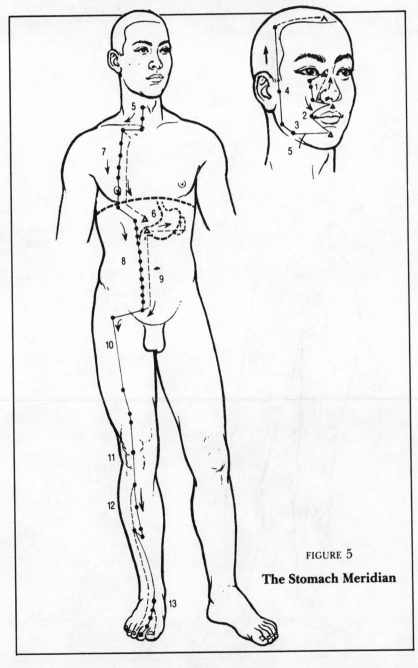

FIGURE 5

The Stomach Meridian

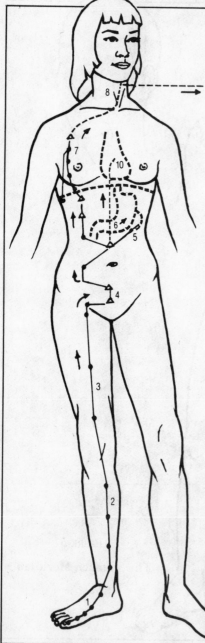

FIGURE 6

The Spleen Meridian
(*Zu-tai-yin pi-jing* 足太阴脾经)

The Spleen Meridian originates at the medial side of the big toe. It then runs along the inside of the foot (1) turning in front of the inner ankle bone. From there, it ascends along the posterior surface of the lower leg (2) and the medial aspect of the knee and thigh (3) to enter the abdominal cavity (4). It runs internally to its pertaining Organ, the Spleen (5), and connects with the Stomach (6). The main Meridian continues on the surface of the abdomen, running upward to the chest (7), where it again penetrates internally to follow the throat (8) up to the root of the tongue (9), under which it spreads its Qi and Blood. An internal branch leaves the Stomach, passes upward through the diaphragm, and enters into the Heart (10), where it connects with the Heart Meridian.

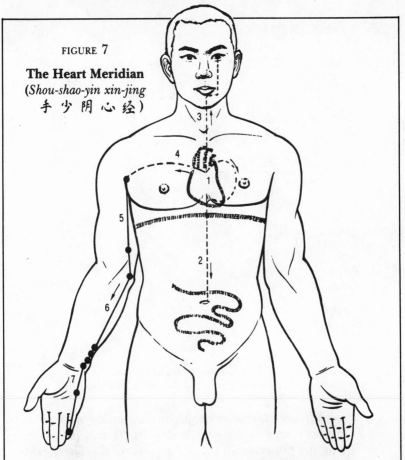

FIGURE 7

The Heart Meridian
(*Shou-shao-yin xin-jing*
手 少 阴 心 经）

The Heart Meridian has three branches, each of which begins in the Heart (1). One branch runs downward through the diaphragm (2) to connect to the Small Intestine. A second branch runs upward from the Heart along the side of the throat (3) to meet the eye. The third branch runs across the chest from the Heart to the Lung (4), then descends and emerges in the underarm. It passes along the midline of the inside of the upper arm (5), runs downward across the inner elbow, along the midline of the inside of the forearm (6), crosses the wrist and palm (7), and terminates at the inside tip of the little finger, where it connects with the Small Intestine Meridian.

FIGURE 8

The Small Intestine Meridian
(*Shou-tai-yang xiao-chang-jing* 手 太 阳 小 肠 经)

The Small Intestine Meridian begins on the outside of the tip of the little finger, crosses the palm and wrist (1), and passes upward along the posterior aspect of the forearm (2). The Meridian continues upward along the posterior border of the lateral aspect of the upper arm (3), circles behind the shoulder (4), and runs to the center of the uppermost part of the back (where it meets the Governing Meridian). Here, the Meridian divides into two branches, one entering internally (5) to connect with the Heart (6), diaphragm, and Stomach (7), before entering its pertaining Organ, the Small Intestine (8). The second branch ascends along the side of the neck (9) to the cheek (10) and outer corner of the eye (11) before entering the ear. A short branch leaves the Meridian on the cheek (12) and runs to the inner corner of the eye, where it connects with the Bladder Meridian.

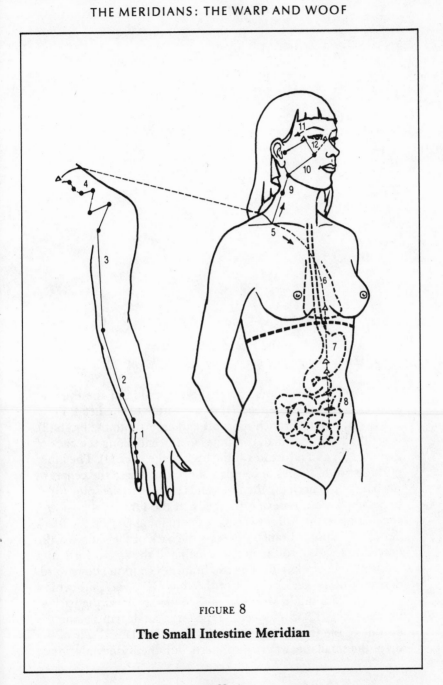

FIGURE 8

The Small Intestine Meridian

FIGURE 9

The Bladder Meridian
(*Zu-tai-yang pang-guang-jing* 足 太 阳 膀 胱 经)

The Bladder Meridian starts at the inner side of the eye and ascends across the forehead (1) to the vertex of the head. From this point, a small branch splits off and enters into the brain (2), while the main Meridian continues to descend along the back of the head (3) and bifurcates at the back of the neck (4). The inner of these two branches descends a short distance to the center of the base of the neck (5), then descends parallel to the spine (6). A branch splits off, entering the body in the lumbar region and connecting to the Kidney (7) and its pertaining Organ, the Bladder (8). The outer branch traverses the back of the shoulder (9), descends adjacent to the inner branch and the spinal cord, and crosses the buttocks (10). The two branches continue downward, descend the posterior aspect of the thigh (11), and join behind the knee. The single Meridian now continues down the back of the lower leg (12), circles behind the outer ankle, runs along the outside of the foot (13), and terminates on the lateral side of the tip of the small toe, where it connects with the Kidney Meridian.

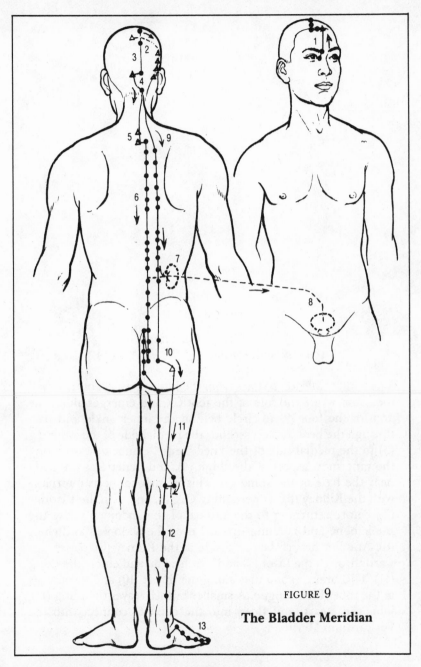

FIGURE 9

The Bladder Meridian

FIGURE 10

The Kidney Meridian
(*Zu-shao-yin shen-jing* 足 少 阴 肾 经)

The Kidney Meridian starts from the inferior aspect of the small toe, runs across the sole of the foot (1), and emerges along the arch of the foot (2) to circle behind the inner ankle and pass through the heel. It then ascends the medial side of the lower leg (3) to the medial side of the knee crease, climbs upward along the innermost aspect of the thigh (4), and penetrates the body near the base of the spine (5). This branch connects internally with the Kidney (6), its pertaining Organ, and with the Bladder (7), before returning to the surface of the abdomen above the pubic bone and running upward over the abdomen and chest (8). Another branch begins inside at the Kidney (6), passes upward through the Liver (9) and diaphragm, and enters the Lung (11). This branch continues along the throat (10) and terminates at the root of the tongue. A smaller branch leaves the Lung (11), joins the Heart, and flows into the chest to connect with the Pericardium Meridian.

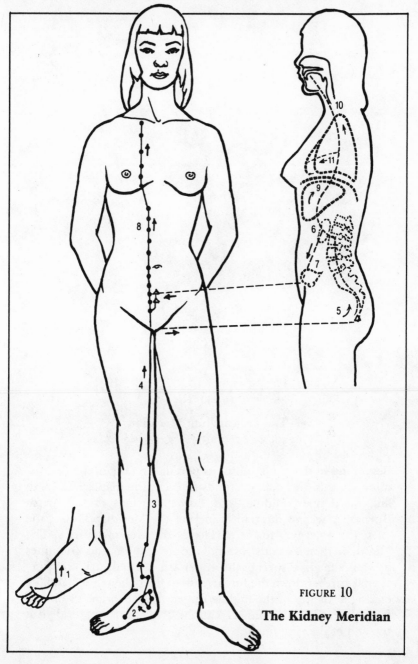

FIGURE 10

The Kidney Meridian

FIGURE 11

The Pericardium Meridian
(*Shou-jue-yin xin-bao-jing* 手 厥 阴 心 包 经)

Beginning in the chest and in its pertaining Organ, the Pericardium (1), this Meridian descends through the diaphragm (2) to link the Upper, Middle, and Lower portions of the Triple Burner. A second internal branch of the Meridian crosses the chest (3), emerging to the surface at the area of the ribs. The Meridian then ascends around the armpit (4) and continues down the medial aspect of the upper arm (5) to the elbow crease. It runs further down the forearm (6) to the palm of the hand (7), ending at the tip of the middle finger. A short branch splits off from the palm (8) to connect with the Triple Burner Meridian at the end of the ring finger.

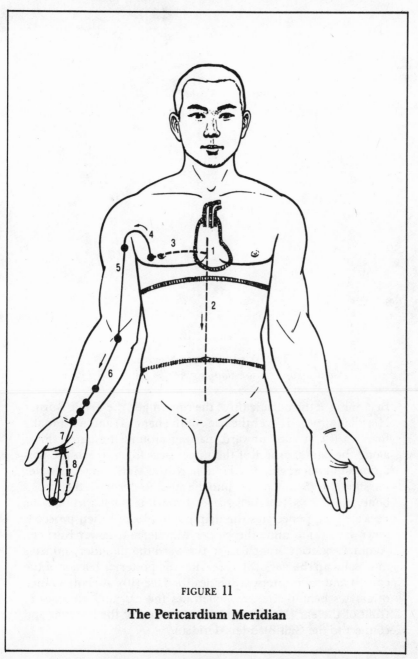

FIGURE 11

The Pericardium Meridian

FIGURE 12

The Triple Burner Meridian
(*Shou-shao-yang san-jiao-jing* 手 少 阳 三 焦 经)

Beginning at the outside tip of the ring finger, the Triple Burner Meridian proceeds over the back of the hand (1) and wrist to the forearm (2). It runs upward, passing around the outer elbow, along the lateral aspect of the upper arm (3), to reach the posterior shoulder region (4). From here, the Meridian travels over the shoulder (5) and enters into the chest underneath the breastbone. An internal branch passes from this point through the Pericardium, penetrates the diaphragm (6), and then proceeds downward (7) to unite the Upper, Middle, and Lower Burners. Another, exterior branch ascends toward the shoulder and runs internally up the neck (8). It reaches the posterior border of the ear (9) and then interiorly circles the face (10). A short branch originates behind the ear, penetrates the ear, and emerges in front of the ear (11) to reach the outer end of the eyebrow and connect to the Gall Bladder Meridian.

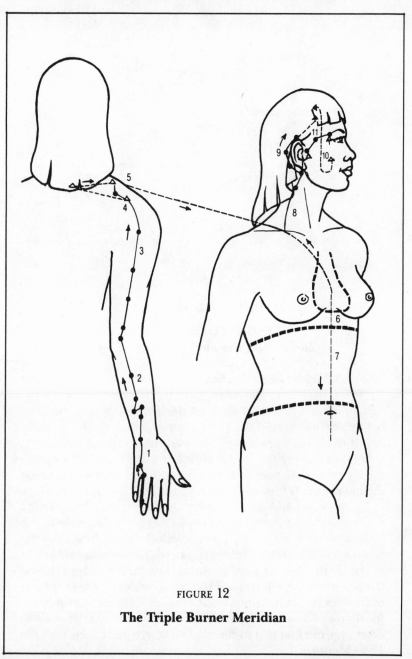

FIGURE 12

The Triple Burner Meridian

FIGURE 13

The Gall Bladder Meridian
(*Zu-shao-yang dan-jing* 足 少 阳 胆 经)

The Gall Bladder Meridian begins at the outer corner of the eye
(1), where two branches arise. One branch, remaining on the
surface, weaves back and forth on the lateral aspect of the head
before curving behind the ear (2) to reach the top of the shoulder. It then continues downward, passing in front of the underarm (3) and along the lateral aspect of the rib cage (4) to reach
the hip region. The second branch internally traverses the cheek
(5) and proceeds internally through the neck (6) and chest (7) to
reach the Liver and its pertaining Organ, the Gall Bladder (8).
Continuing downward, this branch emerges on the side of the
lower abdomen, where it connects with the other branch in the
hip area (9). The Meridian then descends along the lateral aspect
of the thigh (10) and knee to the side of the lower leg (11) and
further downward in front of the outer ankle. It crosses the top
of the foot (12) and terminates at the lateral side of the tip of the
fourth toe. A branch leaves the Meridian just below the ankle to
cross over the foot (13) to the big toe, where it connects with the
Liver Meridian.

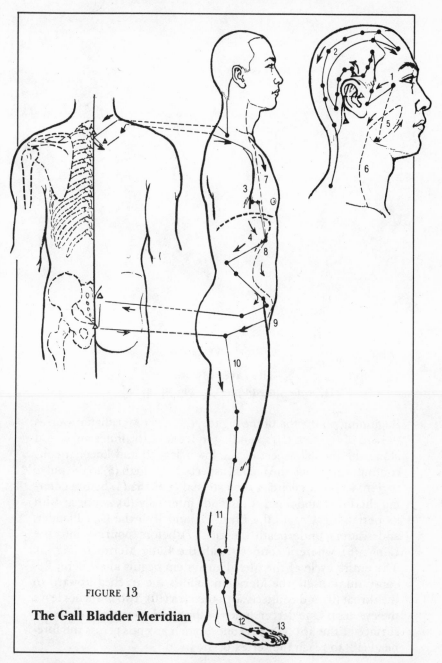

FIGURE 13

The Gall Bladder Meridian

FIGURE 14

The Liver Meridian
(*Zu-jue-yin gan-jing* 足厥阴肝经)

Beginning on the top of the big toe, the Liver Meridian traverses the top of the foot (1), ascending in front of the inner ankle and along the medial aspect of the lower leg (2) and knee. It runs continuously along the medial aspect of the thigh (3) to the pubic region, where it encircles the external genitalia (4) before entering the lower abdomen. It ascends internally (5), connects with its pertaining Organ, the Liver (6), and with the Gall Bladder, and scatters underneath the ribs (7) before pouring into the Lungs (8), where it connects with the Lung Meridian (Fig. 3). The entire cycle of the Meridian system begins anew here. Reconstituting itself, the Meridian follows the trachea upward to the throat (9) and connects with the eyes (10). Two branches leave the eye area: One descends across the cheek to encircle the inner surface of the lips (11); a second branch ascends across the forehead (12) to reach the vertex of the head.

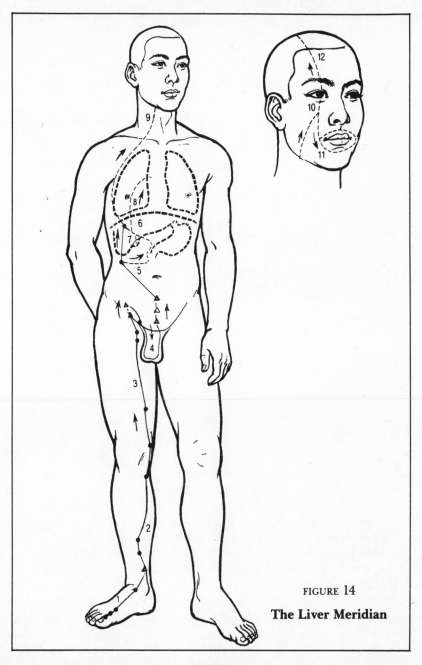

FIGURE 14

The Liver Meridian

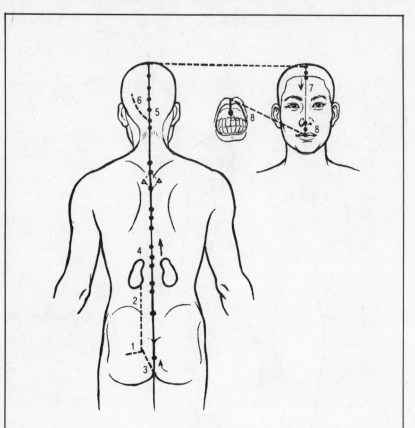

FIGURE 15

The Governing Vessel
(*Du-mai* 督脉)

The Governing Vessel begins in the pelvic cavity (1). An internal branch ascends from here to the Kidney (2). Another internal branch descends to emerge at the perineum (3) and pass through the tip of the coccyx. Ascending along the middle of the spinal column (4), it reaches the head (5) to penetrate into the brain (6). The main branch continues over the top of the head, descends across the forehead (7) and nose to end inside the upper gum (8).

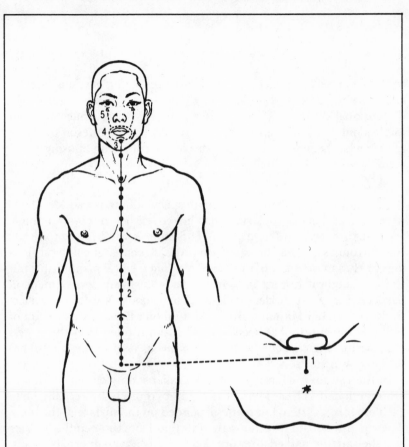

FIGURE 16

The Conception Vessel
(*Ren-mai* 任 脉)

The Conception Vessel begins in the pelvic cavity, emerges at the perineum between the anus and external genitalia (1), and runs forward across the pubic region. It ascends along the midline of the abdomen (2), chest, and throat to the lower jaw (3), where it penetrates internally to encircle the lips (4) and send a branch to the eyes (5).

Notes

1. "Channel" is in fact a better translation of *jing-luo* than "Meridian." The word *channel* is closer to the Chinese, suggesting a three-dimensional conduit that contains a real substance, while Meridian implies only a two-dimensional grid. In this book, however, the term *Meridian* has been used in order to avoid the confusion of using a new term.

2. *Ling Shu* [2], sec. 7, chap. 49, p. 340.

3. Until recently the most common speculation was that Meridians were a hypothetical construct that linked earlier discovered single acupuncture points. These points had supposedly been empirically tested from as early as the late Stone Age. Recent archeological findings in Hunan province of intact pre-*Nei Jing* medical manuscripts put Chinese medical history in general, and Meridian development in particular, in a much clearer light. (These books are known collectively as the Han Ma-wang Burial Mound Silk Books. A collection of the most intact texts has been published and is titled after the largest manuscript, *Prescriptions for Fifty-two Illnesses* (Wu-shi-er Bing-fang) [Beijing:Wenwu Press, 1979].)

In the two texts concerned with Meridians, only eleven Meridians are mentioned. These Meridians are not connected internally or to each other in a system but seem suspended on the surface of the body. Their pathways and directions are different from those in the *Nei Jing* and they are not named after or related in any way to internal Organs. In one of the texts some of the Meridians (the text calls them "mai" or vessels) have such symptomatic names as the "tooth vessel," "ear vessel," and "shoulder vessel." In general, this early Meridian system seems primitive compared to the one of several hundred years later recorded in the *Nei Jing*.

The relationship between Meridian and points is given an interesting twist by these early texts. No points are mentioned, just entire Meridians, portraying zones of influence, needing stimulation by moxibustion. This evidence suggests Meridians existed before points.

These new glimpses into the past are reminiscent of Sigerist's speculation on medicine's development in an even earlier period of human history:

An individual hurts his leg and spontaneously without thinking he rubs it. . . . Another individual suffers from lumbago, crawls to the fire and once he feels the heat the pain becomes more tolerable. . . . We can well imagine that early man suffering an acute pain in the stomach felt impelled to act, pressed his epigastrium with both hands, applied heat or cold, drank water or some decoction until he felt relieved. Pain, in other words, released a series of instinctive reactions, some of which were more effective than others. With developing civilization men learned to differentiate between treatments, became aware of them, remembered them and passed them on. [Henry E. Sigerist, *A History of Medicine*, vol. 1, pp. 115–117.]

4. The Chinese character (*ren*) for this Meridian means "responsibility," probably implying responsibility for the Yin Meridians. The word also has the connotation of conception (pregnancy), which is where the common English translation comes from.

5. The convention of speaking of fourteen Meridians begins with Hua Shou's Elaboration of the Fourteen Meridians [14], first published 1341 C.E. In this treatise, for the first time, the Governing Vessel and Conception Vessel were separated from the eight Extra Meridians and included with the regular twelve Meridians.

6. The *Nei Jing* abstractly and theoretically states that there are 365 points (*Su Wen*, sec. 15, chap. 58, p. 291), but only mentions 160 points by name in all of its discussion. The number of regular acupuncture points was clarified and increased throughout Chinese history. The table at the top of page 110 summarizes this historical progression (based on a comparable chart in Shanghai Institute, Study of Acupuncture Points [86], p. 4).

7. For a fairly comprehensive presentation of the outside-Meridian points see Hao Jin-kai, Illustrative Charts of Extra Meridians Acupuncture Points [76].

8. Academy of Traditional Chinese Medicine, An Outline of Chinese Acupuncture (Beijing: Foreign Languages Press, 1975), p. 181. This text also locates the point in the traditional way.

9. The earliest stated location of this point (Gall Bladder 31, *Fengshi*, Wind Market) is in Wang Shu-chuan, Classic of Nourishing Life with Acupuncture and Moxibustion [21] (first appeared 1220 C.E.), p. 73. The oldest location of a point would usually be presented in Huang-fu Mi, Systematic Classic of Acupuncture [15], which first ap-

(See note 6, page 109)

Points			Sources		
	Nei Jing	Systematic Classic of Acupuncture (c. 282 C.E.)	Illustrated Classic of Acupuncture Points as Found on the Bronze Model (1026 C.E.) and Elaboration of the Fourteen Meridians (1341 C.E.)	Classic of Nourishing Life with Acupuncture (1220 C.E.) and Great Compendium of Acupuncture (1601 C.E.)	Golden Mirror of Medicine (1742 C.E.)
Single Points	25	49	51	51	52
Bilateral Points	135	300	303	308	309
Total Number of Meridian Points	160	349	354	359	361

peared in c. 282 C.E. This text gives the earliest systematic presentation of acupuncture that includes point location, but it does not include Gall Bladder 31.

10. The gate theory was postulated by Ronald Melzack and Patrick Wall in 1965 (*Science* 150 [1965]:971–79). Though still controversial, it is a plausible mechanism to integrate disparate information about pain perception. As a comprehensive theory it explains that the pain sensation is not the product of a single nerve system, but that each specialized portion of the entire nervous system contributes to the pain experience. One of the central assertions of the gate control theory is that there exists a spinal gating mechanism in the dorsal horns, the substantia gelantinosa, that regulates the amount of information conveyed from the peripheral nerve fibers to spinal cord transmission cells. These cells in turn activate central nervous system structures such as the thalmus, responsible for expressions of pain. The gating mechanism is thought to transmit more sensory pain information as the proportion of small diameter (A delta or C) fibers firing exceeds the amount of large diameter (A-beta) fiber activity. Melzack considers acupuncture a form of hyperstimulation analgesia, where the acupuncture pain relief is thought to be due to this phenomenon of inhibition of pain by stimulation of large fiber activity. (See R. Melzack and S. G. Dennis, "Neurophysiological Foundations of Pain" in *The Psychology of Pain*, edited by R. A. Sternback [New York: Raven Press, 1978].)

11. The first evidence that neurochemicals were released by acupuncture came from a controlled experiment in which pairs of rats were connected serially through their circulatory systems. An acupuncture needle applied to the point Large Intestine 4 (*he-gu*) in one rat raised the pain threshold in *both* rats (*American Journal of Chinese Medicine* 2 [1974]:203). In 1976, it was reported that substances which were blocked by morphine antagonists were released with acupuncture. A group of substances, identified chemically as peptides and called endorphins, was then localized in the pituitary gland (*Science* 193 [1976]:1081–86). The *New England Journal of Medicine* (vol. 296, no. 5 [Feb. 3, 1977], pp. 266–271) reported that the most potent of the endorphins "is 5,000 to 10,000 times more potent than morphine." Moreover, it said that endorphins lead to the release of ADH (antidiuretic hormone) from the posterior pituitary and facilitates the release of FSH (follicle stimulating hormone) and ACTH (adrenocorticotropic hormone) from the posterior pituitary. Thus, concludes the article, this group of chemicals appears to function through the limbic-hypothalamus-pituitary axis.

Dr. Bruce Pomeranz and a group at the University of Toronto have been studying the responses of animals to painful stimuli after acupuncture. They have found that after an induction period of twenty minutes, recordings from the pain responsive nerve cells in the spinal cord are reduced (*Experimental Neurology* 54 [1977]:172); that there is an increase in the pain threshold, equated with analgesia, which can be blocked by naloxone (a morphine antagonist), thus implying the presence of endorphins; and that, depending on the frequency of stimulation, at least two different hormonally induced systems may be involved (*Life Sciences* 19 [1976]:1957; 25 [1979]:1957). This relation between acupuncture analgesia and the endorphin system has caused a great deal of excitement in the field of scientific investigation of acupuncture. Dr. Pomeranz has further supported the theory of endorphin relatedness by experimenting with strains of mice deficient in opiate receptors. Unlike their normal counterparts, these mice do not develop analgesia with acupuncture (*Nature* 273 [1978]:675). Additional evidence was produced by using dextronaloxone, the stereoisomer of the active compound levonaloxone, which does not fit into the receptor site and does not block the analgesic effect of acupuncture (*Life Sciences* 26 [1980]:631).

Human clinical studies of experimentally induced pain and acupuncture analgesia have confirmed that there is an increase in the pain threshold as well as a decrease in the desire to report a stimulus as painful (D. J. Mayer et al. in *Brain Research* 121 [1977]:368; C. R. Chapman et al. in *Pain* 2 [1976]:265). The effect of naloxone on the reversal of acupuncture analgesia in human studies is still controversial (Chapman et al. in *Pain* 9 [1980]:183).

12. The mechanism by which acupuncture may function is still in the early stages of discovery (see the previous note). The available modern Chinese research on the effects and applications of acupuncture in terms of modern biochemistry and physiology are not well presented and are poorly designed by Western standards. Because it lacks proper controls and base-line studies, this research can most accurately be called clinical observation. At times it borders on the anecdotal. This type of observation-research may, however, point the way toward potentially useful scientific investigation in the West. A summary of the Chinese research appears in Shanghai Institute, Acupuncture [85], pp. 399–408. The English translation of this text by O'Connor and Bensky (Chicago: Eastland Press, 1981) is excellent. This section is chapter 10. It catalogues studies on animals and humans performed in modern China. The results are wide-ranging, with all the physiological systems undergoing change. A very small sample of the results is as follows:

a. Needling acupuncture point Stomach 36 (*Zu-san-li*) strengthens intestinal peristalsis (muscle contractions in animals, barium transit time in humans). Other points relax the intestines.

b. Needling Large Intestine 4 (*He-gu*) and Triple Burner 5 (*Wai-guan*) causes vasodilation and lowers blood pressure. Needling Pericardium 6 (*Nei-guan*) causes vasoconstriction, helpful in hypotensive states.

c. The heart rate is able to be regulated: A fast beat is slowed, a slow one increased. The general tendency is to reduce heart rate and strengthen cardiac muscle contraction.

d. Needling Stomach 36 (*Zu-san-li*) and Large Intestine 4 (*He-gu*) increases the level of 17-hydroxycorticosteroids in the blood, sometimes by a factor of two or three. These levels are maintained for a considerable time.

e. The Shenyang Scientific Medical Research Institute, using direct measurement methods, found that the ACTH content of the blood of white rats rose markedly after they received electro-acupuncture.

f. Levels of oxytocin, vasopressin, norepinephrine, follicle stimulating hormone, and prolactin are affected when different points are needled.

g. The immune system is stimulated. Patients with bacillary dysentery show an increase in phagocytosis three hours after acupuncture treatment, which peaks twelve hours after treatment. The effect was greatest with electric acupuncture (a modern technique of hooking the needle to a low-voltage electric current), less sustained with regular acupuncture, and even less with moxibustion alone.

In rabbits, leukocyte counts increase with acupuncture treatment, peaking in three hours.

h. After needling numerous points, acetylcholine concentration in the brain is increased in animals (compared with controls). This indicates an inhibitory state, as in analgesia and anesthesia.

The most complete recent summary of acupuncture research in China is Developments in Acupuncture Research (*Zhen-jiu Yan-jiu Jin-Zhan*), ed. by Traditional Chinese Medicine Research Institute (Beijing: People's Press, 1981).

13. Herbology clearly becomes the dominant tendency of Chinese medicine from the Tang Dynasty (618–907 c.e.) onward. The early period seems more concerned with acupuncture. For example, the *Nei Jing* mentions only two herbal prescriptions.

14. Jiangsu New Medical Institute, Encyclopedia of the Traditional Chinese Pharmacopeia [32].

15. Strange as these two animal-derived materials sound, a scientific basis has been found for some of their actions. This is also the case for most of the materia medica. Both of these traditional medical materials have a digitalislike effect on the heart that is very potent, as well as having a wide assortment of additional uses verified by Western research. See Zhongshan Institute, Clinical Use of Chinese Medicines [92], pp. 459, 566. Incidently, ephedrine entered the modern Western pharmacopoeia via early-twentieth-century research on the Chinese herb *Ephedra* (C. P. Li, *Chinese Herbal Medicine* [Washington, D.C.: John E. Fogarty International Center, U.S. Dept. of HEW, NIH, 1974], p. 5).

16. Figures 3–16 are based on diagrams appearing in Academy of Traditional Chinese Medicine, *An Outline of Chinese Acupuncture* (Beijing: Foreign Languages Press, 1975). The earliest description of Meridian pathways, but without all the points, is the *Ling Shu*, sec. 3, chap. 10.

5

Origins of Disharmony:
Stormy Weather

In my early student days in China, I worried that the Chinese perception of disease—the ideas as well as the vocabulary—was not only unusual and mysterious, but also just plain silly. It seemed too simple to talk, as the Chinese do, of Dampness, Wind, or Heat as generative factors in illness. Then one night, while I was having dinner with the Chinese family I lived with, a woman at the table excused herself because of a "head Wind." That incident made me realize how culturally relative my medical perceptions were. To my Chinese friends, the idea of head Wind was not at all outlandish—it was as grounded in reality as the Western concept of the flu. Chinese ideas simply represent a different way of organizing information about health and disease.

Chinese medicine and Chinese philosophy, as we have seen, do not concern themselves very much with cause and effect, or with trying to discover *this* cause that begets, in linear progression, *that* effect. Their concern is with relationships, with the pattern of events. Thus, their idea of the way illness begins is very different from the Western view.

In fact, the Chinese do not have a highly developed theory for the origins of disease. They conceive of certain factors that affect the body, factors that could be described in the Western vocabulary as causes. It is therefore tempting to the Western

mind to describe them as such, but to the Chinese these generative factors are not exactly causes. Take Dampness, for example.
In China, as in the West, people might say that someone became
ill because he or she went out in the rain or got his feet muddy
or because he lives in a damp basement. But to the Chinese,
dampness precipitates only a pattern of Dampness; there is no
distinction between the illness itself and the factor that "caused"
it. The question of cause becomes incidental. In this sense, the
word *cause* is almost a synonym for *effect*. In Chinese pattern-
thinking (further explained in Chapter 7), what might at first
seem to be a cause becomes part of the pattern, indistinguishable and inseparable from the effect. Pattern-thinking subsumes
the cause, defining it in terms of the effect and making it part of
the total pattern. What we in the West call a cause has little
importance in Chinese thought. The lines of causality are bent
into circles.

Nevertheless, the general population in China, and its medical practitioners, when asked "Why is there disharmony?"
speak of three categories of precipitating factors in illness.
These are environment, emotional outlook, and way of life.

The general population, including doctors, will sometimes
think of these factors as causes. People assume that Dampness,
for instance, can "cause" illness in some people at certain times.
Friends, relatives, and neighbors will advise a person to wear a
raincoat or to move out of a damp basement. Teachers, parents,
and philosophers, jointly with physicians, will recommend certain life styles or disapprove unhealthful activities. They will
suggest a change in emotional attitudes or in environment if a
person seems to be unwell or wants to maintain health. The
giving of such advice is considered the province not exclusively
of the physician, but also of educators, leaders, and friends.
Behavior prescribed by society is, however, presumed to be
healthy and positive, and may also complement the work of the
physician.

In the narrower, more precise and refined realm of medicine,
pattern-thinking about illness is more pronounced than it is in
the general society. To the physician, the view of Dampness, for

example, as a cause of disease is less important than two other ways of thinking about it. The physician would first take note of the damp basement as a simple fact, a piece of information, a sign to be considered along with other signs. He may tell the patient to move (i.e., he may treat the Dampness as a cause), but his main concern would be to place this sign into the patient's total configuration of signs—including color of face, pulse, tongue, emotional outlook, and so forth. The physician would see Dampness as one element of a pattern of disharmony and would not necessarily single it out as a cause needing treatment. The Dampness is just part of the picture. Other people living in the wet basement may not get sick. So something else is going on to make the patient sensitive. The physician's gaze inevitably goes to the complete arrangement of signs. If the patient can't move out of the basement, the doctor would try to reharmonize him or her so as to eliminate the sensitivity to Dampness. And even if the patient could change homes, he or she would still need reharmonizing to deal with the pattern carried within that is susceptible to Dampness.

The amount of attention given to such relationships leads to the second and more important way a Chinese physician understands Dampness—as both an individual and a universal pattern. Dampness is a pattern of qualities and events that relates a person to the natural environment. The person is a microcosm manifesting the same configuration of signs as does the macrocosm. Dampness in the environment is wet, heavy, sodden, and lingering; Dampness in the body makes a person heavy, bloated, and slow. If one's internal pattern is very "swampy," one can manifest such bodily signs without ever having been exposed to a drop of external moisture. It is important to note that the Dampness outside the body may precipitate a condition of Dampness within the body, but exposure in a causal sense is unnecessary. One is more likely to have a Damp illness in London, but it is still possible in Arizona. Dampness is recognized by what is going on inside, not by knowledge of external exposure. The condition is not *caused* by Dampness; the condition *is* Dampness. The cause is the effect; the line is a circle. The physician sees the bodily pattern as a miniature form of the more general natural image, and because the patterns of the body and of nature are similar, they share an identity of poetic equivalence.

In answer to the question "Why do people get sick?" the Chinese can answer that precipitating factors in one of the three categories—environment, emotion, and way of life—generate illness. But although one or another of these factors may be present at the beginning of an illness, that factor is never seen as separate from the illness. It is part of the web, one of the signs and symptoms the Chinese physician weaves into a diagnosis.

The Six Pernicious Influences (*liu-yin* 六 淫)

The six Pernicious Influences are the environmental factors that play a part in disease. They include six climatic phenomena—Wind, Cold, Fire or Heat, Dampness, Dryness, and Summer Heat[1]—and are also called the six Evils (*liu-xie*).[2]

The healthy body is a balance of Yin and Yang. It is sustained by a network of activity of complementary forces that generate and limit one another. Thus, the Qi moves the Blood, but also holds it in place; the Heart stores Shen (Spirit) and also moves Blood; the Spleen rules ascending, the Stomach rules descending; the Liver rules spreading and the Kidneys rule storage; the Lungs rule the circulating and descending of Qi; the Kidneys govern the grasping of Qi. When the balance is upset, Yin and Yang lose adjustment. The body may then be susceptible to the harmful effects of a Pernicious Influence. A Pernicious Influence, of course, is just a natural event. It becomes harmful only when the body has an inappropriate relationship to it.

When the body is weakened by an imbalance of Yin and Yang, a climatic phenomenon can invade the body and become a Pernicious Influence. The body in this state undergoes a conflict between the Pernicious Influence and the Normal Qi. The first encounter of the invading Influence is with the body's Protective Qi. If the Protective Qi is strong, the Influence is expelled and the individual recovers. But if the Qi is weak, or the Pernicious Influence is very strong, the illness develops and goes deeper, becoming more involved with the internal Organs.

Illnesses generated by any of the Pernicious Influences that have invaded the body usually come on suddenly, with no warning. They are characterized by aversion toward the particular Influence (e.g., fear of cold, dislike of wind), fever, chills, body aches, and general malaise. These symptoms are understood to be the result of Normal Qi and Protective Qi attempting to expel the Influence.

When a Pernicious Influence invades the body like this, from the outside, it is called an External Pernicious Influence. A Pernicious Influence can also, however, arise internally.[3] In this case, the body manifests similar signs and symptoms. One important difference is that the illness does not usually come on suddenly, and often there are no fever or chills. A Pernicious Influence that develops inside the body is called an Internal Pernicious Influence. An External Pernicious Influence usually accompanies sudden acute illnesses, whereas an Internal Pernicious Influence is more often related to chronic illnesses. All the Pernicious Influences, however, are really models or images for bodily processes that mimic climatic conditions, and are treated accordingly.

In the following description of each Influence, both the external and internal aspects are discussed.

Wind (feng 风)

Wind in the body resembles wind in nature. It is both movement and that which generates movement in what would otherwise be still. It produces change and urgency in what would otherwise be slow and even, and it causes things to appear and disappear rapidly. Wind affects the body just as it moves the branches and leaves of a tree. Accordingly, Wind is a Yang phenomenon.

Wind is associated with the spring, but a disharmony characterized by Wind (a Wind disharmony) can appear in any season. The association of a Pernicious Influence with a season is one of potentiality—the body may be more susceptible to Wind Influences in the spring. And although there is a connection between the environment and the body, the body's inner dynamic may be affected by Wind in any other season and may not be affected by it in the spring. The correspondence between a Pernicious Influence and its season is poetic, but real—it means that the microcosm is taking part in the life of the macrocosm.

Wind is the one Pernicious Influence that rarely appears by itself. It is usually accompanied by some other External Pernicious Influence, such as Cold or Dampness. The presence of Wind allows and even promotes the invasion of the body by the other Influences. Therefore, the *Nei Jing* says that "the hundred diseases develop from Wind."[4] Because Wind is "light and airy," the *Nei Jing* also says that "injury by Wind first affects the upper parts."[5] Wind is thought to show itself initially on the upper and outer portions of the body, especially the face, skin, sweat glands, and lungs. Sometimes, people affected by Wind will recall recent exposure to drafts.

Because Wind is associated with movement, it is often recognized by such signs as pain that moves from place to place, itching or skin eruptions that change locations, spasms, tremors of the limbs, twitching, dizziness, or tetany. Summarizing this, the *Nei Jing* comments: "Wind is adept at movement and many changes."[6]

When Wind is an External Pernicious Influence, it is called External Wind. External Wind is characterized by its suddenness of onset, as are all the External Pernicious Influences. It is often accompanied by fever (a sign of the conflict between an External Influence and Normal Qi), fear of drafts, sweating, sudden headaches, stuffed nasal passages, itchy or sore throat. Because it is usually accompanied by another Pernicious Influence, it contains the signs of the other Pernicious Influences. External Wind often resembles what Western medicine describes as the onset of an infectious or contagious disease.

Internal Wind usually accompanies a chronic disharmony, frequently, though not exclusively, of the Liver. The Liver is responsible for smooth movement in the body, and thus is especially susceptible to irregular movement, a condition that would be described as Wind. Signs of Internal Wind may include dizziness, tinnitus, numbness of the limbs, tremors, convulsions, and apoplexy.

> CLINICAL SKETCH: A patient has what Western medicine calls an upper respiratory infection. He is chilled and has a stuffed nose, a slight fever, and head and body aches. The Chinese diagnosis might be External Wind and Cold invading the body. Treatment would call for expulsion of Wind, using acupuncture points such as Gall Bladder 20, the Chinese name for which is Wind Pond (*Feng-chi*), and certain herbs. Fresh ginger, for example, enters the Lung Meridian and causes sweating, which expels Wind and Cold.[7]

Cold (han 寒)

Cold, in the body as in nature, is a Yin phenomenon. It is associated with winter, the way Wind is associated with spring. But, again, Cold does not appear only in its corresponding season. A cool breeze in the summer, for example, can generate a pattern of External Cold, especially if a person is very sensitive because of a preexisting Internal disharmony. Cold weather in general, however, aggravates a Cold condition in the body.

The most important sign of any Cold Influence is that the individual feels cold. The entire body, or part of it, may be cold to the touch or may have a pale, frigid appearance. The person often has a marked aversion to cold and seeks warmth, perhaps in the form of a hot-water bottle or an extra sweater.

Cold in the body also acts as it does in nature. It contracts things, obstructing normal movement. It freezes things, leading to slow movement, underactivity, and hibernation. Cold in the Meridians can block the circulation of Qi or Blood, causing severe, sharp, cramping pain that is somewhat responsive to heat. Cold in the Meridians of the limbs may lead to contractions and stiffness. As the *Nei Jing* remarks, "Cold enters the Meridians and there is retardation of movement . . . the Qi cannot penetrate, and finally there is pain."[8] Secretions and excretions related to Cold disharmonies are clear or white with a frozen look, such as clear mucus, sputum, vomit, urine, or diarrhea with a clear or white fluid. The *Nei Jing* says, "Cold is watery, transparent, clear, and cool."[9]

External Cold disharmonies, like all External Pernicious Influences, come upon the patient suddenly. They are usually accompanied by the fear of cold, as well as chills, mild fever, headache, and body aches. Usually the chills are more pronounced than the fever, and the fever is interpreted as the body's effort to expel the External Influence. Since Cold obstructs the pores, there is usually little sweating associated with Cold disharmonies.

Internal Cold is related to insufficient Yang. Yang is Heat and activity, so when it is insufficient, it follows that the body will be Cold and slow. Internal Cold is usually chronic and is associated with underactivity and general slowness. The body or portions of it will be cold; the person will often need more sleep than usual, and will crave warmth. Just as Internal Wind is often connected with the Liver, Internal Cold is often related to the Kidneys, since the Kidneys have the Life Gate Fire and are the source of the body's Yang.

CLINICAL SKETCH: A male patient complains of difficulty in urinating and of dribbling urine, problems that gradually become more frequent over several years. A Western physician diagnoses a prostate condition (benign prostatic hypertrophy). The patient visits a Chinese physician, who notices that his face is pale and he is wearing a lot of sweaters. The patient tells the physician that he has always disliked cold and that he sleeps curled up. These and other signs, such as a deep, slow pulse and a pale, moist tongue, point to a pattern of Internal Cold. Treatment might include moxibustion, stimulation by burning mugwort, at such points as Governor Vessel 4 (*Ming-men*, Life Door) and Kidney 2 (*Ran-gu*, Blazing Valley) in order to strengthen the Kidney Qi. The physician might also prescribe decoctions containing praying mantis cocoons, as they enter the Kidney Meridian and strengthen or tonify the Life Gate Fire.[10]

Heat (re 热) or Fire (huo 火)

The terms *Heat* and *Fire* can be used interchangeably, although Heat usually connotes an External Pernicious Influence and Fire an Internal Pernicious Influence. Fire, however, is also a normal characteristic of the body. It is the body's Yang aspect, as opposed to the Yin, one of the two bodily principles that must be kept in balance. The Fire that is the normal Yang of the body should not be confused with Fire Pernicious Influence, which is a source of disharmony.

Heat or Fire, because of its characteristic of being hot and active, is a Yang phenomenon. It is associated with summer but is common year-round, and its signs within the body resemble its manifestations in nature. When Heat Pernicious Influence is present, the whole body or portions of it feel hot or appear hot. The person affected by it dislikes heat and has a preference for cold. He or she will display such signs as high fever, a red face, red eyes, and dark, reddish urine. Heat can also collect in small areas of the body's surface, creating Fire Poison (what in the West would be called inflammation). Its symptoms are carbuncles, boils, reddish ulcers, or other skin lesions that are red, swollen, raised, and painful. Secretions and excretions related to Heat or Fire Pernicious Influence tend to be sticky and thick and to feel hot: cough with thick yellow mucus or stools with mucus and blood accompanied by burning sensation in anus. Heat or Fire Pernicious Influences can also dry out bodily matter and deplete the Fluids. Thus, a dry tongue, unusual thirst, dry stools, or scanty urination are other possible signs of the presence of this Influence.

Heat Pernicious Influence, being a Yang phenomenon, induces movement, as does Wind. Wind is more mobile, however, and its movement is trembling or spasmodic, sudden or abrupt. Heat, on the other hand, is said to induce "reckless movement," especially of Blood and Shen. In the Blood, such movement often leads to hemorrhaging and red skin eruptions. In the Shen, "reckless movement" may be recognized by confused speech or delirium, for instance, in a patient with a high fever.

External Heat or Fire disharmonies are marked by high fever, headache (since Heat rises), swollen and sore throat, dry mouth, great thirst, desire for cold, occasional bloody sputum, skin eruptions, irritability, or delirium. There is usually a higher fever with Heat than with Cold and only slight or no chills, more headaches, and fewer body aches. This is because Heat tends to rise and it obstructs the Meridians less than Cold does. As with the other External Pernicious Influences, the onset of illness is usually sudden.

Internal Heat or Fire develops from disharmonies of the Yin and Yang of the various Organs. It will be discussed in Chapter 7.

CLINICAL SKETCH: A patient suddenly gets a high fever and a severe sore throat. She has a red face, a dry, hacking cough, and no fear of cold. A Western physician takes a throat culture and discovers the presence of Group A Betahemolytia *streptococcus*. Antibiotic drugs are prescribed, with good results. If the same patient had gone to a Chinese physician, he very likely would have diagnosed a Heat Pernicious Influence. Herbs like *Coptis* and *Scutellena*, which disperse and cool Fire, would have been prescribed. The results would have been adequate though perhaps slower to achieve than with the antibiotic treatment. Modern research shows, incidentally, that both *Coptis* and *Scutellena* inhibit the growth of streptococcus bacteria. Acupuncture treatment, such as needling Large Intestine 4 (*He-gu*, Adjoining Valleys), to cool Fire, would in this case have offered some symptomatic relief and heightened the body's resistance, but would have been less effective than herbs.[11]

Dampness (*shi* 湿)

Damp Pernicious Influences lead to clinical symptoms that resemble the properties of dampness in the natural environment. Because Dampness is wet, heavy, and slow, it is Yin. It is technically linked with what the Chinese call "the long summer," but actually is associated with damp weather in any season. Living or working in damp surroundings or wearing damp clothing can also pave the way for Dampness to invade the body. Dampness is heavy, turbid, and lingering. It tends to move things downward, and so the *Nei Jing* states that "the lower body is the first area affected by Dampness."[12] As a Yin phenomenon, Dampness is like Cold, but its effects are distinguishable from those of Cold. For example, Cold pain is characterized by sharp, intense cramping, while Damp pain is protracted and gives a feeling of heaviness. During a Damp illness, the head may feel dull—"as if in a sack," the Chinese say. The limbs may feel heavy and sore, and the patient will express a dislike for damp environments. Excretions and secretions associated with Dampness are copious and often turbid, cloudy, or sticky, like "sand" in the eyes, cloudy urine, heavy diarrhea, heavy vaginal discharge, or fluid-filled or oozing skin eruptions. External Dampness can easily obstruct the movement of Qi, producing fullness of the chest or abdomen, and dribbling or incomplete urination or defecation. Or External Dampness can penetrate the Meridians, affecting the limbs and causing heaviness, stiffness, or soreness in the joints. It can also easily affect the Spleen. The Spleen rules "the raising of the pure," transforming pure essences into Blood and Qi by a vaporization process that requires a dry environment. A traditional Chinese saying sums this up as "The Spleen likes Dryness."[13] The Spleen is therefore especially sensitive to Dampness. Dampness can readily "distress" the Spleen and interfere with its "raising" of pure foods and fluids. This can be seen in signs like loss of appetite, indigestion, nausea, diarrhea, and abdominal edema. At the same time, however, other Spleen disharmonies, because they prevent the raising or transforming of Fluids, can allow Dampness to linger in the body, leading to a condition of Internal Dampness.

External and Internal Dampness are distinguishable primarily by their speed of onset. External Dampness will be acute and accompanied by other External signs, but will easily turn into Internal Dampness. And Internal Dampness will make a person more susceptible to External Dampness. Either type of Dampness lingers and stagnates, and is likely to last a long time.

CLINICAL SKETCH: Two patients have painful, vesicular lesions on their bodies. The first patient has the eruptions on his face, the second patient has them on his lower trunk. A Western doctor diagnoses both conditions as herpes zoster and prescribes analgesics for the pain, as there is no Western-style treatment for the virus causing the disease. The patients go to a Chinese doctor, who will probably recognize two distinct patterns of disharmony. The patient whose eruptions are on the face might have a Wind-Heat disharmony, while the patient with the eruptions on the lower trunk has a Damp-Heat condition. Both are Heat patterns, as the eruptions are red, painful, and swollen. The location of the eruptions is different because the precipitating factors, the Pernicious Influences, are different. Wind is light, and leads to manifestations on the face; Dampness is heavy, and so descends, resulting in eruptions on the lower trunk. For the first patient, the doctor would prescribe herbs and acupuncture that expel Wind-Heat, while herbs and acupuncture that eliminate Damp-Heat would be given to the second patient. These methods of treating herpes have been demonstrated effective, possibly because some of the herbs used inhibit the growth of the virus,[14] while the acupuncture would help relieve pain. Also, selecting an herbal treatment solely on the basis of Western knowledge of viruses would have been less effective than combining the herbs according to traditional methods.[15]

Mucus (*tan*) is a form of Internal Dampness. Although it is not, strictly speaking, a precipitating factor in illness, it is related to Dampness and is seen in conjunction with a great many disharmonies.

The term *Mucus* includes the Western meaning of a secretion of the mucous membranes visible, for instance, in the form of phlegm. But it also has other characteristics and connotations that make it an entirely different concept from that of Western physiology. Mucus generally arises with disharmonies of the Spleen or Kidneys that affect the movement of Water in the body. Such a condition allows Dampness to linger, and the Dampness may condense, creating Mucus. Mucus is thick and heavy, heavier than Dampness. It can more easily cause obstructions and can generate lumps, nodules, or tumors.

When Mucus collects in the Lungs, there is coughing with heavy expectoration. Mucus in the Heart can obstruct the Shen, leading to muddled thought, stupor, comalike states, chaotic behavior, or madness. Mucus in the Meridians may result in numbness, paralysis, or the development of nodules and soft, mobile tumors. Mucus in the throat can cause the sensation of a lump in the throat. An examination of the tongue and pulse will tell a physician whether or not Mucus is present in a disharmony. A thick, "greasy" coating on the tongue or a slippery pulse are the two most important signs. (See Chapter 6.) Whenever there is Mucus, it implies Dampness.

Dryness (zao 燥) and Summer Heat (shu 暑)

Dryness and Summer Heat are two distinct Pernicious Influences, but they are much less important than Wind, Cold, Heat, and Dampness. This is because they are less frequently used as a description of the inner environment. In clinical practice they are even more expendable than they are in the traditional theory.

Dryness Pernicious Influence is associated with autumn, and is a Yang phenomenon. It is also closely related to Heat. Dryness and Heat are on a continuum, with the Dry end emphasizing dehydration and the Heat end emphasizing redness and hotness. Thus, Dryness is accompanied by dry nostrils, lips, and tongue, cracked skin, and dry stools.

External Dryness often interferes with the circulating and descending functions of the Lungs, manifesting perhaps a dry cough with little phlegm, asthma, or chest pain, as well as the signs of suddenness, fever, body aches, and other symptoms characteristic of the External Pernicious Influences. The few disharmonies that involve Internal Dryness will be discussed in Chapter 8.

Summer Heat is purely an External Pernicious Influence that always results from exposure to extreme heat. Its symptoms include sudden high fever and heavy sweating. Summer Heat easily injures the Qi, causing exhaustion, and depletes the Fluids. It often occurs together with Dampness.

The six Pernicious Influences, External or Internal, can never be seen in isolation from the body. They can only be recognized by the signs and symptoms that accompany them. And those signs and symptoms are part of a bodily pattern that is greater than any one Pernicious Influence. The Dampness or the Wind-Cold that begins a disharmony is part of the disharmony itself, and the disharmony contributes to the condition of Dampness or Wind-Cold. The linear idea of cause and effect becomes a circle in Chinese medicine, because Chinese pattern-thinking subsumes all the pieces into a more important whole.

Dampness or Wind-Cold or other climatic phenomena are finally descriptions of bodily states, metaphors that relate what's going on in the body to its complement in the universe. As causes, they are secondary to the overall pattern. In fact, in some cases, exposure to Dampness may generate a Cold condition, or exposure to Cold may generate a Wind-Heat condition. And if someone has been exposed to Dampness but manifests a Heat pattern, then Heat is what counts. Treatment will be for Heat, not for Dampness. In Western medicine, it is often impossible to treat a condition without knowing the cause; in Chinese medicine, the treatment is always for the condition itself, regardless of the cause. The Pernicious Influence, as a cause, is unimportant.

An individual may have tendencies toward a certain state—one person is usually Cold and Damp, while another is Hot and Dry. Each of these people will receive a Pernicious Influence in his or her own way, so that it will become part of that person's unique pattern. The Pernicious Influence does not have any characteristics that belong to it alone and that are not defined by its manifestations in a particular body.

The Pernicious Influence can only influence—it cannot determine. And with all the elements that are considered in Chinese medicine, it is just one piece, another sign to be woven into the pattern.

The Seven Emotions (*qi-qing* 七 情)

Chinese medical practitioners have always recognized that emotional factors play a part in health and illness. The emotional life cannot be separated from the physical. Concern for the psychological texture of a patient's being must be part of a physician's examination, as the Fundamental Substances and the Organs are all intimately connected to the emotions.

The *Nei Jing* cites seven emotions that particularly affect the body and that are still considered most important: joy, anger, sadness, grief, pensiveness, fear, and fright. The differences between sadness and grief, fear and fright, appear to be of degree; sometimes these pairs are combined as one emotion. Of course, emotional qualities are not in themselves pathological, and all of them appear in healthy individuals. It is only when an emotion is either excessive or insufficient over a long period of time, or when it arises very suddenly with great force, that it can generate imbalance and illness. And the reverse is also true: Internal disharmony can generate unbalanced emotional states.

Emotional excess or insufficiency acts on the Qi and on the other Substances. The *Nei Jing* states that "excess joy is associated with slow and scattered Qi; excess anger induces the Qi to ascend; excess sadness and grief weakens the Qi; excess pensiveness generates 'knottedness' or 'stuckness'; fear results in descending Qi; and fright induces chaotic Qi."[16] The seven emotions are also thought to correlate with the five Yin Organs: joy with the Heart; anger with the Liver; sadness and grief with the Lungs; pensiveness with the Spleen; and fear and fright with the Kidneys. Disharmonies in one of these Organs tend to produce an imbalance in the corresponding emotion and vice versa.

The two Organs considered most susceptible to emotional disturbance are the Heart and the Liver. One of the functions of the Heart is to store the Shen. Unharmonious emotions can lead easily to disturbances of the Shen, resulting in insomnia, muddled thinking, inappropriate crying or laughing, and, in extreme cases, fits, hysteria, and insanity. The Liver harmonizes the emotions through its "sprinkling" function. Thus, Liver Qi going in the wrong direction can be the result of excessive anger or the source of it. Disharmonies of Liver Qi and anger accompany one another. Stagnation of the Liver may be associated with any emotional frustration, or with inappropriate and extreme mood changes.

The seven emotions can also affect the other Organs and Substances. Excessive joy, for instance, can scatter the Heart Qi, causing the Shen to become muddled and uncontrolled. When excessive anger affects the Liver, there may be signs such as dizziness, chest congestion, a bitter taste in the mouth, and pain in the upper abdomen and sides. Excessive sadness or grief may weaken the Lung Qi, while great fear can make Kidney Qi descend, even to the point of causing a person to lose control of urination. Excessive pensiveness may result in stagnation of the Qi, thereby disturbing the Spleen's function of transforming food and leading to such abdominal symptoms as stomach distention or poor digestion. The Shen can become confused and flustered as a result of excessive fear or fright.

The correspondences between the emotions, Qi, and the Organs are useful to the physician, but are not meant to be mechanically applied or rigidly adhered to. Although the seven emotions are said to be internal generative factors of disease, Chinese medicine does not see them as precisely defined causes, but accepts them as yet another source of information with which to weave patterns of disharmony.

CLINICAL SKETCH: An individual is constantly angry and has nightmares. She complains of occasional dizziness, but otherwise feels healthy. A Western physician finds a slight elevation in blood pressure, but no other problem. He suggests that the patient see a psychiatrist to deal with her mental state. When the patient decides to try Chinese medicine, an examination reveals excessive Liver activity. Acupuncture points such as Liver 2 (*Xing-jian*,

Walk Between) and Gall Bladder 44 (*Qiao-yin*, Opening of Yin), and herbs such as *Gardenia* fruit and *Gentiana*, are used in the treatment. All of these cool and disperse excess Fire in the Liver, markedly improving her condition.

Way of Life (*bu-nei-wai-yin* 不 內 外 因)

This category of precipitating factors is traditionally called "not External, not Internal." In other words, it includes those factors that are neither Pernicious Influences (External) nor emotions (Internal). To the West, these are usually considerations of life style, and so they have been categorized as such.

The Chinese, as much as any other culture, have put a lot of emphasis on the way people conduct their lives. Their ideal life would be lived in harmony with the universe. If this is achieved, the assumption is that the person will have attained inner harmony as well. The Yin and Yang will be balanced, the emotions will be even. Of course, all this is not the province of medicine alone, but is also the concern of the culture as a whole and all its members. The physician, however, is aware of this, and is often called upon to treat disharmonies resulting from an unwise life style and to point out inappropriate habits.

Diet

Diet is considered an important influence on health and illness in Chinese medicine, and many books are devoted to dietary considerations. (This concern for diet, however, never approaches the Hippocratic emphasis.) Because the Stomach receives food and the Spleen is responsible for transforming it into Qi and Blood, these two Organs are most affected by diet.

Irregularity in quantity or quality of food, or in time of eating, can disrupt bodily harmony. Insufficient food or lack of proper food can mean that insufficient raw material reaches the Spleen. There will then be Deficient Qi and Blood, in the whole body or in certain Organs. Excess food that obstructs the Stomach's "ripening" and the Spleen's "transforming" is called "Stagnant Food" and may lead to such symptoms as distension, sour belching, or diarrhea.

A predilection for certain types of food can also generate disharmony. The Chinese say that too much raw food can strain the Yang aspect of the Spleen and generate Internal Cold Dampness resulting in such signs as abdominal pain, diarrhea, or weakness. Fatty and greasy foods, alcohol, or sweets can produce Dampness and Heat. Improperly cleaned food may injure digestion.

The Chinese people know many types of food, combinations of foods, and methods of preparation that are sometimes prescribed in medical literature and practice. This book is not primarily concerned with therapeutics, so Chinese dietary suggestions are not discussed. But even if they were, most Chinese dietary concepts would not be transferable to Western culture (except perhaps in Oriental restaurants). Diet, more than any other therapy, is strongly tied to a society's particular customs and habits. No Chinese book could tell Westerners what to eat for breakfast—Westerners would probably not be able to find the ingredients or prepare them, nor would many of them want to eat the result. And the Chinese could never give a reasoned opinion, based on empirical experience, on precisely when to eat or not to eat a lasagna. More important, though, Chinese physicians, like doctors in all cultures, are used to being ignored when they make dietary recommendations. Unfortunately, both patient and doctor too often feel that diet, while very useful in prevention and recovery, is not potent or specific enough to correct many serious disharmonies, and it is thus generally given a reduced importance in medicine.

Sexual Activity

In Chinese medical texts, excessive sexual activity is considered a precipitating factor of disease. Overindulgence is said to injure the Kidney Jing, which results in such symptoms as lumbago, dizziness, and general reduction of vitality. Giving birth too many times weakens the Jing and Blood, generating problems with menstruation and discharges. In the Chinese texts, sexual activity is referred to as "affairs of the bedroom," and "excess" activity is never clearly defined. This is because propriety in "affairs of the bedroom" is the province of the society in general as well as of medicine. Social conventions and the standards of class position have always been as important as medical considerations in determining the appropriate level of activity.

If a patient is considered to be engaging in excessive sexual activity, however, the doctor may suggest he or she have sex less often. But the doctor might as easily try to reharmonize the patient so that he or she would be physically able to sustain an increased amount of sexual activity. Using pattern-thinking, one can always balance the configuration in several ways.

Physical Activity

The category of physical activity includes general life activity. All life activity, to the Chinese, should point toward the goal of living in harmonious balance with the cosmos, the seasons, and one's own constitution and stage of life. Yang times—morning, spring, youth—should be active periods in a person's life; Yin times—evening, winter, old age—should be quiescent periods. The *Nei Jing*, for instance, mentions that in the winter one should "go to sleep early but arise late" and remain dormant "like someone with private intentions or as if one's intentions were already fulfilled."[17]

Physical activity is important to harmonize the flow of Qi and Blood and to develop strength in the body. Excessive labor, however, can strain the Spleen's ability to produce Qi and Blood, leading to deficiencies of these Substances. The body must rest, but excessive ease or slothfulness can weaken the vitality of Qi and Blood. Excessive use of a particular part of the body—a barber's hand, for instance, or a singer's voice—can lead to strain and disharmony. In some cases, the physician will suggest a change of life style, but often this is impossible. In the case of a singer, for instance, the physician would prescribe treatments so that continual use of the voice would not throw the body out of balance; the physician would create a balance within the given situation.

An inappropriate life style can be both a generative factor of disharmony and a manifestation of disharmony itself. Inappropriate life style accompanies disharmony; there is no beginning or end. A person who is always "running around" may drain the Qi of the various Organs or conversely, may be manifesting hyperactivity of those Organs. Someone who is always "sitting around" can cause the Qi and Blood to stagnate or may be manifesting depressed activity of the Organs.

Chinese medical practitioners are always concerned with the maintenance of health. The *Nei Jing* poetically says: "To administer medicine after an illness begins is . . . like digging a well after becoming thirsty or casting weapons after a battle has been engaged."[18] Patients are often taught correct diet, proper attitudes, and healthful life styles. The central concern is always balance, rhythm, and harmony. Food, for instance, should be prepared and eaten in balance. Leafy green vegetables, a Yin substance, should be cooked with ginger, which is Yang. T'ai Chi exercises encourage rhythmic and controlled movement. Adolescents are expected to have different emotional attitudes than the elderly. Frail people should do less demanding work than people with robust constitutions.

Recommendations of this type are not made only by doctors. The determination of what is or is not a healthful life style is made by the society at large and becomes part of a cultural model of "how to live." The theory and practice of health are thus also the concern of philosophers, educators, cooks, homemakers, parents, grandparents, neighbors, and friends.

Miscellaneous Factors

The Chinese also recognize several other precipitating factors in illness (which, strangely, belong in the "not External, not Internal" category). These include burns, bites, parasites, and trauma—sudden, easily identifiable conditions. Although these factors can be readily thought of as causes, the Chinese physician must nevertheless consider how they interact with other bodily signs and symptoms, and must discern a pattern to reharmonize. Even a snakebite or a burn cannot be isolated from the rest of a person's being. The miscellaneous factors are dealt with in the literature but are not unique to Chinese medicine, nor are they essential to the understanding of the Chinese medical view.

All of the precipitating factors discussed in this chapter would be called causes in the West. But it must be stressed again that in Chinese medicine, a distinct and separable cause is unimportant; the relationships within a pattern are crucial. Any one factor is, finally, another piece of the whole. And the complete patient is treated, never for the cause, but for his or her unique configuration of signs and symptoms. The idea of causality in Chinese medicine is ultimately a means for identifying and qualifying the important relationships between environment, emotional character, personal life style, and health and illness.

Notes

1. Different historical periods have emphasized different Pernicious Influences in the theory and clinical practice. The *Nei Jing*, for example, deals extensively with Wind but briefly with Fire. Cold, in this earlier period, is usually considered the source of febrile illnesses. Later periods will emphasize Heat. For a discussion see Jia De-dao's Concise History of China's Medicine [95], 1979, pp. 66–69, 194.

2. Besides the Pernicious Influences, there is the concept of Pestilences—*li-qi* or *yi-qi*. Pestilence is considered an additional External Pernicious Influence. It is first mentioned in the *Su Wen* (sec. 21, chap. 71), but the idea was not fully developed until Wu You-xing wrote his Discussion of Warm Epidemics [25] in 1642 c.e. In that book, he discussed "warm epidemics" or "pestilence" as separate from climatic conditions but able to affect even the healthiest body with great virulence. However, appropriate treatment methods are still based on determining which of the six Pernicious Influences the Pestilence resembles.

3. The understanding of External and Internal aspects of a Pernicious Influence varies with historical period. An excellent discussion concerning this problem in relation to Wind and apoplexy appears in Shanghai Institute, Lecture Notes on Traditional Chinese Internal Medicine [54], p. 162.

4. *Su Wen* [1], sec. 12, chap. 42, p. 238.

5. Ibid., sec. 8, chap. 29, p. 180.

6. Ibid., sec. 12, chap. 42, p. 236.

7. Reports such as Analysis of Effectiveness of Traditional Chinese Herbal Medicines in 150 Cases of Influenza and Preliminary Analysis of 1006 Cases Using Acupuncture for Treatment of Influenza, in Journal of Traditional Chinese Medicine (JTCM), February 1960, indicate that traditional methods of treatment can be more effective than those of modern medicine.

8. *Su Wen*, sec. 11, chap. 39, p. 218.

9. Ibid., sec. 22, chap. 74, p. 539.

10. For an interesting clinical report on how Chinese medicine views and treats swollen prostate, see Preliminary Experience in Combining Traditional Chinese and Western Medicine to Treat Swollen Prostate in Sixty-five Cases, JTCM, February 1980, pp. 34–35. In this patient group four main types of patterns were discovered: a Damp-Heat pattern; a Deficient Yin pattern; a Deficient Yang pattern (as in the example given); and a Deficient Spleen Qi pattern. Using only Chinese herbal medicines, results based on subjective reports showed that forty patients recovered normal urination, eleven improved, and nine had no change. (The Western treatment involved use of a catheter when necessary.)

11. For a discussion of the antibiotic effects of the two herbs mentioned, see Shanghai First Medical Hospital, Clinical Handbook of Antimicrobial Medicines [82], pp. 77–78. The possible mechanism of acupuncture's role in infectious illnesses is not so well described in the literature as the probable herbal mechanisms. However, some research has been reported, as in Role of Humoral Immunity in Acute Bacillary Dysentery Treated with Acupuncture, JTCM, April 1980. This study reports that acupuncture on humans produced marked increase in the level of immunoglobulin, total complements, specific antibodies, fecal SIgA, and the bactericidal properties of plasma. The same article reports that according to analysis of serum lysozyme and the phagocytosis of reticuloendothelial cells of the liver in rabbits, acupuncture appears to stimulate and strengthen humoral immunity.

12. *Su Wen*, sec. 8, chap. 29, p. 180.

13. Beijing Institute, Foundations [38], p. 57.

14. This illustration is based on the incident mentioned in the Introduction. An excellent discussion of herpes zoster appears in Guanganmen Hospital, Collected Clinical Experiences of Zhu Ren-kang: Dermatology [73], pp. 70–76. Only one of the prescriptions recommended for herpes zoster does not include some herbs listed in Chen Xin-qian, Pharmacology: New Edition [71], pp. 121–131 as inhibiting the growth of virus. The main such herbs are *Baphicacanthes cusia, Taraxacum mongolicum,* and *Portulaca oleracea*. All these herbs are considered useful in cooling Heat.

15. The hospital that edited Dr. Zhu's cases (see note 14) reported that in the 144 cases of herpes zoster treated by traditional methods between January 1974 and June 1975, a noticeable and significant reduction of length of illness and severity of pain was observed as compared with cases treated with Western methods or those receiving no treatment (Collected Clinical Experiences of Zhu Ren-kang: Dermatology [73], p. 76).

16. *Su Wen*, sec. 11, chap. 39, p. 221.

17. Ibid., sec. 1, chap. 2, p. 11.

18. Ibid., p. 14.

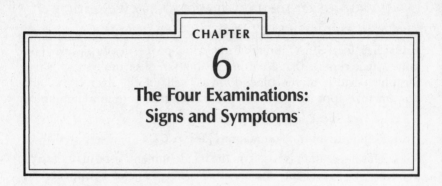

The first five chapters discussed the vocabulary and ideas behind the Chinese weaving of patterns. Now the theories of Fundamental Substances, Organs, Meridians, and Pernicious
Influences must become concrete. How do these ideas work
when they are applied to a specific patient? How do they enable
a physician to diagnose a pattern of disharmony? What does the
doctor look for, and how are the more important clues distinguished from the less important? How does the doctor begin
to deal with all the signs and symptoms a patient presents?

In this chapter, we will follow the procedure a physician uses
with a new patient. We will see the way Chinese physicians
examine patients—what they look for, how they judge the significance of what they see, how they interpret the signs and
symptoms. These pieces, or elements of patterns of disharmony, can include a wide range of data—style of movement,
sensations of warmth, pain, facial color, mood, qualities of the
tongue or pulse, and many other signs. When these bits and
pieces of information are put together, they create the image of
a disharmony.

But the very process of examining the pieces of a pattern
poses a problem: What do we make of a piece in a system that
says that only the whole can determine the meaning of the
piece? Before we go on to the examinations, therefore, we

should look again at the philosophy that informs Chinese medicine so that our customary Western viewpoint will not interfere with our understanding.

As has been said, Chinese philosophy and medicine are based on Taoist consciousness[1] and on Yin-Yang theory, which imply a world view very different from that of the West. The Chinese could never produce an Aristotelian, and would be hard pressed to accept Aristotle's famous law of contradiction: "There is a principle in things, about which we cannot be deceived but must always, on the contrary, recognize the truth— viz., that the same thing cannot at one and the same time be and not be, or admit any other similar pair of opposites."[2] This principle, that *A* cannot be *not A*, became the cornerstone of all Western logic. Yet little trace of it can be found in either Taoist thought or Chinese medical writings.

A very different spirit informs the Chinese view of knowledge and being. Lao Tzu, the earliest Taoist sage, formulated this understanding of the nature of reality:

> *To be bent is to become straight.*
> *To be empty is to be full.*
> *To be worn out is to be renewed.*
> *To have little is to possess.*[3]

Chuang Tzu, the Taoist philosopher, says:

When there is life there is death, and when there is death there is life. When there is possibility, there is impossibility, and when there is impossibility, there is possibility. Because of the right, there is wrong, and because of the wrong, there is right. . . . The "this" is also the "that." The "that" is also the "this." . . . Is there really a distinction between "that" and "this"? . . . When "this" and "that" have no opposites, there is the very axis of Tao.[4]

Change and transformation are the only constants for the Chinese; things (*A* and *not A*, "this" and "that") can simultaneously be and not be. Yin and Yang produce each other, imply each other, and finally *are* each other.

There was at least one pre-Socratic Western philosopher, Heraclitus, who seems to have developed a view of the universe comparable to that of the Taoists. The fragments of his writings that have come down to us set forth his ideas:

> The attunement of the world is of opposite tensions, as is that of the harp and bow.[5]

> The road up and the road down is one and the same. The beginning and end are common.[6]

> That which is at variance with itself agrees with itself.[7]

> Cold things become warm, warmth cools, moisture dries, the parched get wet. It scatters and gathers, it comes and goes.[8]

This Heraclitean notion of primitive flux is very close to that of the Tao. But Heraclitus represents only one skein of Western thought. The dominant ideas were those of Aristotle and his followers, for whom the primary consideration was how things emerge from such flux and achieve distinct existence. The flux had to be differentiated, carved into distinct categories, before there could be reality as Aristotle conceived it. The Aristotelian emphasis on form derives from this concern.

The Chinese, however, never thought of the Tao, or flux, as a vicious undertow from which things must fight free and distinguish themselves. To them, the flux is a vast harmony that embraces all things. They do not ask of an entity how well it measures up to the pure form prescribed for it, but rather what is its relationship to other entities. It is not important or even necessary that every entity attain pure form, but it is important that every entity have a place in the overarching pattern of existence.

In the nineteenth century, Hegel finally confronted and denied Aristotle's law of contradiction and developed the theory that has come to be known as Hegelian dialectics. For Hegel, the intricacies of relationship override the Aristotelian concern that A not be confused with *not* A. A can, in fact, be other than A, depending on its place in an overall schema. These ideas are so similar to those of Chinese philosophy that Hegelian and Chinese thought have often been compared.[9]

But Chinese and Taoist philosophy are not exactly the same as Hegelian dialectics. The Chinese, for example, never elaborated their intuition of the dialectical process into a philosophy of reason as Hegel did. They went no further than to make simple refinements in Yin-Yang theory. They never tried to tame the elusive and changeable qualities of the Tao. The word *Tao*, although sometimes translated as "the Way," cannot really be translated into satisfactory English, and even its meaning in Chinese frustrates the attempt to pin it down. "The Tao that can be told of is not the Tao. The Name that can be named is not the constant name."[10] And so the Chinese have developed ways of alluding to the Tao—in aphorisms, parables, and tales that are more like poetry than like the systematic presentations of Western thought.

But the Tao is not poetry either; to see it as such is also to lose it. The Tao, as the ultimate reality, can be apprehended—in medicine, for instance—but that apprehension has to take place within the context of flux, interconnectedness, and dynamism. The Tao comes to stand for something that does not deny reason, but always manages to remain just outside its grasp.

The Chinese emphasis on interconnectedness and change takes on a very specific character in the context of medicine. When the Chinese physician examines a patient, he or she plans to look at many, many signs and symptoms and to make of them a diagnosis, to see in them a pattern. Each sign means nothing by itself and acquires meaning only in its relationship to the patient's other signs. What it means in one context is not necessarily what it means in another context.

When statements are made in this chapter, therefore, they are always modified by the word "usually." This is because no statement is going to be specifically true and applicable in every case. In a landscape painting, a mountain *usually* denotes Yang because it is big and hard; but in a picture that focuses on an ocean, mountains may appear in the distance, thus denoting

Yin because they are relatively small and passive. The meaning of the mountains is determined by context.

The same is true of the body. A "rapid" pulse, for example, is considered a sign of Heat. The correspondence between rapid pulse and Heat is about as rigid a correspondence as can be found in Chinese medicine. Yet there are cases in which even a rapid pulse can have a different or opposite meaning. A patient may be lying listlessly in bed, covered by many blankets. He is short of breath, his face is pale, and his body is puffy. He has no appetite, his stools are watery, and he has a pale, moist, swollen tongue. These symptoms make up a pattern of Deficiency/Cold disharmony, a Yin disharmony—even though his pulse is 120 beats per minute. In this case, the abnormally fast pulse, usually a sign of extreme Heat, or Yang, signifies extreme weakness, or Yin. *A* is usually *A* but sometimes it is *not A*.

In Chinese medicine, as in Chinese philosophy, one cannot understand the whole until one knows the parts and cannot understand the parts without knowing the whole. Learning a detail, *A*, for instance, is not worth much until the full circle of Chinese medicine has been traveled, at which time *A* will show itself to be rich and useful. The part can only be known when the whole is apparent. This dialectic, this circularity, is a kind of catch-22, but it is also a central aspect of the medicine's artistry. The Chinese interplay of whole and parts does not lend itself to booklike elucidation; the sequential, linear book form can only attempt to approach the intricacies of the Chinese system. But the nature of the difficulty, at least, can be made explicit.

The Four Examinations (si-jian 四 诊)

The Chinese physician performs an inspection of the patient that divides into four stages. The four stages are called the Four Examinations,[11] because each one focuses on a different way of recognizing signs in a patient. The Four Examinations are Looking, Listening and Smelling (these two words are the same word in Chinese), Asking, and Touching. The physician completes each of the Examinations, gathering signs to weave into the final diagnosis.

The signs themselves may fall neatly into place, pointing unanimously to a particular disharmony. Or they may seem to contradict each other, requiring the physician to interpret closely and carefully before making a determination. Some signs—like those of the pulse or tongue—are more important than others and are given greater weight. They bring the bodily landscape into focus. Some signs—like headache or blood in the urine—are looked on more as complaints beneath which a disharmony is lurking and are given little diagnostic weight. These complaints demand interpretation and clarification from accompanying signs and symptoms. A complaint is the problem that brings a person to a physician; the patient will usually mention his or her complaint. A sign, however, is something that the doctor looks for but that the patient would not necessarily know or talk about. There are a countless number of possible signs, symptoms, and complaints; this discussion is limited to those signs that are most characteristic of Chinese diagnosis and that make the most important contribution to pattern discernment.[12]

An individual sign or symptom may point to a particular Organ or to a quality of disharmony. This chapter describes signs that point to the most commonly found qualities of patterns, the basic textures and shades. The major qualities, of course, are Yin and Yang. Disharmonies always involve imbalances of Yin and Yang. For clarity, the Yin–Yang archetypes are often broken down into sub-categories: Deficiency and Excess, and Cold and Hot. When the reference is to proportion of Substances, Deficiency is the Yin aspect and Excess the Yang; with reference to temperament and level of activity, Cold is Yin and Hot is Yang. The terms *Cold* and *Hot*, of course, designate normal aspects of the body, as well as environmental factors (Pernicious Influences) and qualities of disharmony. Their meanings in any given situation can be distinguished only by the context in which the words are used, but in this chapter they will be considered as qualities of disharmony.*

Looking (wang-zhen 望 診)

The first stage of the Four Examinations is Looking. In the Looking Examination, the physician attends to four characteristics that are visible to the eye. The first is general appearance, including the patient's physical shape, the patient's manner, the way he or she behaves during the Examination, and the state of the patient's Shen. The second is facial color. The third characteristic is the tongue, including the material of the tongue itself, the coating of the tongue, and its shape and movement. The fourth is the bodily secretions and excretions. These characteristics are presented in the order of observation by the physician. In order of their importance to the doctor, however—that is, how much weight they are given when the doctor begins to discern patterns—they are: tongue, facial color, secretions and excretions, and appearance.

Appearance

The patient's physical shape is an indication of his or her health. A person whose appearance is strong and robust is likely to have strong Organs. When disharmonies occur in such a person, they are likely to be those of Excess. A weak-looking, frail individual is more likely to have weak Organs and therefore to have disharmonies of Deficiency.

---

*The reason for this apparent lack of precision in terminology lies in the nature of the Chinese language. In this ideographic language, there are relatively few words and each character has a wide semantic range. A word can be a noun, adjective, or verb depending on its context. There are no verb tenses or moods. The shade or actual meaning of a word is determined by context. Thus a word such as Heat can be used to mean the body's normal Heat, or can be a Pernicious Influence, or a quality of disharmony, or the name of a pattern of disharmony. Although there is ambiguity in the Chinese language, however, there is also the possibility of expressing subtle and elusive shades and fusions of meaning.

Someone who is overweight is often prone to Deficient Qi, all the more so if he or she tends to be pale and swollen. Heaviness can also be a sign of tendency toward Excess Mucus or Dampness. A thin person, especially one with a sallow complexion, narrow chest, and dry skin—a dried prune appearance—is often prone to Deficient Yin or Blood. Great wasting of flesh in the course of a long illness suggests that the Jing is exhausted.

Signs of shape are generally the least reliable aspects of a patient's appearance. They amount to what may be called constitutional tendencies or predispositions to certain kinds of disharmony.

The *Nei Jing* states, "Yang is movement, Yin is quiescence."[13] This is the key to examining a patient's manner and emotions. A person who is agitated, outward, talkative, aggressive, and irritable is usually manifesting a Yang tendency. A passive, inward, quiet manner is usually Yin. Heavy, forceful, ponderous movement is typically part of a disharmony of Excess; frail and weak movement usually indicates a Deficiency. Quick movement is usually part of a Heat pattern; slow, deliberate movement is generally part of a Cold pattern. If the patient, when in bed, stretches his feet, removes the covers, or moves away from heat, he may well be suffering from a Heat disharmony. If, on the other hand, the patient curls up in bed, likes to be covered, or wants to be near heat, the doctor would suspect a Cold condition.

Observation of the Shen or Spirit means observing the patient's facial expression, posture, speech, responsiveness, the look and shine of the eyes, the appropriateness of reaction, the clarity of thought. It is one of the first signs a Chinese physician will note and is as much a part of the Examinations as looking at the tongue or feeling the pulse. If the eyes are without luster or the face is clouded, the Shen may be depleted or in disharmony. If the personality is vital, the eyes alive, then the Shen is harmonious.

Since the Shen is nourished by Qi and Blood, an evaluation of Shen is a clue to the relative strength of these Substances. Chinese doctors speak of "having Shen," "lack of Shen," and "false

Shen." False Shen usually occurs during a severe or terminal illness, when a patient may suddenly become alert although all other signs point to grave deterioration. This temporary, or false, Shen, is seen as the last flicker of a dying candle.

Facial Color

The color of the face and its moistness are closely related to the body's Qi and Blood. The *Nei Jing* states that "all the Qi and Blood of the Meridians pour upward into the face."[14] Normal and healthy facial color obviously depends on a person's racial and ethnic origin, climatic conditions, and occupation. In general, however, a healthy face is shiny and moist. If an individual is ill, but the face appears healthy, it suggests that the Qi and Blood are not weakened and that the illness is not serious. A withered face implies weakness of the vital Substances and a less favorable prognosis. Abnormal facial colors have definite clinical significance. White is associated with disharmonies of Deficiency or of Cold. A bright white face with a puffy, bloated appearance is a sign of Deficient Qi or Deficient Yang. If the white face is lusterless and withered, it signifies Deficient Blood. Sometimes the face is white when there is pain. Red appears with Heat and Fire. When the entire face is red, it is a sign of Excess Heat. The words Heat and Fire refer to the same phenomenon, but the word *Heat* is usually used to talk about external Heat, while Fire is used to talk about internally generated Heat. Yellow indicates Dampness or Deficiency. A yellow face is especially related to Internal Dampness produced by a weak Spleen not "raising the pure fluids." When the entire body, including the eyes, is yellow, the symptom is always seen as indicating a Damp condition. If the yellowness tends toward bright orange, the Dampness is also Hot and is called Yang jaundice; if the yellow is pale, it is a sign of Cold Dampness and is called Yin jaundice. A pale yellow face without brightness may be a sign of Deficient Blood.

Qing is an important color in Chinese culture and medicine. The Chinese describe it as "the color of a dragon's scales." It is translated as "blue-green," although connoting many shades between blue and green. Blue-green indicates stagnation or obstruction of Blood and Qi (Congealed Blood and Stagnant Qi). It is usually associated with patterns of Excess. Because the Liver rules flowing and spreading, and because Wind is associated with Liver disharmonies, Qing also appears when there is Liver disharmony or Wind. In the case of extreme obstruction, Qing may acquire a purplish tinge.

Darkness or Black is associated with Deficient Kidneys and Congealed Blood. This color often arises after a prolonged chronic illness. The blackness may be especially evident under the eyes. An abnormally dark complexion generally indicates that the illness will be difficult to treat.

Tongue

Observing the tongue is one of two pillars of the Four Examinations;[15] the other is feeling the pulse. One elderly Chinese physician, a teacher of the author, described the tongue as a piece of litmus paper that reveals the basic qualities of a disharmony. Many signs may be interpreted only when the entire configuration can be seen, but the tongue interpretation is always essential. It is often the clearest indication of the nature of a disharmony and its pattern, reliable even when other signs are vague and contradictory.

When talking about the tongue, Chinese physicians make a distinction between the tongue material and the coating of the tongue. The Chinese word for the tongue coating can best be translated as "moss" or "fur." The tongue material and tongue moss are treated as two separate elements of tongue examination.

The tongue material can be various shades of red and can have varying degrees of moisture.

A normal tongue is pale red and somewhat moist. The characteristic healthy color is the result of abundant Blood carried to the tongue by smoothly moving Qi. If the tongue maintains its normal color during an illness, it is a sign that the Qi and Blood have not been injured, and the prognosis is very favorable.

A pale tongue is less red than a normal tongue, and indicates Deficient Blood or Deficient Qi or Excess Cold.

A red tongue is redder than a normal tongue, and points to a Heat condition in the body.

A scarlet tongue is deeper red than a red tongue, and points to an extreme Heat condition. In a disharmony characterized by External Heat, it indicates that Heat has entered the deepest levels of the body.

A purple tongue usually indicates that the Qi and Blood are not moving harmoniously and that there is a pattern of Stagnant Qi or Congealed Blood. A pale purple tongue means the obstruction is related to Cold; reddish-purple is a sign of Heat-related injury to the Blood or Fluids. In general, if the lack of flow is due to Cold, the tongue will appear moist. If it is due to Heat, the tongue will appear dry. A purple tongue may also be associated with the Liver's failure to flow or spread properly.

A tongue with a dark tinge signifies some form of stagnation.

The coating, fur, or moss on the surface of the tongue is the result of Spleen activity. During its vaporization of pure essences, the Spleen also causes small amounts of impure substances to ascend, like smoke. These substances come out in the tongue. Some medical literature, in fact, refers to tongue moss as "smoke." The moss is thus intimately related to digestion and can reflect the state of the digestive system. Other activities of the body also leave impressions on the moss—evidence of bodily states—that are visible to the physician.

The tongue moss covers the whole surface or patches of the surface of the tongue. It can vary in thickness, color, texture, and general appearance. In a healthy individual the density of moss is relatively uniform, although it may be slightly thicker in the center of the tongue. The moss is thin, whitish, and moist, and the tongue material can be seen through it.

A thin moss can be normal, but during an illness it may be a sign of Deficiency. A very thick moss is nearly always a sign of Excess.

Moss that is puddled with moisture is a sign of Excess Fluids, usually due to Deficient Yang (or Fire, the body's internal Heat), but is also a possible sign of other patterns, such as Dampness.

Moss that is very dry or sandpaperlike is a sign of Excess Yang or Fire, or of Deficient Fluids.

A moss that appears firmly implanted on the tongue body, like grass sprouting from the ground, signifies strong Spleen and Stomach Qi. Moss that appears to be floating on the surface of the tongue is a sign of weak Spleen and Stomach Qi.

A greasy moss appears to be a thick, oily film covering the tongue or a portion of it. It can resemble a layer of white petroleum jelly or butter, and is a sign of Mucus or Dampness in the body. A pasty moss, which is greasy but somewhat thicker (the Chinese say it looks like the lumpy result of mixing oil and flour), signifies extreme Mucus or Dampness. Greasy moss is an important sign in discerning patterns of disharmony.

When the moss seems to have been removed so that the tongue or a portion of it appears shiny, it is called "peeled tongue"—described by Chinese texts as resembling the flesh of an uncooked chicken after the skin has been removed. A peeled tongue may be a sign of Deficient Yin or Fluids, or of Spleen Qi too weak to raise smoke.

White moss, though also the color of normal moss, can appear in illness. It may signify Cold, especially if there is excessive moisture in the tongue material. But if the white moss resembles cottage cheese (or, as the Chinese say, unshaped tofu), it signifies Heat in the Stomach.

A yellow moss points to Heat: the deeper the yellow, the greater the Heat.

A black or gray moss is a sign of either extreme Heat or Cold—extreme Heat if the tongue material is red, extreme Cold if it is pale.

The shape and movement of the tongue are also considered. A normal tongue is neither too big nor too small for the mouth, looking neither swollen nor shriveled. It should move with flexibility but not uncontrollably, and it should not slant in any particular direction. The normal tongue should be a smooth piece of flesh without cracks, and although it may have raised papillae, it should have no red pimples or eruptions.

The swollen tongue is puffy with scalloped edges, as though it had been imprinted by the teeth. The usual origin of a swollen tongue is Deficient Qi or Excess Fluids. In rare instances, however, it may be part of a pattern of Excess Heat, in which case the tongue body will also be very red.

A thin tongue is slender, smaller than a normal tongue, and is usually a sign of Deficient Blood or Fluids.

A stiff tongue lacks flexibility, resembling, as the Chinese say, "a piece of wood." This type of tongue usually implies a Wind Pernicious Influence or Mucus obstructing the Heart Qi.

A trembling tongue seems to wiggle uncontrollably. When this type of tongue is pale, it is a sign that Qi is insufficient to regulate proper movement. If the tongue is red, the diagnosis is usually Internal Wind moving the tongue.

A tongue that lolls like a panting dog's is most often a sign of Heat.

A contracted tongue that cannot be stretched out is usually seen in serious situations. When the accompanying tongue color is pale or purple, Cold is probably contracting the body. If a contracted tongue is swollen, it usually signifies Mucus or Dampness. If the tongue material of a contracted tongue is red, it is a sign that Heat has injured the Fluids.

Cracks on the tongue are common and are considered normal if they have been present since birth. If, however, they develop during an illness, they are a sign of chronic and severe illness. The exact interpretation depends on the tongue color. Cracks in a red tongue are usually a sign of Heat injuring the Fluids or of Deficient Yin; cracks in a pale tongue signify Deficient Blood and Qi.

Red eruptions, pimples, or thornlike protrusions on the tongue, redder than the occasional raised papillae of the normal tongue, are usually signs of Heat or of Congealed Blood.

These signs often occur on only certain portions of the tongue. For example, the center of the tongue alone may be thickly coated, or only the sides of the tongue might be red, or a crack might appear just at the tip. For such cases particular areas of the tongue are said to correspond to particular Organs. Figure 17 illustrates these correspondences, which are helpful but are *never* considered absolute.

FIGURE 17

Areas of the Tongue and Corresponding Organs

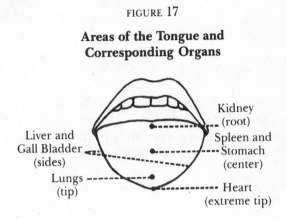

Secretions and Excretions

The principal secretions and excretions are phlegm, vomit, urine, and stool. Because phlegm and vomit may be seen by the physician, they are considered part of the Looking Examination. Urine and stool are usually discussed with the patient and are therefore covered in the Asking Examination.

Clear, thin phlegm exuding from the nose and throat is usually part of a Cold pattern. If the phlegm is yellow and sticky, it is a sign of Heat. A large amount of phlegm easily coughed usually indicates Dampness. Bloody phlegm is commonly a sign of Heat injuring the Lungs.

Thin, watery, clear vomit usually signifies a Cold pattern and Deficient Stomach Qi, as does the vomiting of undigested food without a sour taste in the mouth. Sour-tasting vomit usually indicates Stomach Heat. Yellow, bitter-tasting vomit is a sign of Liver Heat or Gall Bladder Heat.

Listening and Smelling (wen-zhen 闻 诊)

This Examination deals with a number of common signs, all about equally important in the weaving of a diagnosis.

Voice and respiration are the first. Coarse, strong respiration may signify Excess. Weak respiration or shortness of breath, accompanied by weak, low voice and little speech, suggests Deficiency. A sudden loss of voice suggests an External Pernicious Influence, while chronic loss of voice is usually a sign of Deficiency. Wheezing most often suggests Mucus.

A heavy cough or a sudden and violent one is a sign of Excess. A dry, hacking cough suggests Heat or Dryness. A weak cough is usually part of a Deficiency pattern.

Chinese medicine distinguishes between two main kinds of bodily odors that are present during illness. These smells are difficult to describe, and so the Chinese physician relies heavily on experience when interpreting them. One odor is characterized as foul, rotten, and nauseating, like the odor of rancid meat or rotten eggs. Such an odor signifies Heat. The second odor is less nauseating but more pungent or fishy, and may seem to hurt the nose. It is like the smell of fumes from bleach, and indicates Cold and Deficiency.

Asking (wen-zhen 问 诊)

In the third of the Four Examinations, the physician asks questions, as would a Western doctor, to discover important but not readily apparent information. Of course, many, many questions may be asked, but only those that are most common and that are essential to pattern perception are discussed here. These cover the following topics: sensations of cold or hot; perspiration; headaches and dizziness; quality and location of pain; urination and stool; thirst; appetite and tastes; sleep; gynecological concerns; and medical history.[16] Questions about hot and cold, pain, and medical history are generally the most important. The other signs discovered by Asking may contribute necessary shadings to a pattern, but they rarely determine it.

Sensations of Cold and Hot

In general, Cold corresponds to Yin and Hot to Yang, for internally generated disorders. Subjective sensations of Heat, feeling warm to the touch, or a dislike of hot weather or hot places can be a sign of Heat. Cold is signified by the opposite—constant chills or a preference for warm places, for instance.

Acute fevers of external origin fall into the special category of febrile illnesses. Until very recently, such illnesses were always considered life-threatening and were in fact a major cause of death. Fevers are therefore a central focus of most Chinese medical texts, as they are in the writings of Hippocrates and in other early medical traditions. (Febrile illnesses are the subject of Appendix A.)

When a patient has a sudden fever together with chills, it indicates that the body's Qi is attempting to expel an External Pernicious Influence; it is not necessarily a sign of Cold. If the fever persists but the chills disappear, the illness is said to have gone deeper and the fever is a sign of Heat. A low-grade fever especially noticeable in the afternoon or heat felt only in the palms of the hands, soles of the feet, and the sternum (known collectively to the Chinese as the "five hearts") indicates insufficient Yin.

If the patient has no fever yet fears Cold, he or she is usually suffering from Deficient Yang or Deficient Qi, especially if the condition is chronic. Interestingly, whether or not blankets make the patient any warmer is a helpful diagnostic distinction. If blankets increase the patient's warmth, the disharmony is probably in Internal Deficiency of Yang. If not, the disorder may be an invasion of an External Cold Pernicious Influence.

Perspiration

Perspiration occurs when the pores are open but not when the pores are closed. Both these conditions are affected by various disharmonies. If a patient perspires in the daytime even though he or she engages in little or no physical activity (spontaneous sweating), it indicates that Protective Qi is not properly regulating the pores and that there may be a pattern of Deficient Yang or Deficient Qi. Excessive perspiration during sleep (night sweating), however, signifies Deficient Yin—a relative excess of Heat in the body causing the pores to open.

If no perspiration occurs during an illness with fever and other signs of an External Pernicious Influence, the Pernicious Influence is probably Cold that has obstructed the pores. If there is perspiration during such an illness, it suggests External Heat opening the pores, or perhaps a Deficiency of Qi hampering the proper regulation of the pores. The choice between these two possibilities would be based on other signs. If the fever breaks after perspiration, the Pernicious Influence has been expelled.

Headache and Dizziness

Headaches may accompany any of the patterns of disharmony, but some broad distinctions between types of headaches can be helpful. Sudden headaches often appear with External Pernicious Influences, which disturb the Yang or Qi of the head. Chronic headaches more often accompany Internal disharmonies. Severe headaches may be a sign of Excess, while slight, annoying headaches are usually signs of Deficiency. The Organ most associated with headaches is the Liver, because Liver Qi often rises when the Liver is in disharmony. A physician may consider the exact location of a headache significant, since it corresponds to the Meridian passing through that part of the head and thus to the rest of the system connected by that Meridian.

Dizziness, like headaches, can be part of any pattern of disharmony. Although it is most frequently seen in patterns of Deficient Yin or Blood, it always depends on the rest of the configuration for interpretations.

Pain

After Cold and Hot, this is the next most important subject of the Asking Examination. In fact, pain is often the patient's chief complaint, the thing that brought him or her into the physician's office. Pain manifesting in a particular part of the body indicates a disharmony in that area. Pain in the chest, for instance, indicates disharmony in the Heart or Lungs; pain of the flank and ribcage indicates Liver and Gall Bladder disharmony; pain in the epigastrum (solar plexus) indicates Stomach and Spleen disharmony; abdominal pain above the navel indicates disharmony of the Spleen and Intestines; abdominal pain around and below the navel indicates disharmonies of the Intestines, Bladder, Uterus, or Kidney; groin, genital-area, and hypogastrium (lower abdomen) pain indicates Liver Meridian disharmony; and lower back pain signals Kidney disharmony.

The Chinese physician is also concerned with a patient's description of the exact quality of his or her pain. Table 2 summarizes the significance and type of disharmony associated with some common qualities of pain.

TABLE 2

Signification of Qualities of Pain

Quality of Pain	Signification
Diminished by heat	Cold
Diminished by cold	Heat
Relieved by touch or pressure	Deficiency
Aggravated by touch or pressure	Excess
Diminishes after eating	Deficiency
Increases after eating	Excess
Increases in humid weather	Dampness
Accompanied by bloating or sense of fullness	Stagnant Qi
Sharp and stabbing, usually fixed in location	Congealed Blood
Sensation of heaviness	Dampness
Moves from place to place	Wind or Stagnant Qi
Slight and accompanied by fatigue	Deficient Qi or Dampness

Urine and Stool

Chinese physicians do not generally take urine or stool samples for examination; they get the information they need from the Asking Examination.

A patient whose urine is clear usually has a Cold pattern, while dark yellow or reddish urine indicates Heat. Copious urine and frequent nighttime urination suggest that the Kidneys are not properly vaporizing Water and point to Deficient Kidney Qi. Scanty urination is usually a sign of some type of Excess, such as Dampness or Heat obstructing the Bladder Qi, although it can be a sign of Deficient Fluids. Frequent, scanty, dark, and painful urinations indicate Dampness and Heat in the Bladder. Inability to complete urination, dribbling, or a lack of force in urination often signifies Deficient Qi, Cold, or Dampness.

Infrequent, dry, or hard stools are usually part of a configuration of Heat Excess, but, depending on the accompanying signs, may also signify Deficient Fluids or Deficient Qi. Frequent watery or unformed stools usually signify Deficient Yang, Deficient Qi, or Dampness. Urgent diarrhea, especially when yellowish and accompanied by a burning sensation in the anus, is a sign of Heat. Stools that are first dry and then wet suggest Deficiency. Undigested food in stools often signifies Deficient Yang of the Spleen.

Thirst, Appetite, and Tastes

Chinese physicians commonly ask patients whether they are thirsty. This is because thirst is often a sign of Heat, while lack of thirst often signifies Cold. Thirst without desire to drink is a sign of Deficient Yin or of Dampness.

Lack of appetite usually signifies a Stomach or Spleen disharmony due to Deficient Qi or Dampness. Excessive appetite is a sign of Excess Stomach Fire.

Unusual tastes in the mouth may also indicate disharmony. A bitter taste suggests Heat, most commonly as a condition of the

Liver or Gall Bladder. A sweet pasty taste suggests Damp Heat in the Spleen. Foul tastes often mean Liver or Stomach Heat, while salty taste sensations may indicate Kidney disharmony. Inability to distinguish tastes is usually part of a pattern of Deficient Spleen Qi.

Sleep

In keeping with their emphasis on balance, the Chinese believe that people should have just enough sleep. Too little or too much indicates imbalance and disharmony.

Insomnia is described in Chinese texts as "Yang unable to enter Yin"—the active unable to become passive—and "Shen not peaceful." This usually means that Blood or Yin or both are Deficient and incapable of nourishing the Shen stored in the Heart. There is therefore a relative excess of Yang, which is not balanced and is unable to quiet down. Excess Yang or Fire in any other Organ can also disturb the Shen and cause insomnia. The constant desire to sleep, or excessive sleep, is often a sign of Deficient Yang, Deficient Qi, or Dampness.

Gynecological Concerns

Chinese physicians routinely ask female patients about gynecological matters. If a woman's menstrual periods arrive earlier than usual, it may signify that Heat is causing reckless movement of Blood or that Deficient Qi cannot govern Blood. The accompanying signs would make a distinction easy to arrive at: A red tongue would mean Heat, a pale tongue would mean Deficient Qi. Late periods suggest Deficient Blood or Cold causing Stagnation. Irregular menstruation is often a sign that Liver Qi is not moving harmoniously.

Excessive menstrual flow may signify Heat in the Blood or Deficient Qi. Insufficient flow or lack of menses (except during pregnancy) may mean Deficient Blood, Cold obstructing the Blood, or Congealed Blood. Pale and thin menstrual blood points to a Deficient condition. Very dark blood suggests Heat, and blood that is purplish, especially if clotted, may indicate Congealed Blood.

Copious, clear or white, and thin discharges (leukorrhea) usually signify Deficiency and Dampness. Discharges that are thick and yellow, or accompanied by itching or soreness of the vagina, are often signs of Heat and Dampness.

Medical History

The Chinese physician wants to have a complete medical history of each patient. This is because patterns may reappear time after time, pointing to various irregularities or body activities, and because previous disharmonies may be affecting the patient's health. The patient's history is an additional sign in the diagnosis. The physician's general rule is that acute illnesses are associated with patterns of Excess, and chronic illnesses with patterns of Deficiency. Older people tend to have Deficiency patterns, whereas younger people are inclined toward Excesses.

Touching (qie-zhen 切 诊)

The last of the Four Examinations is conventionally considered the most important. Part of it involves touching different parts of the body and various acupuncture points. This is another way to get at information sometimes discovered by asking such questions as: Is the skin cold, hot, moist, or dry? Is pain diminished or aggravated by pressure? But the heart of the Touching Examination is the feeling of the pulse, a procedure far more complex than what we know in the modern West.

Taking the pulse is such an important feature of China's medicine that Chinese patients often speak of going to the doctor as "going to have my pulse felt." Indeed, pulse taking approaches the subtlety and complexity that bespeaks an art. It requires thorough training, great experience, and the gift of sensitivity. When the physician takes a pulse, he or she is alert to a tremendous array of sensations that must be expertly understood and arranged as a unity— the "feel" of an individual pulse.

Although a pulse can be felt at various points on the body, Chinese medicine emphasizes taking it at the radial artery near the wrist.[17] Ideally, both patient and physician are relaxed. The *Nei Jing* suggests that early morning, when the body is calmest, is the best time to feel a pulse. The physician places his or her middle finger parallel to the lower knob on the posterior side of the radius (radial eminence). The index finger will then naturally fall next to the wrist, and the ring finger will fall next to the index finger. (See Figure 18.) The pulse can thus be felt in three positions on each wrist: The index finger touches the

FIGURE 18

Pulse Taking, Chinese Style

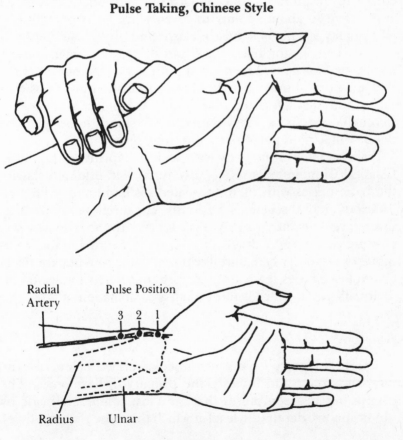

body at the first position, the middle finger touches at the second position, and the ring finger at the third position.

Chinese pulse theory gives meaning to the pulse as it is felt in each position on the wrist, but we will assume for now that the three fingers all feel the same thing and that the pulse is the same on each wrist. The pulse is palpated at three levels of pressure: superficial, middle, and deep. At the first or superficial level, the skin is lightly touched; at the second or middle level, a moderate amount of pressure is applied; at the third or deep level, the physician presses quite hard.

A normal or harmoniously balanced pulse is felt mainly at the middle level. Normal speed is between four and five beats per complete respiration (one inhalation and one exhalation), amounting to about seventy to seventy-five beats per minute. The quality of a normal pulse is elastic and "lively," neither hard and unyielding nor flaccid and indistinct. A normal pulse is said to be "spirited." The normal pulse may vary, however: An athlete's normal pulse may be slow; a woman's pulse is usually softer and slightly faster than a man's; children's pulses are faster than adults'; a heavy person's pulse tends to be slow and deep, while a thin person's is more superficial.

Disharmonies in the body leave a clear imprint on the pulse. Classical Chinese texts reflect a centuries-old effort to classify the basic pulses with their associated disharmonies. The codifications and discussions variously cite twenty-four, twenty-seven, twenty-eight, or thirty pulse types.[18] In the following discussion, twenty-eight classical pulses are presented in the traditional order, described, and illustrated.[19] These types are really general categories that rarely correspond exactly to a given individual's pulse, which is most often a combination of types.

Types of Pulse

The first eighteen types of pulse, described below, are the most important and indicate the primary disharmonies. The distinctions between pulses that are most commonly made by physicians are depth (the level at which the pulse is perceptible), speed, width, strength, overall shape and quality, rhythm, and length.

Depth

A *floating* pulse (*fu mai*) is "higher" than normal; that is, although distinct at a light or superficial level of pressure, it is less perceptible when palpated at the middle and deep levels. This pulse signifies an External Pernicious Influence, suggesting that the disharmony is in the superficial parts of the body where Protective Qi is combating the External Influence. A floating pulse is classified as Yang because its exteriorness corresponds to a primary Yang characteristic. A floating pulse frequently occurs without any other signs suggesting External Influences. In this case, if it is also without strength, the floating pulse signifies Deficient Yin. This is because the pulse is active or "dancing," a sign of relative Excess Yang and therefore of Deficient Yin. If the pulse is floating but has strength, and again no External Influences are present, it may be a sign of Interior Wind.

A *sinking* or *deep* pulse (*chen mai*) is distinct only at the third level, when heavy pressure is applied. It indicates that the disharmony is Internal, or that there is obstruction. It is accordingly classified as Yin.

Speed

A *slow* pulse (*chi mai*) is one that has fewer than four beats per

FIGURE 19

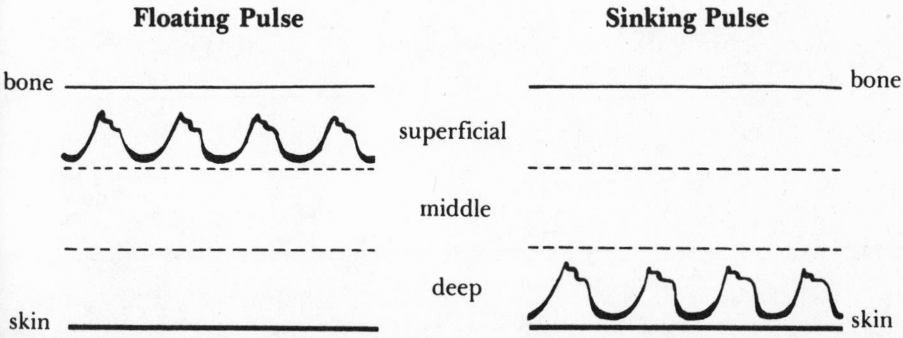

Floating Pulse   **Sinking Pulse**

respiration. It is a sign of Cold retarding movement or of insufficient Qi to cause movement. It is described as Yin.

A *rapid* pulse (*shu mai*) is one that has more than five beats per respiration. It indicates that Heat is accelerating the movement of Blood. It is accordingly a Yang pulse.

FIGURE 20

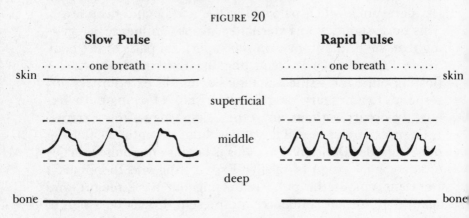

Width

A *thin* pulse (*xi mai*) feels like a fine thread but is very distinct and clear. It is a sign that the Blood is Deficient and unable to fill the pulse properly. Often the Qi is also Deficient. This pulse is described as Yin.

A *big* pulse (*da mai*) is broad in diameter and very distinct, and suggests Excess. It is commonly felt when Heat is present in the Stomach or Intestines, or both. It is a Yang pulse.

FIGURE 21

Thin Pulse	Big Pulse
skin	skin
superficial	
middle	
deep	
bone	bone

Strength

An *empty* pulse (*xu mai*) is big but without strength. It feels weak and soft like a balloon partially filled with water. It is usually felt at the superficial level and is often slower than normal. It signifies Deficient Qi and Blood, and is considered a Yin phenomena.

A *full* pulse (*shi mai*) is big and also strong, pounding hard against the fingers at all three depths. It is a sign of Excess and is classified as Yang.

FIGURE 22

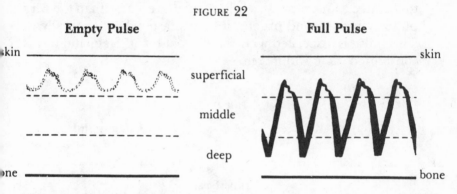

Empty Pulse		Full Pulse
skin	superficial	skin
	middle	
	deep	
bone		bone

Shape

A *slippery* pulse (*hua mai*) is extremely fluid. It feels smooth, like a ball bearing covered with viscous fluid. Classical texts compare it to "feeling pearls in a porcelain basin." A contemporary Chinese physician says it "slithers like a snake." It is a sign of Excess, usually of Dampness or Mucus. This pulse often occurs in women during pregnancy, when extra Blood is needed to nourish the fetus. It is considered "Yang within Yin." (This type of classification will be discussed in Chapter 7.)

A *choppy* pulse (*se mai*) is the opposite of a slippery pulse. It is uneven and rough, and sometimes irregular in strength and fullness. Chinese texts liken it to "a knife scraping bamboo or a sick silkworm eating a mulberry leaf." When this pulse is also described as being thin, it is a sign of Deficient Blood or Deficient Jing. It can also be a sign of Congealed Blood. Sometimes a choppy pulse is irregular in rhythm. In this case it is called "the three and five not adjusted"—meaning that there are sometimes three beats per breath and sometimes five beats per breath. This is usually a Yin pulse.

A *wiry* pulse (*xuan mai*) has a taut feeling, like a guitar or violin string. It is strong, rebounds against pressure at all levels, and hits the fingers evenly. But it has no fluidity or wave-like qualities. It signifies stagnation in the body, usually related to a disharmony that impairs the flowing and spreading functions of the Liver and Gall Bladder. It is a Yang pulse.

A *tight* pulse (*jin mai*) is strong and seems to bounce from side to side like a taut rope. It is fuller and more elastic than the wiry pulse. Vibrating and urgent, it seems faster than it actually is. This pulse is associated with Excess, Cold, and Stagnation. It is considered Yang within Yin.

FIGURE 23

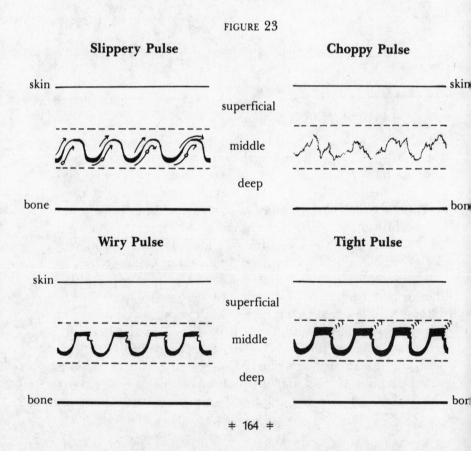

Length

A *short* pulse (*duan mai*) does not fill the spaces under the three fingers and is usually felt in only one position. It is often a sign of Deficient Qi and is classified as Yin.

A *long* pulse (*chang mai*) is the opposite of a short pulse. It is perceptible beyond the first and third positions; that is, it continues to be felt closer to the hand or up toward the elbow. If it is of normal speed and strength, it is not considered a sign of disharmony. But if it is also tight and wiry, it points to Excess and is considered a Yang pulse.

FIGURE 24

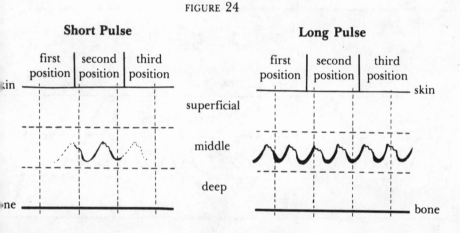

Rhythm

A *knotted* pulse (*jie mai*) is a slow, irregular pulse that skips beats irregularly. It is a sign of Cold obstructing the Qi and Blood, though it may also indicate Deficient Qi, Blood, or Jing. This pulse is often a sign of the Heart not ruling the Blood properly, and the more interruptions in rhythm, the more severe is the condition. A knotted pulse is classified as Yin.

A *hurried* pulse (*cu mai*) is a rapid pulse that skips beats irregularly. It is usually a sign of Heat agitating the Qi and Blood, and is considered a Yang Pulse.

An *intermittent* pulse (*dai mai*) usually skips more beats than the previous two pulses, but does so in a regular pattern. It is

FIGURE 25

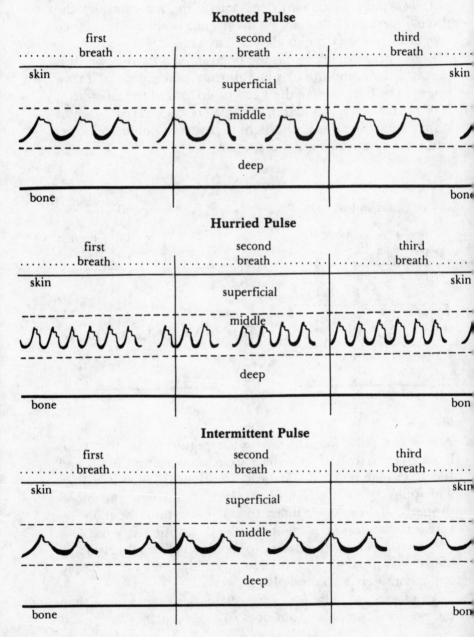

Knotted Pulse

Hurried Pulse

Intermittent Pulse

often associated with the Heart, signifying a serious disharmony, or it can signal an exhausted state of all the Organs. It
is a Yin pulse.

The knotted, hurried, and intermittent pulses are sometimes
congenital, in which case they are not necessarily signs of disharmony.

Moderate Pulse

A *moderate* pulse (*huan mai*) is the healthy, perfectly balanced
pulse—normal in depth, speed, strength, and width. It is quite
rare, and pulse discussions list it as secondary. For a Chinese
physician to issue a clean bill of health, a patient does not have
to have this pulse. In fact, healthy people seldom do have it.
Everyone's "normality" or "balance" has a certain constitutional
and age-linked disposition toward Yin or Yang disharmonies,
and each person's "normal" pulse will reveal this propensity. For
perceiving disharmonies, the significance of a moderate pulse
lies in the way it combines with other signs. If signs of Dampness are present, for instance, this pulse, which is sometimes
considered slightly slippery, may reinforce a diagnosis of
Dampness.

FIGURE 26

Moderate Pulse

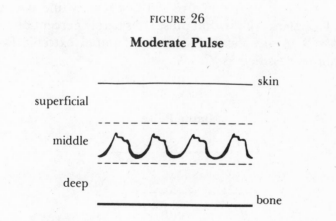

Other Pulses

The other ten classical pulse types are combinations and refinements of the previous eighteen and are generally consid-

ered less important. They are, however, readily discernible by the experienced physician and are useful in determining precise shades of significance in a diagnosis.

A *flooding* pulse (*hong mai*, Figure 27) surges with the strength of a big pulse to hit the fingers at all three depths, but it leaves the fingers with less strength, like a receding wave. It signifies that Heat has injured the Fluids and Yin of the body. It is considered Yin within Yang.

FIGURE 27

Flooding Pulse

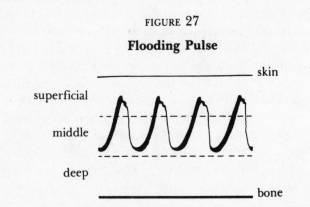

A *minute* pulse (*wei mai*, Figure 28) is extremely fine and soft, but lacks the clarity of the thin pulse. It is barely perceptible and seems about to disappear. This pulse signifies extreme Deficiency and is classified as Yin.

FIGURE 28

Minute Pulse

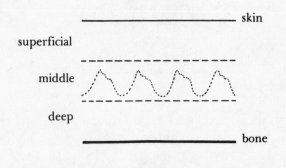

A *frail* pulse (*ruo mai*, Figure 29) is soft, weak, and somewhat thin. It is usually felt at the deep level. It is like an inverted empty pulse, but signifies a more extreme Deficient Qi condition because the Qi cannot even raise the pulse. A frail pulse is a Yin pulse.

FIGURE 29

Frail Pulse

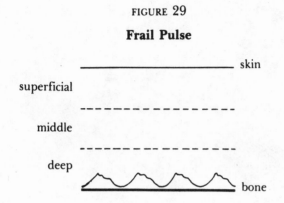

A *soggy* pulse (*ru mai*, Figure 30) is a combination of the thin, empty, and floating pulses. It is extremely soft, is less clear than a thin pulse, and is perceptible only in the superficial position. The slightest pressure makes it disappear. A soggy pulse feels like a bubble floating on water. It is a sign of Deficient Blood or Jing and sometimes of Dampness. It is a Yin pulse.

FIGURE 30

Soggy Pulse

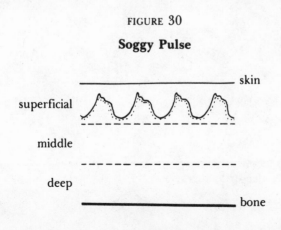

A *leather* pulse (*ge mai*, Figure 31) is a combination of the wiry and floating pulses, with aspects of the empty pulse. It feels like the tight skin on the top of a drum. It is a sign of Deficient Blood or Jing, and is classified as a Yin pulse.

FIGURE 31

Leather Pulse

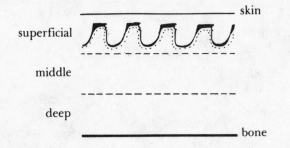

A *hidden* pulse (*fu mai*, Figure 32) is an extreme form of the sinking pulse. Intense pressure must be applied to feel it. If a hidden pulse is strong, it is usually a sign of Cold obstructing the Meridians. If it is weak, it signifies Deficient Yang that cannot raise the pulse. Hidden pulses are described as Yin.

FIGURE 32

Hidden Pulse

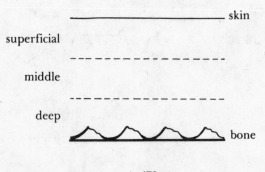

A *confined* pulse (*lao mai*, Figure 33), also known as a *prison* pulse, is the opposite of the leather pulse and is a form of the hidden pulse. It is very deep and wiry, and usually long and strong. It is a sign of obstruction due to Cold, and is considered Yang within Yin.

FIGURE 33

Confined Pulse

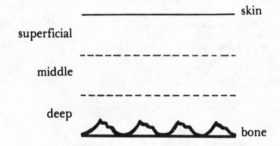

A *spinning bean* or *moving* pulse (*dong mai*, Figure 34) is a combination of the short, tight, slippery, and rapid pulses. It is felt in only one position and is said to be "incomplete, without a head and tail, like a bean." It signifies an extreme condition and is rarely seen. It usually occurs in cases of heart palpitations, intense fright, fever, or pain. It is a Yang pulse.

FIGURE 34

Spinning Bean Pulse

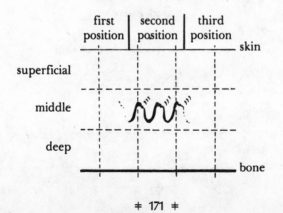

A *hollow* pulse (*kong mai*, Figure 35) feels like the stem of a green onion—solid on the outside but completely empty within. It is often a floating pulse as well. A hollow pulse implies Deficient Blood and is often seen after great loss of Blood. It is considered Yin.

FIGURE 35

Hollow Pulse

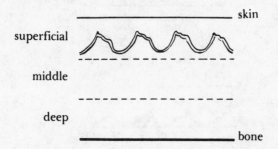

A *scattered* pulse (*san mai*, Figure 36) is similar to an empty pulse because it is floating, big, and weak. It is larger and much less distinct than the empty pulse, however, and tends to be felt primarily as it recedes. It is a sign of serious disharmony—Kidney Yang exhausted and "floating away." A scattered pulse is classified as Yin.

FIGURE 36

Scattered Pulse

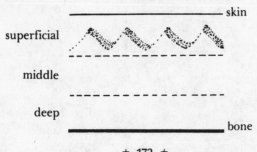

For purposes of this general description of the pulses, we have assumed that all three fingers are feeling the same pulse. In practice, however, each finger feels something slightly different. The two wrists will also give different readings. The three pulse positions on the two wrists are thought to correspond to certain Organs, indicating disharmonies in those Organs. Although there has been disagreement in China about the exact correspondences, Table 3 illustrates the system most commonly used in China today. (See Appendix D for a historical overview of opinions on the pulse position correspondences.) The correspondences are generally said to be the same at all three pressure levels, although in a more complex view, the superficial level correlates with the Yang Organs, while the deep level correlates with their coupled Yin Organs. (See Table 1 in Chapter 3.)

TABLE 3

Pulse Position Correspondences

	Left Wrist	Right Wrist
First position	Heart	Lungs
Second position	Liver	Spleen
Third position	Kidney Yin	Kidney Yang (Life Gate Fire)

The twenty-eight basic pulses can be felt at three levels, in three positions, and on two wrists. Already the feeling of a pulse is quite complicated. But when we realize that the twenty-eight pulses are more often found in combination than in their pure form, and that the characteristics of even one pulse type may vary from position to position or from wrist to wrist, it is clear that the system is extremely complex, capable of infinite refinement. Pulse diagnosis is a very sophisticated art. It demands subtlety and wisdom on the part of the physician to discern the relative importance of each variable and to make of them all an intelligent and precise diagnosis—to weave a useful pattern.

This chapter has described some of the more common signs and symptoms that a physician uses to perceive a pattern. It must be repeated that we have described only the pieces of the patterns—and that for Chinese thought and medicine pieces have no meaning outside of the whole. Any of the signs mentioned here can have a different signification, depending on the rest of the configuration. For example, the sign of thirst or a dry tongue points to Heat or Deficient Yin. This sign has this signification because it usually appears in a configuration with other Heat signs. But if the person with a dry mouth feels cold, is pale, tired, weak, emotionally flat and low-keyed, has a pale tongue and a slow, weak pulse, the dryness changes its meaning: It becomes a sign of extreme Deficiency with an inability to raise Water. The context defines the piece. Seeing the part simultaneously with the whole is one aspect of the artistry of Chinese medicine. There are no straight lines—no "this" means "that"— just cloudlike patterns that continuously change their shape.

Notes

1. "Chinese medicine . . . has been fostered and brought to maturity by what for want of a better term we may call 'Taoist consciousness.'" Manfred Porkert, "Chinese Medicine: A Traditional Healing Science," in *Ways of Health*, ed. by David S. Sobel (New York: Harcourt Brace Jovanovich, 1979), p. 150.

2. Aristotle, "Metaphysics," in *The Basic Works of Aristotle*, ed. by Richard McKeon, book 11, chap. 5, p. 856.

3. Chap. 23 of the *Tao-te Ching*, in Chan, *Chinese Philosophy*, p. 151.

4. Chuang Tzu in Chan, *Chinese Philosophy*, p. 183.

5. Jones, *Hippocrates and Heracleitus with an English Translation*, vol. 4, p. 489.

6. Ibid., p. 493.

7. Ibid., p. 485.

8. Ibid., p. 483.

9. See, for example, Needham, *Science and Civilization*, vol. 2, pp. 201, 291, 303, 466, 478; Chan, *Chinese Philosophy*, pp. 173, 183; Fung Yu-lan, *A History of Chinese Philosophy*, vol. 1, p. 185, and vol. 2, p. 212.

10. Chap. 1 of the *Tao-te Ching*, in Chan, *Chinese Philosophy*, p. 139.

11. The earliest reference to a method of Four Examinations is in the biography of the legendary physician Bian Que that appears in the Historical Records (*Shi Ji*) written in the early Han dynasty. This biography, part fact and part fiction, takes place during the Warring States period of the fifth century B.C.E. and contains valuable information about Chinese medicine that may even predate the *Nei Jing*. The earliest reference to a clear procedure of Four Examinations is in "Difficulty 61" of the *Nan Jing* [3].

12. One of the most complete compilations of signs and symptoms is the volume, more than a thousand pages long, called the Dictionary of Sources of Disease [35] by Wu Ke-qian. See Bibliography for other such compilations.

13. *Su Wen* [1], sec. 2, chap. 7, p. 53.

14. *Ling Shu* [2], sec. 1, chap. 4, p. 39.

15. Scattered references to various types of tongues and their significance exist in all early Chinese medical writings. The *Nei Jing* mentions many types of tongues but presents them in no orderly fashion. Zhang Zhong-jing in his Discussion on Cold-induced Disorders [27] and Essential Prescriptions of the Golden Chest [29] (which were originally one book written in 219 C.E.) mentions many additional types of tongue. In some cases he bases entire treatments on tongue changes. (See Appendix A for a discussion of Zhang Zhong-jing.) Subsequent medical authorities such as Chao Yuan-fang (c. 600 C.E.) and the great physician Sun Si-miao (590–682 C.E.) discussed tongue examinations more completely. The first systematic presentation of tongues was Ao's Golden Reflections of Cold-induced Disorders (*Ao-shi Shang-han Jin-jing Lu*), which appeared in 1341 C.E. and recorded thirty-six types of tongues with illustrations. All the subsequent literature on tongues is an elaboration of Ao's work. One of the more important of these texts is Zhang Deng's Mirror of the Tongue for Cold-induced Disorders (*Shang-han She-jian*), a volume from 1668 C.E. that has 120 illustrations of different tongues. For a discussion of the development of Chinese tongue examination and a fuller presentation of the examination itself, see Beijing Institute, Traditional Chinese Tongue Examination [70]. Also see a similar work with the same title and also by the Beijing Institute [69].

16. It is possible to ask an almost endless number of questions concerning any aspect of a person's health and illness. Any detail can be dissected into further Yin and Yang aspects. In the Ming dynasty a minimum of "ten questions" was considered necessary for pattern discernment. The first list of ten questions seems to have been drawn up by the great codifer Zhang Jie-bing in his Complete Book (*Jing-yue Quan-shu*, 1624 C.E.). His list included (1) cold and hot, (2) perspiration, (3) head and body, (4) urination and stool, (5) food and drink, (6) chest, (7) deafness, (8) thirst, (9) cause, pulse, and color, (10) smell, Spirit, and sight (numbers 9 and 10 include Touching, Looking, and Smelling). Later, Chen Shou-yuan in his Practical and Easy Medicine (*Yi-xue Shi-yi*), published in 1804 C.E., listed his own ten questions, including Zhang's questions 1–8 and then (9) old illnesses and (10) cause. The modern text used as a primary source for this book, Shanghai Institute, Foundations [53], lists the following ten questions: (1) cold and hot, (2) perspiration, (3) head and body, (4) stool and urination, (5) food, drink, and tastes, (6) chest and abdomen, (7) ears and eyes, (8) sleep, (9) old illnesses and history, (10) thought, emotions, life style, habits, and work. For further information, see the listing for "ten questions" in Traditional Chinese Medical Research Institute, *Concise Dictionary of Traditional Chinese Medicine* [34], p. 3.

17. It should also be mentioned that another method of pulse taking is featured in the *Nei Jing* alongside the system of palpation of the radial artery. An entire chapter (*Su Wen*, sec. 6, chap. 20) is devoted to this other method, which involves palpation of various arteries over the entire body, each of which is said to correspond to an internal Organ or to a particular part of the body. It was only in the *Nan Jing* period that the taking of the radial artery pulse clearly became the dominant method. See Appendix D, Note 1.

18. The *Nei Jing* mentions over twenty types of pulses, but the meaning of some pulse names is unclear. Despite this, it is the source of the later, more highly developed theories of pulse examination. The earliest text devoted exclusively to pulse examination is Wang Shu-he, Classic of the Pulse, which appeared about 280 C.E. and which describes twenty-four basic pulse types. This volume combined Wang Shu-he's own clinical experience with information on pulses found in the *Nei Jing*, the *Nan Jing*, and the writings of such clinicians as Zhang

Zhong-jing and Hua Tuo. Li Shi-zhen, in his Pulse Studies of the Lakeside Master (first published in 1564 C.E.), lists twenty-seven pulse types. In Essential Readings in Medicine (*Yi-zhong Bi-du*), published in 1637 C.E., Li Zhong-zi discusses twenty-eight "classic" pulses. Other texts mention more pulse types. Modern texts, however, usually refer to twenty-eight pulses.

All the descriptions of pulses in this book are based on those in Li's Pulse Studies [16]; Shanghai Institute, Foundations [53]; Shanghai City Traditional Chinese Medical Archives Research Committee, Selections from Pulse Examination [17]; and Wang Shu-he, Classic of the Pulse [22].

It should be noted that pulse examination plays a crucial role in all literate traditional medical systems. In the Egyptian *Edwin Smith Surgical Papyrus* (before 1600 B.C.E.) pulse examination was already an established practice. Galen of Pargamum (129–200 C.E.) completed eighteen treatises on pulse that include finer details of perception than those found in Wang Shu-he's Classic of the Pulse. Galen elaborated over one hundred pulse types by distinguishing size, strength, speed, duration of diastole and/or systole, frequency, and hardness and softness. His attention to rhythm and quality generated such famous pulse categories as the gazelling, ant-crawling, worming, and mouse-tailed pulses that continued to be used in the West until the eighteenth century.

19. Most of the diagrams of pulses are based on those in Liu Guan-jun, Pulse Examinations [61].

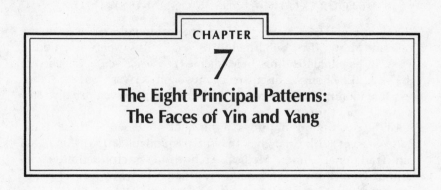

The Eight Principal Patterns:
The Faces of Yin and Yang

Chinese medicine recognizes many patterns of disharmony. All of them, however, can be preliminarily grouped into what are known as the Eight Principal Patterns.

Distinguishing the Eight Principal Patterns
(ba-gang bian-zheng 八 纲 辨 证)

To discern the Eight Principal Patterns within the signs and symptoms presented by the patient is one of the physician's major tasks.

The Eight Principal Patterns are composed of four pairs of polar opposites: Yin/Yang, Interior/Exterior, Deficiency/Excess, and Cold/Hot. These Eight Principal Patterns are actually a concrete subdivision of Yin and Yang into six subcategories. This division allows a clearer, more systematic approach to Yin-Yang theory and practice in Chinese medicine. Yin and Yang retain their primacy because of their broad, all-encompassing nature, while the other six patterns are finally subsumed in Yin-Yang patterns.

Up to this point, the reader has been presented with two kinds of information: an abstract description of the human body oriented around the theory of Yin and Yang, and a detailed listing of various signs of disharmony. In this chapter, these two categories of information begin to merge, for each individual is defined by a unique relationship between his or her own bodily signs and the overall movement of Yin and Yang.

The Eight Principal Patterns are the fundamental model for mediating between these two realms: They are the primary faces of Yin and Yang. They allow the physician to penetrate the abstract principles of Yin and Yang, principles that are so simple, yet so hard to grasp because they presume to be the general laws of totality, of everything around us and inside us, in our bodies, our minds, and our spirits. The Eight Principal Patterns serve, then, as a conceptual matrix that enables the physician to organize the relationship between particular clinical signs and Yin and Yang.

Conceptualizing and distinguishing the Eight Principal Patterns is the first step toward discerning the basic composition and shading of the clinical landscape. Before the various signs and symptoms gathered by the Four Examinations can be fully understood, they must be perceived within this schema.

The translation of the expression *ba-gang* as "Eight Principal Patterns" must be explained. *Ba* means eight. *Gang*, originally a term for the head rope of a fishing net, can also mean guiding principles, essentials, or parameters. In the medical tradition, *gang* connotes the primary matrix that guides all clinical discernment.

Bian-zheng, translated here as "distinguishing patterns," is one of the commonest terms in Chinese medical literature. *Bian* means to distinguish, recognize, or clarify, while *zheng* can mean evidence, proof, or emblem and, in a different form, symptom or ailment.

From a modern Western perspective, it is tempting to translate the Chinese words as "differentiating syndromes," but that rendering would distort the uniqueness and potential validity of the Chinese idea.[1] "Syndrome" is a purely descriptive term, suggesting an arbitrary grouping of signs and symptoms that is meaningless without an underlying cause. "Syndrome" implies that something is missing. For the West, "the knowledge of the cause [is] needed to elevate a clinical entity or a syndrome to the rank of a disease."[2]

But the Chinese physician never leaves the realm of signs and symptoms to seek an independent, *a priori* cause or mechanism susceptible to isolation and treatment. During the course of the Four Examinations, the physician simultaneously collects, interprets, and organizes signs—a complex, subtle perception that leads to an understanding of the physiological events taking place in the patient's body.

The work of the Chinese physician, therefore, is to distinguish patterns, not syndromes, by recognizing the state of bodily disharmony within the domain of signs and symptoms. The process of Chinese medicine is the process of weaving together the elements and recognizing a pattern in myriad signs. For the Chinese, patterns are sufficient and are the ultimate guiding conception for diagnosis and treatment.

The construct of the Eight Principal Patterns allows the physician to begin to recognize how the Yin and Yang tendencies of the body may be in disharmony.[3] It enables the physician to distinguish patterns of the broadest, most general type. Occasionally, these are all that are needed to proceed with treatment. In most cases, however, further refinement of the pattern is required in order to discover the unique features of a particular disorder and so determine an appropriate treatment.

Because Chinese medicine never leaves symptoms, never searches behind the phenomena for cause, but seeks only a configuration, much of the rest of this book is a series of lists or compilations of signs and symptoms. As with any skill, training the mind to see patterns requires frequent repetition. But the reward of patience and perseverance is the discovery of the artistic and poetic effort of Chinese medicine as it attempts to capture the essence of a human organism in disharmony.

Patterns of Interior (*li-zheng* 里 证) and Exterior (*biao-zheng* 表 证) Disharmony

The Interior/Exterior distinction is a relatively simple one, preliminary to the other principles. It gives the Yin/Yang clinical picture a basic spatial location by designating the site of a disharmony.

Interior patterns are generated primarily by Internal disharmonies; Exterior patterns by External Influences. These terms will remind the reader of the discussion of Pernicious Influences in Chapter 5, in which illnesses associated with Internal Yin/Yang disharmonies were differentiated from those characterized by the conflict of External Influences and Normal Qi. However, "Interior" and "Exterior" are used here to describe the location and characteristics of a disharmony, rather than its generation.

The weaving together of some of the following signs suggests a pattern of Exterior disharmony: acute illness with sudden onset; chills and/or aversion to cold, wind, heat, etc.; fever; head or body ache; thin tongue moss; a floating pulse.

Interior disharmonies are all those not considered Exterior. Interior disharmonies are often associated with chronic conditions and may be distinguished by such signs as pain or discomfort in the trunk, vomiting, changes in the stool or urine, high fever with no fear of cold, changes in the tongue material, and sinking pulse.

It may be seen that the signs of a pattern of Exterior disharmony are identical with those indicating an External Pernicious Influence, while the signs of an Interior disharmony are those of an Internal Yin/Yang disharmony.

Patterns of Deficiency (xu-zheng 虚 证) and Excess (shi-zheng 实 证)

If an illness is characterized by insufficient Qi, Blood, or other Substances, or by the underactivity of any of the Yin or Yang aspects of the Organs, the pattern is likely to be one of Deficiency. General signs of Deficiency are: frail and weak movement; ashen, pale, or sallow face; shallow breathing; pain that is relieved by pressure; spontaneous sweating; copious urination or incontinence; pale tongue material with little or no moss; and an empty, thin, or otherwise weak pulse. Deficiency patterns are usually chronic in nature, and may be thought of as a clinical landscape that is sparsely composed, bleak and desolate.

Broadly speaking, a pattern is likely to be one of Excess when a Pernicious Influence attacks the body, when some bodily function becomes overactive, or when an obstruction causes an inappropriate accumulation of substances such as Qi and Blood. The pattern of Excess is suggested when some of the following signs are woven together: ponderous and forceful movement; a particularly loud and full voice; heavy breathing; chest or abdominal pains that are aggravated by pressure; scanty urination; thick tongue moss; strong (wiry, slippery, or full) pulse. In general, patterns of Excess tend to be acute, and may be seen in the mind's eye as a cluttered clinical landscape.

Patterns of Cold (han-zheng 寒 证) and Heat (re-zheng 热 证)

The pattern of Cold disharmony generally manifests itself when the body's Yang Qi is insufficient, or when Cold Pernicious Influences are present. A combination of the following signs describes a Cold pattern: slow, deliberate movement; withdrawn manner; white face; fear of cold; cold limbs; sleeping in a curled up position; pain lessened by warmth; watery stool; clear urine; thin and clear white secretions and excretions; no thirst or a desire for hot liquids; pale and swollen tongue material with white or moist moss; and a slow pulse. Cold signs indicate that the basic shade of the bodily disharmony is "cloudy," like an overcast, frozen winter.

The pattern of Heat disharmony is associated with either a heat Pernicious Influence, hyperactivity of the body's Yang functions, or insufficient Yin or Fluids, leading to a relative preponderance of Yang. A Heat disharmony is revealed by the following signs: quick, agitated movement; delirium; a talkative, extroverted manner; red face and eyes; whole or part of the body hot to the touch (or it feels hot to the patient); high fever (which may or may not be related to the fever of expelling a Pernicious Influence); irritability; thirst and desire for cold liquids; constipation; dark urine; dark, thick, and putrid secretions and excretions; red tongue material with yellow moss; and rapid pulse. Heat signs suggest that the basic shading of the body disharmony is "bright," and its mood is "jumpy." Table 4 summarizes the signs associated with Deficiency and Excess and the signs associated with Cold and Heat disharmonies.

TABLE 4

Summary of Main Excess/Deficiency and Heat/Cold Signs

General Signs	Tongue	Pulse
Excess Patterns		
Ponderous, heavy movement; heavy, coarse respiration; pressure and touch increase discomfort	thick moss	strong (full, wiry, slippery, etc.)
Deficiency Patterns		
Frail, weak movement; tiredness; shortness of breath; pressure relieves discomfort; inactive, passive appearance; low voice; dizziness; little appetite	pale material; thin moss	weak (empty, frail, minute, etc.)
Heat Patterns		
Red face; high fever; dislike of heat; cold reduces discomfort; rapid movement; outgoing manner; thirst or desire for cold drinks; dark urine; constipation	red material; yellow moss	rapid
Cold Patterns		
Pale, white face; limbs cold; fear of cold; heat reduces discomfort; slow movement; withdrawn manner; no thirst, or a desire for hot drinks; clear urine; watery stool	pale material; white moss	slow

Patterns of Yin (yin-zheng 阴 证) and Yang (yang-zheng 阳 证) Disharmonies

Yin and Yang disharmonies are the most general, all-inclusive patterns in Chinese medicine. Indeed, all questions may ultimately be reduced to whether an individual pattern is Yin or Yang.

Yin patterns are combinations of signs associated with Interior, Deficiency, and Cold, while Yang patterns are woven from signs appropriate to Exterior, Excess, and Heat. These relationships are enumerated in Tables 5 and 6.

Of course, very few human illnesses can be characterized as pure Yin or pure Yang. If diagnosis were that simple, the task of the Chinese physician would be merely to catalogue symptoms, an exercise that would produce a clinical landscape resembling a Cubist painting. Most patients exhibit a complex mixture of Yin and Yang signs and symptoms. For example, an extroverted, agitated personality (Yang) can also be frail and weakly nervous (Yin). A slow, obsessive, calculating, and meticulous personality (Yin) can also be aggressive and belligerent (Yang). An individual with a severe contracting abdominal pain worsened by pressure (Excess and Yang) may, at the same time, get relief from a hot bath (Cold and Yin) and may have a slow pulse (Cold and Yin). Moreover, a single symptom might have varying significations because aspects of more than one pattern may be present. For instance, menstrual cramps relieved by Heat (Cold and Yin) may respond uncomfortably to touching (Excess and

TABLE 5

Yin and Yang Used to Summarize the Six Other Principles

Yin	=	Interior	+	Deficient	+	Cold
Yang	=	Exterior	+	Excess	+	Hot

TABLE 6

Signs of Yin and Yang Patterns

Examination	Yin Signs	Yang Signs
Looking	quiet; withdrawn; slow, frail manner; patient is tired and weak, likes to lie down curled up; no Spirit; excretions and secretions are watery and thin; tongue material is pale, puffy, and moist; tongue moss is thin and white	agitated, restless, active manner; rapid, forceful movement; red face; patient likes to stretch when lying down; tongue material is red or scarlet, and dry; tongue moss is yellow and thick
Listening and Smelling	voice is low and without strength; few words; respiration is shallow and weak; shortness of breath; acrid odor	voice is coarse, rough, and strong; patient is talkative; respiration is full and deep; putrid odor
Asking	feels cold; reduced appetite; no taste in mouth; desires warmth and touch; copious and clear urine; pressure relieves discomfort; scanty, pale menses	patient feels hot; dislikes heat or touch; constipation; scanty, dark urine; dry mouth; thirst
Touching	frail, minute, thin, empty, or otherwise weak pulse	full, rapid, slippery, wiry, floating, or otherwise strong pulse

Yang), or a pulse may be both rapid (Heat and Yang) and thin (Deficient and Yin).

Therefore, the Eight Principal Patterns in their pure form are usually inadequate descriptions of clinical reality. They provide preliminary guidance for further diagnostic refinement.

The first level of refinement is combining the Eight Principal Patterns to allow a closer approximation of clinical reality and a finer shading of the picture of disharmony. The way in which the Eight Principal Patterns are combined, reinforced, or modified illustrates how complex patterns are developed from simple ones. The method is basic to the process by which Yin and Yang combine to embrace reality.

Combinations of the Eight Principal Patterns

The Pattern of Excess/Heat (*shi-re-zheng* 实热证)

When the patterns of Excess and Heat combine, two Yang patterns are merged, creating a distinct pure Yang Pattern. A typical configuration of the signs of this new pattern might be as follows.

Signs	Movement	Pain Qualities	Tongue	Pulse
Excess (Yang)	forceful	intensified by pressure	thick moss	full and strong
+	+	+	+	+
Heat (Yang)	fast	relieved by cold	red with yellow moss	rapid

The Pattern of Deficiency/Heat (*xu-re-zheng* 虚热证)

If patterns of Deficiency and Heat are merged, the resulting combination has both Yin (Deficiency) and Yang (Heat) aspects, which modify each other. The patient will most likely manifest the following signs.

Signs	Movement	Pain Qualities	Tongue	Pulse
Deficiency (Yin)	weak and fragile	relieved by pressure	little or no coating	thin
+	*but*	*but*	*but*	*but*
Heat (Yang)	fast	relieved by cold	red	rapid

The normal Yin/Yang balance of the body, as well as the patterns of Excess/Heat (Excess Yang) and Deficiency/Heat (Deficient Yin), are schematically diagrammed in Figures 37, 38, and 39. (Because they are charts, these diagrams are based on a linearity foreign to the information they are used to present. Nonetheless, given this one qualification, they may be helpful.)

The pattern of Excess/Heat (also called Excess Yang, Figure

FIGURE 37

Normal Yin/Yang Balance

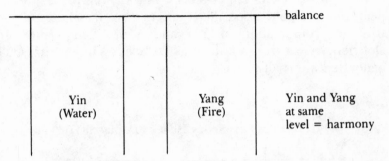

balance

Yin
(Water)

Yang
(Fire)

Yin and Yang
at same
level = harmony

38) actually has too much Fire (Yang). Its precipitating factor is often External. Since this is a pure Yang pattern, all the signs will be Yang signs. For example, the movement of the patient may be fast and forceful like that of a prizefighter, the pulse full and rapid, and the tongue would likely be red, with a thick yellow coating.

FIGURE 38

Pattern of Excess/Heat or Excess Yang

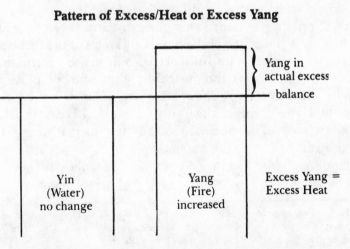

Yang in
actual excess

balance

Yin
(Water)
no change

Yang
(Fire)
increased

Excess Yang =
Excess Heat

The pattern of Deficiency/Heat (Figure 39) has some qualities of Yang (Fire), but the symptoms actually appear because of insufficient Yin (Water).* The fire signs are "the appearance of Heat," also called "empty Fire" (*xu-huo*), and constitute a combination of Yin and Yang. This pattern of Deficiency/Heat is also known as Deficient Yin and is usually generated internally.

FIGURE 39

Pattern of Deficiency/Heat or Deficient Yin

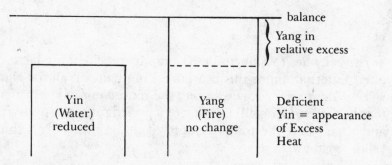

The patient may exhibit movement and activity less forceful than that associated with Excess/Heat, here taking the form of insomnia, restlessness, high, nervous laughter, or jumpy anxiety. There may be sensations of heat, but unlike the fevers of Excess, only the palms of the hands and soles of the feet become warm, or the fever is low, or it occurs only in the afternoon. The tongue is red (Yang), the moss thin (Yin), and the pulse rapid (Yang) but thin (Yin). These signs are often described as "the Yin unable to embrace the Yang": That is, there is insufficient Water to control the normal Fire, and the normal Yang gets out of control.

Understanding this process of assessing a place between pure

---

*Fire or Heat is the aspect of life that is activity. It is Yang. Cold would normally be the opposing Yin aspect to Fire, but Cold implies the cessation of life. Therefore, Water is thought to be the Yin aspect that balances Fire in life.

Yin and pure Yang is the first glimpse of how clinical complexity is perceived.

The Pattern of Excess/Cold (*shi-han-zheng* 实 寒 证)

The patterns of Excess and Cold also combine Yin and Yang aspects. A patient with this pattern might manifest the following configuration of signs:

Signs	Movement	Pain Qualities	Tongue	Pulse
Excess (Yang)	forceful	unrelieved by pressure	thick moss	tight, wiry, full, or otherwise strong
+	*but*	*but*	*but*	*but*
Cold (Yin)	slow	responds to heat	pale	slow

This pattern is usually of External origin, although it may arise from Internal imbalances. The signs of Excess/Cold are modifications of the signs of its two primary aspects: The movement and emotions of the patient will be slow but forceful, perhaps robotlike; the patient may experience cramping pain and will not want to move; the painful area dislikes touch but will be relieved by a heating pad; the pulse will be slow and full; and urine will be clear but scanty. Because the pattern of Excess/Cold describes the presence of too much Cold, it is also called the pattern of Excess Yin (see Figure 40, page 190).

The Pattern of Deficiency/Cold (*xu-han-zheng* 虚 寒 证)

Like the Excess/Heat pattern, the Deficiency/Cold pattern is relatively simple because two sets of Yin signs reinforce one another to produce a pure Yin pattern. This might yield the following signs.

Signs	Movement	Pain Qualities	Tongue	Pulse
Deficiency (Yin)	frail/weak	relieved by pressure	little or no moss	empty, thin, or otherwise weak
+	+	+	+	+
Cold (Yin)	slow	responds to heat	pale	slow

FIGURE 40

Pattern of Cold/Excess or Excess Yin

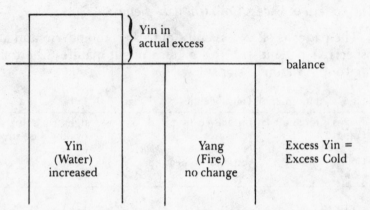

This pattern usually results from an Internal disharmony. Both Yin aspects in Cold patterns reinforce each other so that the patient's movements and emotions are slow and frail, like those of an old, weak, chronically ill person, and the pulse is both slow and empty. Other signs would also be distinctively Yin, such as clear and copious urine.

The pattern of Deficiency/Cold is generated by a relative deficiency of Fire, so that the cold is only the "appearance of Cold" rather than a genuine excess of Cold. Hence, this pattern is also known as one of Deficient Yang (see Figure 41).

The basic combinations of Deficiency and Excess patterns with Cold and Heat patterns are summarized in Table 7.[4]

When a pattern is pure Yin (Deficiency and Cold, Yin within Yin) or pure Yang (Excess and Heat, Yang within Yang), the various signs merge and reinforce each other. When a pattern has aspects of both Yin and Yang (Excess and Cold or Deficiency and Heat), the physician must distinguish whether the Yang aspect predominates—that is, whether the pattern is one of Yin within Yang, or whether the Yin predominates and the pattern is Yang within Yin.[5]

The nature of these patterns can be clarified if we consider

FIGURE 41

Pattern of Cold/Deficiency or Deficient Yang

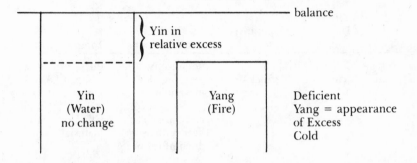

TABLE 7

Combination of Deficiency and Excess Patterns
with Cold and Heat Patterns

	Yin-Yang Designation	Generative Factor	Common Signs	Tongue	Pulse
Excess Heat	Excess Yang	Heat Pernicious Influence collects	high fever; fast, strong movements; delirium; pressure intensifies discomfort; patient desires cold; dark, scanty urine; constipation	thick, yellow moss; red material	rapid and full
Deficient Heat	Deficient Yin	Yin fluids depleted, Yin does not embrace Yang, insufficient Yin produces appearance of "empty Fire"	afternoon fever; weak, rapid, nervous movement; night sweats; warm palms and soles; insomnia; dizziness; dark urine	little moss; tongue is reddish	rapid and thin

TABLE 7 (cont.)

Combination of Deficiency and Excess Patterns with Cold and Heat Patterns

	Yin-Yang Desig-nation	Generative Factor	Common Signs	Tongue	Pulse
Excess Cold	Excess Yin	Cold Pernicious Influence collects	ponderous, forceful, slow movement; aversion to cold; limbs are cold; heat reduces discomfort, but pressure intensifies it; clear, scanty urine	thick, white, moist moss; pale material	slow and strong (tight, wiry, etc.)
Defi-cient Cold	Deficient Yang	insufficient Yang produces appearance of Cold	frail, weak, slow movement; aversion to cold; heat and pressure relieve discomfort; copious, clear urine; flat affect; no Spirit	thin moss; pale, puffy material	slow and weak (thin, minute, frail, etc.)

why Deficient Yin patterns and their signs (insomnia and night sweats) occur during the night, and Deficient Yang patterns and their signs (constant sleepiness and daytime sweats) happen during the day. Night is the time of inactivity and quiescence, but if a patient has a Deficient Yin pattern, he or she will have difficulty winding down because there is not enough Yin to control the Yang. This relatively excessive activity will not be noticeable during the day when it is normal to be active. At night, however, excess activity would be obviously inappropriate and would manifest itself as a disharmony state. A patient with a Deficient Yang pattern will tend to be underactive, and although this underactivity is appropriate to the normal quiescence of the night, it would be easily noticed during the day.

Patterns of True Heat / Illusionary Cold
(zhen-re jia-han-zheng 真 热 假 寒 证);
True Cold / Illusionary Heat
(zhen-han jia-re-zheng 真 寒 假 热 证)

Sometimes, and commonly in very extreme disharmonies, some signs will appear that are actually illusionary. For example, in the course of a severe Heat disharmony (that is, a disharmony in which the patient is affected by signs associated with Heat), the patient may experience delirium, a burning sensation in the chest and abdomen, and great thirst for cold liquids. The tongue moss will be yellow and dry, and the pulse very rapid and full. Suddenly the patient's limbs turn cold, while other signs remain the same. (In shock, which this is not, other signs would also change.) This sign of cold limbs is termed Illusionary Cold. It is also said to be Illusionary Yin because it is the result of extreme Yang energy forcing Yin to the extremities. The pattern it indicates is called True Heat / Illusionary Cold.

On the other hand, in a very severe Cold disharmony in which the limbs are cold, the pulse is minute, and the stool full of undigested food, the patient might become agitated instead of remaining quiet and withdrawn, as would be expected. The agitation gives the appearance of Heat, although the pattern is one of genuine Cold. This pattern is termed True Cold / Illusionary Heat. It arises because the Yang is so weak that it floats to the surface of the body "like the last flicker of a dying candle." Figures 42 and 43 (pages 194 and 195) illustrate the dynamics of these illusionary sign phenomena.

Patterns of Internal/External, Deficient/Excess, Cold/Hot

It is possible for opposite patterns to exist simultaneously. For example, a person may have a chronic Deficiency/Cold pattern, with such signs as cold limbs, watery stool, and pale, puffy tongue. Suddenly, a Heat/Wind Pernicious Influence invades the body and produces a fever, fear of drafts, headache, red,

FIGURE 42

Pattern of True Heat/Illusionary Cold

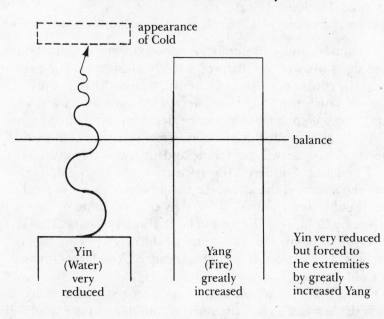

sore throat, and thirst and dry tongue, while the earlier signs remain. This is a case of an Interior/Deficiency/Cold disharmony existing simultaneously with an Exterior/Heat disharmony. Other possible signs in the total pattern can vary greatly, depending on which pattern is dominant at a given moment.

In addition, one pattern of disharmony can often change into another pattern. For instance, a weak Spleen may be unable to vaporize water. A pattern of Deficiency affecting the Spleen can then cause Dampness. But a buildup of Dampness, with symptoms such as edema and corresponding changes in pulse and tongue, can then create a pattern of Excess. Or, as is more common, a pattern of simultaneously occurring Deficiency and Excess with many possible variations and combinations of symptoms can result. Similarly, Heat can turn into Cold, or vice versa. An Excess/Heat illness of high fever can change into a pattern of Cold/Deficiency. This may be manifested in cold

FIGURE 43

Pattern of True Cold/Illusionary Heat

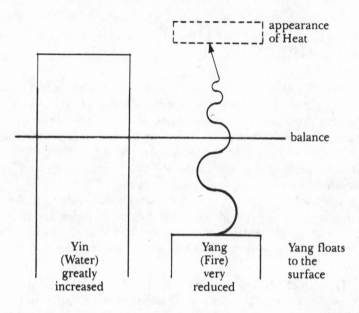

limbs, a very pallid face, deep, weak pulse, or even shock. Or a Deficiency/Heat pattern of irritability, dry mouth, and rapid, thin pulse may appear. A patient could also begin with an Exterior/Cold pattern of a Cold Pernicious Influence with signs like chills, fever, body aches, thin, white tongue moss, and floating and tight pulse. The chills may then disappear and the other signs change to high fever, thirst, irritability, yellow tongue moss, and rapid pulse—that is, a change from a Cold pattern to a Heat pattern. The Chinese clinician constantly sees such continuously changing multiple patterns.

The Eight Principal Patterns are the major categories into which all patterns of disharmony are grouped. For the Chinese, they are the guidelines, the nets that help to capture human reality. They define a disharmony in the most general way, but, as has been shown, they can also be endlessly combined and refined to describe a disharmony more precisely.[6]

Notes

1. This translation is now common. For example, *A Chinese English Dictionary* (printed by Beijing Foreign Languages Institute [Beijing: Commercial Press, 1978], p. 9) defines *ba-gang* as the "eight principal syndromes."

2. Owsei Temkin, "Health and Disease," in *The Double Face of Janus and Other Essays in the History of Medicine* (Baltimore: Johns Hopkins University Press, 1977), p. 436. Dr. Temkin also points out that the impetus to define a disease by a cause, in its modern form, was due to the influence of Robert Koch's monumental discovery of the tubercle bacillus in 1882 and the dramatic effect of bacteriology and germ theory on modern concepts of disease in general.

Of course, this modern notion of causality is very different from the Aristotelian metaphysical idea of *final* and *formal* causes. In the scientific system an explanation means a reduction of things into their elementary parts, and the concept of change in terms of *efficient* causality alone.

3. The effort to concretize and clarify Yin and Yang into Eight Principal Patterns is the history of Chinese medicine systemizing itself. Combinations of paired patterns are frequently mentioned and emphasized as the key aspects of disease and treatment in all early texts. The *Nei Jing*, for example, has many references such as: "Yang is Heavenly Qi and rules the Exterior, Yin is Earthly Qi and rules the Interior. Therefore, the Yang way is Excess and the Yin way is Deficiency" (*Su Wen*, sec. 8, chap. 29, p. 179); "The occurrence of the hundred illnesses is in their Excess or Deficiency" (*Su Wen*, sec. 17, chap. 62, p. 334); or "Yin rules Cold, Yang rules Heat" (*Ling Shu*, sec. 11, chap. 74, p. 505). Many other concepts, all of them aspects of Yin and Yang, are also mentioned—Blood, Qi, Chronic, Acute, Falling, Rising, Damp, Dry, Thin, Thick, Soft, Hard, Lower, Upper, Mucus, Fire, Quiescent, Moving, etc. Throughout the history of Chinese medicine, attempts have been made to give the myriad movements of Yin and Yang a less abstract and more systematic form. For example, Kou Zhong-shi, in his Elaborate Pharmacopoeia (*Ben-cao Yan-yi*) of 1116 C.E., codifies the Eight Essentials, which he calls Excess, Deficiency, Cold, Heat, Pernicious Influence, Normal Qi, Interior, and Exterior. For him these are the primary aspects of Yin and Yang that need adjustment when there is disharmony. In 1565 c.e., Lou Ying, in his Outline of Medicine (*Yi-xue Gang-mu*), stated that in order to reharmonize the Yin and Yang of the body, the physician must first determine whether the disharmony is of the Qi or the Blood, Exterior or Interior, Upper or Lower regions of the body, and then in which Yin or Yang Organ. Then one must ascertain whether the imbalance is Deficiency, Excess, Cold, or Heat. The great codifier of the Ming dynasty, Zhang Jie-bing, in his Complete Book, 1624 c.e., states that Yin and Yang are the general principles and that Exterior/Interior, Excess/Deficiency, Heat/Cold are the main aspects. For the Chinese, the actual form of the organization of Yin/Yang is less important than the underlying ability to see Yin/Yang as having many possible aspects and movements. For a full discussion of the historic development of the systematization of Yin/Yang theory, see Jia De-dao, Concise History [95], pp. 231–234.

4. The basic matrix of this table is delineated in the *Nei Jing*: "Deficient Yang then outer Cold, Deficient Yin then inner Heat [identified with empty Fire], Excess Yang then outer Heat, and Excess Yin then inner Cold" (*Su Wen*, sec. 17, chap. 62, p. 341). The symptomology of the charts, and indeed of this entire chapter and the next one, is ultimately based on the *Nei Jing* as systematized by the tradition. The *Nei Jing* is not always consistent in its presentation, but occasionally such sentences appear: "Abundant pulse, hot skin, abdominal distention, lack of urine and stool, and stuffiness with pressure are called the Five Excesses. A thin pulse, cold skin, lack of Qi, diarrhea or frequent urination, and inability to eat are called the Five Deficiencies" (*Su Wen*, sec. 6, chap. 19, pp. 128–129).

5. For example, in a Deficient Yin pattern (Deficiency/Heat), the matrix of signs may emphasize Heat more than Deficiency (e.g., if the pulse is very rapid but only somewhat thin, or the patient's movement is very quick but only slightly weak). In this case, the Yang predominates and the pattern is Yin within Yang. In another Deficient Yin pattern, the pulse may be somewhat rapid but very thin, and the patient's movement very frail but only slightly quick. In this case, the pattern would be one of Yang within Yin. An evaluation process would take place to determine whether an Excess/Cold (Excess Yin) pattern were Yin within Yang or Yang within Yin. Pure Yin is also called Yin within Yin, and pure Yang is called Yang within Yang. These patterns and their combinations are summarized in the following table.

Yin-Yang Designation	Pattern Combination	Yin-Yang Combination	Pulse as Sample Sign
Excess Yang	Heat/Excess	Yang within Yang (pure Yang)	rapid and full
Deficient Yang	Cold/Deficient	Yin within Yin (pure Yin)	slow and weak
Excess Yin	mostly Cold with some Excess	Yang within Yin	slow and slightly tight
	or		
	mostly Excess with some Cold	Yin within Yang	tight, strong, and slightly slow
Deficient Yin	mostly Heat with some Deficiency	Yin within Yang	rapid and slightly thin
	or		
	mostly Deficiency with some Heat	Yang within Yin	thin and slightly rapid

In clinical practice, patients fit into the spaces between the pure categories described. Most patients simultaneously have Deficient Cold (Deficient Yang) with some Excess Cold (Excess Yin), or some Excess Heat (Excess Yang) with Deficient Heat (Deficient Yin). The process of evaluation is the same—an appraisal of the predominating proportions. For an example, see Chapter 8, page 229.

6. The Song dynasty (960-1279 C.E.) codification of Yin-Yang theory into the categories that became the Eight Principal Patterns bears a marked resemblance to a similar systematization of Greek medicine developed in Islamic civilization. These two clarifications of the earlier medical tradition coincided in time, and the form and content of the two are strikingly similar.

The Greco-Arab synthesis, like the Chinese, was bipolar. Its Hot and Cold temperaments were the active primary poles, while Dry and Moist were the passive secondary poles. The four humors, tastes, predominant organs, times of year, etc., fit into a dynamic schema of correspondence with the four temperaments. Avicenna (Ibn Sina, 980–1037 C.E.), the "prince and chief of physicians," wrote descriptions of the signs for each of four temperaments, which are roughly equivalent to the Eight Principal Patterns.

For Avicenna, an abundance of Heat had some of the following signs: feeling uncomfortably hot; bitter taste in mouth; rapid gestures; excitability; liveliness; excessive thirst; sense of burning in epigastric region; quick pulse; intolerance of hot food; cold relieves symptoms; symptoms are worse in summer. This is notably like the Chinese Excess Heat pattern. Avicenna's Cold temperament has some of these signs: lack of desire for fluids; deficient digestive power; lack of excitability; slow gestures; flaccid joints; fever, if present, is of the phlegmatic type; cold things easily upset and hot things are beneficial; small, slow, sluggish pulse; symptoms are worse in winter. This easily compares to the Chinese Deficient Cold pattern. Avicenna's abundance of Moisture resembles Dampness or Excess Cold: puffiness; excessive mucoid salivation and nasal secretion; diarrhea; swollen eyelids; difficult digestion; lassitude; moist articles of diets are harmful; soft and wide pulse. And finally, Avicenna's abundance of Dryness resembles Deficient Yin: insomnia; wakefulness; rough, dry skin; hot water and oils are easily absorbed in the skin; symptoms are worse in autumn. See O. Cameron Gruner, *The Canon of Medicine of Avicenna*, part 1, thesis 3, par. 452–500, pp. 257–278, esp. p. 273.

Avicenna was concerned with causality in an Aristotelian sense and would often go so far as to find an entire array of material, efficient, formal, and final causes of an illness. Yet despite this radical difference from the Chinese style, Greco-Arab medicine (like all humoral medicine) correlates all the observable phenomena of a human being into an image derived from the natural environment. This image portrays a human microcosm resembling a universal macrocosm. The net result of this methodology will often produce a striking confluence of ideas.

Similarities to the Chinese model are found even in nonbipolar systems, as in the Hindu Ayurvedic system. For example, *pitha*, responsible for heat production, resembles China's Fire; *vata*, whose presence is indicated by such phenomena as respiration, circulation, and excretion, resembles China's Qi; and *kapha*, which protects the tissues from being consumed by the internal fires of *pitha*, very much resembles the Chinese Yin or Fluids. In pathology, this image configuration method carries over. For example, the Pitha-type headache is "associated with burning sensation in various parts of the head and bleeding from the nose. It is generally aggravated during mid-day and summer and autumn seasons." The Vata-type headache is "associated with a giddiness, sleeplessness, dryness and roughness of the eyes and various types of pain." Kapha-type headaches have "heaviness of the head, watering of the eyes, inflammation of the middle ear, running of the nose [and] inflammation of the mucus membrane of the nose." Vd. Bhagwan Dash, *Ayurvedic Treatment for Common Diseases*, pp. 94–95. For a general discussion of Ayurvedic medicine see C. Dwarkanath's *Introduction to Kayachikitsa*. When I worked in an Ayurvedic hospital in India years ago, I found that my Chinese medical background enabled me in a short time to predict the categories that Ayurvedic physicians would use to describe their patients.

The relation and relative importance of causality within Greco-Arab medicine and Ayurvedic medicine are compared by V. K. Venkataswami, "Humoral Theory and Modern Medicine," in *Theories and Philosophies of Medicine*, comp. by Dept. of Philosophy of Medicine and Science.

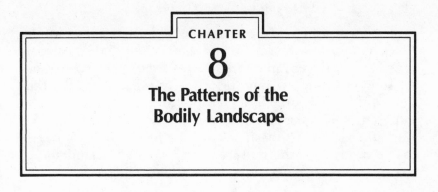

The Eight Principal Patterns, as we have seen, define the basic picture of bodily disharmony. Although the general qualities delineated by these patterns sometimes allow the physician to select the proper acupuncture points or herbs, or a combination of the two, that will rebalance the disharmony, more frequently the clinical picture must be refined. This refinement is achieved by using the Eight Principal Patterns as a basic matrix and also seeing or emphasizing signs that relate to the Fundamental Substances, the Pernicious Influences, or the Organs.

The first section of this chapter deals with patterns that describe disharmonies of Qi and Blood. The second section is concerned with Pernicious Influences, not as generative or localizing factors, but as categories of clinical pictures. The third section reexamines the medical paradigms of East and West, and the fourth describes the general patterns displayed by disharmonious Organs. These patterns are the basic diagnostic units of Chinese medicine.

Patterns of Qi and Deficient Yang,
Patterns of Blood and Deficient Yin

Qi and Blood are the Fundamental Substances most involved in the harmonious and disharmonious states of the body. Qi is involved with all Organs and has special relationships with the Liver, Lungs, and Spleen. Blood is ruled by the Heart, governed by the Spleen, and stored in the Liver. Other Fundamental Substances such as Jing (primarily associated with the Kidneys) and Shen, which is related to the Heart, are also important but are more specific and less general. As the *Nei Jing* summarizes: "Disharmonies of the Blood and Qi give rise to the changes of the hundred diseases."[1] A brief outline of common Qi and Blood disharmony patterns follows.

Patterns of Deficient Qi (qi-xu-zheng 气 虚 证) and Deficient Yang (yang-xu-zheng 阳 虚 证)

Deficient Qi is a Deficiency pattern that intimately involves the Qi. The following signs gleaned from the Four Examinations, when woven together, suggest Deficient Qi: general weakness or lethargy; pale, bright face; shallow respiration; low, soft voice; little desire to speak; dislike of movement; spontaneous sweating; pale tongue material; and empty, frail, or otherwise weak pulse. The most reliable of these signs are a bright, pale face and a weak pulse.

If the pattern of Deficient Qi is a generalized one in which the entire body's Normal Qi is affected, the physician need not proceed any further with the diagnosis and can start appropriate treatment. The pattern, however, may also be associated with a particular Organ Qi or a particular type of Qi (for example, Protective Qi). In such cases, additional signs specific to a particular type of Qi disharmony will be displayed.

It is important to distinguish the patterns of Deficient Qi from those of Deficient Yang. Deficient Yang includes Deficient Qi. Qi is a Yang phenomenon because it is dynamic. If Qi is deficient, therefore, some aspect of Yang will also be deficient. Furthermore, since Deficient Yang encompasses Deficient Qi, if Yang is deficient, it would follow that Qi, as well as other Yang functions, is deficient. Deficient Yang implies a diminution of Fire, which leads to a relative Excess of Cold or the "appearance of Cold." Therefore, Deficient Yang displays the signs of Deficient Qi as well as signs of Interior Cold, such as cold limbs, aversion to cold, puffy tongue, and slow pulse. Often, the shared signs are more severe. Deficient Yang is a broader category of Deficiency than Deficient Qi in two senses: It is more inclusive, and it affects the body at deeper levels.

Patterns of Stagnant Qi (qi-zhi-zheng 气滞证)

Stagnant Qi is a pattern of Excess that occurs when the smooth flow of Qi is stuck in a particular Organ, Meridian, or other part of the body. This pattern usually requires further elaboration to localize it. Stagnant Qi may result from emotional or dietary imbalances, External Pernicious Influences, or trauma. When Qi is Deficient—that is, when there is not enough Qi in a particular part of the body to keep the Qi itself moving—Stagnant Qi may also arise. This is a case of a pattern of Deficiency turning into one of Excess.

A primary symptom of Stagnant Qi is distention and/or soreness and pain. (This does not mean, however, that all soreness and distention result from Stagnant Qi.) The distention or soreness associated with Stagnant Qi characteristically changes in severity and location and can be a response to emotional changes because the Liver relates both to the flow of Qi and to the emotions. If palpable lumps are present, they usually are soft, and they come and go. A darkish or purplish tongue and a stagnant pulse, such as a wiry or tight pulse, are also salient signs of this pattern.

Patterns of Deficient Blood (xue-xu-zheng 血虚证)
and Deficient Yin (yin-xu-zheng 阴虚证)

A Deficient Blood pattern is basically a Deficiency pattern that emphasizes Blood. Such a pattern may be preceded by loss of Blood, insufficient Spleen Qi to produce Blood, or Congealed Blood that prevents new Blood from forming. The following signs, when woven together, point to the general pattern of Deficient Blood: dizziness; thin, emaciated body; spots in the visual field or otherwise impaired vision; numb limbs or weak tremors in the limbs; dry skin or hair; scanty menses; lusterless, pale face and lips; pale tongue material; and thin pulse. The most decisive of these signs are the lusterless, pale face and the thin pulse. Deficient Blood, like Deficient Qi, may affect a particular Organ, requiring further refinement of the pattern based on additional signs.

Deficient Blood and Deficient Yin have a relationship similar to that between Deficient Qi and Deficient Yang—they are on a continuum. Deficient Yin, however, is neither more extreme in quality nor deeper than Deficient Blood. It is distinguished from Deficient Blood only by the "appearance of Heat"—a relative excess of Yang brought about by a lack of Yin, or Water. Deficient Blood and Deficient Yin often display similar signs, especially emaciated appearance, dizziness, spots in the visual field, and thin pulse. Deficient Yin, though, will also display Heat signs: agitated manner, red cheeks, warm palms and soles, night sweats, red tongue material, and rapid, thin pulse.[2]

Pattern of Congealed Blood (xue-yu-zheng 血瘀证)

This is an Excess Blood pattern and is the most important example in that category. It may be preceded by trauma, hemorrhage, Stagnant Qi (which cannot move the Blood), or Cold Obstructing the Blood. The primary sign of Congealed Blood is pain. This pain is different from that of Stagnant Qi because it tends to remain fixed and is a stabbing pain. Other common signs of Congealed Blood are tumors, lumps, and hard, relatively immobile masses. Recurring, frequent hemorrhages (because the Blood flow is blocked, causing "spillage"), hemorrhages with clots of a dark, purple tinge (the color of congestion), a dark complexion, dark purple tongue material with red spots, and a choppy pulse all point to the pattern of Congealed Blood.

Pattern of Hot Blood (xue-re-zheng 血热证)

This pattern is a form of the Excess/Heat pattern. Its major symptom is bleeding. It is often generated by a Heat Pernicious

Influence that has invaded deep inside the body, agitating the Blood and making it "reckless"—that is, causing it to leave the normal pathways and to hemorrhage. Symptoms of Hot Blood include: blood in the sputum, vomitus, urine, or feces; bloody nose; excessive menses; and red skin eruptions. Other accompanying Heat signs may include thirst, irritability, scarlet tongue, rapid pulse, and, in extreme cases, delirium.

Patterns of Pernicious Influences

These terms have been discussed as generative factors of disharmonies (Chapter 5), as qualities of disharmony (Chapter 6), and in association with the Eight Principal Patterns (Chapter 7). Now we will consider Pernicious Influences as descriptions of a particular image in a bodily landscape.

In a sense, all patterns characterized by Pernicious Influences denote a presence in the body of something not normally there. This invasion may be internally or externally generated. Patterns of Pernicious Influence are therefore patterns of Excess Yin or Excess Yang. Conversely, all patterns of Excess Yin or Excess Yang are usually considered manifestations of External and/or Internal Pernicious Influences.

The many signs that characterized Pernicious Influences when they were considered as precipitating factors (Chapter 5) reappear as aspects of the patterns of Pernicious Influences. Clinically, these signs are interpreted as part of a Pernicious Influence pattern, especially if the appropriate tongue and pulse signs are also present.

In general, the conception of a Pernicious Influence as a pattern has more clinical utility than does the construct of a Pernicious Influence as a causative agent of disease. In other words, although environmental Cold, Heat, Wind, and Dampness may predispose or affect the body, they may also become the disharmony itself. Thus, the patterns of Pernicious Influences will display distinct and recognizable signs and symptoms. The physician may then decide that the diagnosis of these general patterns reveals enough to prescribe treatment, or that it is necessary to gather additional signs pointing to disharmony in particular Organs.

Patterns of Heat Pernicious Influence
(*re-xie-zheng* 热 邪 证)

These are patterns of Excess Yang. The signs of this pattern are identical with those of Excess/Heat disharmony (see Chapter 7). Most Excess/Heat disharmonies are External in origin and are therefore Exterior patterns, to which Exterior signs are consequently added (see Chapter 7). (The one major exception is Internal Excess Fire, which is usually a Liver disharmony.) The pattern of External Dryness (*wai-zao-xie-zheng*) is a form of the External Heat Pernicious Influence pattern and displays more signs of dehydration.

Internal Dryness is seldom mentioned and is not perceived as a pattern of Pernicious Influence. Usually thought to be identical with Deficient Yin, it almost always manifests itself in relation to a specific Organ.

Patterns of Wind Pernicious Influence
(*feng-xie-zheng* 风 邪 证)

These are also patterns of Excess Yang. Like all Wind patterns, Wind Pernicious Influences are generally characterized by their sudden onset. The signs may rapidly change location, and various signs may appear in succession. Wind usually arises together with other Pernicious Influences. Although Wind patterns may be marked by a floating pulse, the presence of other Influences and pulse signs often overshadows the floating aspect.

The pattern of Exterior Wind/Cold (*wai-feng-han-zheng*) is characterized by such signs as sudden onset of illness; headache; soreness due to obstructed Meridians; relatively severe chills; low fever; white, moist tongue moss; and a floating, tight pulse.

The pattern of External Wind/Heat (*wai-feng-re-zheng*) manifests many of the same signs as Exterior Wind/Cold, except that the fever tends to be higher and the chills less pronounced. In addition, Heat signs appear instead of Cold signs, especially a floating fast pulse, thirst, and a dry, reddish tongue with yellow moss.

The pattern of Wind Penetrating the Meridians (*feng-xie ru-jing-luo-zheng*) is recognizable by mobile soreness or numbness in the limbs and by skewed or twisted facial features. If Wind obstructs the flow of Qi in the Meridians, paralysis may occur. This pattern often has a floating pulse, and it may combine with Dampness or Cold to produce other tongue and pulse signs.

Patterns of Cold Pernicious Influence
(*han-xie-zheng* 寒 邪 证)

These are patterns of Excess Yin. They have signs identical with those of Excess/Cold, discussed in Chapter 7. With some exceptions, Excess/Cold is Externally generated.

The pattern of Cold Blockage (*han-bi*) is characterized by severe pain in the joints and flesh and by spasms and contractions, as well as by the other signs of a Cold pattern (such as a pale, moist tongue and a slow or tight pulse).

In the pattern of Cold Pain (*han-tong-zheng*), severe abdominal pain is so prominently linked to a Cold Pernicious Influence that it is not necessary to distinguish a particular Organ before prescribing definite treatment. Cold Pain is often accompanied by clear vomitus, diarrhea, constipation, a pale tongue with white moss, and a tight, deep, slow pulse.

Patterns of Damp Pernicious Influence
(*shi-xie-zheng* 湿 邪 证)

These are patterns of Excess Yin. With few exceptions, all patterns of Damp Pernicious Influence affect the Spleen; they are discussed later in this chapter.

Patterns of Mucus (*tan-zheng* 痰 证)

Mucus patterns are patterns of Excess Yin. They are also a special category of the Dampness pattern because Mucus is a development of Dampness. Although almost always related to the Spleen, Mucus can be intimately related to additional Organs as well. It is recognized as a part of various patterns if a greasy, thick tongue moss and slippery pulse are present, along with signs of the original pattern. The pattern of Turbid Mucus Disturbing the Head is discussed in relation to the Spleen later in this chapter.

The pattern of Wind Mucus (*feng-tan-zheng*) is a general one in which Wind signs and Mucus signs are present simultaneously. It usually develops in relation to particular Organs and is marked by sudden collapse, convulsions, and tremor (the results of Wind), as well as foaming at the mouth, a thick, greasy tongue moss, and a slippery pulse (the signs of Mucus).

The pattern of Mucus Lingering in the Meridians (*tan-liu-jing-luo-zheng*) displays such signs as numbness in the limbs or relatively soft, mobile swellings, lumps, or tumors (such as goiter, lymphadenopathy, and sabaceous cysts) accompanied by specific Mucus signs.[3]

East and West Reconsidered

At this point, the nature of the difference between the perceptions of Eastern and Western medicine needs to be reexamined. In Chapter 1 it was demonstrated in a very simple way that six patients suffering from ulcer could be perceived quite differently by Chinese and Western doctors. This illustrated the fact that a single Western disease entity may generate various diagnoses of medical disharmonies within the framework of Chinese medicine.

Now let us take a closer look at the actual study of the sixty-five gastric-ulcer patients from which the six patients were chosen as examples (see Chapter 1, note 6). All of these patients had theoretically identical diseases in the terms of Western medicine.

About half of the sixty-five Chinese diagnoses cited various Spleen disharmonies (Deficiency, Dampness, Cold, etc.), while the rest pointed to Stomach and Liver disharmonies. None of the patients was described as having a Lung or Kidney disharmony. Thus, the diagnoses of the Western medical entity did not yield a totally random sample of Chinese medical disharmonies. From the universe of possible Chinese diagnoses, the single Western diagnosis of gastric ulcer was paralleled by a few specific clusters of disharmony patterns.

If this experiment had been reversed and a number of patients, all diagnosed by a Chinese physician as manifesting the same pattern of disharmony, had been seen by a Western physician, several distinct Western disease entities would be diagnosed. However, a high incidence of certain specific clusters of diseases would emerge. Although there are no one-to-one correspondences between Chinese and Western diagnoses, a type of correlation can indeed be found.

This correlation may be demonstrated by using the pattern of Deficient Spleen Qi as an example. This pattern is associated with such signs as chronic fatigue, lack of appetite, poor digestion, watery stool, abdominal distention, pale tongue material with thin, white moss, and empty pulse.

If a large group of patients with this disharmony were looked at from a Western perspective, half of them would probably be diagnosed as having chronic gastrointestinal disorders such as gastroenteritis, ulcers, or nervous stomach. A significant number would be thought to have chronic hepatitis, hemorrhoids, amenorrhea, anemia, and various bleeding disorders. A much smaller percentage would be diagnosed as having depressive neurosis and degenerative neuromuscular disorders.[4] It would be unlikely that any of the patients exhibiting Deficient Spleen Qi would be discovered to have acute urinary infections, glaucoma, or pleurisy.[5]

Another example is the pattern of Liver Fire, the signs of which may include red face; red eyes; scanty, dark urine; constipation; severe headaches and/or ringing in the ears; a tendency toward emotional outbursts; nausea or vomiting; red tongue material with yellow moss; and wiry, full, and fast pulse. In Western terms, people with this pattern might be diagnosed as having hypertension, migraine, atherosclerosis, acute conjunctivitis, glaucoma and other eye disorders, or acute hepatitis, with a smaller percentage thought to have bleeding disorders and urogenital infections.[6] Liver Fire patterns would probably not be associated with such Western diseases as chronic gastrointestinal disorders, tuberculosis, pernicious anemia, or dysentery.

In different Chinese patterns, some of the same Western medical categories can exist. For instance, in both the Deficient Spleen Qi and the Liver Fire patterns, hepatitis and hematolytic disorders would be likely Western diagnoses. It can be seen that a large group of patients with a particular Chinese pattern would frequently generate a cluster of several Western medical disease entities, producing a statistical correspondence of large groups, rather than any one-to-one correspondences.

This kind of statistical grouping results from comparison because, although the two systems imply different understandings of health, disease, diagnosis, and treatment, they nonetheless deal with the same body. There is an overlap in which some of the bodily functions and locations, as perceived by East and West, are at times comparable, or at least mutually recognizable. And both systems rely on internally consistent frames of reference.

This statistical correlation has been noted in China, especially during the last thirty years, when many patients have been diagnosed by the two systems consecutively or simultaneously.[7] The implications and nature of the diagnosis provided by each system are always different—the Chinese diagnosis is refined by understanding how the disharmony embraces the other Organs and the entire human being, while the Western diagnosis is refined by isolating an exact cause or a precise pathological process.

On the simple level, the correlations between Chinese and Western medicine do not help in formulating correct treatment. You cannot merely look up a disease and its treatment in one system and then find an analog in the other. Nevertheless, amid the strange-sounding formulations of Chinese diagnosis, the correlations may help readers familiar with Western medicine to orient themselves. Further explorations of these correlations may open up an avenue for deeper scientific research into Chinese medicine.

The following discussion of disharmony patterns of the Organs will include statistical correlations with Western diseases which are indicated in clinical reports, studies, and medical texts produced in the People's Republic of China.*

Patterns of Organ Disharmony

Describing patterns of disharmony in terms of the Organs that are involved is the next step in refining the understanding of a disharmony. Patterns of disharmony involving particular Organs are primarily an elaboration of the Eight Principal Patterns, the patterns of Qi and Blood disharmonies, and the patterns of Pernicious Influences. These basic patterns are then refined and made specific by the addition of signs and symptoms alluded to in the earlier discussion of Organs.

---

*It is interesting to note that some Western diseases, such as epilepsy (*dian-xian*), dysentery (*li-ji*), malaria (*nue-ji*), measles (*ma-zhen*), and consumption (*fei-lao*), exist in the Chinese medical system as well as in the Western one. This correspondence reflects the fact that the two systems ultimately treat the same human body and that certain disease categories are recognized globally by symptoms alone and antedate the rise of modern medicine. Dysentery, for instance, is known by the same symptoms to both East and West. In the modern West, however, the diagnosis of dysentery would be followed by the search for a pathogen—amebic or bacterial—whereas in Chinese medicine, more signs would be collected to categorize the dysentery according to an appropriate pattern. Similarly, Chinese medicine recognizes a pattern similar to the Western entity of pulmonary tuberculosis. A Chinese physician would proceed to classify it as a pattern by synthesizing the accompanying signs and symptoms into a more precise configuration. A modern Western physician would search for the pathogen, identify the disease as tuberculosis, and treat it according to its bacterial origin. This equivalence is approximate. Because the differential criteria are not the same, it is possible for a diagnosis of dysentery or diabetes in Chinese medicine not to be that same entity in Western medicine. (To avoid confusion, all diseases or patterns common to both medical systems will be referred to by their Western nomenclature.)

The patterns of Organ disharmony are not, however, mechanically generated by logical principles, but represent the way in which tradition has modified theory throughout centuries of clinical practice. For example, although the Lungs can have Deficient Yang, such a pattern is not generally discussed in the medical literature. In practice, Deficient Yang of the Lungs is seen as Deficient Lung Qi in combination with Deficient Kidney Yang. The patterns of Organ disharmony presented here are the basic, most common patterns of disharmony in clinical Chinese medicine.

Heart Disharmonies

The primary function of the Heart is to rule the Blood and Shen. These substances are therefore commonly involved in patterns of Heart disharmonies.

Patterns of Deficient Heart Blood (*xin-xue-xu* 心 血 虛) and Deficient Heart Yin (*xin-yin-xu* 心 陰 虛)

Both these patterns are associated with an insufficient amount of Blood or Yin to nourish the Heart and Shen. The actual symptoms of these two patterns are deceptively similar. They commonly include heart palpitations, forgetfulness, insomnia, excessive dreaming, disturbed sleep, and a feeling of unease. These symptoms are thought of as the Blood or Yin unable to embrace the Qi or Yang.

Because the patterns of Deficient Heart Blood and Deficient Heart Yin have so many of the same signs and symptoms, pulse and tongue signs become crucial. This is typical of the pivotal role of these two signs. Deficient Heart Blood will have a pale tongue and thin pulse, with the likely addition of a pale, lusterless face, dizziness, and lethargy. Deficient Heart Yin will have a reddish tongue, rapid and thin pulse, with the possible appearance of night sweats, warm palms and soles, and agitated manner. A skilled physician, however, will be able to identify a pattern from a symptom common to both Heart disharmonies.

Consider the sign of disturbed sleep. A patient who has trouble falling asleep will tend to have Deficient Heart Blood if, once at rest, his Shen remains at rest (because there is no relative Excess to continue to disturb the Shen). However, a patient who often awakes in the night will tend toward Deficient Heart Yin because the relative Heat may continue to disturb the Shen.

Deficient Heart Blood is often associated with Deficient Spleen Qi because the Spleen produces the Blood, while Deficient Heart Yin is usually related to Deficient Kidney Yin since the Kidneys are the source of the Yin of the Organs.

When Western doctors examine patients exhibiting these patterns, they often find cardiovascular disorders characterized by tachycardia, arrhythmia or anemia, hypertension, hyperthyroidism, depressive neurosis, and extreme malnutrition.[8]

Patterns of Deficient Heart Qi (xin-qi-xu 心 气 虚) and Deficient Heart Yang (xin-yang-xu 心 阳 虚)

Deficient Heart Qi displays the general signs of Deficient Qi—weak pulses, pale tongue, and lethargy—as well as Heart-specific signs such as palpitations and muddled Shen. Because the Heart Qi is responsible for Blood movement, Deficient Heart Qi is associated with irregular pulse types such as knotted or intermittent. Deficient Heart Yang displays the same signs, though often with greater severity, and also shows signs of the "appearance of Cold" (a slow and much weaker pulse and swollen, moist tongue, etc.). Sometimes Yang can be so Deficient that it suddenly "collapses," producing profuse sweating, extreme cold in the limbs or the entire body, purple lips (cyanosis), minute or even imperceptible pulse—signs suggesting that Yin and Yang are separating and the patient is near death.

The patterns of Deficient Heart Qi and Deficient Heart Yang often appear with Deficient Lung Qi because there is a link to the "sea of Qi" in the chest. Deficient Kidney Yang may also be observed with these Heart patterns because the Kidneys are the body's source of Yang.

Western doctors who examine patients displaying these patterns often observe cardiac insufficiency, coronary arteriosclerosis, angina pectoris, nervous disorders, general bodily weakness, and depressive neurosis.[9]

Patterns of Congealed Heart Blood (xin-xue-yu 心血瘀)

Insufficient Heart Qi or Heart Yang to move the Blood in the chest often precedes and accompanies the pattern of Congealed Heart Blood.[10] This extremely serious condition is an instance in which a Yin condition produces a partial Yang condition. The resulting pattern may be Yin within Yang, indicated by a strong pulse, or Yang within Yin, indicated by a weak pulse. In either case, Congealed Heart Blood will manifest Yang signs of stabbing pain and purple face and tongue, along with such Yin signs as lassitude, palpitations, and shortness of breath. The pulse is likely to be in between Yin and Yang, for example, choppy or wiry.

Mucus may also contribute to the obstruction of Blood. The resulting Mucus Obstructing the Heart and Congealed Blood pattern would have accompanying Mucus signs, such as thick, greasy tongue moss, woven into the clinical picture.

Patients manifesting the pattern of Congealed Blood are often diagnosed in Western terms as suffering from angina pectoris, pericarditis, or coronary artery disease.[11] A Western doctor would, after this diagnosis, further examine the heart to investigate possibilities for surgery. A Chinese doctor, after diagnosing the pattern Congealed Heart Blood, would need to determine whether the pattern was one of relative Excess or Deficiency, what aspects of Heat or Cold were present, and what other Organs were involved.

Patterns of Cold Mucus Confusing the Heart Openings (han-tan-mi-xin-qiao 寒痰迷心竅) and Mucus Fire Agitating the Heart (tan-huo-rao-xin 痰火扰心)

These are patterns of Excess in which Cold or Hot Mucus are part of a configuration of disharmonies of the Shen. Both patterns are characterized by thick tongue moss, a slippery pulse, and abnormal behavior, sometimes accompanied by drooling. Since Cold Mucus is Yin, behavioral signs associated with this pattern might include an inward, restrained, foolish manner; muttering to oneself; staring at walls; and sudden blackouts. The pulse might be slow as well as slippery, and the tongue moss would be white. Since Hot Mucus is relatively Yang, we would expect signs tending toward hyperactivity: an agitated, aggressive manner, incessant talking, and perhaps violent lashing out behavior, accompanied by other Heat signs, such as rapid pulse and yellow moss.

Often Mucus disharmonies of the Heart may be seen to correspond to Western categories of mental illness. At other times these disharmonies correlate with such Western disease entities as encephalitis and gram negative sepsis, when they affect cerebral functions, or apoplexy, or epilepsy.[12]

CLINICAL SKETCH: A recent clinical report published in a Chinese journal of traditional medicine[13] detailed the course of thirty-one patients with premature ventricular contractions (PVCs) who were treated by Chinese traditional medicine. Western scientists evaluated the patients by electrocardiography and blood chemistry before and after treatment, and reported that traditional Chinese therapy led to complete recovery in 38.7 percent of the patients, brought improvement to 38.7 percent, and had no effect on the remaining 22.6 percent. No patient in this study suffered any side effects from the treatment.

In general, the Chinese physicians distinguished two broad types of disharmony: Excess (Congealed Blood) and Deficiency (Deficient Qi and/or Blood). Each patient was treated with herbal prescriptions to correspond with the exact variation of the pattern the patient exhibited. Here are the details of one particular case.

The patient, a male bookkeeper aged fifty-three, was first examined on January 5, 1978. His chief complaint was heart palpitations. His chest had felt distended and full for the past nine months, with the discomfort especially severe after exertion. He had a long history of coughing up sticky white phlegm, especially in the winter. His tongue material was dark purple and reddish with a white, greasy moss. His pulse was primarily knotted.

The Western evaluation by electrocardiogram showed a heart rate of eighty-eight beats a minute with five PVCs per minute. Blood chemistry data included readings of 286 mg/ml cholesterol and 196 mg/ml triglyterides. An X-ray examination revealed a normal heart with changes consistent with emphysema.

The traditional Chinese physician found several patterns existing simultaneously. The pattern of Congealed Heart Blood was predominant, revealed by the darkish tongue, chest pressure, knotted pulse, and heart palpitations. Secondary aspects of Mucus Obstructing the Heart were seen in the signs of phlegm and greasy tongue moss. In addition, the symptoms of coughing, phlegm, sensitivity to winter cold, and white, greasy moss pointed to Cold Damp/Mucus Obstructing the Lungs. In addition, the reddish tongue and rapid pulse were associated with Deficient Heart Yin.

The patient received a seven-day herbal prescription that contained eleven ingredients including *Pueraria, Trichosanthes*, and *Salvia miltiorrhiza*. The purpose of the herbs was mainly to move Blood and also to transform Mucus and slightly nourish the Heart Yin. After taking the herbs for seven days, the patient reported a reduction in palpitations and reduced feeling of heaviness in the chest. He also coughed less and the PVCs were reduced to three to four beats per minute.

The patient was then given a similar prescription for a period of thirty-five days. After this, all symptoms disappeared. Upon reexamination by Western scientists, the patient's electrocardiogram showed no evidence of premature ventricular contractions or of any other abnormality. Blood evaluation showed 255 mg/ml cholesterol and 95 mg/ml triglycerides. The patient was discharged with an additional herbal prescription to maintain his improvement.

It is interesting to note that several of the herbs used in this patient's prescription have been studied by pharmacologists and demonstrated to dilate the coronary arteries, thus increasing the supply of blood and oxygen to the heart.[14]

Lung Disharmonies

The Lungs rule the outside of the body, and of all the Yin Organs, they are the most sensitive to External Pernicious Influences. For this reason, the Lungs are called "the tender Organ." Because there is a close relationship between the Lungs and Qi, this Organ is particularly sensitive to disharmonies of Deficient Qi. Lung disharmonies also commonly involve Deficient Yin.

The Pattern of Cold Violating the Lungs
(han-xie-fan-fei 寒邪犯肺)

This is an External Cold Pernicious Influence pattern that especially affects the Lungs. It is likely to be woven together by such signs of External Cold as chills, a slight fever, head and body aches, and, since the pores are blocked by Cold, a lack of perspiration. Also expected would be a thin white tongue moss, and a floating, tight pulse. These signs will be accompanied by Lung disharmony symptoms such as stuffy or runny nose, asthma, or a cough with a thin, watery sputum. In the West, patients with this pattern would often be diagnosed as suffering from the common cold, acute or chronic bronchitis, bronchial asthma, or emphysema.[15]

The Pattern of Heat Clogging the Lungs
(re-xie-yong-fei 热邪壅肺)

This pattern manifests the usual signs of an External Heat Pernicious Influence such as fever, slight chills, perspiration, thirst, constipation, dark urine, red tongue with dry, yellow moss, and fast pulse. In addition, there will be Lung-specific signs such as a red, sore, swollen throat, asthmatic breathing, or a full cough with a yellow, sticky expectorant. There may be a runny nose with thick yellow phlegm or, since Heat can injure fluids and cause Blood to move recklessly, a dry or bleeding nose.

A Western doctor, looking at patients with this pattern, might diagnose the common cold, acute or chronic bronchitis, pneumonia, tonsillitis, or pulmonary abcess.[16]

The Pattern of Mucus Dampness Hindering the Lungs (tan-shi-zu-fei 痰 湿 阻 肺)

This pattern usually runs a longer course than the previous two patterns. While it can be generated by an External Damp Pernicious Influence, more often it is the result of any External Influence invading the body and encountering a preexisting chronic disharmony with tendencies toward Mucus accumulation. Chronically Deficient Spleen or Kidney Qi, for example, may lead to Dampness and Mucus buildup, predisposing the body to this pattern of disharmony. Common signs include full, high-pitched coughing, wheezing, or asthma with copious phlegm; chest and flank distention and soreness; increased difficulty in breathing when lying down (since it is even harder for Lung Qi to descend when the body is horizontal); thick, greasy tongue moss that is either white or yellow depending on whether the obstructing Mucus is Cold or Hot; and a slippery pulse (the major sign of Mucus Dampness). In the West this pattern would be perceived most often as chronic bronchitis or bronchial asthma.[17]

The Pattern of Deficient Lung Yin (fei-yin-xu 肺 阴 虚)

This pattern can occur when chronically Deficient Yin, usually of the Kidneys, affects the Yin of the Lungs. It may also be a consequence of Heat Invading the Lungs and remaining within the body for so long that the Heat injures the Lung Yin. Signs include a dry cough with little or no phlegm, bloody sputum (if Heat has injured the Blood Vessels), and such general signs as an emaciated appearance, low voice, red cheeks, afternoon fever, night sweats, reddish tongue with a small amount of dry moss, and a thin, rapid pulse. In Western terms these conditions might be diagnosed as pulmonary tuberculosis, chronic pharyngitis, chronic bronchitis, or bronchiectasis.[18]

Deficient Lung Qi (fei-qi-xu 肺 气 虚)

This pattern usually occurs either as the result of an External Pernicious Influence remaining in the Lungs for a long period and injuring the Qi (an Excess condition turning into one of Deficiency) or because of various Internal disharmonies that affect the Lungs. The signs of this pattern are exhausted appearance and Spirit, low voice and lack of desire to talk, and weak respiration. If a cough is present, it is weak. If the Protective Qi has also been weakened, there are other signs such as daytime sweats and lowered resistance to colds. In Western terms such symptoms might point to emphysema, chronic bronchitis, pulmonary tuberculosis, or allergies.[19]

CLINICAL SKETCH: The following example is taken from the author's private practice. A woman, aged twenty-six, complained of wheezing, difficulty in breathing, and coughing, especially in the middle of the night. Sleeping was very difficult. The pattern had begun suddenly when the patient was sixteen years old and had gotten steadily worse. The patient constantly felt tightness in her chest, unrelated to seasonal changes, and when an attack started, there was much sneezing and coughing. Phlegm with a thick and yellow quality was produced. The patient's medical history was otherwise insignificant. Her appetite was good and her stools and urination were normal. She was very thin, with dark rings under her eyes. Her energy level was good except during an attack, and she did not report any emotional stress but seemed a little jumpy and anxious. Otherwise, her Shen was harmonious and clear. Her tongue was red and cracked in the middle and had scattered red dots. Her pulse was rapid (ninety-six beats per minute) and also slippery and slightly thin.

When she first came for treatment, she was taking Western medication but wanted an alternative because the drugs made her dizzy, tired, and nauseated.

Many of the signs pointed to the pattern of Heat in the Lungs: yellow phlegm, rapid pulse, red tongue, and thirst. Other signs, such as the thin body, the chronic nature of the disorder, the peeled and cracked tongue, and thin pulse, pointed to Deficient Yin. The wheezing, thick phlegm, and slippery pulse indicated that Mucus was present. A combination of acupuncture and herbal treatments was administered to cool the Lung Heat, nourish the Yin of the Lungs, and eliminate Mucus. This therapy brought the symptoms under control within two weeks.

Although the patient is still subject to occasional attacks, they are much less frequent and intense. When needed, she takes herbs or uses an herbal inhalator.

Tables 8 and 9 show correlations between pulse types and various Lung disharmonies. As has been said, pulse signs are reliable in delineating the texture and shading of disharmonies. Imagine a number of patients, all of whom manifest the most common sign of Lung disharmony—coughing. Theoretically, it would be possible to diagnose their various patterns of disharmony solely on the basis of pulse signs (as shown in Table 8). It would even be possible, using pulse signs, to diagnose patterns of disharmony of other Organs that affect the Lungs and also produce coughing (see Table 9).

For all of the disharmonies listed in Tables 8 and 9 there are also other signs, as well as the pulse, that point to the appropriate pattern of disharmony. But since pulse taking is so accurate, why examine the other signs?

TABLE 8

Correlation of Pulses and Lung Disharmony

Pulse	Pattern of Lung Disharmony
Floating and tight	Exterior/Cold/Wind
Floating and rapid	Exterior/Hot/Wind
Slippery	Mucus Obstructing
Thin and rapid	Deficient Yin
Empty	Deficient Qi

TABLE 9

Correlation of Pulses with Kidney, Liver, Heart, and Lung Disharmonies

Pulse	Pattern of Disharmony
Frail and slow	Kidneys not Grasping Qi (affecting Lung Qi)
Wiry	Liver Invading Lungs
Choppy and intermittent	Congealed Heart Blood Obstructing Qi of Chest

The first reason is that, in practice, rarely are pulse signs so pure that they can be categorized simply according to the theoretical charts. A patient will often manifest shadings of various pulse types—hints and overtones of a number of patterns—because in reality several different patterns of disharmony usually occur simultaneously. Moreover, a pulse may suggest contradictory interpretations that other signs must help resolve, or the other signs may point to a totally different pulse interpretation. And finally, it is rare to find a pulse taker so skilled that he or she could read the shadings of the pulse at an appropriately subtle level.[20]

Spleen Disharmonies

The central tasks of the Spleen are (1) ruling the transformation of food into Qi and Blood and (2) governing the Blood. Internal disharmonies of the Spleen are usually linked to an insufficiency of Spleen Qi to perform these activities. Because the Spleen is especially sensitive to Dampness, its patterns of Excess tend to involve Dampness. Such disharmonies are usually internally generated.

Patterns of Deficient Spleen Qi (*pi-qi-xu* 脾气虚) and Deficient Spleen Yang (*pi-yang-xu* 脾阳虚)

The pattern of Deficient Spleen Qi is associated with such Spleen-specific signs as poor appetite (insufficient Qi to transform food); slight abdominal pain and distention that are relieved by touching (insufficient Qi to move food), and loose stools (insufficient Qi to complete digestion). In addition, there are the other signs of Deficient Qi, primarily lethargy, a pale tongue with thin white moss and an empty pulse. From this pattern, Western physicians might diagnose gastric or duodenal ulcers, nervous dyspepsia, hepatitis, chronic dysentery, or anemia.[21]

The pattern of Deficient Spleen Yang is a deeper and more serious disharmony than that of Deficient Spleen Qi. It is associated with signs of the appearance of Cold, especially cold limbs; swollen, moist, pale tongue; and slow, frail pulse. Also, certain of the Spleen-specific signs will be more extreme or Cold in nature (for instance, watery stools containing undigested food and abdominal distention or pain that responds favorably to heat as well as pressure). Deficient Spleen Yang may also affect the movement of water in the body, producing such symptoms as edema, difficulty in urination, and leukorrhea. Patients with Deficient Spleen Yang might be diagnosed in the West as having such chronic diseases as gastric or duodenal ulcers, gastritis, enteritis, hepatitis, dysentery, or nephritis.[22]

Pattern of Spleen Qi Sinking (*pi-qi-xia-xian* 脾气下陷)

This is a subcategory of Deficient Spleen Qi and Deficient Spleen Yang and occurs when the Qi cannot perform its function of retaining things in their proper place. This pattern is also sometimes called Middle Burner Collapsing. In addition to the signs of Deficient Spleen Qi and Deficient Spleen Yang, this pattern displays signs associated with falling, such as hemorrhoids, prolapse of the uterus, extreme chronic diarrhea, or urinary incontinence.

Pattern of Spleen Unable to Govern the Blood (*pi-bu-zong-xue* 脾不统血)

This is another subcategory of Deficient Spleen Qi or Yang, occurring when the Yang Qi of the Spleen cannot hold the

Blood in place. Various kinds of chronic bleeding result: blood in the stool, bloody nose, chronic subcutaneous hemorrhaging, excessive menses, or uterine bleeding. These symptoms are generally accompanied by other signs of Deficiency. (If hemorrhaging were accompanied by signs of Excess or Heat, it would of course be interpreted differently, probably as Hot Blood.)

In Western medicine, the pattern of Spleen Unable to Govern the Blood would commonly appear as functional uterine bleeding, bleeding hemorrhoids, hemophilia, or Henoch-Schönlein purpura.[23]

Pattern of Dampness Distressing the Spleen (shi-kun-pi 湿 困 脾)

Most Spleen disharmonies are patterns of Deficiency. The Spleen likes dryness and dislikes Dampness. Dampness Distressing the Spleen is often the result of a Deficient Qi or Yang pattern. In this situation, fluids are not properly transformed and Dampness builds up in the Spleen; thus, the pattern is one of Deficiency turning into Excess. This is an Interior pattern whose signs may include: lack of appetite and sensation of taste, skin eruptions containing fluid, watery stool, nausea, and a feeling of fullness in the chest or head. A slippery or soggy pulse is very important in discerning this pattern because other signs may be similar to those of Deficient Qi. Thick, greasy tongue moss is also a crucial sign here, since it nearly always points to Excess.

In Western terms, this pattern might translate into chronic gastroenteritis, chronic dysentery, or chronic hepatitis.[24]

External Dampness Obstructing (wai-shi-zu 外 湿 阻)

This pattern is similar to the preceding one, although somewhat less common, and occurs when Dampness is an External Pernicious Influence. The Spleen is affected, and the same signs of Dampness Distress are present. In addition, this pattern tends to be relatively acute, characterized by sudden onset and, occasionally, a low fever.

Damp Heat Collecting in the Spleen
(*pi-yun-shi-re* 脾 蕴 湿 热)

Dampness and Cold are both Yin, and so Dampness patterns are likely to manifest signs of Cold. However, Dampness can also be Hot, and if Heat signs are present, a distinct, common pattern may be perceived. Although Damp Heat Collecting in the Spleen is usually the result of an External Pernicious Influence,[25] this pattern is also associated with eating fatty foods and excessive alcohol consumption. The signs of Dampness will be present as well as the signs of Heat, and, in addition, the movement of bile can be obstructed, causing jaundice and a bitter taste in the mouth.

A Western physician examining a patient with the pattern of Damp Heat Collecting in the Spleen might diagnose acute gastric inflammation, acute hepatitic infection, cholecystitis, or cirrhosis of the liver.[26]

Because Dampness is Yin and Heat is Yang, one would have to determine in a clinical situation whether the pattern were Yin within Yang or Yang within Yin—that is, which element is dominant. Table 10 suggests some criteria for making this important distinction.

TABLE 10

Damp Heat Collecting in the Spleen

Signs	More Dampness Yang within Yin	More Heat Yin within Yang
Chest/Abdomen	feeling of fullness	relatively more pain, with some distention
Thirst	no thirst, or thirst without desire for fluids	thirst
Urine	scanty and slightly yellowish	scanty and very dark yellow
Tongue	slightly red material, with yellow and very greasy moss	red material, with yellow and somewhat greasy moss
Pulse	soggy, not too rapid	rapid and slippery

Turbid Mucus Disturbing the Head
(*tan-zhuo-shang-rao* 痰 浊 上 扰)

This is a development of Damp Spleen patterns. The patient suffers from severe dizziness, rather than a feeling of heaviness in the head, because Mucus is heavier than Dampness. Very greasy tongue moss is a predominant sign of this pattern. In Western terms, this pattern is often part of such disorders as hypertension and Ménière's disease.[27]

CLINICAL SKETCH: A patient in the author's practice complained of chronic abdominal distention and discomfort, tiredness, and a feeling of heaviness. He had a sallow complexion and a slow, phlegmatic ambience. His tongue was slightly pale with a very thick, greasy moss, and his pulse was very empty. All other signs were normal. The Western doctors this patient had consulted diagnosed his condition as a nervous stomach. The signs of distention and heaviness pointed to the pattern of Dampness Distressing the Spleen, which was confirmed by the greasy coating on the tongue. The empty pulse, on the other hand, pointed to the pattern of Deficient Spleen Qi. The pattern of Dampness Distressing the Spleen and the pattern of Deficient Qi are part of a continuum between two textbook points. This patient fell somewhere in between—he manifested aspects of both. He could be described as having the pattern of Deficient Qi turning into Dampness Distressing the Spleen (a Deficiency turning into an Excess, or vice versa). The correct treatment was to strengthen the Spleen Qi, supplementing the Deficiency, and to expel and disperse Dampness, removing the Pernicious Influence.

The relative amount of tonification and dispersion that needs to be done in any one case by herbs or acupuncture needles depends on the relative amount of Deficiency and Excess present; that is, on the exact proportions of the patient's unique signs. In fact, the most precise description of the patient's patterns is the exact combination of acupuncture points and herbs used. The "cause"—the Deficient Qi that leads to Dampness—is not treated. Instead, the physician treats the exact pattern generated at the moment by the particular configuration of manifesting signs.

In this case, a series of ten acupuncture treatments and the use of herbs led to complete relief of the symptoms. The tongue greasiness disappeared, but the pulse remained somewhat empty, pointing to a constitutional tendency toward this disharmony that the treatment had not yet been able to correct.

Liver Disharmonies

One important function of the Liver is to rule "flowing and spreading." This organ oversees the flow of interdependent bodily processes the way the commander of an army guides troops. It is understandable, therefore, that most Liver disharmonies are related to stagnation. Such stagnation characteristically develops aspects of Excess and Heat. The Liver is the Yin Organ most involved with Excess Heat disharmonies and Internal Heat (Fire). Internal Wind Pernicious Influences are also often generated in the Liver. Liver Fire easily ascends and can affect the head and eyes. From another perspective, we can say that just as the Spleen needs dryness for its digestive activities, so the Liver needs moisture (which is dependent on Kidney Yin and Jing) for its smooth, sprinkling activity. A dry, disharmonious Liver can easily lead to patterns of Heat. In addition, when Liver Qi lacks moisture and cannot properly flow and spread, it tends to "jump" or "fly off the handle." The latter expression accurately characterizes the inappropriate anger that is a common emotional sign of Liver disharmony.

The Liver, because of its relation to moisture, is very dependent on its Yin aspect. This, in turn, brings us to the Liver's other main function, storing the Blood, which is the major Yin Substance and the "mother of Qi."

Pattern of Constrained Liver Qi (gan-qi-yu-jie 肝气郁结)

This pattern, which is the most common form of Stagnant Qi, is also the most common pattern of Liver disharmony. It manifests itself in many ways, with signs that vary but usually include a blue-green, purplish, or otherwise dark tinge to the tongue, and a pulse that suggests blockage, such as a wiry or tight pulse. Constrained Liver Qi may affect the emotions and produce depression, a sense of frustration, or inappropriate anger. If this pattern involves the throat, the patient will feel a lump in the throat, a sensation the Chinese call the "plum-pit feeling." In the Liver Meridians along the groin, breast, or flank, Constrained Liver Qi is associated with distention or lumps; in the neck, there may also be lumps. In addition, this pattern may affect the Liver's storage of Blood, leading to menstrual pain, irregular menses, and swelling of the breasts during menses. Patients with Constrained Liver Qi could be diagnosed in Western terms as suffering from an extremely wide range of disorders, including mastitis, scrofula, nervous and emotional disorders, and various menstrual problems.[28]

As one aspect of its spreading function, the Liver assists the Spleen's activity of transforming food. Constrained Liver Qi can affect this Spleen function, creating a subpattern known as Liver Invading the Spleen (*gan-fan-pi*), which has such signs as nausea, vomiting, sour belching, abdominal pain, and diarrhea.

Since these digestive signs also characterize patterns of Spleen disharmony, one must distinguish the pattern of Liver Invading the Spleen by other accompanying signs. A patient with this pattern would not have the tiredness associated with Deficient Spleen Qi or other Spleen symptoms. Most important, the tongue material would be somewhat darkish or purple (or even normal, if the disharmony is not too chronic) instead of pale (a sign of Deficient Spleen Qi), and instead of the empty pulse that accompanies Deficient Spleen Qi, the patient with Liver Invading the Spleen would have a wiry pulse.

Pattern of Liver Fire Blazing Upward (gan-huo-shang-yan 肝火上炎)

This is an Excess/Heat condition of the Liver often precipitated by Constrained Liver Qi generating Fire or by dramatic emotional changes. The Fire produced by a disharmonious Liver most often rises to the head, and there are such signs as splitting headaches, dizziness, red face and eyes, dry mouth, and deafness or sudden ringing in the ears. We might also expect irritability, frequent anger, and insomnia (because Liver Fire disturbs the Shen), as well as general signs of Excess/Heat (constipation; dark, scanty urine; red tongue with rough, yellow moss; and a rapid and full as well as wiry pulse). Liver Fire often injures the Blood Vessels, causing various bleeding symptoms. Patients manifesting this pattern might be diagnosed in the West as suffering from essential hypertension, migraine headaches, bleeding of the upper digestive tract, menopausal complaints, eye diseases such as acute conjunctivitis and glaucoma, or ear disturbances such as labyrinthitis, Ménière's disease, or otitis.[29]

Pattern of Deficient Liver Yin (gan-yin-xu 肝 阴 虚)

This is an Empty Fire pattern (the appearance of Heat in a Deficient Yin pattern; see Figure 39), woven from the usual symptoms of Deficient Yin such as red cheeks, afternoon fever, hot palms and soles, nervousness, reddish tongue, and thin, fast pulse, as well as Liver-specific signs such as dizziness (a general Deficient Yin symptom, but especially associated with the Liver), muddled vision, dry eyes, and other eye problems, wiry, rapid, and thin pulse, depression, and nervous tension. A Western physician confronting patients with this pattern may diagnose essential hypertension, nervous disorders, chronic eye ailments, and menopausal complaints.[30]

The pattern of Turbid Mucus Disturbing the Head, which is a Damp Spleen pattern, often accompanies Liver Fire, Liver Yang, and Liver Yin patterns. It may be discerned by such additional signs as extreme dizziness, a thick, greasy tongue moss, and slippery aspects of the pulse.

Pattern of Arrogant Liver Yang Ascending (gan-yang-shang-kang 肝 阳 上 亢)

This pattern combines aspects of both Excess Fire (Excess Yang) and Empty Fire (Deficient Yin). That is, it has signs that resemble those of Liver Fire Blazing Upward as well as those of Deficient Liver Yin.

It is worthwhile to discuss these three Liver patterns in some detail because they are commonly seen disorders and will further illustrate Chinese medical diagnostic techniques. These three patterns, as well as Constrained Liver Qi, must be seen as generatively interrelated. For example, the stagnation of Constrained Liver Qi can easily transform into Liver Fire. This Fire, over a period of time, can damage Liver Yin and produce Arrogant Liver Yang Ascending or Deficient Liver Yin. Although our language is that of causality, in a patient these patterns may follow or intersect one another, or may even appear simultaneously.

In fact, even identifying a particular pattern is problematic, since every textbook pattern is only a theoretical image and is seldom found unambiguously in an actual patient. Thus, Excess Fire and Deficient Yin patterns are theoretically quite distinguishable, but one often faces clinical situations in which the distinction is hardly clear at all, since the signs seem to point to a pattern somewhere in between the two. Such an admixture of signs is so common in Liver disharmonies that Chinese medical tradition has designated a separate pattern to describe it— Arrogant Liver Yang Ascending. Figure 44 illustrates the continuum of Liver Heat Patterns from Excess Fire (Excess Yang) to Empty Fire (Deficient Yin). Chinese medical tradition defines three points on this continuum as three separate patterns in order to teach students how to organize signs, weave patterns, and prescribe treatment. In actuality, the level of Fire and Water in a patient can vary infinitely, and the specific clinical pattern woven for a particular patient will involve shadings that suggest aspects of all three Liver Heat patterns. For example, it would be possible to have the pulse characteristic of Liver Fire, the eye signs of Deficient Liver Yin, and the emotions characteristic of Arrogant Liver Yang Ascending. The physician must use skill, experience, and sensitivity to evaluate the relative importance of the various signs and prescribe the correct treatment.

FIGURE 44

Continuum of Liver Heat Patterns

Liver Fire Blazing Upward (Excess Fire)	Arrogant Liver Yang Ascending, Excess Fire, and Deficient Yin (Empty Fire) simultaneously	Deficient Liver Yin (Empty Fire—appearance of Heat)

	Liver Fire Blazing Upward (Excess Fire)	Arrogant Liver Yang Ascending, Excess Fire, and Deficient Yin (Empty Fire) simultaneously	Deficient Liver Yin (Empty Fire—appearance of Heat)
Heat	whole body constantly hot	periodic hot flushes in head and face	palms and soles hot; slight afternoon fever
Headache	severe, splitting	throbbing	mild
Eyes	red, swollen, painful	reddish; some pain	spots in field of vision; dryness
Dizziness	severe	moderate	mild
Emotions	violent fits of anger	anger or depression	nervous irritability or depression
Pulse	full, rapid, and wiry	rapid and wiry	thin, rapid, and wiry

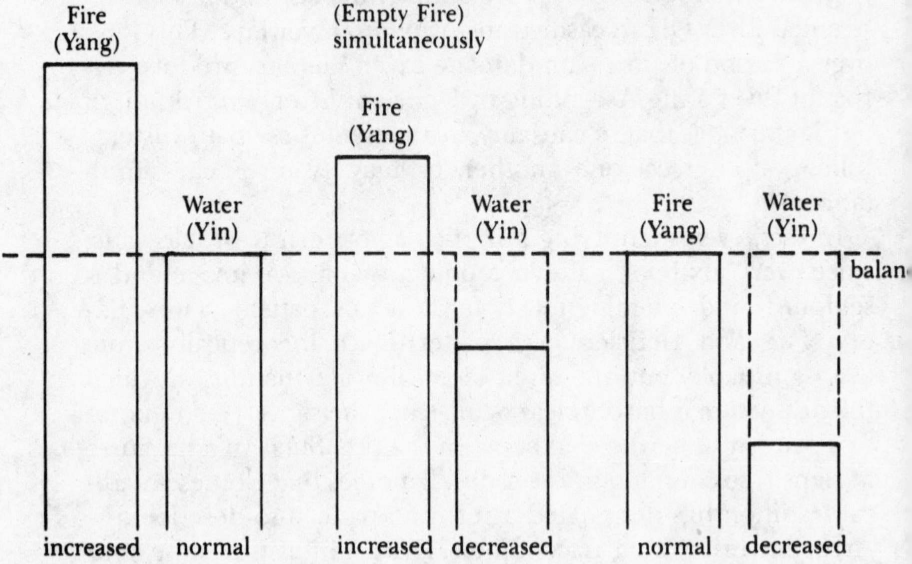

In clinical practice, most Organ disharmonies present this type of admixture of signs suggesting several patterns. Only for Liver disharmonies, however, has this clinical truth become a common theoretical consideration. A special pattern—Arrogant Liver Yang Ascending—has been defined because of the frequent clinical prevalence of this mixture of signs.

The paired opposites of the Eight Principal Patterns are not mutually exclusive. Instead, they define the limits of continuums that the skilled physician knows how to manipulate.

Pattern of Liver Wind Moving Internally (*gan-feng-nei-dong* 肝 风 内 动)

This pattern occurs when Liver Fire or Liver Yang precipitates uncontrollable and/or sudden movement or rigidity in the body. Its signs include those of other Liver disharmonies, with the addition of Wind signs such as trembling, difficulty in speaking, extreme stiff neck or tetany, spasms and convulsions, pulsating headaches, extreme dizziness, ringing in the ears, sudden facial rigidity or twitching, and unconsciousness (as in apoplexy). Liver Wind usually develops out of an extreme form of some other Liver pattern. Thus, if the Liver Wind were a result of Constrained Liver Qi, there would be a dark or purplish tongue; if it resulted from Liver Fire Blazing Upward or Arrogant Liver Yang Ascending, a reddish tongue would be seen.

Pattern of Deficient Liver Blood (*gan-xue-xu* 肝 血 虚)

This pattern of Deficiency may be visualized on a continuum with Deficient Liver Yin. It will tend to manifest general Deficient Blood signs such as pale, lusterless face, thin pulse, and dizziness, as well as Liver-specific signs such as hazy vision or spots in the field of vision, flank pain, and tendons and muscles that are numb or exhibit weak, spasmodic movement (since the Liver rules the tendons). Pale fingernails (since the Liver manifests in the nails) and irregular or insufficient menstruation, or amenorrhea, are additional symptoms. In the world of Western medicine, this pattern might be seen as anemia, chronic hepatitis, nervous disorders, hypertension, menstrual disorders, or various chronic eye problems such as retinitis.[31]

Pattern of Cold Stagnating in the Liver Meridian (han-zhi-gan-mai 寒 滞 肝 脉)

This pattern arises when Cold obstructs the Liver Meridian in the area of the groin. Signs include pain and distention in the lower side and groin; a swollen scrotum, which feels as if it were being pulled downward; moist tongue with white moss; deep, wiry, slow pulse; and discomfort relieved by heat. In the West, this pattern would be seen as one type of hernia (a term used in both Western and Chinese medicine) or as a urogenital disorder such as pelvic inflammatory disease.[32]

CLINICAL SKETCH: This example is taken from the collected case histories of Dr. Wu, a famous traditional physician in China.[33]

The patient, a male aged forty-two, first visited on February 3, 1964. His complaints included throbbing temples and soreness at the top of the head.

From the Four Examinations, it was learned that the patient had dark yellow urine, difficulty in defecating, a poor appetite, painful teeth, painful right flank, painful eyeballs, insomnia, and excessive dreaming. His tongue was red; the moss was thick, greasy, and white; and the pulse was sinking and wiry. A Western medical examination at the same hospital diagnosed hypertension (blood pressure $^{180}/_{130}$ mm Hg) and the beginnings of coronary heart disease.

Dr. Wu's diagnosis was Constrained Liver Qi accompanied by Liver Fire Ascending to Disturb the Head. His treatment called for harmonizing the Liver, cooling Liver Fire, and transforming Mucus.

An analysis of the process leading to this diagnosis is interesting. The yellow urine and difficult stools point to Heat, as does the red tongue. The flank pain and wiry pulse point to Constrained Liver Qi. The headaches, pounding temples, and eye pain suggest Liver Excess, because of the wiry pulse. The lack of appetite and the greasy moss point to Mucus and to Liver Invading the Spleen, while the insomnia and excessive dreaming are consonant with a Heart-Shen disharmony, especially from Heat or Deficient Yin. However, since there were no other signs of Heart disharmony, Dr. Wu determined that this sign was actually part of the pattern of Liver Fire that disturbs the Heart rather than a Heart pattern.

One question that could be raised is why the patient has a sinking rather than a rapid pulse. Dr. Wu's interpretation was that some signs point to Heat, while others point to Constrained Liver Qi and Mucus. The Fire is only affecting the Head and tongue material, while the tongue moss and sinking pulse indicate the Constrained qualities. The Constrained Liver Qi is interpreted as invading the Spleen because of the digestive symptoms. The Mucus may in fact be Cold, although Dr. Wu's diagnosis did not mention this. His treatment, however, while mainly using Fire-cooling herbs, also used two warm herbs to transform Mucus.

The entire treatment was herbal. A prescription of twelve herbs, including *Gardenia jasminoides, Gentiana scabra,* and *Heliotis diversicolor* (abalone shell), was given to the patient. After he had taken the decoction for three days, a noticeable improvement was reported (blood pressure $^{130}/_{90}$ mm Hg). A similar prescription was then given for nine more days, after which the patient reported that all symptoms had disappeared. On the third visit, the physician prescribed an herbal pill to be taken for a longer period of time in order to make the treatment permanent.

There is no traditional Chinese understanding of blood pressure, as the concept was first noted by French scientists during the eighteenth century. And in medicine it was not routinely used until 1912, when the Massachusetts General Hospital began measuring it on all entering patients. It should be mentioned, however, that the Chinese pharmacopoeia has many herbs that modern research has demonstrated can lower blood pressure.[34] This fact was irrelevant to the physician, though, who achieved excellent results by basing his treatment on reharmonizing the entire body. Using only those Chinese herbs that Western research has linked to reducing blood pressure (i.e., using a Western paradigm to select Oriental herbs) would have produced poorer results.[35]

It should be clear that the Western entity known as hypertension can be found in various types of patterns and that this example of Liver Fire is but one common type. Other common patterns could include Liver and Kidney Yin both Deficient, and Kidney Yin and Yang both Deficient.[36]

Kidney Disharmonies

The Kidneys store Jing, or Essence, and since the body cannot have too much Jing, patterns of Kidney disharmony tend to be ones of Deficiency. In addition, because the Kidneys are considered the root of the Yin and Yang of all the Organs, disharmonies of the Kidneys are rarely isolated. Of all the patterns of disharmony, they are most often linked to disharmonies of other Organs, either preliminary to those disharmonies or as a final consequence of them.

Pattern of Deficient Kidney Yang (shen-yang-xu 肾 阳 虚)

This pattern, also called Weak Life Gate Fire (ming-men-huo-ruo) manifests signs of Deficiency and the "appearance of Cold" (that is, a Deficiency/Cold pattern). Thus, its signs include Cold signs such as bright, white, or darkish face, subdued, quiet manner, no Shen, fear of cold, and cold limbs, as well as such Kidney-specific signs as cold and sore lower back, impotence, sterility, spermatorrhea, loose teeth, and deafness or loss of hearing. In addition, there might be copious, clear urine, night urination, or dripping urine. (If the ruling Water functions of the Kidneys are affected in the opposite way, signs of edema and problems of insufficient urination might develop.) The tongue will be swollen and pale with scalloped markings on the edges and a moist, thin, white moss. The pulse will generally be frail and slow or minute, and will often be particularly frail and sinking in the third pulse position. Also, the patient may be generally debilitated.

Deficient Kidney Yang often occurs concurrently with Deficient Heart Yang, Deficient Spleen Yang, or Deficient Lung Qi.

In the first case, the common symptoms are simultaneous edema and heart palpitations; in the second case, edema with chronic digestive problems; and in the third case, chronic cough, shortness of breath, or asthma. The latter Kidney/Lung disharmony is sufficiently common to merit a separate name— Kidney Unable to Grasp the Qi (*shen-bu-na-qi*)—and is seen as a subpattern of Deficient Kidney Yang.

The various patterns involving Deficient Kidney Yang would be diagnosed in the West as a very wide range of disorders including chronic nephritis, lumbago, sexual dysfunction, chronic urinary and prostate problems, chronic ear disorders, adrenal gland hypoactivity, hypothyroidism, or depressive neurosis. Kidney Unable to Grasp the Qi might also yield diagnoses of cardiac insufficiency, chronic asthma, or emphysema. Deficient Kidney Yang and Deficient Spleen Yang might be seen as pulmonary heart disease, chronic enteritis, chronic dysentery, edema due to liver cirrhosis, heart disease, or nephritis.[37]

Pattern of Deficient Kidney Yin (*shen-yin-xu* 肾 阴 虚)

This pattern, also called Kidney Water Exhausted, is a condition of Empty Fire. It is woven by such general signs as thin, shriveled constitution, dry throat, hot palms and soles, red cheeks, afternoon heat flushes, night sweats, reddish tongue with little moss, and a thin, rapid pulse. Kidney-specific signs might include ringing in the ears or loss of hearing; weak, sore back; little sperm; premature ejaculation; forgetfulness; and vertigo.

Deficient Kidney Yin, when it involves other Organs, most often occurs along with Deficient Yin of the Heart, Liver, and Lungs. When the Heart is involved, one sees Heart-specific signs such as insomnia, heart palpitations, and excessive dreaming. If the Liver is affected, there are often vision problems, headaches, and irregular menses. With Lung involvement, there would be a weak, dry cough, possibly with bloody sputum.

Western doctors might correlate Deficient Kidney Yin with essential hypertension, lumbago, chronic ear problems, diabetes, or chronic urogenital infections. Heart problems involving tachycardia or hyperthyroidism may be seen in patients with Deficient Kidney Yin and Deficient Heart Yin. The Pattern of Deficient Kidney Yin and Deficient Liver Yin may be seen in the West as menstrual problems, while tuberculosis and emphysema might be diagnosed in patients with Deficient Kidney Yin and Deficient Heart Yin.[38]

Pattern of Deficient Kidney Jing (shen-jing-bu-zu 肾精不足)

When Jing is Deficient, the Yin and Yang of the body are both diminished (see Figure 45). Assuming that Yin and Yang are equally Deficient, the pattern of Deficient Kidney Jing will, first of all, manifest Kidney signs. These signs will not, however, have any obvious Cold or Hot associations as they did in preceding patterns.

Deficient Kidney Jing will then tend to display signs relating to development, maturation, or reproduction. Characteristic signs include premature aging or senility, bad teeth, poor memory, and brittle bones. In a child, such signs as slow physical or mental development, late or incomplete fontanel closure, or poor general skeletal development are common. Sexual dysfunction without appearances of Cold or Heat would likely be a

FIGURE 45

Kidney Disharmonies

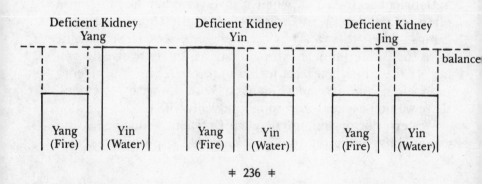

Jing Deficiency. In addition, many of the Kidney-specific signs would be seen.

In clinical situations, Yin and Yang are rarely equally diminished, and a Deficient Jing pattern will tend slightly toward either the Yin or the Yang side, with the appropriate tongue and pulse signs reflecting the tendency. Such a tendency can also be read in other signs. For example, in the area of sexual problems, a pattern of Deficient Jing somewhat more Deficient on the Yang side might lead to impotence in a man and to lack of sexual interest in a woman because there is a lack of the Fire that rises and arouses. Deficient Jing weighted on the side of Deficient Yin, however, might lead to premature ejaculation or insufficient vaginal secretions since the Yin cannot properly embrace the Yang.

CLINICAL SKETCH: Some interesting examples come from two studies that explored the efficacy of Chinese medicine in treating the Western medical entity known as systemic lupus erythematosus (SLE), a serious and often fatal autoimmune disease.[39]

Two studies, the first dealing with 120 cases of lupus, the second with 22 cases, both concluded that traditional herbal treatments reduced the mortality rates from lupus more effectively than Western therapy, and that in a high proportion of cases, Chinese medicine is very helpful in treating the disorder.

The first study found that several distinct disharmony patterns arise when diagnosing SLE. Here is a case history from the second study, which emphasized Kidney patterns.

On May 23, 1960, a woman, aged thirty-two, came to the hospital complaining that her facial skin, especially her cheeks, seemed to have injuries similar to frostbite. The condition had gradually gotten worse over the previous six months. She also complained of sore joints and back pain, dizziness, palpitations, insomnia, night sweats, and an occasional low fever. She was often thirsty, but had no desire to drink. Since the illness began, her hair had been falling out and her menstrual blood had diminished.

The Chinese examination noted a depleted Spirit, thinness of the whole body, low voice, and dark complexion. Her cheeks had a purple-red rash, the center of which was gray and scaled. Her eyes were sunken and darkish in the sockets; her hair was thin; the tongue moss was thin and white; the tongue material was cracked and bright red; and the pulse was thin and slightly rapid, with the third position especially weak.

Following the Chinese clinical examination, the patient was given a battery of Western medical tests. Some of the lab findings include: white blood cell count 2,400/mm^3; red blood count 3.06 × 10^6/mm^3; total protein 8.6 grams percent; platelets 54,000/mm^3; sedimentation rate 32 mm/hour (Cutler). An electrocardiogram showed arrhythmia, LE prep negative.

The dizziness, night sweats, heart palpitations, recurring low fevers, cracked and red tongue, and thin and rapid pulse all pointed to Deficient Yin. The backache, the weak third position on the pulse, the darkened eye sockets, and the loss of hair suggested that the Deficiency was in the Kidneys. The joint soreness was interpreted as Wind Invading the surface Meridians, obstructing the Qi and Blood. The rash on the face was thought to be the Heat of Deficient Yin Affecting the Blood, thus resulting in skin eruptions. (See Appendix D.)

The Chinese physician chose an herbal treatment that combined fourteen herbs to nourish the Kidney Yin and Blood, cool the Blood, and expel Wind. The herbs used included *Rehmannia glutinosa*, *Polygonum multiflorum*, and *Paeonia lactiflora*. The patient was given a prescription to be taken daily for eighteen days. When she returned for the next examination, the rash had somewhat subsided. She was given a slightly different prescription. By the time she returned in five days, the rash had been very visibly reduced, her appetite had improved, and her joints were less sore. The backache, palpitation, and night sweats were all gone. White blood cell count was 4,500/mm^3, red blood cell count was 3.84 × 10^6/mm^3, and platelets were 98,000/mm^3. The patient continued to show improvement with additional treatment.

This chapter has focused on those major patterns of disharmony that are most important in the Chinese medical tradition—disharmonies involving Qi, Blood, Pernicious Influences, and the individual Yin Organs. Appendix B describes the common patterns associated with disharmonies of the Yang Organs.

Table 11 summarizes the most common patterns that occur when two Yin Organs are simultaneously involved in a disharmony.

TABLE 11

Patterns Involving Two Yin Organs Simultaneously

Pattern	Signs	Tongue	Pulse
Deficient Heart Qi and Deficient Lung Qi	palpitations; shortness of breath; weak cough; asthma; spontaneous sweating	pale	frail
Deficient Heart Blood and Deficient Spleen Qi	palpitations; insomnia; loss of appetite; abdominal distention; loose stools; lethargy; pale, sallow complexion; menstrual blood is pale and excessive, or amenorrhea	pale	empty or thin
Heart and Kidney Lose Communication (Heart Yin and Kidney Yin both Deficient)	palpitations; insomnia; irritability; forgetfulness; vertigo; tinnitus; dry throat; sore back; nocturnal ejaculations; afternoon fever; night sweats	reddish, dry material; little moss	thin, rapid, sinking
Heart Yang and Kidney Yang both Deficient	palpitations; cold appearance; edema; scanty urine	pale, swollen, moist material; white moss	sinking and minute
Lung Yin and Kidney Yin both Deficient	cough with little mucus; mucus with blood; mouth and throat dry; voice low or hoarse; lower back and limbs sore and weak; night sweats; red cheeks; afternoon fever; sterility	red material; little moss	thin and rapid

TABLE 11 (*cont.*)

Patterns Involving Two Yin Organs Simultaneously

Pattern	Signs	Tongue	Pulse
Deficient Lung Qi and Deficient Kidney Yang (Kidney Unable to Grasp Qi)	asthma (especially exhalation easy, inhalation difficult); shortness of breath; exertion worsens condition; no Spirit; low voice; spontaneous sweating; cold limbs	pale, moist, swollen material	frail or empty
Deficient Spleen Qi and Deficient Lung Qi	shortness of breath; cough; asthma accompanied by copious, thin, white phlegm; reduced appetite; loose stools; edema	pale, with white moss	empty
Deficient Spleen Qi and Deficient Kidney Yang	cold appearance; bright white complexion; lower back and limbs are cold and sore; loose stools with undigested food; edema; difficulty of urination; ascites	pale, moist, swollen, with white moss	frail and especially sinking
Liver Invading Spleen	chest and flank are distended and sore; emotional frustration, moodiness, or anger; reduced appetite; distended abdomen; loose stools; passing gas	dark or normal material; white moss	wiry
Liver Fire Invading Lungs	burning pain in chest and flank; irritability and quick anger; vertigo; red eyes; bitter taste in mouth; serial coughing; coughing blood	red, with thin yellow moss	wiry and rapid

TABLE 11 (*cont.*)

Patterns Involving Two Yin Organs Simultaneously

Pattern	Signs	Tongue	Pulse
Deficient Liver Yin and Deficient Kidney Yin	vertigo; headaches; spots before eyes; forgetfulness; tinnitus; dry mouth and throat; flank pain; lower back and limbs are sore and weak; hot palms and soles; red cheeks; menses irregular or reduced	red, with little moss	thin and rapid

Beyond this point, the discernment of patterns becomes much more complex and cannot easily be continued without clinical experience and extensive discussion of classical texts. In the next chapter, therefore, we will leave behind the discussion of particular patterns of disharmony and will return to the theory and style of traditional Chinese medicine.

Notes

1. *Su Wen* [1], sec. 17, chap. 62, p. 335.

2. It should be noted that it is possible for there to be a Qi-Blood continuum very different from a Blood-Yin continuum. Because "Qi is the commander of Blood" and "Blood is the mother of Qi," very often Deficient Blood and Deficient Qi exist simultaneously and merge together. This situation gives rise to a very common clinical situation in which the patient has signs of both Deficient Qi and Deficient Blood. Sometimes this situation gives a Cold appearance (for instance, cold limbs) because the Deficient Qi aspect develops signs of Deficient Yang.

3. "Stagnant Food" was alluded to in Chapter 5 in the discussion of dietary factors in disharmony. The term can also be used to describe a disharmony pattern that acts as an extreme form of Mucus. This results from overeating, or because the Stomach and Spleen are too weak to ripen and transform the food, so that it remains undigested. Signs of the pattern of Stagnant Food include nausea, vomiting, belching, foul-smelling gas or stool, distended or painful abdomen, irregular stools, lessening of discomfort in abdomen after bowel movement or passing gas, a greasy or pasty, thick moss, and a slippery pulse.

4. For an interesting discussion of treating Western medical categories with methods that tonify Spleen Qi, see Shanghai Institute, Study of Prescriptions [87], pp. 227–230.

5. It is possible for a person with a particular Chinese medical disharmony to be considered healthy or a hypochondriac after a Western physician's examination. The opposite could also be true: A Chinese medical practitioner might see no disharmony in a situation where a Western medical disease is diagnosed. Each system has blind spots from the perspective of the other.

6. For a discussion of the treatment of Western medical categories with methods that cool Liver Fire, see Shanghai Institute, Study of Prescriptions [87], pp. 47–48.

7. In China, people often go from a Western practitioner to a traditional practitioner and vice versa, or are treated in a hospital where both medical systems are used simultaneously.

8. Shanghai Institute, Foundations [53], p. 172; Zhejiang Provincial Committee, Foundations of Traditional Chinese Medicine [91].

9. Ibid., p. 171; Zhejiang Committee, Foundations [91], p. 72.

10. This pattern is called Heart Blockage (*xin-bi*) in the *Su Wen* (sec. 20, chap. 43).

11. Zhejiang Committee, Foundations [91], p. 73; Shanghai Institute, Foundations, p. 173.

12. Ibid., p. 74. Many parallels to the pathology of classic Greek humoral medicine and Chinese concepts can be found. Here the parallel is striking. Hippocrates describes epilepsy, paraplegia, apoplexy, and convulsions as humidity of the brain with excess phlegm often accompanied by dryness causing overexcitability. The humoral origin is similar to the Chinese, but the Greek attention to morphology "correctly" put the disturbance in the brain rather than the Heart.

13. Clinical Observation of Effectiveness of Traditional Chinese Medicine in Treating Thirty-one Cases of Premature Ventricular Contractions, SJTCM, March 1979.

14. Forty-nine Cases of Coronary Heart Disease Treated by Heart-comforting Decoction of *Pueraria lobata* and *Trichosanthes kirilowii*, SJTCM, July 1979, p. 19; Zhongshan Institute, Clinical Uses of Chinese Medicines [92], pp. 36, 273, 485.

15. Zhejiang Committee, Foundations, p. 89; Selected Explanations of Traditional Chinese Medical Terms [33], p. 140.

16. Ibid., p. 90.

17. Selected Explanations [92], p. 141.

18. Zhejiang Committee, Foundations, p. 91; Selected Explanations, p. 142.

19. Ibid., p. 91.

20. On the other hand, we could add that a truly refined physician may be capable of distinguishing a pattern of disharmony simply by listening to the quality of a patient's cough. This is because the entire configuration will affect the quality of any single element of a pattern. See Chapter 9.

21. Selected Explanations, p. 135; Zhejiang Committee, Foundations, p. 84.

22. Ibid.; Shanghai Institute, Distinguishing Patterns and Dispensing Treatments [52], p. 223.

23. Zhejiang Committee, Foundations, p. 84.

24. Guangzhou Ministry, Essentials of Traditional Chinese Medicine [75], p. 98.

25. Because the Yang Organs are generally more affected by External Pernicious Influences, this pattern is often considered Damp Heat in the Stomach and Intestines. See Appendix B.

26. Guangzhou Ministry, Essentials, p. 98.

27. Shanghai Institute, Foundations, p. 218.

28. Ibid., p. 185.

29. Guangzhou Ministry, Essentials, p. 94; Selected Explanations, p. 133. By Five Phase correspondence, it would seem that ear problems should be mainly a disharmony of the Kidney. In clinical practice, however, Kidney disharmony is generally associated with Deficiency patterns involving the ear, whereas Liver or Gall Bladder disharmony is associated with Excess patterns. Acute eye problems are often associated with the Lungs.

30. Zhejiang Committee, Foundations, p. 79.

31. Guangzhou Ministry, Essentials, p. 95; Selected Explanations, p. 132.

32. Beijing Institute, Foundations, p. 121; Zhejiang Provincial Committee, Clinical Study of Traditional Chinese Medicine [90], p. 356.

33. Clinical Cases of Wu Shao-huai (*Wu Shao-huai Yi-an*) [78], pp. 57–59. Dr. Wu, at the time his clinical reports were published, had over sixty years of clinical practice and was principal of the Jinan City Institute of Traditional Chinese Medicine.

34. Chen Xin-qian, Pharmacology [71], pp. 381–383.

35. Eleventh People's Hospital of Shanghai Institute, Theory and Treatment of Hypertension [72]. See entire study.

36. Zhejiang Committee, Clinical Studies, p. 241–244.

37. Shanghai Institute, Foundations, p. 192; Selected Explanations, p. 145; Zhejiang Committee, Foundations, p. 17.

38. Ibid., p. 193; Guangzhou Ministry, Essentials, p. 105.

39. Treatment of Systemic Lupus Erythematosus with combined Traditional Chinese and Western Medicine, SJTCM, September 1979; Shanghai First Medical Hospital, Studies on the Kidneys [84], pp. 22–26.

CHAPTER

9

Chinese Medicine as an Art

The process of seeing patterns in the multiplicity of clinical events allows the Chinese physician to visualize a bodily landscape, to perceive an individual disharmony, thereby making a diagnosis, and to prescribe treatment. For any complaint—from the stomachache described in Chapter 1, to blood in the urine, to frequent violent emotional outbursts—the process is the same.

The patterns delineated in the last two chapters are the most common and basic configurations that the Chinese medical tradition can portray. Picking out a particular pattern is actually only a more precise and detailed way of describing the disharmony as basically Yin or Yang, or Yin within Yang, or Yang within Yin.

To illustrate this process of discovering patterns, let us consider a patient with the complaint of dry eyes. This complaint is typically considered a sign of Deficient Liver Blood or Deficient Liver Yin because, in the accumulated clinical experience of Chinese physicians, dry eyes are frequently accompanied by such Deficient Liver Blood signs as thin, wiry pulse, pale tongue, pale nails, and dizziness, or by Deficient Liver Yin signs like thin, rapid pulse, reddish tongue, thirst, red cheeks, and dizziness. In clinical practice, however, the pattern is the ultimate concern, and it is the pattern that finally determines the significance of any one particular sign, symptom, or complaint.

If the signs accompanying dry eyes were to point to aspects of Excess, as would a strong pulse, severe headaches, pus discharge from the eyes, and so on, the complaint would probably be seen as part of a pattern of Liver Fire or Arrogant Liver Yang Ascending.

Dry eyes could also be part of a Deficient Kidney Yin pattern if a different set of signs such as a rapid, frail pulse, backache, urination difficulties, and tinnitus were present. It is possible for dry eyes to be understood as part of a pattern of External Heat Violating the Lungs if the complaint is found amid such signs as acute onset, cough, fever, chills, and rapid, floating pulse. Less typical possibilities would be various Deficient Qi or Deficient Yang patterns, which generally have "wet" complaints. In that case, an atypical dryness of the eyes would be interpreted as the Qi or Yang unable to raise Water.[1] Sometimes aspects of two different patterns emerge. Dry eyes are frequently mentioned in clinical records as part of a pattern of Kidney Jing and Liver Yin, both Deficient; or Liver Blood and Spleen Qi, both Deficient.

All patterns are forms and combinations of Yin and Yang. Fire or Wind is Yang. Insufficient Qi, Insufficient Blood Jing, or Insufficient Shen is Yin. Dampness, Mucus, or Cold is Yin (Water, Cold) within Yang (Excess). Dryness (Deficient Yin) is Yang (Heat) within Yin (Deficiency). The sign of dry eyes can thus imply that the nourishing aspects of the body are in a Yin condition (Deficient Blood) or that there is a Yin condition with aspects of relative excess Yang (Deficient Yin). Or the sign may point to Yin with aspects of excessive Yang (Arrogant Yang) or pure Yang (Heat Pernicious Influence), or indeed a Yin condition of the active aspects of the body (Deficient Yang or Qi).

Ultimately, Chinese medicine begins and ends with Yin and Yang and never goes outside Yin and Yang. Discerning the Organs involved in the patterns only helps to pinpoint the preponderant location of the Yin-Yang disharmony.

Although Yin and Yang are manifested in signs and symptoms and all patterns are composed of signs and symptoms, it must be emphasized that Chinese medical treatment is never symptomatic. Treatment is based on the complete pattern and on the principle of reharmonizing bodily imbalance. For a Heat pattern, cooling herbs or acupuncture techniques are employed; for a Cold pattern, warming herbs or acupuncture techniques are used. For Deficiency, the body is nourished; for Excess, the body is drained. Finer shadings and complexities of these general patterns mandate finer and more subtle shadings of treatment, but finally what is Yang is reharmonized by Yin and what is Yin is reharmonized by Yang.[2]

For the hypothetical patient with dry eyes, each possible pattern would require a different and distinct treatment of herbs and/or acupuncture points to reharmonize the whole organism. The symptom itself would not be primarily or directly treated.[3]

Historically, most traditional systems for medicine have had parallel notions of reharmonizing opposites. For the classical Greeks,

> Bodily health was dependent on the rightly proportioned mixture of physical opposites: hot and cold, wet and dry [which are identified with the four humors: blood, phlegm, yellow bile, and black bile]. If they are in a state of *harmonia* in the body, then as the doctor in Plato's *Symposium* puts it, the most mutually hostile elements in it are reconciled and taught to live in amity: "and by the most hostile I mean the most sharply opposed as hot to cold, bitter to sweet, dry to wet." This dogma of the importance of maintaining—or restoring in the case of sickness—the right quantitative relationship between opposite qualities became the cornerstone of Greek medicine.[4]

Any example of premodern-scientific, prequantitative, pretechnological medical thinking reveals a commitment to the idea of balance. There are striking similarities to be found in the Greek medicine of antiquity, in the practice of the Arab physicians who followed them, and in the Hindu Ayurvedic systems (see Chapter 7, note 6). In all these cultures, the method of examining a patient and evaluating health and illness involved *qualitative* correspondences. Aspects of bodily activity or illness were found to correspond to some element in nature or to an emblem that was believed to be the foundation of natural existence. Health and illness were usually defined in terms of balance.

There is also a *quantitative* stream in Greek thought, expressed in parts of the Hippocratic corpus and echoed 500 years later by Galen in Rome, that is fundamentally different from the Chinese conception of balance. In Greco-Roman medical thought, the opposing elements are often forms of entities that are physically "compounded" in the body—building blocks as it were. For example, in the *Nature of Man* Hippocrates says:

> The body of man has in itself blood, phlegm, yellow bile, and black bile; these make up the nature of his body and through these he feels pain or enjoys health. Now he enjoys the most perfect health when these elements are duly proportioned to one another in respect of compounding power and bulk and when *they are perfectly mingled*. Pain is felt when one of these elements is in defect or excess, or is isolated in the body without being compounded with all the others. For when an element is isolated and stands by itself, not only must the place where it left become diseased, but the place where it stands in a flood must, because of excess, cause pain and distress.[5]

Classical Western physicians who followed parts of the Galenic tradition believed that the elements themselves—as distinct from the single, unified organism—could be treated. In Chinese thought, the complementary opposites are really descriptions of tendencies of the activity of the whole organism. The Chinese can speak of rebalancing a bodily disharmony that has the nature of Heat, but not of a body having too much Heat or black bile. One system seeks to reapportion various elements of the body; the other is concerned with rebalancing the whole body.

In the West, the *qualitative* correspondence formulations of Hippocrates were gradually superseded by other, more etiological and analytic strains of Greek medical thought. After the scientific revolution of the seventeenth century, the last remnants of the theory of symbolic, humoral emblems were abandoned and medicine followed science in the attempt to quantify observable phenomena. Images of quality were left behind for precise units of quantity that operated according to the mechanical laws of chemistry and physics. Reality had become fragmented.

In our description of Chinese patterns of disharmony—the clinical landscape—only the simplest, most basic configurations have been presented thus far. The bodily landscapes we have sketched may be compared to the simple figures of people, houses, birds, and trees that children draw when they first try to depict the world. So far, only patterns that are clear, distinct, simple, and neat have been presented.

In a clinical situation, however, patterns often appear to merge or to be blurred and complexly shaded. The case histories in Chapter 8 were an attempt to find real yet simple clinical applications of the Chinese conceptual framework, but even the simplest examples were fairly complex because real people do not often manifest signs and symptoms that fit neatly together.

The process of discerning more complex patterns is different—not in kind, but in degree—from the process of recognizing basic patterns. Signs that do not easily blend into a simple pattern are analyzed in the same way that the signs pointing to any of the Eight Principal Patterns are analyzed (see Chapter 7). One must consider, for example, whether the sign presents a Yin aspect within a Yang configuration, or whether it is an illusionary sign that just resembles Yin within a "pure" Yang pattern, or whether perhaps it is part of a secondary pattern unrelated to a primary pattern.

To illustrate this process, let us consider one sign seen in the examination of the tongue. A very pale, swollen tongue (a Yin sign) usually fits together with an excessively moist tongue (also a Yin sign). If, however, a very pale tongue is accompanied by excessive dryness, a more complex perception and analysis must take place. Does the dryness point to a pattern that has both Yin and Yang aspects, such as Deficient Kidney Jing? Is the dryness an illusionary sign of Yin caused by serious pure Deficient Yang unable to move and raise Water? Or is the dryness part of a secondary pattern such as External Wind/Heat occurring along with a primary pattern of, say, Deficient Kidney Yang? The physician must draw upon sensitivity and experience to determine the relationship among the signs and so discern the essence of the pattern.

In a clinical situation, the configuration of signs will often suggest many different patterns. For example, a continuum of Liver Heat patterns was described in Chapter 8. Chinese medical theory has assigned names to three points on this continuum; but an actual case of Liver Heat may manifest signs appropriate to neither pure Excess Fire, nor pure Empty Fire, nor even to an equal mixture of the two (Arrogant Liver Yang Ascending). Often, the actual patient will exhibit a combination of the various signs of the three patterns.

Signs suggesting contradictory tendencies are also common. There is, for example, an established classical pattern of disharmony called Hot Stomach/Cold Intestines, which is characterized by hot, putrid vomitus, red tongue, and a desire for cold drinks, along with watery, odorless stools and an empty pulse. Such a situation shows that there is a whole constellation of more complex patterns of disharmony which require yet finer shadings in the clinical landscape.

This book has tried to present the process—the logic and the art—a Chinese doctor follows to reach diagnostic conclusions. It has described how a Chinese physician gathers and weaves together parts in order to see a whole that is greater than the sum of its parts, a whole that approximates the actual complexity of a human being. Yet the process of diagnosis has another side to it as well, one that is tied to clinical practice.

At the same time that the physician is weaving parts into a whole, he or she can also see the *whole in a part*. For example, although the pulse is the most reliable indicator of the overall shape of a disharmony, a truly adept physician can diagnose from almost any sign. In the finest shadings of a particular emotion or tongue or manner of walking, the master physician can discern a pattern, because the whole leaves its characteristic imprint on each part.

An expert physician can recognize an entire disharmony by merely listening to a cough. A pattern of External Cold Wind Invading the Lungs, for example, would probably be associated with a round, full cough in a patient who does not have an agitated manner. An External Hot Wind pattern would manifest in an agitated cough with a drier sound, and there would be difficulty in coughing up sputum. Mucus Obstructing the Lungs would produce a full, high-pitched, watery sound, less forceful than that of an Exterior pattern, and a lot of sputum. The cough of a Deficient Lung Yin pattern would be raspy, weak, and frail. The Kidneys not Grasping the Qi would produce a short, weak cough that might seem to knock the person over. A Liver Invading the Lungs cough would have a spurting, projectile quality, with many coughs in a series and then a rest, because the Liver controls smooth movement. The cough of Congealed Blood Obstructing the Chest would be weak, and the sound might have a sloshy texture.[6]

The ability to read such imprints is the highest diagnostic skill of the Chinese physician. It was epitomized for me by an elderly Chinese doctor with whom I once studied. This physician watched a stranger enter a room and promptly asked him when he'd had his gall bladder removed!

Weaving parts to see a whole and seeing the whole in individual parts are polar complements: They are opposite modes of perception, but both are required in the process of diagnosis. This recognition of the whole in an individual part reveals the diagnostic process to be more than just the summation of signs. Because the whole is always greater than the parts, and the addition of parts can seldom capture a unique whole, the physician must bring a clinical judgment and sensitivity to each patient in a situation that partakes of the artistic disciplines of Chinese civilization.

A Chinese artist is concerned, not so much with the physical reality of the horse, the mountain, or the flower that he is painting, but with capturing the spirit of what is depicted. The essence of a painting is in each stroke. The Chinese physician is as much an artist as the Chinese painter. He or she is "dedicated to the expression of the inner spirit instead of the physical verisimilitude [and the] painting should reflect a . . . spontaneous and instantaneous flow of the brush."[7] The diagnostic process attempts to capture the essence of an individual just as a Chinese painting renders the essence of a particular landscape.

This view of the doctor as artist gives great stature to the Chinese physician, but no more so than the Western view. And, while both Chinese and Western medicine assert that a doctor can only become a good doctor through extensive clinical experience, Chinese medicine does place a greater emphasis on the development of sensitivity.

This emphasis is a crucial difference between the two medical systems. A Western physician who has completed training believes himself or herself already armed with the necessary science and skills. Clinical practice then represents the zone in which greater speed, accuracy, and familiarity are achieved. A Chinese doctor does not emerge from training with precisely this kind of confidence. He or she not only has been taught a science, but has also been equipped with a complex yet supple instrument with which to approach the human being. To master it will take a lifetime of practice. If we ignore for a moment that the aim of both Western and Eastern medical practice is to alleviate suffering and cure patients, then Chinese medicine does appear to have more in common with artistic disciplines than does Western medicine. The truly skilled Chinese physician, like the Chinese painter, poet, calligrapher, and swordsman, is a master of the sure stroke of discernment.

This book has focused on elementary diagnosis, yet the reality of an individual human being eludes not only the simple patterns presented here, but also the most sophisticated net of patterns. With a gritty stubbornness, real human disorders persistently fall into the tiny spaces between patterns and between words. Distinguishing patterns of disharmony takes the physician just so close to a particular disharmony; the attempt is completed in treatment—in particular combinations of herbs and/or acupuncture points. In fact, it could be said that any pattern of disharmony is actually defined by the treatment prescribed for its rebalancing.

It is for this reason that the great bulk of written material in the Chinese medical corpus concerns therapeutics. Most of the books mentioned in this book's historical Bibliography (Appendix I) and other appendices deal with methods of treatment. The theory described in this book is the surface tip of the iceberg, as it were: Understanding theory is only the beginning of understanding therapy. Entire Chinese volumes detail the intricacies of treatment appropriate to the various shadings of a single pattern. Words alone cannot describe a pattern—it must be approached by determining the herbs and acupuncture points in the exact proportion, quantity, and quality that will match the exact movement of Yin and Yang in each individual patient.

To prescribe such a precise treatment, the physician must be familiar with the effect of the vast Chinese pharmacopoeia on specific symptoms and patterns; must know how substances modify one another's properties in combination; must know the use of the classical prescriptions; and, finally, must understand how to adjust prescriptions for situations that inevitably differ slightly from any previously encountered. This holds true for acupuncture as well: The physician must know the characteristics of each point, its function, its effect on disharmonies, and must understand exactly how to combine points when approaching a particular disorder.

It is through herbology and acupuncture—in the addition of a certain herb or point, in tiny adjustments of the quantity of herbs or of hand technique—that the physician reflects the subtle shadings unique to every patient. A skilled physician can read a prescription and thereby visualize an individual's particular pattern of disharmony, know which parts of the body are affected and how, understand the severity of the symptoms and their duration, tell what other symptoms and tendencies exist, and often even sense the emotional makeup of the patient—a prescription is *that* sensitive and faithful to a patient's being. Treatment, therefore, touches the patient in a twofold way: It both expresses and attempts to heal the disharmony.

Notes

1. Another possibility is a Deficient Qi and Deficient Blood pattern in which the dryness is interpreted as a Deficiency of the Moistening aspect of the Blood. See Chapter 8, note 3.

2. The principle of treatment is so integral to Chinese thought that one can find a summary of it in the *Tao-te Ching*, chap. 77: "When [the string] is high, bring it down / when it is low, raise it up. / When it is excessive, reduce it. / When it is insufficient, supplement it." Chan, *Chinese Philosophy*, p. 174.

Sun Si-miao, the greatest physician of the Tang dynasty (618–907 C.E.), put this therapeutic principle in a famous negative formulation: "If Excess is added to, Deficiency reduced, flow drained, obstruction blocked, Cold chilled, Heat warmed, then illness increases and instead of viewing a patient's life, I see his death." Thousand Ducat Prescriptions [19], sec. 1, chap. 2, p. 1.

3. Chinese texts in general distinguish between treating the "outward manifestation" (*biao*), which means the symptoms, and treating the "root" (*ben*), which means the disharmony pattern. By treating the root, one usually expects the "appearance" or symptoms to disappear. But in certain situations one must apply the traditional saying: "In urgency, treat the outward manifestations" (quoted by Ma Ruo-shui in his Theoretical Foundations [62], p. 33). For example, if a patient is hemorrhaging and there is considerable bleeding, the physician will first attempt to stop the bleeding—the symptom—for temporary relief so that he can later treat the pattern. Or, in the case of severe ascites, if fluid in the abdomen is hindering respiration, the doctor would temporarily treat the symptom. It is also common to treat both the symptom and the root simultaneously in order to relieve the patient's discomfort while reharmonizing the underlying pattern. Many other such clinical situations are mentioned in chap. 65 of the *Su Wen*, sec. 18, which is mainly devoted to this distinction between manifestation and root.

4. W. K. C. Guthrie, *The Greek Philosophers* (New York: Harper & Row, 1950, 1975), p. 41.

5. Jones, *Hippocrates and Heracleitus*, vol. 4, pp. 11–13. Emphasis added. The *Nature of Man* is one of the last and most theoretical of the Hippocratic writings. It is usually attributed to Polybus, Hippocrates' son-in-law.

6. Chap. 38 of the *Su Wen* is titled "Discussion on Coughing" and is devoted to distinguishing coughs produced by the various Organs. Its method is to rely primarily on variations of accompanying symptoms. For instance, a cough that is part of a Liver disharmony is said to induce flank pain, making it difficult to twist the trunk (*Su Wen*, sec. 10, chap. 38, pp. 214–217). Coughing itself, however, also indicates that at least the Lungs are affected, for coughing is the sound of the Lungs (*Su Wen*, sec. 7, chap. 23, p. 150).

7. Chan, *Chinese Philosophy*, p. 210.

For the purpose of discussion, we may consider traditional Chinese medical examination, diagnosis, and treatment as three distinct categories. In practice, however, they are phases of a continuous process. The patterns of disharmony are the framework of this process, and so, in a sense, they comprise a theory. The Western mind, however, requires that a theory sum up phenomena and formulate a general principle to explain their nature and relationship. A theory implies a truth. Are patterns of disharmony real and true? This is a tricky question that brings us to the abyss that separates Chinese and Western thought.

The Chinese world-view is circular and self-contained. It imagines that the universe is a whole, a macrocosm, made up of the constant unfolding and flux of Yin and Yang. Chinese medicine, like Chinese thought in general, begins and ends with this notion of a whole, within which all the parts are related to each other and also to the whole. The Chinese physician begins with a knowledge of the whole, made up of the countless details codified in traditional medical texts. Through clinical experience, he or she develops a sensitivity to the individual. And in the end, the physician touches one concrete manifestation of the whole—a manifestation that is *itself* a whole. The movement between these two wholes, from the macrocosm of all bodily phenomena to the microcosm of one unique human being, is mediated by the conceptual framework of the patterns of disharmony.

The concept of patterns of disharmony describes the movement of Yin and Yang in the body, but also exemplifies the way in which Yin and Yang unfold in the universe. The Eight Principal Patterns—Interior/Exterior, Deficiency/Excess, Cold/Hot, and Yin/Yang—interrelate in the body as they do in the universe. Any pattern of disharmony that emerges when these aspects of Yin and Yang intertwine with a patient's specific signs is thus a particular manifestation of the universal movement of Yin and Yang. All phenomena partake of the whole.

Patterns of disharmony are real and true in the sense that they provide a way to perceive the Chinese notion of what has been called "the web that has no weaver."[1] The web is the macrocosm—the universe—that is considered to be uncreated, but to exist through the dictates of its own inner nature: that is, through the constant unfolding of Yin and Yang. There is no "truth" behind or above the things we see; there is no creator or first cause; yet the things we see continue, and their continuing is the eternal process of the universe.

Perhaps only the words of a Taoist philosopher can take us any closer to this paradoxical reality:

> The operations of Heaven are profoundly mysterious. It has water-levels for levelling, but it does not use them; it has plumblines for setting things upright, but it does not use them. It works in deep stillness. . . .
>
> Thus it is said, Heaven has no form and yet the myriad things are brought to perfection. It is like the most impalpable of featureless essences, and yet the myriad changes are all brought about by it. So also the sage is busied about nothing, and yet the thousand executives of State are effective in the highest degrees.
>
> This may be called the untaught teaching, and the wordless edict.[2]

The Chinese description of reality does not penetrate to a truth; it can only be a poetic description of a truth that cannot be grasped. The Heart, Lung, and Kidneys of this volume are not a physical heart, lung, or kidneys; instead they are personae in a descriptive drama of health and illness. For the Chinese, this description of the eternal process of Yin and Yang is the only way to try to explain either the workings of the universe or the workings of the human body. And it is enough, because the process is all there is; no underlying truth is ever within reach. The truth is immanent in everything and is the process itself.

Can a system of knowledge rooted in such a metaphysics have anything to communicate to Western science? By now, Chinese medicine, especially acupuncture, has achieved limited acceptance at the periphery of the Western medical enterprise. Acupuncture is the object of widespread curiosity, and attempts are being made to integrate certain of its techniques into the mainstream of Western medical practice. In some areas of society, the practitioner of Chinese medicine is even enjoying a kind of vogue. People have always had inflated expectations about medicine, and the Chinese doctor can all too easily become a focus for those who hope for a cure-all, an infallible elixir, a side-show potion that the medical establishment either doesn't know or conspires to suppress.

The current turning away from Western medicine, however, cannot be explained solely on the basis of unrealistic expectations. It is more likely that many people have begun to see that too often Western medicine is simply not concerned with general well-being because it can only assess very small, discrete bits of information. Also it is rooted in a society whose routine processes not only provoke stress but contaminate the environment to such an extent that every new comfort may conceal a new threat to life. Our medicine parallels our society: New cures often produce side effects of unexpected virulence. Moreover, our central medical institution, the hospital, is structured like nothing so much as a health factory—a contradiction in terms.

Chinese medicine offers a different vision of health and disease, one that is implicitly critical of Western medicine because it refuses to see the individual as an entity separate from his or her environment. Most important, Chinese medicine attempts to locate illness within the unbroken context or field of an individual's total physical and psychological being. It aims to cure through treatments that encompass the whole of the individual as closely as possible. In contrast, the ideal of Western medicine is to probe with laserlike accuracy, penetrating to the microscopic agent of disease in the tissue, the cell, and ultimately the DNA molecule. The chief weakness of Western medicine, in short, is that it tends not to see the whole.

Chinese medicine has other notable strengths. Chinese remedies are sometimes more effective than Western ones, and they are generally gentler and safer. Chinese prescriptions, for example, do not produce side effects because they are balanced to reflect a patient's entire state of being. Chinese medicine, in addition, is better able than Western medicine to treat illnesses arising from the complex interrelationships of physical and mental phenomena. (Indeed, the very idea of the unity of body, mind, and spirit is one Western scientific blind spot.) Chinese medicine, because it emphasizes balance and relationship more than measurable quantity, can also frequently discover and treat a disorder before it is perceptible by the most sophisticated Western diagnostic techniques. Chinese medicine is capable of touching those places that evade the microscope and that, after all, constitute human reality.

Chinese medicine shares with other traditional qualitative medical schemes, such as the classical Greek or Hindu models, an ability to measure quality. Modern Western medicine, following on the heels of the scientific revolution, broke the living continuity of experience, the actual texture of human reality, into measurable units. Reality becomes perceptible only in relationship to a projection of units of space, time, motion, and matter. For many modern doctors, the idiosyncratic response to illness—e.g., how the patient covers himself or herself with a blanket, or the patient's ambience, Spirit, emotions, or values—has become buried in the transition from the traditional to the scientific. This may have been appropriate at one point in history and led to many monumental achievements in health care, but problems have arisen. Much that is human and medically effective has been lost or remains to be discovered because modern health care too often avoids seeing human beings as unique, organic beings. It can easily fail to recognize that people are not simply isolable events reducible to mechanical and experimental models.

On the other hand, no honest Chinese physician can fail to be awed by the achievements of Western medicine, by the ease with which a drug such as streptomycin, or a technique such as open heart surgery, can penetrate to the core of disorders that Chinese medicine finds complex and intractable.

Because Chinese medicine collects only external signs in order to perceive an overall form, it has blind spots of its own. And one of its greatest strengths—its perception of the body as a whole—can be its greatest weakness. For Chinese medicine can never separate the part from the whole, even when a clinical situation demands that the overall relationships be ignored and a particular part be treated directly. A tumor or a large gallstone must sometimes be identified, isolated, and removed. Chinese medicine rarely does this—it lacks both the theory and the technique.

And, because it stresses quality and proportion, and sees quantity as secondary, Chinese medicine is weak on prognosis. For example, most tumors that are fixed in location are thought to result from Congealed Blood and are treated by appropriate reharmonizing techniques. But Chinese medicine cannot focus on the tumor itself to determine whether it is malignant or benign. A good Chinese doctor can often sense that a disharmony is life-threatening, but this is not a central issue in the Chinese medical method. He or she cannot attempt to offer a quantifiable prognosis the way Western medicine can.

Modern Western medicine is clear, precise, and definite. It has the sure stroke of measurement as opposed to the more fallible stroke of judgment. Its precision and technology allow swift intervention that can be crucial in life-threatening situations.

Modern Western and traditional Chinese medicine are two discrete systems of theory and practice that have complementary strengths and weaknesses. They seem to need each other very much. Can either system absorb anything of real consequence from the other?

On the Chinese side, such hope is unreasonable. Although Chinese medicine has developed considerably in its history, this progress is a long spiral that moves forever around its point of origin, the ancient texts. Since this point of origin is assumed to contain the seed of everything that can be known, all development is a form of slow exegesis within a broad conceptual framework. The ancient books are the language of Chinese medicine, and while the vocabulary can be expanded and enriched, the grammar and syntax are fixed. Complete and self-contained, traditional Chinese medicine is incapable of assimilating anything that challenges its fundamental assumptions. New ideas and substances can be identified and even incorporated, but they can never expand or transform the fundamental matrix. So, vitamin B_{12} is very Yang, penicillin is very Yin, but there is nothing beyond Yin and Yang.

Perhaps it is precisely because Chinese thought is uninterested in cause, is circular, and sees the universe as being in a state of spontaneous cooperation without a creator or regulator, that it lacks an impulse to go beyond its own organization of observations. There is no desire to discover an ultimate reality transcending phenomena, no need to go beyond the imminent. Chinese thought cannot expand or transcend its own limitations. Its concept of the unity of opposition calls for sharpened clarity, one-pointed vision, and it precludes the idea that humankind can ever attain higher levels of truth. Ultimately, "returning is the movement of the Tao."[3]

At first glance, Western medicine seems equally impervious to alternate modes of perception. Given its current bureaucratic entrenchment, its disposition toward technological solutions, and its arrogant faith in its own destiny, a strong argument can be made that Western medicine will never see anything more in the Chinese system than a curious bag of tricks. Yet Western science, as distinct from institutionalized Western medicine, has in recent years undergone some important changes. The effect of these theoretical developments has been a questioning of explanations based solely on linear cause and effect, and a movement toward a new understanding of phenomena—an understanding not unlike some of the Chinese notions presented in this book. Joseph Needham, for example, suggests that

the characteristic Chinese conception of causality in the world of Nature was something like that which the comparative physiologist has to form when he studies the nerve-net of coelenterates, or what has been called the "endocrine orchestra" of mammals. In these phenomena it is not very easy to find out which element is taking the lead at any given time. The image of an orchestra evokes that of a conductor, but we still have no idea what the "conductor" of the synergistic operations of the endocrine glands in the higher vertebrates may be. Moreover, it is now becoming probable that the higher nervous centres of mammals and man himself constitute a kind of reticular continuum or "nerve-net" much more flexible in nature than the traditional conception of telephone wires and exchanges visualized. At one time one gland or nerve-centre may take the highest place in a hierarchy of causes and effects, at another time another, hence the phrase "hierarchically fluctuating." All this is quite a different mode of thought from the simpler "particulate" or "billiard-ball" view of causality, in which the prior impact of one thing is the sole cause of the motion of the other.[4]

Other perceptions have arisen from recent Western musings on the consequences of quantum theory:

Parts . . . are seen to be an immediate connection, in which their dynamical relationships depend, in an irreducible way, on the state of the whole system (and, indeed, on that of broader systems in which they are contained, extending ultimately and in principle to the entire universe). Thus, one is led to a new notion of *unbroken wholeness* which denies the classical idea of analyzability of the world into separately and independently existent parts. . . .[5]

Ecological criticism of modern medicine has brought forth new ideas:

> Microbial agents, disturbances in essential metabolic processes, deficiencies in growth factors or in hormones, and physiological stress are now regarded as specific causes of disease. . . . Unquestionably the doctrine of specific etiology has been the most constructive force in medical research for almost a century and the theoretical and practical achievements to which it has led constitute the bulk of modern medicine. Yet few are the cases in which it has provided a complete account of the causation of disease. Despite frantic efforts, the causes of cancer, of arteriosclerosis, of mental disorders, and of the other great medical problems of our times remain undiscovered. It is generally assumed that the cause of all diseases can and will be found in due time by bringing the big guns of science to bear on the problems. In reality, however, search for *the* causes may be a hopeless pursuit because most disease states are the indirect outcome of a constellation of circumstances rather than the direct result of single determinant factors.[6]

Even in the inner sanctum of health care, calls are being made for changes to new paradigms: "It took two hundred years for medicine to incorporate the insights of classical physics, the physics of Newton. More than fifty years after the 'quantum revolution' in modern physics medicine has yet to incorporate its standards."[7]

Paradoxically, these new ideas in Western science, ideas that point toward an awareness of the totality of being, have arisen as a direct result of the Western urge to penetrate phenomena and to find the transcendent truth behind them. Western thought, at its most noble and honest, is nourished by the constant tension between unknown and known, imperfect and perfect. Western humanity is quickened by a metaphysical dilemma— on the one hand, it was created in the image of the Almighty, and on the other, it was created from dust.[8] Western humankind is enmeshed in creating and becoming; it labors in growth and development. Perhaps this is a consequence of Judeo-Christian emphasis on an omnipresent, transcendent God making impossible the attainment of human perfection. Perhaps this idea is related to the Greek metaphysical notion that "we are what we are because of what we can become." In any case, it is an idea altogether missing in China, an attitude that contrasts sharply with the Chinese view of truth as inherent in the harmonious arrangement of the given.[9]

Western science can be criticized for insensitivity, for arrogance, for storming Heaven—but the fact remains that it is humble, and humility is integral to the best scientific thought. For all its misuses, the idea of progress implies that not everything has been achieved, that more is yet to come. In order to remain science, science must believe that what it discovers tomorrow may undermine and revolutionize everything it believes today. Western science, unlike traditional Chinese thought, is necessarily receptive to the new. And there is now a new sense of organism, interconnectedness, quality, and unity emerging on the frontiers of modern science. The development of Western thought is creating room for new models and theories.

As science encounters Chinese medicine, Western investigation will inevitably tend to reduce the techniques of acupuncture and herbology to a biochemical Western model (see Chapter 4, notes 10 and 11). There is hope, however, that the uncanny Taoist spirit of interrelatedness will illuminate those places that evade the Western yardstick so that more than just new techniques are learned. By moving toward a view of human health and illness that is both analytical and synthetic, the West may be able to create a more exact paradigm of biological reality and, by quantum leaps, move the methods of Chinese medicine to new heights of precision and efficacy.

While mystery and profundity can be found in both East and West, perhaps a more vibrant insight lies in the West with its idea of creator and creating, being and becoming. In the dynamics of the Judeo-Christian-Islamic transcendent Creator, or of Greek metaphysics, can be found the seeds, hope, and impetus for a constant striving toward progressive maturation, increased knowledge, and ever-deeper recognition of truth. Dy-. namic revelation and unfolding are implicit in the dialectics of the West.

The story is told that on Mount Sinai, in addition to the Law, Moses was given a list of all diseases and their cures. This Book was later destroyed by a pious king who was anxious to restore humility among his subjects.[10] At its best, Western science knows that we can never reconstruct this Book, but it also knows that, in the face of our own incompleteness, we must continue to try. The books of traditional Chinese medicine have been written. The Western book, which is always being created, may yet include Chinese characters.

Notes

1. "The conception . . . [is] of a vast pattern. There is a web of relationships throughout the universe, the nodes of which are things and events. Nobody wove it, but if you interfere with its texture, you do so at your peril. . . . This web woven by no weaver . . . approach[es] a developed philosophy of organism." Needham, *Science and Civilization*, vol. 2, p. 556.

2. Lü's Spring and Autumn Annals (c. 240 B.C.E.), quoted in Needham, *The Great Titration*, p. 324.

3. *Tao-te Ching*, chap. 40.

4. Needham, *Science and Civilization*, vol. 2, p. 289.

5. David Bohm, and B. Hiley, "On the Intuitive Understanding of Non-locality as Implied by Quantum Theory," cited in Zukav, *The Dancing Wu-Li Masters* (New York: William Morrow & Co., 1971), p. 315.

6. René Dubos, *Mirage of Health* (New York: Harper Colophon Books, Harper & Row, 1959, 1979), p. 102.

7. H. Bursztajn et al., *Medical Choices, Medical Chances* (New York: Seymour Lawrence / Delacorte Press, 1981), p. xiii.

8. Immanuel Kant spoke of a similar sense of tension and transcendence as the source of creativity:

Two things fill the mind with ever new and increasing admiration and awe: . . . the starry heavens above me and the moral law within me. . . . The former view of a countless multitude of worlds annihilates, as it were, my importance as an animal creature, which must give back to the planet (a mere speck in the universe) the matter from which it came. . . . The latter, on the contrary, infinitely raises my worth as that of an intelligence by my personality, in which the moral law reveals a life independent of all animality and even of the whole world of sense . . . a destination which is not restricted to the conditions and limits of this life but reaches into the infinite. [*Critique of Practical Reason*, trans. by Lewis White Beck (Indianapolis: Bobbs-Merrill, 1956), p. 166).]

Viktor Frankl has described the same idea in psychological terms:

Mental health is based on a certain degree of tension, the tension between what one is and what one should become. . . . What man needs is not homeostasis but . . . spiritual dynamics in a polar field of tension. [*Man's Search for Meaning* (New York: Simon & Schuster, 1962), pp. 104–105.]

Franz Kafka's rendering of this idea is as follows:

He is a free and secure citizen of the world, for he is fettered to a chain which is long enough to give him the freedom of all earthly space, and yet only so long that nothing can drag him past the frontiers of the world. But simultaneously he is a free and secure citizen of Heaven as well, for he is also fettered by a similarly designed heavenly chain. So that if he heads, say for the earth, his heavenly collar throttles him, and if he heads for Heaven, his earthly one does the same. And yet all the possibilities are his, and he feels it; more, he actually refuses to account for the deadlock by an error in the original fettering. [*The Great Wall of China* (New York: Schocken Books, 1936, 1970), Reflection #63, pp. 174–175.]

9. "The Chinese are perhaps unique among the world's major peoples in that their early traditions include neither a creation myth nor epic legends about ancient folk migrations." Charles O. Hucker, *China's Imperial Past* (Stanford, Calif.: Stanford University Press, 1975), p. 22.

10. Babylonian Talmud, Zeraim, *Berakoth*, 106, and Mo'ed, *Pesachim*, 566. The king was Hezekiah.

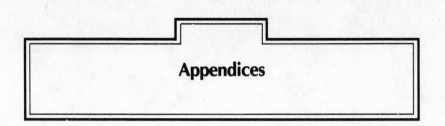

Appendices

APPENDIX A
The Stages of Disease:
A Series of Clinical Scenes

This appendix illustrates the evolution of Chinese medical thinking and demonstrates its vitality. Chinese medicine is a body of knowledge composed of a great many commentaries written during the past twenty centuries. Although there is apparent confusion in its history, it would be a mistake to overlook the fact that Chinese medicine has also undergone a lengthy process of self-clarification. Chinese medicine always goes back to its respected and revered sources, but they are continuously scrutinized and supplemented. In short, the living tradition perpetually rediscovers itself.

This process of self-revitalization is exemplified by historical developments in the Chinese approach to febrile diseases. Among the most common clinical pictures observed by physicians East and West are illnesses that involve fever and a sequence of events that includes onset, peak, and recovery. (Until very recently, these illnesses were the major cause of death.) In the modern West, these disorders would probably be described as infectious and contagious diseases. Chinese physicians describe such febrile illnesses as sequential patterns of disharmony.

Initially, these patterns were thought to occur within a six-stage sequence. Later, a possible four-stage sequence was also developed, to supplement the earlier thinking and to give physicians an alternative theory with which to work. Both the six-stage and the four-stage sequences comprise the basic perceptual framework with which Chinese physicians diagnose and treat febrile illnesses.[1] The concept of pattern sequences in febrile diseases also elaborates on the Exterior patterns of the Eight Principal Patterns, as well as the patterns of Pernicious Influences.

The Pattern of Six Stages
(liu-jing bian-zheng)

The idea of a six-stage pattern of disease was first developed by one of the greatest physicians in Chinese history, Zhang Zhong-jing, in his classic *Shanghan Lun* (Discussion of Cold-induced Disorders), written around 220 C.E. Dr. Zhang studied and synthesized all the medical writings of his time to develop the six-stage pattern. His ideological point of departure was an unclear and obscure passage from the *Nei Jing* that describes six disease stages,[2] and from this he created an elaborate, logical, and practical sequence pattern. The treatment method and prescriptions described in this pattern are still memorized by all practitioners of traditional Chinese medicine.

Dr. Zhang's Discussion of Cold-induced Disorders became the second most important work in Chinese medical literature and generated at least as many commentaries as the *Nei Jing*, even though it emphasized treatment methods and prescriptions rather than theory. The elegance and subtlety of the Discussion lies in the minimal number of signs it uses to delineate a pattern and in the delicacy and precision of its prescriptions and their permutations.

The six stages presented in the Discussion comprise a series of patterns that map out the course of diseases characterized by Pernicious Influences entering the body and generating fever. Usually, Dr. Zhang suggests, such diseases begin with the first stage and proceed in sequence to the sixth; however, a disease can go straight to any stage, skip stages, or even move in reverse.

The first stage is called Tai Yang (Greater Yang). In the Discussion, this stage is characterized by fear of Cold or Wind, fever, headache, and a floating pulse.[3] (Within the rubric of the Eight Principal Patterns, this is a pattern of External Cold Pernicious Influence.) The Discussion mentions many distinctions and variations in the Tai Yang stage.[4] This stage marks the onset of illness, after which the Pernicious Influence can enter either the Yang Ming or the Shao Yang stage.

The Yang Ming stage (Yang Brightness) is characterized by "fever, perspiration, no fear of cold, but rather a fear of heat."[5] Irritability, thirst, and rapid, big, and full pulse are the important Yang Ming signs. This stage marks the internal development of the disease, and according to the Eight Principal Patterns, this is an Interior/Heat pattern.

The third stage is Shao Yang (Lesser Yang). Logically, this category should precede Yang Ming. The order of presentation, however, is based on the original *Nei Jing* narrative and therefore was not changed. The signs that designate the Shao Yang pattern include "chills and fever coming alternately, chest and flanks distended, bitter taste in the mouth, no appetite, irritability, and urge to vomit."[6] The fever and chills resemble those of malaria, occurring separately and distinctly. Shao Yang belongs to a subcategory within the principle of Exterior/Interior and is known as a half-Exterior/half-Interior pattern. Since Shao Yang has neither the simultaneous chills and fever of an Exterior pattern nor the Interior signs of fever and no fear of cold, it is considered an in-between. This pattern is intimately tied to the Gall Bladder and Triple Burner Meridian pathways and is therefore associated with flank pain, bitterness in the mouth, blurry vision, and wiry pulse.

The first three stages—Tai Yang, Yang Ming, and Shao Yang—are patterns of Excess. The fourth and fifth stages are patterns of Deficiency and Interiority, and are not really concerned with Pernicious Influences; the sixth stage is considered a miscellaneous one. A Pernicious Influence can enter the body during the last three stages either by proceeding sequentially through the first three or by going directly inside.[7]

The fourth stage is Tai Yin (Greater Yin). It is characterized by a full and distended abdomen, lack of thirst, along with "vomiting, no appetite, great diarrhea, and occasional pain."[8] The commentaries consider this state a pattern of Deficient Spleen Yang.

The fifth stage is Shao Yin (Lesser Yin) and is thought to be a step deeper. Many commentaries call this the most serious stage. Its salient signs are "minute pulse and a great desire to sleep."[9] Other signs are aversion to cold, cold limbs, and lack of fever. The commentaries consider this stage a pattern of Deficient Yang, especially of the Kidneys.

The sixth stage is Jue Yin (Absolute Yin). Logically, it should be the deepest and most serious stage. The Discussion, however, reveals that this is actually a miscellaneous pattern in which the Yin and Yang of the body act in a complex manner so that some areas are Hot and others are Cold. The text also discusses worms.[10]

The pattern of six stages, along with its many subcategories and great number of prescriptions, was for many hundreds of years the basis for treating febrile diseases of outside origin. (The prescriptions for the last three stages served as the basis for treating Internal disharmonies.) Slowly, however, physicians began to criticize it for its omissions and one-sidedness. Many clinicians and theorists believed that Dr. Zhang's Discussion emphasized Cold Pernicious Influences to the virtual exclusion of Heat Pernicious Influences, focused on Cold Injuring the Yang while forgetting to deal with Heat Injuring the Yin, and dealt with Deficient Yang while ignoring Deficient Yin. (Also, it is possible that the nature of illness changed through the ages, with better sewage, sanitation, social stability, and improvements in nutrition.)

The Pattern of Four Stages
(wei-qi-ying-xue bian-zheng)

Later Chinese physicians working from the beginning of the Ming dynasty (1368–1644 C.E.) through the Qing dynasty (1644–1911 C.E.) developed what became known as the pattern of four stages.[11] This construct was intended to address the inadequacies of the pattern of six stages. It was not a refutation of the Discussion of Cold-induced Disorders; rather it was a supplement that provided a more comprehensive method for treating febrile diseases. Depending on the clinical signs, a Chinese doctor could now interpret the disorder by means of either the six- or the four-stage sequence. The pattern of four stages became known as a development of "Warm Disease School" (wen-re-xue). Although this school occurs late in Chinese medical history, it is universally accepted as part of the classical Chinese medical tradition, demonstrating how patterns, theories, and clinical perceptions change and are refined for greater clarity and accuracy.

The Warm Disease School traced its origins to a few scattered sentences in the *Nei Jing* that refer to Heat illnesses, such as "Winter injures with Cold, in

Spring there will be Warm illness,"[12] and to a few brief references in the Discussion, such as "Tai Yang illness, fever and thirst, no fear of cold, is Warm illness."[13]

Taking four words from the *Nei Jing* that describe physiological entities, the Warm Disease School went on to develop an alternate series of patterns of Heat illness. They depicted four broad sequential scenes of febrile disharmonies.[14] In this schematic representation, febrile diseases are thought to be able to enter four distinct depths of the body.

The first stage, called the pattern of the Wei Portion (*wei-fen-zheng*) occurs when a Pernicious Influence is in the Wei portion or the first depth of the body. (*Wei* is the Chinese word for Protective Qi.) Disharmonies of this pattern are characterized by fever, a slight fear of cold, headache, coughing, slight thirst with or without perspiration, either the tongue material or the tip of the tongue slightly red, and a floating and rapid pulse. Within the rubric of the Eight Principal Patterns, it is a pattern of Exterior Heat. It is not described in Dr. Zhang's Discussion.

The second pattern of the four stages, the pattern of the Qi Portion (*qi-fen-zheng*), occurs when the Pernicious Influence enters the Qi portion, or the second depth of the body. This happens if the Pernicious Influence is not dispelled from the Wei portion and manages to penetrate deeper into the body. Its primary sign is fever without fear of cold, which is similar to the Yang Ming stage of the six-stage sequence or to an Interior/Heat pattern of the Eight Principal Patterns. Various subpatterns develop, depending on the types of Heat involved and which Organ is invaded. The details of this stage are extensively dealt with in the literature. For example, Heat in the Lungs displays the signs of high fever, wheezing, coughing, yellow tongue moss, and thirst; Heat in the Stomach produces high fever, sweat, dark, scanty urine, constipation, abdominal and epigastric pain, and flooding pulse.

The third stage of the four stages is called the pattern of the Ying Portion (*ying-fen-zheng*). The word *Ying* describes the Nutritive aspect of Qi that is associated with Blood, and the Ying stage is the next depth of the sequence. The main signs include a scarlet red tongue, irritability, restlessness, delirium or coma, fever that is greater at night, thirst (but not so great as that associated with the Qi Portion), slight red skin eruptions, and a thin, rapid pulse. Because the Pernicious Influence is in the deeper Yin portions of the body, the tongue becomes scarlet and the Shen is very easily disturbed, while thirst is reduced because some Fluids vaporize and ascend to the tongue. Because the Ying stage is preliminary to the Blood stage, one often sees the beginning of skin rashes and eruptions, which are signs of Heat in the Blood.

The pattern of the Blood Portion (*xue-fen-zheng*) is the final, deepest, and most serious of the four stages. All signs of the Ying Portion now worsen; the patient succumbs to a high fever, delirium, or coma, is extremely irritable, and has distinct and dramatic skin eruptions and rashes. As the Heat disturbs the Blood, there is reckless movement with such signs as vomiting of blood, nosebleeds, blood in the stool or urine, and skin eruptions. The Shen may also be greatly disturbed. The Heat in this stage can injure the Yin and the Blood, thereby easily allowing Wind to arise with such signs as tremors, stiffness, eyes staring upward, and teeth locked shut. Sometimes this stage has more manifestations of Deficiency, and the Heat can be thought of as injuring the Yin, Fluids, and Blood. The signs accompanying this are low fever (morning cool / evening hot), hot palms and soles, dry teeth, sunken eyes, trembling hands, and a very thin pulse.

The Pericardium is often affected in Warm illnesses. The most common problem is Heat disturbing the Shen during a Warm illness. This phenomenon is usually described as Heat collapsing into the Pericardium. It occurs most often during the Ying or Blood stage. Whenever the Pericardium is so affected, the Shen may become unclear, and coma or delirium can develop. Serious irritability and a trembling tongue are often the first signs of such a collapse. Another common alternative pattern that also influences the Shen and accompanies External Heat illnesses is Mucus Obstructing the Pericardium. Table 12 distinguishes these two patterns.

TABLE 12

Heat Patterns Affecting the Pericardium

PATTERN

Sign	Heat Pernicious Influence Collapsing into Pericardium	Turbid Mucus Obstructing Pericardium
Shen	coma, often with convulsions or nervous activity	coma, or patient is sometimes awake
Fever	high fever	lower fever
Stool	often no change, or constipation	loose stools
Pulse	thin and rapid or wiry and rapid	soggy and rapid or slippery and rapid
Tongue	scarlet, dry material; yellow moss	red material; white, greasy moss or yellow, greasy moss

Notes

1. This topic of Chinese medical theory is called Distinguishing Patterns of External Heat Disorders (*wai-gan re-bing bian-zheng*).

2. The *Nei Jing* states that on the first day of Cold invading the body it injures the Tai Yang. On the second day it injures the Yang Ming, on the third day the Shao Yang, the fourth day the Tai Yin, the fifth day the Shao Yin, the sixth day the Jue Yin. If the disease continues, it repeats this cycle. See *Su Wen*, sec. 9, chap. 31, pp. 183–185. Tai Yang, Yang Ming, Shao Yang, Tai Yin, Shao Yin, and Jue Yin are also names for the Meridians. But a connection between the six stages and the Meridians was not explicitly stated in Chinese medical literature until a commentary on Dr. Zhang's Discussion was written by Zhu Kong in 1107 C.E. It should also be noted that although the six stages seem to be based on the *Nei Jing*, many scholars believe, because of syntactical evidence, that the Discussion of Cold-induced Disorders was written before the bulk of the *Nei Jing*.

3. Zhang, Discussion [27], sec. 1, p. 1.

4. The most important distinction in this stage is between a situation in which there is no perspiration, which is considered Excess, and a situation where there is perspiration, which is considered Deficiency.

5. Zhang, Discussion, sec. 182, p. 116.

6. Ibid., sec. 96, p. 57.

7. The last three stages are actually of little use in treating febrile illnesses and have little diagnostic value in general. They are important mainly because the recommended prescriptions are the basis for much of the traditional therapy.

8. Zhang, Discussion, sec. 273, p. 161.

9. Ibid., sec. 281, p. 166.

10. Zhang Zhong-jing's Essential Prescriptions of the Golden Chest [29], which originally was part of a single volume that included the Discussion, goes on to discuss various Interior disorders, gynecological disorders, and complex situations.

11. Among the most important of these physicians were Ye Tian-shi, whose major book was Discussion of Warm Diseases (*Wen-re Lun*, 1746 C.E.), and Wu Ju-tong, whose major work is Refined Diagnoses of Warm Diseases [23], 1798 C.E.

12. *Su Wen* [1], sec. 1, chap. 3, p. 21; also sec. 2, chap. 5, p. 35.

13. Zhang, Discussion, sec. 6, p. 3.

14. The discussion of the pattern of four stages is based on that in Nanjing Institute, Lecture Notes on Warm Illnesses [80], pp. 5–10. The discussion on the Pericardium is based on Shanghai Institute, Foundations [53], pp. 236–239.

APPENDIX B
Yang Organs in Disharmony

The main function of the Yang Organs is to receive and digest food, absorbing the useful portion and transmitting and excreting waste. Because Yang Organs are primarily involved with "impure" substances such as untransformed food, urine, and excrement, they are considered less Internal than the Yin Organs, which are concerned with the "pure" or Fundamental Substances of Qi, Blood, Jing, and Shen. Yang Organs play a less crucial role than Yin Organs in both theory and practice. In acupuncture, however, the Yang Meridians are at least as important as the Yin Meridians.

Each Yang Organ is coupled with a Yin Organ in what is called an Interior-Exterior relationship (see Table 1 in Chapter 3), and the Meridian pathways of each pair of coupled Organs are connected. Some Yang Organs have an intimate relationship with their corresponding Yin Organ. Other Yang-Yin couplings seem to be merely a mechanical working-out of Five Phase correspondences.

The correspondences between Liver and Gall Bladder, Spleen and Stomach, and Kidney and Bladder have actual physiological significance and are valuable in the practice of Chinese medical pathology. The correspondences between Heart and Small Intestine and between Lungs and Large Intestine are to be found in their Meridians and are of less consequence in the actual practice of medicine.

The Yang Organs are generally more involved with Excess and Heat disharmonies than their Yin counterparts. The most common Bladder disharmony is Damp Heat Pouring Downward (Heat/Excess), while Kidney disharmonies are usually patterns of Deficiency.

The Stomach and Spleen also exhibit these tendencies and show their complementary opposition in relation to Dampness and Dryness. The Stomach likes Dampness and is sensitive to Dryness, while the opposite is true of the Spleen. Thus, Deficient Yin of the Stomach is a common pattern, while Dampness disharmony is typical of the Spleen. The complementary relationship of the Stomach and Spleen is also emphasized by the direction of their Qi: downward from the Stomach and upward from the Spleen. Therefore, a disharmony of the Stomach will display signs of nausea, vomiting, and belching (reversals of the usual direction of movement), while the Spleen's disharmony is associated with loose bowels and hemorrhoids.

Gall Bladder and Liver disharmonies are difficult to distinguish clinically because the Liver, unlike the other Yin Organs, often tends to be associated with Heat and Excess. There is a different distinction, however, in that Gall Bladder disharmonies are often seen to be more Exterior and Liver disharmonies more Interior.

The patterns of Small Intestine and Large Intestine disharmonies are not usually related to their corresponding Yin Organs except in acupuncture, where Meridians of the Yang Organs are used to treat their corresponding Yin Organs. Most commonly, Small and Large Intestine disharmonies are related to the Spleen, with a tendency to involve Excess, Stagnation, or Heat (for instance, Damp Heat in the Large Intestine). Often the symptom of gurgling or rumbling (borborygmus) distinguishes these disharmonies from those of the Stomach and Spleen.

The Triple Burner does not exist apart from other Organs and is rarely involved in patterns that distinguish it from the other Organs. (Again, this is not true of its Meridian, which has a distinct existence and therapeutic use.)

The most common Yang Organ disharmony patterns are summarized in Tables 13–17.[1]

TABLE 13

Stomach Disharmony Patterns

Pattern	Signs	Tongue	Pulse
Stomach Fire Blazing	thirst; excessive drinking; excessive appetite; bad breath; gums swollen and painful; burning sensation in epigastrium	red material; thick yellow moss	flooding, or rapid and full
Deficient Stomach Yin	dry mouth and lips; no appetite; dry vomit or belching; constipation	peeled, reddish material	thin and rapid
Stagnant Stomach Qi[1]	epigastrium is distended and painful; pain often extends to sides; pain is often emotionally related; belching; sour taste in mouth	darkish material	wiry
Congealed Blood in Stomach	stabbing, piercing pain in epigastrium; distention; touch aggravates pain; black or dark stools; darkish face	darker material with red dots; thin yellow moss	wiry and choppy
Deficient Cold in Stomach[2]	slight, persistent pain in epigastrium; discomfort relieved by warmth, eating, and touching	pale material; moist white moss	deep or moderate without strength

[1]Often called Liver Invading Stomach.

[2]Often called Deficient Spleen Yang.

TABLE 14

Small Intestine Disharmony Patterns

Pattern	Signs	Tongue	Pulse
Deficient Cold of Small Intestine[1]	slight, persistent discomfort in lower abdomen; gurgling noises in abdomen; watery stools	pale material; thin white moss	empty
Stagnant Qi of Small Intestine[2]	groin and hypogastrium have urgent pain, often extending to lower back; one testicle descends more than the other	white moss	deep and wiry or deep and tight
Excess Heat of Small Intestine[3]	irritability; cold sores in mouth; sore throat; urination is frequent and even painful, with dark urine; lower abdomen feels full	red material; yellow moss	rapid and slippery
Obstructed Qi of Small Intestine	violent pain in abdomen; constipation; no gas passes; possible vomiting of fecal material	greasy yellow moss	wiry and full

[1]Often discussed as Deficient Spleen Qi.

[2]This pattern often describes hernias and is often discussed as Cold Obstructing the Liver Meridian.

[3]This pattern is often called Heart Fire Moving by Meridian to Small Intestine and is an exception in which the Heart and Small Intestine are clinically coupled.

TABLE 15

Large Intestine Disharmony Patterns

Pattern	Signs	Tongue	Pulse
Damp Heat Invading Large Intestine[1]	urgent need to defecate, intensifies after defecation; stool has pus or blood; burning anus; often accompanied by fever	red material; greasy yellow moss	slippery and rapid
Intestinal Abcess[2]	urgent pain in lower right abdomen; fever, or no fever; resists touch	red material; yellow moss	rapid
Exhausted Fluid of Large Intestine	constipation; dry stool; often associated with postpartum condition	red and dry material	thin

TABLE 15 *(cont.)*

Large Intestine Disharmony Patterns

Pattern	Signs	Tongue	Pulse
Cold Dampness in Large Intestine[3]	rumbling in intestine; abdomen sometimes painful; diarrhea; clear urine	moist, greasy white moss	deep and slippery
Deficient Qi of Large Intestine[4]	chronic diarrhea; slight persistent lower abdominal discomfort; rumbling in intestine; pressure relieves discomfort; cold limbs; tired Shen	pale material; white moss	frail

[1]Often called Damp Heat Dysentery.

[2]This pattern is mentioned in the *Ling Shu* and discussed in detail by Zhang Zhongjing. It is analagous to the Western entity of appendicitis.

[3]Often called Dampness Distressing the Spleen.

[4]Often called Deficient Spleen Yang.

TABLE 16

Gall Bladder Disharmony Patterns

Pattern	Signs	Tongue	Pulse
Excess Gall Bladder Heat	flank and chest are painful and distended; bitter taste in mouth; vomits bitter fluid; patient angers easily	red material; yellow moss	wiry, rapid, and full
Damp Heat in both Gall Bladder and Liver	jaundice (Yang type with bright yellow color); painful flanks; scanty, dark urine; fever; nausea; vomiting	red material; greasy yellow moss	wiry, rapid, and slippery
Deficient Gall Bladder Heat	vertigo; frightens easily; timidity; indecision; unclear vision; annoyance at little things	thin white moss	wiry and thin

TABLE 17

Bladder Disharmony Patterns

Pattern	Signs	Tongue	Pulse
Damp Heat Pouring Downward into Bladder	frequent, urgent, painful urination; fever; thirst; dry mouth; backache	red material; greasy yellow moss	wiry and rapid or slippery and rapid
Damp Heat Accumulating and Crystallizing in Bladder	urine occasionally contains sandlike pieces; difficult urination or sudden urine obstruction; occasional violent stabbing pain in lower groin or back; occasional blood in urine	reasonably normal	rapid
Turbid Damp Heat Obstructing Bladder	urine contains cloudy or murky substances	red material; greasy moss	soggy and rapid
Deficient Bladder Qi[1]	incontinence or frequent urination or bed wetting	moist white moss	deep and frail

[1]Often called Deficient Kidney Yang.

Notes

1. Tables 13–17 are based on those in Tianjin City, Traditional Chinese Internal Medicine [55], pp. 29–45, and in Anhui Institute, Clinical Handbook [68], pp. 34–38.

APPENDIX C
Patterns and Chief Complaints

When a patient consults a Chinese physician, he or she usually has a chief complaint such as fever, coughing, or intestinal problems. This complaint is part of a pattern of disharmony, and the overriding diagnostic consideration of the physician is to distinguish the pattern that accompanies the complaint. Some common complaints and the typical patterns they are integrated into are listed in Tables 18–39. Neither the complaints nor the patterns are meant to be exhaustive; only to illustrate a process. Many of the chief complaints may be found as broad pathological categories in textbooks of traditional Chinese medicine, where they are discussed at length in terms of patterns and their variations, interactions, and treatments.[1]

APPENDIX C

Fever

Fever is usually a prominent feature of most patterns of External Pernicious Influence. Deficient Yin is the major Interior pattern that involves fever, but the table also includes two other Interior patterns that are not usually associated with fever. Their inclusion is meant to illustrate the flexibility needed in Chinese medicine.

TABLE 18

Fever

Pattern	Signs	Tongue	Pulse
Exterior Cold/ Wind	fever; aversion to cold; headache or body ache; sometimes coughing; sometimes runny or stuffed nose; no thirst	thin white moss	floating and tight or floating and moderate
Exterior Heat/ Wind	fever; slight aversion to cold; headache; thirst; sore throat; sometimes cough with yellow phlegm	tip of tongue is red; slightly yellow moss	floating and rapid
External Cold and Interior Deficient Yang simultaneously	very slight fever; acute onset; desire for more clothing; desire for sleep; great aversion to cold	pale, moist material	minute
Pernicious Influence in Shao Yang stage of six stages	fever and chills are distinct (i.e., not simultaneous); no appetite; nausea	thin and white, or yellow and white, moss	wiry
Pernicious Influence in Yang Ming stage of six stages	only fever; no aversion to cold; thirst; irritability; red face; perspiration	red material; dry yellow moss	flooding, with strength, or slippery and rapid
Deficient Yin	chronic low afternoon fever; warm palms and soles; insomnia; night sweats; red cheeks	reddish material; thin moss	thin and rapid
Deficient Qi	chronic low fever (especially in morning); spontaneous sweating; fear of draft; fatigue; white, shiny face	pale material; thin white moss	frail
Congealed Blood	chronic low fever; no thirst, or thirst but no desire to drink; stabbing, fixed pain; hemorrhage	dark purple material, or red pimples on surface	choppy

Headache

Headache can be the chief complaint of a wide assortment of patterns. In general, headaches that are sudden in onset, or of short duration, or severe without letup, are part of External or Internal Pernicious Influence patterns (that is, patterns of Excess). Chronic mild headaches are usually part of Interior/Deficiency patterns.

TABLE 19

Headache

Pattern	Signs	Tongue	Pulse
Cold/Wind	sudden headache that feels tight and connects to neck and back; fear of cold accompanied by slight fever; no thirst	thin white moss	tight and floating
Heat/Wind	sudden headache, sometimes even splitting pain; slight aversion to cold; high fever; red face; thirst; sore throat	thin yellow moss	floating and rapid
Damp/Wind	sudden headache that feels heavy and full; fever that comes and goes; stiff joints; pressure in chest; no thirst; sticky taste in mouth	greasy white moss	floating and slippery
Constrained Liver Qi	one-sided headache; flanks are distended; melancholy or constricted emotions; nausea	normal tongue material; white moss	wiry
Liver Fire Blazing Upward	one-sided splitting headache; irritability; angers easily; bitter taste in mouth; scanty, dark urine; constipation; red eyes	red material; yellow moss	wiry and rapid
Arrogant Liver Yang Ascending	one-sided headache that connects to top of head; vertigo; ringing in ears	red material; thin, dry moss	wiry, or wiry and thin
Deficient Spleen Qi	slight headache; shiny white face; fatigue; spontaneous sweating; little appetite	pale material; white moss	empty
Deficient Blood	slight on-and-off-again headaches; lusterless face; palpitations; unclear vision; insomnia	pale material; white moss	thin
Turbid Mucus	headache accompanied by heaviness; possible vertigo; distended chest area; vomiting of saliva	greasy, pasty white moss	slippery

TABLE 19 *(cont.)*

Headache

Pattern	Signs	Tongue	Pulse
Deficient Kidney Yin	headache accompanied by empty feeling in head; vertigo; tinnitus; soreness in lower back and knees; leukorrhea	red material; peeled, dry moss	thin and perhaps rapid
Deficient Kidney Yang	same as signs above for Deficient Kidney Yin; shiny white face; cold limbs; puffy skin or edema	pale, swollen, moist material; little moss	frail
Congealed Blood	constant or chronic headache with sharp, stabbing pain in a fixed location	purple, darkish material, or red spots on tongue	choppy

Vertigo

The Exterior patterns often accompanied by vertigo are identical with those of headaches and will not be repeated in the table. Interior vertigo can be part of either Excess or Deficiency patterns. Interior/Excess patterns are usually Liver Wind patterns that are part of a general Liver Heat pattern (Liver Fire, Liver Yang, or Liver Yin) or part of a Mucus pattern that obstructs the "clear Yang Qi" from ascending to the head. The main Interior/Deficiency patterns involving vertigo are patterns of either Deficient Blood or Deficient Qi that is unable to fill the head, or patterns of insufficiency in the Kidney that prevent it from nourishing the Marrow and Brain.

TABLE 20

Vertigo

Pattern	Signs	Tongue	Pulse
Liver Wind	vertigo; tinnitus; angers easily; condition is often related to emotions; headache; sometimes vomiting; bitter taste in mouth; dry throat; numb limbs	red material; little moss	wiry
Turbid Mucus	vertigo; tinnitus; head feels heavy as if inside a sack; head seems to be spinning; fatigue; no appetite; vomiting	greasy moss	slippery

TABLE 20 (*cont.*)

Vertigo

Pattern	Signs	Tongue	Pulse
Deficient Qi and Deficient Blood	vertigo; tinnitus (exacerbated by exertion); lethargy; pale face; shortness of breath; insomnia	pale material; white moss	thin and frail
Deficient Kidney Yin	vertigo; tinnitus; poor memory; lower back is sore and weak; palms and soles are warm	reddish material	thin and perhaps rapid
Deficient Kidney Yang	vertigo; tinnitus; Spirit is very slow; lower back is sore and weak; cold limbs; impotence; sterility	pale, moist material	frail

Thirst

Thirst is an unusual chief complaint and is discussed here to illustrate the clinical flexibility of Chinese medicine. The sign of thirst usually points to Heat or Deficient Yin. If the accompanying signs depict an atypical pattern, however, the complaint may have a different signification.

In a Chinese medical text, the discussion of thirst would distinguish between this symptom alone and diabetes ("wasting and thirsting disease," see table note on page 332), in which thirst would be accompanied by a large appetite and excessive urination.

TABLE 21

Thirst

Pattern	Signs	Tongue	Pulse
Excess Dryness and Heat in Lungs and Stomach	dry mouth and throat; desire to drink; hot body; perspiration; slight or no fear of cold; aversion to heat; full abdomen; constipation	red material	full and rapid or floating
Deficient Yin	thirst but little desire to drink; warm palms and soles; insomnia; afternoon fever; night sweats	reddish material; no moss	thin and rapid

TABLE 21 (*cont.*)

Thirst

Pattern	Signs	Tongue	Pulse
Deficient Spleen Qi and Dampness Accumulating	thirst but no desire to drink, or a desire for hot fluids; tired limbs; heavy head and body; loose stools	pale material; greasy white moss	empty or soggy
Kidney Yang Insufficient to Transform Water	thirst but no desire to drink, or vomiting after drinking; aversion to cold; fatigue; cold limbs	swollen, pale material; little moss	fragile
Dampness and Mucus Collecting	thirst but no desire to drink, or vomiting after drinking; excess saliva; distended abdomen; difficult, scanty, or incomplete urination	greasy white moss	slippery
Congealed Blood	thirst; irritability; desire to gargle water but no desire to swallow; other signs of Congealed Blood	darkish, purple material	choppy

Vomiting

Vomiting is usually Stomach Qi in rebellion and can be the result of Stomach disharmonies alone or other disharmonies that affect the Stomach.

TABLE 22

Vomiting

Pattern	Signs	Tongue	Pulse
External Cold Wind Invading Stomach	acute onset of vomiting; nausea accompanied by fever and fear of cold; head and body ache; distended chest and abdomen; diarrhea	white moss	tight
External Heat or Summer Heat Invading Stomach	acute onset of vomiting; nausea accompanied by fever; thirst; irritability; diarrhea	red material; yellow moss	rapid and wiry or rapid and soggy
Mucus Obstructing Stomach	vomiting; chest is uncomfortable; no desire to drink; vertigo	greasy white moss	slippery

TABLE 22 (*cont.*)

Vomiting

Pattern	Signs	Tongue	Pulse
Liver Invading Stomach	vomiting; food matter appears in vomitus; sour taste in mouth; distended chest and flanks; condition is often emotionally related	thin white moss	wiry
Heat Generating Liver Wind, which Invades Stomach	projectile vomiting; high fever; headache; stiff neck; convulsions in limbs; tetany	red or scarlet material	wiry and rapid
Deficient Stomach Yin	occasional vomiting; dry mouth; hunger but no desire to eat; other Deficient Yin signs	red material; little moss	thin and rapid
Deficient Spleen and Stomach Qi	vomiting, especially after even slight overeating; unpredictable vomiting that is chronic; fatigue; watery stools; pale, white face	pale material; little moss	empty
Stagnant Food Collecting (Stagnant Food becomes a pattern)	vomiting of sour, rotten food; feeling of relief after vomiting; abdomen is full, sore, and distended after eating; constipation or diarrhea	greasy moss	slippery and full
Worms Disturbing Stomach	vomiting of worms; vomiting of clear fluid, saliva, or yellow-green water after eating; sore abdomen; discomfort is occasional		

Coughing

Coughing is a common symptom, often seen in External Pernicious Influence patterns when they invade the Lungs. Coughing can also be part of Interior Lung disharmonies or other Organ disharmonies affecting the Lungs. This table omits the External Influences, as they have been covered by other tables. Internal disharmonies often associated with coughing are Deficient Yin and Deficient Qi. Organs that most commonly influence the Lungs are the Spleen (Deficiency causing Mucus to develop and invade the Lungs), the Liver (Liver Fire can invade the Lungs), or the Kidneys (Kidneys failing to grasp the Lung Qi).

TABLE 23

Coughing

Pattern	Signs	Tongue	Pulse
Deficient Lung Yin	dry cough; dry mouth and throat; red cheeks; other Deficient Yin signs	red material; little moss	thin and rapid
Deficient Lung Qi	weak cough usually associated with asthma; frequent colds; spontaneous sweating; other Deficient Qi signs	pale, moist material	empty or frail
Mucus Dampness Hindering the Lungs	cough with copious white expectoration; distended chest and epigastrium; no appetite; fatigue; symptoms often occur with Deficient or Damp Spleen signs	greasy white moss	soggy or slippery
Mucus Heat Collecting in Lungs	cough with copious, thick, yellow expectoration; sometimes phlegm has foul smell; other signs of Heat	greasy yellow moss	slippery and rapid
Liver Fire Invading Lungs	sputtering, sporadic cough; cough causes flanks to be painful; dry throat; red face; other Liver disharmony signs	thin, dry yellow moss	wiry and rapid
Deficient Kidney Yang Unable to Grasp Lung Qi	usually there has been a long history of illness; exhalation is easier than inhalation; asthma; exertion exacerbates symptoms; sore lower back; fear of cold; dark face	pale, swollen, moist material	frail

Chest and Flank Pain

The chest is the mansion of the Lungs and Heart, while the Flanks are thought to have an intimate relation with the Liver and Gall Bladder. Chest pain often appears in patterns when Outside Pernicious Influences obstruct the circulation of the Lung Qi, when the Blood and Qi of the Heart are obstructed because there is not enough Yang to generate movement, or when there is a Mucus blockage. Flank pain is often part of various Liver and Gall Bladder disharmonies.

TABLE 24

Chest and Flank Pain

Pattern	Signs	Tongue	Pulse
External Heat Invading Lungs	chest and flanks are painful and sore; cough; asthma; yellow or rust-colored phlegm; fever; chills	yellow moss, red tip	floating and rapid
External Dryness Scorching Lungs	hot body; painful chest; cough; little phlegm; thirst	red material; dry moss	rapid
Mucus Obstructing Chest	flanks are painful and distended; frothy cough with phlegm and saliva; cough aggravates pain; sometimes fever; no thirst	greasy white moss	wiry and slippery
Deficient Heart Yang simultaneous with Congealed Heart Blood	sporadic chest pain; sometimes stabbing pain; fixed pain; pressure in chest	darkish material or red spots	choppy and frail
Deficient Heart Yang with Mucus Dampness Obstructing	chest is distended, sore, and painful; pain connects to shoulder; cough with phlegm; shortness of breath or asthma	pale material, greasy white moss	slippery
Damp Heat of Liver and Gall Bladder	painful flanks; distended epigastrium; feeling of distress in chest; nausea; yellow urine; fever; jaundice	red material, greasy yellow moss	wiry and rapid
Constrained Liver Qi	distended and painful flanks; impatience or quickness to anger; emotional stress increases pain; chest is uncomfortable; little desire to drink	thin white and/or yellow moss	wiry
Congealed Liver Blood	stabbing flank pain in fixed position; palpable mass under ribs	purple, darkish material	wiry and choppy
Deficient Liver Yin and Deficient Kidney Yin	flank has slight dull achiness or soreness; dry mouth; irritability; vertigo; low back pain	red material; little moss	wiry and thin

APPENDIX C

Abdominal Pain

Abdominal pain may appear in disharmonies of the Liver, Gall Bladder, Spleen, Stomach, Kidney, Large and Small Intestines, Bladder, and Uterus. This table summarizes the most common categories.

TABLE 25

Abdominal Pain

Pattern	Signs	Tongue	Pulse
Cold Obstructing Abdomen	sudden, urgent, severe pain; warmth relieves and cold aggravates pain; no thirst; clear urine	pale white material	deep and tight
Cold Obstructing Liver Meridian	urgent cold pain in groin; pain connects to testicles	white material	deep and wiry
Heat Tying the Abdomen	painful and distended abdomen; warm body and abdomen; vomiting; constipation; yellow, scanty urine; irritability	yellow moss	rapid and full
Damp Heat in Liver and Gall Bladder	usually upper right quadrant of body is sore; pain; nausea; vomiting; food is repulsive; sometimes jaundice	greasy yellow moss	wiry and rapid
Damp Heat in Stomach and Intestines	pain in abdomen accompanied by diarrhea with pus or blood; patient feels heavy and worse after defecation; burning anus; fever; scanty, dark urine	greasy yellow moss	slippery and rapid
Intestinal Abcess	abdomen (especially lower right quadrant) is sore and painful; abdomen resists touch; right foot wants to curl up; sometimes accompanied by fever; vomiting	greasy yellow moss	rapid
Damp Heat in Bladder	urgent pain in lower abdomen that sometimes connects with lower back; burning urination that is painful and rough, may contain blood or granules	yellow moss	rapid

TABLE 25 (*cont.*)

Abdominal Pain

Pattern	Signs	Tongue	Pulse
Constrained Liver Qi	distended epigastrium and abdomen; distended flanks; patient resists touch; passing gas relieves pain; condition is emotionally related at times	thin moss	wiry
Congealed Blood in Abdomen	sharp, stabbing abdominal pain that connects to sides; pain is located in fixed position, or palpable mass	darkish material	choppy
Deficient Cold Pain	slight, dull abdominal pain; patient desires heat and touching; loose stools; lethargy	pale material	frail
Stagnant Food Pain	distended abdomen; soreness; pain that resists touch; patient is repelled by food; belching of sour, rotten material; eating aggravates pain; diarrhea relieves pain	greasy moss	slippery or deep and full
Worms Collecting	intermittent abdominal pain, sometimes very severe, often clusters around navel or to one side; sometimes vomiting of worms; emaciation; peculiar eating prejudices; inner lips or cheeks have tiny white dots		

Low Back Pain

Low back pain or soreness is generally a sign of Kidney disharmony. When it is a chief complaint, the physician has to decide whether the lumbago is part of an Excess or Deficiency pattern.

TABLE 26

Low Back Pain

Pattern	Signs	Tongue	Pulse
Damp Cold	lower back feels cold; bending is difficult; patient desires heating pad; pain becomes severe when weather is cold or damp	greasy white moss	deep and slippery
Damp Heat	lower back is sore and feels heavy; scanty, dark urine	greasy yellow moss	slippery and wiry
Damp Heat Pouring into Bladder	(A) stabbing back pain; frequent, burning, and painful urination; bitter taste in mouth	yellow moss	rapid and wiry
	(B) intermittent, severe back pain; pain connects with groin; frequent, painful urination, often with blood, or urine has stones; difficulty passing urine	yellow moss	rapid and wiry
Laboring Lumbago	lower back is sore after exertion; all four limbs are tired; rest relieves pain; no other unusual signs	thin white moss	moderate
Congealed Blood	stabbing back pain at fixed point; pressure visibly increases discomfort; movement is difficult; pain is worse at night	darkish material	choppy
Deficient Kidney Yang	dull, aching, weak back; back and knees are without strength; patient cannot tolerate physical labor; bright white face; cold limbs; night urination	pale material	frail
Deficient Kidney Yin	back is sore, weak, and painful; legs are without strength; vertigo; tinnitus; insomnia	red material	rapid and thin

Diarrhea

Diarrhea is usually a sign of Spleen, Stomach, or Intestinal disharmony. The disharmony can be generated by External Pernicious Influences, Stagnant Food, Organ weakness, or an imbalance of Organ relationships. In general, the most common disharmony is Dampness or obstruction of the

Spleen's transformative function. Spleen disharmony is often generated by its own weakness: Kidney Fire not supporting the Spleen, or the Liver losing its adjustment, thereby affecting the Spleen.

TABLE 27

Diarrhea

Pattern	Signs	Tongue	Pulse
Damp Heat	acute onset; stools are yellow and seem to be dissolved in fluid; foul smell; anus is hot; scanty, dark urine; abdominal pain; bitter taste in mouth; dry mouth; fever; vomiting	yellow, or yellow and greasy moss	soggy and rapid
Damp Cold	usually acute onset; watery stool; elimination is uncomfortable; abdominal pain; intestinal rumbling; heat relieves pain; chest and epigastrium feel oppressed; symptoms are sometimes accompanied by External Cold Wind Pernicious Influences	greasy white moss	soggy
Stagnant Food	sticky stool is sour and foul; epigastrium and abdomen are distended and resist pressure; greater comfort after elimination; sour belching	greasy moss	slippery
Deficient Spleen Qi	watery stool, usually chronic; undigested food in stool; distention; no appetite; desire for heat and touch; fear of cold; lethargy	pale white moss	frail and thin
Deficient Kidney Yang	early-morning need to defecate; sparse, watery stool; all four limbs are cold; desire for heat; symptoms found especially in the elderly; other Kidney signs	pale material	deep and thin
Constrained Liver	emotionally related; sudden need to defecate, accompanied by pain; patient is more comfortable after defecation; distended chest and sides; quickness to anger; irritability; belching	thin moss	wiry

Constipation

Constipation alone is often a sign of Heat and Excess and points to a disharmony in the Large Intestine. As a chief complaint, it can also appear in various other patterns.

TABLE 28

Constipation

Pattern	Signs	Tongue	Pulse
Dry Heat Collecting Inward	constipation; dry stool; bad breath; distended abdomen; scanty, dark urine	red material; thin yellow moss	slippery and full
Stagnant Qi	constipation; distended chest and flanks; no appetite; belching; unproductive desire to defecate	thin, greasy moss	wiry and deep
Deficient Blood	constipation; vertigo; palpitations; face, lips, and nails are lusterless white	pale material	thin
Cold Obstructing the Qi	constipation; slight abdominal discomfort; pressure and warmth relieve pain; clear, copious urine; cold limbs	pale material	deep and slow
Deficient Qi	constipation; fatigue; spontaneous sweating; patient becomes more tired after defecation; stool is not dry	pale, swollen material	empty

Hemorrhaging

Bleeding from nose or gums, coughing blood, vomiting blood, urinating blood, or blood in the stool generally accompany Heat patterns—either of Excess or of Deficiency. Heat or Fire can easily generate such reckless Blood movement. If all other signs point away from Excess/Heat (especially in the lower parts of the body), bleeding may be part of a Deficiency or Cold pattern.

TABLE 29

Nosebleed

Pattern	Signs	Tongue	Pulse
Lung Heat Injuring Meridians	nosebleed; fever; cough; little phlegm; dry mouth	red material; yellow moss	floating and rapid
Stomach Fire Rebelling Upward	nosebleed; dry mouth; bad breath; irritability; constipation	red material; yellow moss	slippery and rapid, or flooding
Liver Fire Ascending	nosebleed; vertigo; headache; red eyes; bitter taste in mouth; irritability; quickness to anger	red material; yellow moss	wiry and rapid
Deficient Yin/Empty Fire Flourishing	nosebleed; vertigo; red eyes; dry throat; tinnitus; irritability; insomnia	red material; thin yellow moss	thin and rapid, with little strength

TABLE 30

Coughing Blood

Pattern	Signs	Tongue	Pulse
Wind/Heat/ Dryness Pernicious Influences Injuring Lungs	fever; dry mouth; dry nose; sore throat; coughing of phlegm with blood; chest pain	red material; yellow moss	floating and rapid
Deficient Yin/Empty Fire Injuring Lungs	dry cough; bloody phlegm; afternoon low fever; no bodily strength; cough is worse at night	red material; little moss	thin and rapid
Liver Fire Invading Lungs	chest and flank pain; coughing of phlegm with blood, or coughing of pure blood; irritability; anger; constipation; dark urine	red material; thin yellow moss	wiry and rapid
Congealed Blood Obstructing Chest	cough; coughing of phlegm with blood or of bloody foam; piercing chest pain; heart palpitations	darkish material or red spots on tongue	intermittent, or wiry and slow, or choppy

TABLE 31

Blood in Urine

Pattern	Signs	Tongue	Pulse
Damp Heat Pouring Downward into Bladder	bloody urine; frequent and painful urination; thirst; low back pain	red material; greasy yellow moss	wiry and rapid, or slippery and rapid
Small Intestine Fire Flourishing[1]	bloody urine; urine feels hot when passed; dark urine; painful urination; irritability; dry mouth; tongue ulceration	yellow moss	rapid
Spleen and Kidneys Both Exhausted	frequent urination with pale red blood; poor appetite; no Spirit, fatigue; sallow yellow face; soreness in lower back; vertigo; tinnitus	pale material	empty or frail

[1]This pattern, also called Heat Fire Entering Small Intestine, is one of very few cases in which the Heart and Small Intestine have a clinical relationship.

TABLE 32

Blood in Stool

Pattern	Signs	Tongue	Pulse
Heat Entering Large Intestine	fresh red blood in stool; blood is passed before stool other Heat signs	yellow moss	rapid
Deficient Cold with Blood in Stool	darkish blood in stool; blood is passed after stool; cold limbs; sallow face; tired Shen	pale material; white moss	sinking and thin

Edema

Edema can affect parts of the body, such as the face, eyelids, or limbs, or it can affect the entire body. Edema usually has a primary relation to the three Yin Organs that regulate water—Lungs, Spleen, and Kidneys.

TABLE 33
Edema

Pattern	Signs	Tongue	Pulse
External Influence with Lung Qi not Circulating	fever; fear of drafts; headache; coughing; sore throat; swollen, puffy face; eventually entire body swells; scanty urination	thin white moss	tight and floating
Spleen Losing Transformative Ability	sallow face; distended epigastrium; no appetite; watery stool; scanty urine; all four limbs are cold	pale, moist material	sinking, moderate, or empty
Kidney Yang Exhausted	whole body is edemic, especially below waist; lower back is sore and heavy; scanty urine; all four limbs are cold; fear of cold; no Spirit; dark or bright white face	swollen, pale material; white moss	frail

Spasms, Tremors, and Convulsions

Spasms, tremors, and convulsions are usually related to Wind and can be of either External or Internal origin.

TABLE 34

Spasms, Tremors, and Convulsions

Pattern	Signs	Tongue	Pulse
External Wind Pernicious Influence Collecting in Meridians	headache; neck and back tremors; sometimes tetany; fear of cold; fever; sore limbs and body; clear Spirit	variable	floating and tight
Extreme Heat Generating Wind	high fever; unclear Spirit; sometimes coma; tremors and spasms in four limbs; mouth tightly clenched	red material	wiry and fast
Deficient Blood Generating Wind	vertigo; fatigue; spasms; tremors; palpitations	pale material	thin
Deficient Yin Generating Wind	long-term disorder injures Yin; tremor in limbs; warm palms and soles; tired Spirit	red material; little moss	thin and rapid
Congealed Blood Inwardly Obstructing and Generating Wind	thin body; spasms; headache; pain in fixed location	darkish material, or material shows red and purple spots	choppy and thin

Gynecological Complaints

The following three common women's disorders illustrate how Chinese medicine would integrate women's complaints into common patterns.

TABLE 35

Dysmenorrhea

Pattern	Signs	Tongue	Pulse
Stagnant Qi/ Congealed Blood	before or during menses, lower abdomen is distended or painful and resists touch; menses flow unevenly; blood is darkish and has clots; passing of clots reduces discomfort; distended breasts	purple, dark, or normal material	wiry or choppy
Cold Damp Obstructing Menses	before or during menses, lower abdomen is painful and cold; heat relieves pain; menses are not smooth; blood is dark-colored, thin, and watery with clots	pale material; moist moss	sinking, tight, or slow
Deficient Blood and Qi	persistent dull soreness in abdomen during or after menses; pressure relieves pain; pale face; fatigue; no desire to speak; small amount of pale blood	pale material; white moss	empty or thin

TABLE 36

Amenorrhea

Pattern	Signs	Tongue	Pulse
Deficient Blood and Qi	menstrual blood over a period of time gradually diminishes until there is none; watery leukorrhea; acrid odor; sallow face; fatigue, no Spirit; limbs are without strength; vertigo; palpitations	pale material; thin white moss	sinking and thin, or empty
Stagnant Qi/ Congealed Blood	amenorrhea seems related to emotional stress; menses suddenly cease; distended breasts and flanks; sallow face; headache	darkish or purple material	wiry or choppy

TABLE 36 (*cont.*)

Amenorrhea

Pattern	Signs	Tongue	Pulse
Deficient Liver Yin and Deficient Kidney Yin	gradual ceasing of menses; weight loss; patient feels hot; afternoon fever; dry skin; dark face; lower back and legs are weak; vertigo; tinnitus; dry mouth; constipation	red or scarlet material; little moss	thin and slightly rapid
Mucus Dampness Obstructing Menses	slight discomfort in lower abdomen; abdomen feels full but soft; much leukorrhea; vertigo; nausea; no taste in mouth; no appetite; distended breasts; condition is usually found in overweight women	greasy white moss	slippery

TABLE 37

Abnormal Uterine Bleeding

Pattern	Signs	Tongue	Pulse
Heat in Blood	heavy bleeding; bright red blood; breasts and flanks are distended; red face; dry mouth; irritability	red material; yellow moss	rapid and big
Deficient Spleen Qi Unable to Govern Blood	heavy bleeding; pale, thin blood; puffy face; pale, bright face; no Spirit; no appetite; watery stool	pale material; thin white moss	empty
Stagnant Qi/ Congealed Blood	constant slight bleeding or sudden heavy bleeding; distended flanks; distended lower abdomen; purple or dark blood clots; passing of clots reduces discomfort; dark face	darkish material	sinking and wiry, or choppy
Deficient Liver Yin and Deficient Kidney Yin	menses arrive early; small amount of blood; pale or purple blood; vertigo; tinnitus; spots before eyes; sore back; insomnia; dry mouth	red, scarlet, and shriveled material	rapid, thin, and perhaps wiry

Insomnia

Insomnia is generally related to disturbances of the Heart Storing Shen. Very often such a Heart disharmony is connected to other Organs as well.

TABLE 38

Insomnia

Pattern	Signs	Tongue	Pulse
Deficient Blood and Deficient Spleen Qi	insomnia; palpitations; forgetfulness; lethargy; food seems tasteless; little appetite; pale face	pale material	thin or empty
Heart and Kidney not Communicating (or Deficient Heart Yin and Deficient Kidney Yin)	insomnia and irritability; palpitations; forgetfulness; night sweats; tinnitus; vertigo; lumbago	red material	rapid and thin
Deficient Heart Qi and Gall Bladder Qi	insomnia; awakens easily in fright; much dreaming; timidity	pale material	wiry and thin
Stomach not Harmonized	insomnia; distended epigastrium; belching; abdominal discomfort; defecation is not smooth; excessive eating	greasy moss	slippery
Liver Fire and Gall Bladder Fire	insomnia; headache; vertigo; sore flanks; quickness to anger; bitter taste in mouth	red material	wiry and strong

Dribbling Urine

Dribbling urine can appear in patterns of any of the Organs that regulate water.

TABLE 39

Dribbling Urination

Pattern	Signs	Tongue	Pulse
Heat Violates Lungs, Obstructing Water's Descent	dribbling urination; acute onset; dry throat; irritability; thirst; cough.	thin yellow moss	rapid
Damp Heat Obstructing Middle Burner	dribbling, cloudy urination; epigastrium feels full; distended abdomen; thirst but no desire to drink	greasy moss	soggy and slippery

TABLE 39 (cont.)
Dribbling Urination

Pattern	Signs	Tongue	Pulse
Deficient Middle Burner (Spleen) Qi	clear, dribbling urination; lethargy; chronic Deficient Spleen signs	pale material	soggy and weak
Weak Life Gate Fire	dribbling urination; no strength in elimination; bright white face; tired Spirit; lower back is cold; knees are without strength	pale material	frail, especially in third position
Bladder Heat Collecting	dribbling, often painful urination; painful hypogastrium	red material	rapid and slippery
Bladder Obstructed	dribbling urination or threadlike urine; pain in hypogastrium	dark purple material	choppy

Notes

1. Tables 18–39 are based on Tianjin City, *Traditional Chinese Internal Medicine* [55], pp. 51–86; Anhui Institute, *Clinical Handbook* [68], pp. 63–82, 128–135; and Huzhou Institute, *Traditional Chinese Gynecology* [77], pp. 25–56.

APPENDIX D
Pulses Revisited

Pulse examination is often the most important of the Four Examinations and is crucial to pattern discernment in general. This appendix amplifies the earlier discussion of pulses. It is presented especially for those readers who are practitioners or students of Oriental medicine and are already familiar with rudimentary pulse theory. The general reader may, however, be interested in the ways that significations (or Yin-Yang correspondences) change depending on a complete configuration of signs.

The pulse can be taken at three positions on the radial artery (see Chapter 6). There are correlations between these pulse positions and certain Organs. Authorities within the tradition have various ideas about the exact correlations; the main opinions are presented in Table 40.[1] In the textual sources, these correspondences are mentioned but given little clinical discussion.

TABLE 40

Pulse Position Correlations

SUMMARY OF OPINIONS FROM MAJOR AUTHORITATIVE SOURCES

Position		*Nei Jing* 1st cent. B.C.E.	*Nan Jing* c. 200 C.E.	Wang Shu-he's Classic of Pulse c. 280 C.E.	Li Shi-zhen's Pulse Studies 1564 C.E.	Zhang Jie-bing's Complete Book 1624 C.E.
Left Hand						
First	Deep	Heart	Arm Shao-yin	Heart	Heart	Heart
	Superficial	Sternum	Arm Tai-yang	Small Intestine		Pericardium
Second	Deep	Liver	Leg Jue-yin	Liver	Liver	Liver
	Superficial	Diaphragm	Leg Shao-yang	Gall Bladder		Gall Bladder
Third	Deep	Kidney	Leg Shao-yin	Kidney	Kidney (Life Gate)	Kidney
	Superficial	Abdomen	Leg Tai-yang	Bladder		Bladder Large Intestine
Right Hand						
First	Deep	Lungs	Arm Tai-yin	Lungs	Lungs	Lungs
	Superficial	Chest	Arm Yang-ming	Large Intestine		Sternum
Second	Deep	Stomach	Leg Tai-yin	Spleen	Spleen	Spleen
	Superficial	Spleen	Leg Yang-ming	Stomach		Stomach
Third	Deep	Kidney	(text unclear)	Kidney (Life Gate)	Kidney (Life Gate)	Kidney
	Superficial	Abdomen		Triple Burner		Triple Burner Life Gate Small Intestine

It is important to realize that the twenty-eight pulses rarely appear alone. Usually two or more appear in combination. For each pulse type, therefore, there is a list of the other pulses that often combine with it.

A pulse can appear in all three or in only one of the positions on the radial artery. To give a sense of how the tradition deals with different pulse positions, tables have been included for the more important pulses. The "Bilateral" column in each table describes the symptoms or patterns that are associated with the pulse when it appears in only one position, but on both hands. This information is an opinion based on statements of Li Shi-zhen (1518–1593 C.E.) in his classic Pulse Studies of the Lakeside Master. The "Left Side" and "Right Side" columns present a simplification of major early opinions on the significance of the pulse when it appears in only one position and on only one hand. These statements derive from the comprehensive compilation made by the Shanghai City Traditional Chinese Medical Archives Research Committee.[2]

When a Chinese physician takes a pulse, there is a sense of openness—of endless possibility—about what will be found. There is always the chance that any pulse may have a meaning different from the one traditionally assigned to it. The following discussion of the twenty-eight classic pulses is intended to impart something of that sense of possibility.

Floating Pulse

A floating pulse is generally defined as the sign of an Exterior pattern of disharmony or of the presence of an External Pernicious Influence. Yet a floating pulse is also commonly found when there are no other signs of an Exterior pattern (such as sudden onset of fever, headache, chills, etc.). If this floating pulse is weak, it is generally a sign of Deficient Yin (or Deficient Blood), with the Yang in relative Excess so that the pulse rises higher than normal. This is an example of the Yin being unable to embrace the Yang. If the floating pulse is strong, it is generally a sign of Internal Wind Pernicious Influence or of Excess Yang.

Common Pulse Combinations

Pulse	Associated Symptoms and/or Patterns
Floating and rapid	External Heat Pernicious Influence
Floating and tight	External Cold Pernicious Influence
Floating and slippery	Wind and Mucus of Internal Origin or Stagnant Food
Floating and long	Excess
Floating and short	Deficiency, especially of Qi
Floating, flooding, big	External Summer Heat Pernicious Influence

APPENDIX D

The Various Positions and a Floating Pulse

	Bilateral (Li Shi-zhen)	Left Side	Right Side
First position	Wind with a headache; Wind and Mucus in chest	Heart Yang Ascending; insomnia; irritability	External Wind; Rebellious Qi in Lungs; cough; asthma
Second position	Deficient Spleen Qi and Excess Liver Qi	Constrained Liver Qi; pain	Stagnant Spleen Qi; distended abdomen; vomiting
Third position	constipation or anuresis	Deficient Kidney Qi; difficulty in urination; lumbago; vertigo; menstrual irregularities	

Sinking Pulse

This pulse is generally considered the sign of an Interior pattern. When a sinking pulse is weak, it is a sign of Deficient Yang, since it means that the Yang cannot lift the pulse. If the sinking pulse is strong, it is generally a sign of Cold restraining the upward movement of the Yang. Occasionally an individual has signs of an External Pernicious Influence along with the sinking pulse. This is usually interpreted as signifying the existence of an underlying Deficient Yang or Deficient Qi pattern that renders the patient unable effectively to combat the External Pernicious Influence. A sinking pulse is also considered the general pulse of Kidney disharmonies. In the winter or for heavy people, however, it is considered normal for the Qi and Blood to be deeper, producing a sinking pulse.

Common Pulse Combinations

Pulse	Associated Symptoms and/or Patterns
Sinking and slow	Interior Cold
Sinking and rapid	Interior Heat
Sinking and slippery	Cold Dampness/Mucus or Stagnant Food
Sinking and wiry	Constrained Liver Qi
Sinking and tight	Pernicious Influence is strong and Qi is Deficient; usually accompanied by pain
Sinking and choppy	Deficient Qi/Congealed Blood

TABLE 42

The Various Positions and a Sinking Pulse

	Bilateral (Li Shi-zhen)	Left Side	Right Side
First position	Mucus Obstructing Chest	Deficient Heart Yang; desire for sleep	Deficient Lung Qi; cough; shortness of breath; asthma
Second position	Cold in Middle Burner; pain	Constrained Liver Qi; pain	Deficient Spleen Qi; diarrhea
Third position	Deficient Kidney Qi; lumbago; diarrhea	Deficient Kidney Qi; lumbago; sore knees; vertigo; impotence; sterility; painful menses; leukorrhea	

Slow Pulse

A slow pulse represents Cold. If this pulse is weak, it signifies insufficient Yang to move the Qi and Blood. If this pulse is strong, it is a sign that Excess Cold is restraining the Qi and Blood. (This sign is often associated with pain.) On rare occasions a slow pulse is accompanied by a constellation of signs pointing to a Heat pattern.[3] Often such a Heat pattern has additional aspects of Dampness, which acts to restrain the movement of Qi and Blood and gives the slow pulse a "soft" quality. It is also possible for a slow pulse with great strength to appear in a Heat pattern without Damp aspects as the result of a Heat Pernicious Influence getting "stuck." (This is very rare for Heat but occasionally occurs in acute Heat patterns with abdominal distention or constipation.)

Common Pulse Combinations

Pulse	Associated Symptoms and/or Patterns
Slow and floating	Exterior Cold
Slow and choppy	Deficient Blood
Slow and slippery	Mucus
Slow and thin	Deficient Yang
Slow and wiry	Cold pain

APPENDIX D

Rapid Pulse

This pulse signifies Heat. Heat generally encourages activity so that the movement of the Qi and Blood increases. A rapid pulse with strength signifies Excess Heat; a rapid but weak pulse points to Deficient Heat or Empty Fire. In rare situations, a rapid pulse may accompany a Deficiency/Cold pattern. Such a rapid pulse is an illusionary sign of Heat and is instead a sign of extreme Deficient Yang floating to the outside of the body.[4] (The patient's situation is serious in this case because the pattern and pulse do not match.)

Common Pulse Combinations

Pulse	Associated Symptoms and/or Patterns
Rapid and thin	Deficient Yin (Empty Fire)
Rapid and floating	likely presence of carbuncle or skin ulcers
Rapid and slippery	Mucus Fire
Rapid and hollow	extreme loss of blood
Rapid and wiry	Liver Fire

Thin Pulse

A thin pulse can mean that the volume of Blood is reduced, therefore signifying Deficient Blood, often accompanied by Deficient Qi. Occasionally a thin but strong pulse is associated with Dampness Obstructing Qi and Blood.

Clinically, a thin pulse must be distinguished from a minute pulse, which is less clear and distinct than the thin and usually even weaker.

Common Pulse Combinations

Pulse	Associated Symptoms and/or Patterns
Thin and wiry	Deficient Liver Blood
Thin and choppy	extreme Deficient Blood
Thin and deep	Dampness Obstructing Qi and Blood, with pain
Thin and minute	Deficient Yang

TABLE 43

The Various Positions and a Thin Pulse

	Bilateral (Li Shi-zhen)	Left Side	Right Side
First position	Deficiency with vomiting	Heart palpitations; insomnia	Qi exhausted from vomiting
Second position	Deficient Spleen Qi and Deficient Stomach Qi; distended abdomen; emaciation	Liver Yin exhausted	Deficient Spleen Qi; abdominal distention
Third position	"Cinnabar Field" (Original Qi) Cold; Yin collapsed	spermatorrhea; diarrhea	Kidney Yang Cold and exhausted

Big Pulse

A big pulse often is not specific enough to have a clear designation, and Li Shi-zhen therefore left it out of his codification of pulses. (He discusses only twenty-seven pulses.) A big pulse is usually either strong, which makes it similar to a full pulse, or weak, which makes it similar to an empty pulse. If a pulse's strength lies between strong and weak (that is, if it is moderate) and still is big, the tendency is to say that it signifies Excess (and also Heat) in the Yang-ming Meridians (the Stomach and Large Intestine Meridians). These Meridians are said to have the most Qi and Blood[5] and to most easily manifest and/or register Excess/Heat. If there are no accompanying signs of Excess, this pulse may be considered the sign of a strong constitution.

Common Pulse Combinations

Pulse	Associated Symptoms and/or Patterns
Big and floating	Deficiency or Exterior/Heat
Big and sinking	Interior/Heat or Kidney Disharmony
Big and wiry	Shao-yang Disharmony
Big and moderate	Damp Heat
Big and floating	Stomach Excess

TABLE 44

The Various Positions and a Big Pulse

	Bilateral (Li Shi-zhen)	Left Side	Right Side
First position	(omitted)	irritability; epilepsy; Wind Heat	Rebellious Qi; swollen face; cough; asthma
Second position	(omitted)	Wind with vertigo; hernia	Stagnant Qi; Excess Stomach Qi; distended abdomen
Third position	(omitted)	Kidney Qi obstructed	dark urine; constipation

Empty Pulse

Different sources all agree that an empty pulse represents Deficiency, but there is disagreement as to whether this pulse necessarily has a superficial aspect. Some sources seem to relate the empty pulse to Deficient Blood (*Nei Jing*,[6] Li Shi-zhen[7]); others relate it to Deficient Qi (*Mai Jing*[8]). In general, if the empty pulse is especially superficial, it is said to signify Deficient Blood (that is, to have a Deficient Yin aspect); if it is less superficial, then it signifies Deficient Qi (that is, it has a Deficient Yang aspect). Compared with a thin pulse, an empty pulse is more indicative of Deficient Qi; compared with a frail pulse, it is more indicative of Deficient Blood.

Modern texts and clinical practice seem to agree that an empty pulse is more closely related to Deficient Qi than to Deficient Blood. This interpretation results from concentrating on the big or swollen nature of the pulse, which would be a characteristic of Deficient Qi. The bigness of the pulse is thought to signify the Qi not governing or "wrapping" the Blood.

The Organ most associated with an empty pulse is the Spleen. This association further contributes to the identification of an empty pulse with Deficient Qi, because the Spleen, in itself, is frequently associated with Deficient Qi or with a combination of Deficient Qi and Deficient Blood patterns, but rarely with Deficient Blood patterns alone.

An empty pulse can also be associated with the onset of a Summer Heat Pernicious Influence.

Common Pulse Combinations

Pulse	Associated Symptoms and/or Patterns
Empty and rapid	Deficient Yin
Empty and slow	Deficient Yang
Empty and very soft	Deficient Protective Qi, with spontaneous sweating

TABLE 45

The Various Positions and an Empty Pulse

	Bilateral (Li Shi-zhen)	Left Side	Right Side
First position	Blood unable to nourish Heart	Heart palpitations	spontaneous sweating
Second position	Deficient Qi with distended abdomen	Blood unable to nourish tendons	distended abdomen Deficient
Third position	Deficient Blood and Deficient Jing; bones feel hot	lower back and knees are sore or atrophying	Yang

Full Pulse

The opposite of an empty pulse, a full pulse is most often felt at the onset of an Excess/Heat disorder, but it can be part of any Excess pattern. Occasionally, especially if the pulse is also somewhat moderate, it can be a sign of a strong constitution. Clinically, it is possible for a full pulse to be part of a Deficiency pattern if all the other elements of a configuration indicate Deficiency.[9] Such a full pulse is illusionary and is thought to be a sign that the prognosis is poor.

Common Pulse Combinations

Pulse	Associated Symptoms and/or Patterns
Full and tending to sinking, wiry	Cold Ascending
Full and rapid	Lung abscess
Full and tending to floating	External Wind Cold Damp Pernicious Influence
Full and sinking	Interior pattern of Stagnant Food or unharmonious emotions
Full and wiry	Liver Fire

TABLE 46

The Various Positions and a Full Pulse

	Bilateral (Li Shi-zhen)	Left Side	Right Side
First position	Wind Heat affecting head; sore throat; stiff tongue; sensation of pressure in chest	stiff tongue	sore throat
Second position	Heat in Middle Burner; distended abdomen	Liver Fire; flank pain	pain in epigastrium
Third position	Heat in Lower Burner; lumbago; constipation; abdominal pain	constipation; abdominal pain	Rebellious Fire Ascending

Slippery Pulse

This pulse is generally a sign of Excess Mucus, Dampness, or Stagnant Food and is therefore considered Yang (Excess) within Yin (Dampness), or vice versa. Li Shi-zhen and other sources (including sections of the *Nei Jing*) differ slightly, but they all imply that a slippery pulse has aspects of Heat and is a Yang pulse. Clinically, a slippery pulse is often seen along with coughs, heavy expectoration, indigestion from stagnant food, Damp Heat pouring into the Bladder, and Damp Heat in the Intestines. A slippery pulse may also accompany pregnancy and can be a sign of a strong constitution.

Common Pulse Combinations

Pulse	Associated Symptoms and/or Patterns
Slippery and wiry	Stagnant Food, or Mucus with Constrained Liver Qi
Slippery and tight	Cold Mucus Obstructing

TABLE 47

The Various Positions and a Slippery Pulse

	Bilateral (Li Shi-zhen)	Left Side	Right Side
First position	Mucus in chest; vomiting; belching with sour taste; stiff tongue; cough	Heart Heat; fitful sleep	Mucus with vomiting or nausea
Second position	Liver Spleen Heat; Stagnant Food	Liver Fire; vertigo	Spleen Heat; Stagnant Food
Third position	"wasting and thirsting"; diarrhea; hernia; urinary problems	dark urine; difficult urination	diarrhea; Fire Ascending

Choppy Pulse

Although primarily a Yin pulse, a choppy pulse can have aspects of either Deficiency or Excess. If a choppy pulse is also weak or thin, it is a sign of insufficient Blood or Jing to fill the Blood Vessels. If it is strong, resisting the fingers, it is generally a sign of Congealed Blood Obstructing Movement. On rare occasions, a choppy, strong pulse can even point to Dampness Obstructing Movement, which is the same signification carried by its opposite type of pulse (i.e., slippery). Some sources include an irregular pulse, which in any one breath beats a different number of times ("the three and five not adjusted") under this type of pulse. This is important because there is no other pulse category that includes this irregularity. Clinically, a choppy pulse is often seen along with Heart and chest pain (this figures prominently in the *Nei Jing*), with illnesses accompanied by great loss of blood or fluids, and with Kidney exhaustion (great Deficiency), especially when related to sexual functions.

Common Pulse Combinations

Pulse	Associated Symptoms and/or Patterns
Choppy and wiry	Constrained Liver Qi, Congealed Blood
Choppy and frail	Qi exhausted (great Deficiency)
Choppy and minute	Deficient Blood and Deficient Yang
Choppy and thin	Dried Fluids (Deficiency)

TABLE 48

The Various Positions and a Choppy Pulse

	Bilateral (Li Shi-zhen)	Left Side	Right Side
First position	Deficient Heart Qi; chest pain	Heart pain; Heart palpitations	Deficient Lung Qi; cough with foamy sputum
Second position	Deficient Spleen Qi and Deficient Stomach Qi; painful, distended flank	Deficient Liver Blood	weak Spleen; inability to eat
Third position	Jing and Blood are injured; constipation or dribbling urination, or bleeding from anus	lower back is weak and sore	weak Life Gate Fire; Jing is injured

APPENDIX D

Wiry Pulse

A wiry pulse implies that something is restricting the movement of Qi and Blood. This pulse is generally associated with a reduction in the Liver's smooth spreading function, but it can also accompany a Cold pattern or any pattern with pain. Clinically, a wiry pulse may also appear with a Mucus pattern that accompanies a pattern of Liver Invading the Spleen. At other times, a wiry pulse may signify a complex pattern such as one of simultaneous Hot and Cold, or a pattern of half-Interior/half-Exterior.

Common Pulse Combinations

Pulse	Associated Symptoms and/or Patterns
Wiry and slow	Liver Cold
Wiry and rapid	Liver Fire
Wiry, rapid, and thin	Deficient Liver Yin
Wiry, rapid, and big	Liver Fire Blazing
Wiry and sinking	Interior Stagnation with pain

TABLE 49

The Various Positions and a Wiry Pulse

	Bilateral (Li Shi-zhen)	Left Side	Right Side
First position	Mucus obstructing diaphragm; headache	Heart pain	headache; chest and flank pain
Second position[1]	(omitted)	malaria; palpable masses in abdomen; spasms	Deficient Spleen Qi; Cold Stagnant Food
Third position	hernia; leg cramps	lower back and leg pain; cramps; lower abdominal pain; hernia	abdominal pain; diarrhea

[1]Qin Bo-wei, the famous twentieth-century practitioner, says that a right second pulse position being by itself wiry is a sign of Wood (Liver) Excess Conquering Earth (Spleen) and is often seen in abdominal pain or diarrhea (Medical Lecture Notes [64], p. 90).

Tight Pulse

A tight pulse signifies that movement is restricted because of Cold. When a Cold Pernicious Influence attempts to impinge the movement of Qi and Blood, the conflict of Cold with the Normal Qi generates combative activity. The pulse feels as if it is moving from left to right and can be compared to the tautness of a stretched rope. Clinically, this pulse often accompanies a pattern of External Cold Wind with body aches, or Deficient Cold of the Middle Burner with pain, or Cold Stagnant Food with pain.

Common Pulse Combinations

Pulse	Associated Symptoms and/or Patterns
Tight and rapid	simultaneous Heat and Cold pattern
Tight and wiry	Cold obstruction
Tight and full	distention and pain
Tight and choppy	Cold obstruction

TABLE 50

The Various Positions and a Tight Pulse

	Bilateral (Li Shi-zhen)	Left Side	Right Side
First position	(omitted)	feverish head; stiff neck; Heart pain	External Cold; asthma; cough; tight diaphragm
Second position	Cold Dampness Obstructing Middle Burner; pain	abdominal distention and pain; flank pain; cramps	distended epigastrium and abdomen
Third position	external genitals are Cold; running piglet illness;[1] hernia	pain underneath navel; sore legs; constipation	running piglet illness; hernia

[1]Running piglet (ben-tun) illness is mentioned in the Ling Shu (sec. 1, chap. 4, p. 45) and is discussed at length in other early texts. Its symptoms are very unpleasant sensations of pain that come and go and run from the navel to the throat. The pattern most associated with these symptoms is Deficient Kidney Yang with Excess Cold, although Liver Fire is also cited.

Knotted Pulse

A knotted pulse signifies Yin in ascendancy. If the pulse is also weak, the lack of smooth movement signifies extreme and chronic insufficient Kidney Fire or insufficient Qi and Blood to fill and move within the Blood pathways. If the pulse is also strong, the obstruction probably involves extreme Mucus, Cold, or Stagnant Qi/Congealed Blood.

APPENDIX D

Common Pulse Combinations

Pulse	Associated Symptoms and/or Patterns
Knotted and floating	Cold Obstructing Meridians
Knotted, sinking, and strong	Stagnant Qi with lumps
Knotted, sinking, and frail	Life Gate Fire exhausted
Knotted and slippery	chronic Mucus
Knotted and choppy	Congealed Blood with lumps

Hurried Pulse

This pulse signifies Excess Heat, often accompanied by aspects of obstruction from Stagnant Qi, Congealed Blood, or Mucus or Food blocking movement. A hurried pulse, especially when it is also weak, is sometimes a sign of "Organ Qi in Perverse Violation" and signifies extreme Deficiency and Cold. This is similar to the rapid pulse in a Cold pattern. Clinically, a hurried pulse is often seen in patterns of Excess Yang that include such symptoms as red eruptions, extreme anger, coarse breathing, violent insanity. The pulse is also seen in Hot asthmatic conditions where Mucus obstructs. Finally, this pulse may accompany patterns of Heart Qi and Heart Yang both exhausted.

Common Pulse Combinations

Pulse	Associated Symptoms and/or Patterns
Hurried, flooding, and full	Pernicious Influence Obstructing Meridian
Hurried and weak	Deficiency approaching separation of Yin and Yang
Hurried and floating	Yang-ming Heat

Intermittent Pulse

This pulse is generally a sign that all the Yin Organs are exhausted. Sometimes this pulse specifically accompanies a Deficient Heart Qi pattern with palpitation and pain, or a Middle Burner Deficient Cold pattern with vomiting. If, however, this pulse suddenly arises and is strong, it may be part of a momentary obstruction of Qi associated with a Wind pattern, pain condition, an emotional situation of great stress, or an injury.

Common Pulse Combinations

Pulse	Associated Symptoms and/or Patterns
Intermittent, thin, and sinking	Deficiency with diarrhea
Intermittent, minute, and thin	Fluids dry
Intermittent and moderate	Spleen Qi exhausted

Short Pulse

This pulse is usually a label for a pulse that cannot be felt in either the first or third positions or in both positions. Sometimes a pulse is called short even when it is felt in all three positions but the beats touching the fingers feel too small in length. Signifying Deficient Qi (especially when the pulse is also weak), it is most commonly seen in Lung, Heart, or Kidney Deficiencies. A short pulse can also accompany a condition of Mucus, Stagnant Food, or alcoholic intoxication (which generates Damp Heat), but in these cases the pulse will also have strength and be slippery and rapid.

Common Pulse Combinations

Pulse	Associated Symptoms and/or Patterns
Short and floating	Deficient Lung Qi or Congealed Blood
Short and sinking	Deficient Kidney Qi
Short and rapid	Heart pain and irritability
Short and slow	Deficient Cold
Short, slippery, and rapid	alcohol injuring Shen

Long Pulse

If a long pulse is also moderate, it can be a sign of a strong constitution. If it has a hard, urgent, tight, or wiry feeling, it suggests Excess. Clinically, this pulse combined with a wiry pulse is often seen with Constrained Liver Qi and with such symptoms as flank pain, headaches, red eyes, and tinnitus. A long pulse together with a flooding pulse can be seen in Yang-ming (Stomach and Large Intestine) Heat disharmonies, especially when accompanied by Mucus and such signs as epilepsy or Yang insanity. Cold/Excess with pain and asthma can have a long and wiry pulse. Lung Heat with coughing of blood often displays this pulse together with a rapid pulse. A long pulse is often felt in Heat patterns in general, characterized by such symptoms as irritability, thirst, and constipation.

Common Pulse Combinations

Pulse	Associated Symptoms and/or Patterns
Long and floating	External Pernicious Influence or Deficient Yin
Long and flooding	Yang insanity or epilepsy
Long, sinking, and thin	lumps or tumors
Long and slippery	Mucus Heat
Long and soggy	alcohol intoxication or Cold
Long and wiry	Liver disharmony

Moderate Pulse

A moderate pulse is the stereotypical normal pulse. Clinically, it is quite rare, for most people have constitutional tendencies to particular disharmony patterns, and even when they are healthy, those tendencies can be detected in their pulses. A pure moderate pulse accompanied by signs of disharmony is, according to some sources, a sign of Dampness. Most sources, however, seem to think that within a disharmony, a moderate pulse will take on the shading of other pulse types so that its interpretation would depend on the complete configuration.

Common Pulse Combinations

Pulse	Associated Symptoms and/or Patterns
Moderate and floating	External Dampness or Wind
Moderate and sinking	Dampness Obstructing
Moderate and choppy	Deficient Blood
Moderate, slow, and thin	Deficient Yang

Flooding Pulse

A flooding pulse is a sign of Excess/Heat with aspects of Deficient Yin. Treatment therefore consists of both cooling Heat and nourishing the Yin. This pulse is usually felt during febrile illnesses with thirst, irritability, and vomiting of blood, or in diseases with red, swollen skin ulceration. Occasionally, there is a flooding pulse whose surging forward movement is big but lacks strength and which recedes like a regular flooding pulse. If this pulse is accompanied by such signs as diarrhea, the interpretation is that the bigness signifies Deficiency (as does an empty pulse), and the pulse is then considered a sign of Deficiency. Heart disharmonies are also associated with this pulse. Another possible interpretation of a flooding pulse is that it implies a situation in which Heat on the Interior is being restrained or bottled up by Cold on the Exterior.

Common Pulse Combinations

Pulse	Associated Symptoms and/or Patterns
Flooding and big	Heat Ascending
Flooding and floating	External Heat or Deficient Yin
Flooding and sinking	Internal Heat or Cold Restraining Heat
Flooding and tight	chest distention or constipation with bleeding
Flooding and slippery	Heat/Mucus

Minute Pulse

A minute pulse signifies Deficient Yang and often accompanies patterns of extreme weakness with such signs as loose stools, bright face, little Shen, fear of cold, Cold diarrhea, or Cold uterine bleeding. This pulse frequently arises in the clinically urgent situations of "Vanquished Yang" (*wang-yang*) and "Vanquished Yin" (*wang-yin*). Vanquished Yang can arise when the Yang is so extremely weak (signified by such signs as much oily perspiration, cold body, no thirst, very faint respiration, cold limbs, coma) that it cannot nourish the Yin. This causes the Yin and Yang to separate, leading to possible "collapse" (fainting or shock) or even death. Vanquished Yin can occur because of great loss of fluids evidenced by severe sweating, vomiting, diarrhea, and bleeding, and is accompanied by weakness, fear of heat, warm skin, thirst, coarse respiration, warm limbs, red, dry tongue, and a flooding but weak pulse. In this case the Yin can no longer nourish the Yang, and the result may be similar to that of Vanquished Yang—separation, collapse, or death. Vanquished Yin or Yang can turn into one another, so even a Vanquished Yin situation can finally develop a minute pulse.

Common Pulse Combinations

Pulse	Associated Symptoms and/or Patterns
Minute and soggy	spasms
Minute and soft	spontaneous sweating
Minute and choppy	great loss of Blood

TABLE 51

The Various Positions and a Minute Pulse

	Bilateral (Li Shi-zhen)	Left Side	Right Side
First position	asthma; Heart palpitations	Qi and Blood both Deficient	Mucus obstructed; asthma
Second position	Deficient Spleen Qi; distended abdomen	sensation of pressure in chest; spasms in four limbs	Stomach Cold; food not transformed
Third position	Deficient Jing; fear of cold; diabetes	injured sperm; uterine bleeding	Kidney diarrhea[1]; pain in navel region; extremely Deficient Yang

[1]See Appendix C, on diarrhea.

Frail Pulse

This pulse shows that the Yang cannot raise the pulse, and so it is a sign of Deficient Yang and/or Deficient Jing. It is primarily seen in Deficient Kidney patterns along with such symptoms as sore bones, weak back and legs, asthma, tinnitus, or dizziness. A frail pulse is sometimes also seen in Deficient Cold Spleen patterns. Li Shi-zhen mentions that it is understandable and even normal to see this pulse in an elderly person, but if it is seen in a young person, the physician must be on the alert for a problem.

Common Pulse Combinations

Pulse	Associated Symptoms and/or Patterns
Frail and choppy	Deficient Blood
Frail and rapid	excessive loss of sperm, or uterine bleeding
Frail, wiry, and thin	Deficient Blood and flaccid tendons
Frail and soft	spontaneous sweating

TABLE 52

The Various Positions and a Frail Pulse

	Bilateral (Li Shi-zhen)	Left Side	Right Side
First position	Deficient Yang	Heart palpitations; forgetfulness	shortness of breath; spontaneous sweating
Second position	Deficient Spleen Qi and Deficient Stomach Qi	spasms	diarrhea
Third position	Yang collapses; Deficient Yin	Deficient Yin	Yang collapses

Soggy Pulse

This pulse is a sign of either Deficient Yin or Deficient Yin and Yang both. It is most often seen after loss of blood, as well as in many serious Deficiency patterns that are slightly more Deficient of Yin than of Yang. Li Shi-zhen says that if this pulse appears after a severe illness or postpartum, it is normal and recovery will be easy. (The tradition speaks of Deficiency that can easily receive tonification and Deficiency that cannot. This situation is Deficiency that can receive tonification.) If a person has this pulse but has no accompanying symptoms of Deficiency, it is said that the pulse is "without root," but the person should be treated in order to prevent disease.

A soggy pulse can also appear along with a Damp pattern, because the Dampness "spreads everywhere" and obstructs Qi and Blood movement. In this case, the soggy pulse is likely to have a tight, hindered quality. Sometimes a soggy, weak pulse appears with simultaneous Dampness Distress and Deficient Spleen patterns.

Common Pulse Combinations

Pulse	Associated Symptoms and/or Patterns
Soggy and wiry	dizziness or numb fingers
Soggy and choppy	loss of Blood
Soggy and rapid	Damp Heat

Leather Pulse

This pulse is a sign of Deficient Jing, Yin, or Blood. It is more serious than an ordinary empty pulse since in this case the Yang Qi is less controlled by the Yin, so that along with an empty feeling in the middle, the very surface of the pulse is hard and wiry. A leather pulse often appears with miscarriages, uterine bleeding, or spermatorrhea.

Common Pulse Combinations

Pulse	Associated Symptoms and/or Patterns
Leather, slippery, and big	excess of perspiration, or diarrhea
Leather and moderate, without Spirit	"dead" Yin, not treatable

Hidden Pulse

This pulse is usually a sign of serious obstruction. If a hidden pulse is strong, the obstruction is usually Excess/Cold or Stagnant Food, and is often accompanied by violent pain. When an extreme Heat situation displays a hidden rapid pulse, it is a situation in which the pattern and pulse do not match and is therefore serious and difficult to treat.

If the hidden pulse is without strength, it is usually a sign that Yang Qi is insufficient to raise the pulse. This is often seen in chronic illnesses accompanied by vomiting, diarrhea, cold limbs, or fainting. Occasionally, a person with a chronic pattern combining Arrogant Liver Yang and Deficient Kidney Yin will suddenly collapse (apoplexy or "succumbing" to Wind) and develop hemiplegia, and this pulse will appear. Some sources say that this can be a normal pulse during pregnancy.

Common Pulse Combinations

Pulse	Associated Symptoms and/or Patterns
hidden and slow	Extreme Cold: Extreme Yin Ascending
Hidden and rapid	Extreme Heat: Extreme Yang Ascending

Confined or Prison Pulse

This pulse is basically a subcategory of the hidden pulse with strength. It again signifies Cold obstruction with pain and the presence of lumps, tumors, or hernia. Li Shi-zhen cautions that if this pulse arises in a Deficiency pattern, the situation is dangerous. Other sources mention it as appearing with "running piglet" illness.

Spinning Bean or Moving Pulse

This pulse is said to result from the chaotic movement of Yin and Yang. When severe pain interrupts the Blood flow, or fright causes the Qi to "sneak" away, the Qi and Blood lose their mutual nourishing function and generate this unharmonious pulse. Although a spinning bean pulse is generally rapid, it does not necessarily imply a Heat condition; it just implies great imbalance.

Common Pulse Combinations

Pulse	Associated Symptoms and/or Patterns
Spinning bean and frail	palpitations
Spinning bean and full	pain; obstruction
Spinning bean and hollow	loss of Jing
Spinning bean and floating	External Pernicious Influence

Hollow Pulse

This pulse generally appears after great loss of blood, but not in chronic patterns of Deficient Blood. It can also appear after depletion of fluids due to vomiting, diarrhea, excessive perspiration, and loss of sperm.

Common Pulse Combinations

Pulse	Associated Symptoms and/or Patterns
Hollow and rapid	Deficient Yin
Hollow, empty, and soft	Deficient Jing; loss of Blood
Hollow and knotted	Congealed Blood

Scattered Pulse

A scattered pulse is a sign of extreme Deficiency, especially of Yang or of Original Qi. When seen in a chronic Deficiency illness with Deficiency signs, however, this pulse is unlike the weak pulse mentioned earlier, in which matching pulse and pattern meant the condition would be relatively easy to treat. In this case, because a scattered pulse is superficial, it shows that the Normal Qi or Yang is "floating" away. This is extreme weakness, and the pattern is difficult to reharmonize. Some sources say that this pulse can have the uneven quality sometimes associated with a choppy pulse. This pulse is usually seen in chronic patterns or in patterns of exhaustion.

The signification of the scattered pulse tends to remain the same no matter what other pulses it is found in combination with. The chart of combinations has therefore been omitted.

Notes

1. The *Nei Jing* opinion is found in *Su Wen*, sec. 5, chap. 17, pp. 106–107. The *Nan Jing* opinion is in "Difficulty 18," pp. 45–46. Its schema is about Meridians, makes no distinction between left and right hands, and is very unclear. The data in this table are only one interpretation. Following these correspondences, the *Nan Jing* goes on to say that the first, second, and third positions represent the Upper, Middle, and Lower Burner, respectively. Wang Shu-he's opinion is found in the Classic of Pulse [22], p. 6. Wang also says that the first, second, and third positions correspond to the sections of the Triple Burner. Li Shi-zhen also emphasizes this Triple Burner relation and his opinion is found in Pulse Studies [16], p. 4. The Zhang Jie-bing opinion is from his landmark *Complete Works of Jing-yue* (Jing-yue Quan-shu), 1624 C.E. [Taipei: Guofeng, 1980], sec. 5, p. 86.

Alternative styles of pulse correspondence at the radial artery also exist in early texts. The *Nan Jing* describes the horizontal layers of the pulse as matching the various Organs: "With three beans of pressure the skin is reached, which is the Lung position. Six beans of pressure reaches the Blood Vessels and is the Heart position. Nine beans of pressure reaches the flesh and muscles and is the Spleen position. Twelve beans of pressure is level with tendons and is the Liver position. Pressing to the bone . . . reaches the Kidneys" (*Nan Jing*, "Difficulty 5," p. 12). Related to this *Nan Jing* method is the method whereby the qualities of pulses are fitted into a correspondence schema. For instance, the *Nei Jing* states that the "Liver is wiry; the Heart pulse is 'hooked' [interpreted to mean flooding]; the Spleen is 'substitutelike' [interpreted to mean soft]; the Lung is 'featherlike' [interpreted to mean superficial]; the Kidneys are 'stonelike' [interpreted to mean deep]" (*Su Wen*, sec. 7, chap. 23, p. 154).

An elaborate comparative pulse correspondence system also exists in the earliest texts. The schema depends mainly on the relative sizes of the entire radial artery as compared with the pulse at the acupuncture point *ren-ying* (Stomach 9) at the common carotid artery of the neck. For example, if the radial pulse is twice as big as the carotid pulse, the illness is in the Gall Bladder Meridian. This method continues for the other Meridians (*Ling Shu*, sec. 2, chap. 9, pp. 89–92; *Su Wen*, sec. 3, chap. 10, p. 69).

2. Li Shi-zhen's opinion is from his Pulse Studies. If an opinion concerning both sides is omitted, it is usually because Li did not mention the case. The summary of opinions of individual positions on each hand is taken from Selections from Pulse Examination [17]. This comprehensive study excerpts pulse discussions from many early texts and catalogues them under the twenty-eight types in historical order.

3. See Zhang Zhong-jing, Discussion on Cold-induced Disorders [27], secs. 208, 225, and 234, for some examples of this situation. Liu Guan-jin (Pulse Examination [61], p. 82) mentions that if the Western disease entity meningitis is accompanied by increased cerebral pressure and high fever, a slow pulse can occasionally be felt. This is a dangerous sign in both medical systems.

4. An example of this situation is discussed in Liaoning Institute, Lecture Notes on Traditional Chinese Medicine [48], p. 34.

5. Yang Ji-zhou, Great Compendium of Acupuncture and Moxibustion [26], (1601 C.E.), sec. 5, p. 164. Originally based on *Su Wen*, sec. 7, chap. 24, p. 54.

6. *Su Wen* [1], sec. 40, chap. 53, p. 280.

7. Pulse Studies [16], p. 58.

8. Wang Shu-he, Classic of Pulse [22], p. 30.

9. Many classical physicians such as Zhang Zhong-jing and Zhang Jie-bing discuss this possibility.

APPENDIX E
Chinese Patterns and
Some Common Western Diseases

In Chapter 8, we discussed how large groups of patients with the same Western disease would frequently generate a cluster of several Chinese patterns. This is because the two systems are consistent interpretations of the same body and sometimes overlap in their perception of the functions and locations of bodily organs. Although there is no one-to-one correspondence for individual patients between Western diseases and Chinese patterns, the correlation between disease and pattern for a large group of patients would not be random. A statistically significant correspondence has been found to exist between the two systems.

Neither the Chinese tongue and pulse signs nor the other general signs a Chinese doctor reports would enable a Western doctor to make a diagnosis. Similarly, a single Western disease has no exact analog in the Eastern system. The tables in this appendix are not meant to be a short-cut for going from Western medicine to Eastern medicine; rather, they summarize preliminaries to further research and mutual understanding.

There are research papers, clinical studies, and textbook material in China that deal with every Western medical disease entity and its relation to Chinese patterns and treatment methods. Tables 53–72 list some common Western diseases and describe the patterns that would most frequently be diagnosed in a large group of patients with the identical Western disease.[1] They give an idea of what it would be like to observe patients simultaneously through both the Eastern and Western perceptual frameworks. They also demonstrate that the Chinese synthetic approach focuses on the body's general responses to a specific Western disease entity. It should be kept in mind that only the most common Chinese patterns associated with any Western disease are mentioned and that every example might yield other patterns as well.

TABLE 53

Coronary Artery Disease

Pattern	Signs	Tongue	Pulse
Turbid Mucus Obstructing Heart	pain or feeling of pressure in chest; pain sometimes radiates down Heart Meridian; left shoulder is sore or numb; coughing of phlegm; no appetite; conditions often seen in overweight people	pale material; greasy moss	slippery and wiry, or soggy and moderate
Congealed Heart Blood	intermittent stabbing pain in Heart or chest; palpitations; shortness of breath; chest feels oppressed	darkish red or purple material	sinking, choppy, or wiry
Deficient Heart Yang	no pain, or patient has recovered from acute pain; fear of cold; fatigue; spontaneous sweating; puffy, grayish white face; palpitations or empty feeling in chest; clear, copious urine	pale material; white moss	frail, slow, or empty
Deficient Heart Yin	no pain, or patient has recovered from acute pain; red face (especially cheeks); palpitations; insomnia; night sweats; thirst but no desire to drink	red material or red tip of tongue; little moss	thin and rapid
Deficient Liver Yin and Deficient Kidney Yin	vertigo; tinnitus; headache; numb limbs; weak lower back and knees; dry mouth; night sweats; hot palms and soles; constipation	red material; little moss	thin, wiry, or rapid

TABLE 54

Cardiac Insufficiency

Pattern	Signs	Tongue	Pulse
Deficient Heart Qi and Deficient Spleen Qi	palpitations and shortness of breath after exertion; fatigue; ashen, pale face; spontaneous sweating; little appetite; watery stool	pale material; thin, white moss	thin, or frail and knotted

TABLE 54 *(cont.)*

Cardiac Insufficiency

Pattern	Signs	Tongue	Pulse
Deficient Heart Yang and Deficient Kidney Yang	palpitations; asthma; face, eyelids, and four limbs are edemic; ashen, white face; sweat on forehead; scanty urine; cold limbs	swollen, pale material; white moss	thin and frail or knotted, or intermittent
Deficient Heart Yang and Congealed Heart Blood	palpitations; hurried breath; darkish face; purplish lips; painful flanks; lower lips are slightly swollen; coughing with blood; scanty urine	purple, darkish material, or purple material with red spots	thin and choppy, or knotted, or intermittent
Deficient Kidney Yang, with Water Radiating to Lungs	asthma; urgent breathing; saliva and phlegm or even a great amount of foaming phlegm from nose; gray-white face; very cold limbs; copious, cold perspiration; fear; irritability	pale material; greasy, white moss	intermittent

TABLE 55

Essential Hypertension

Pattern	Signs	Tongue	Pulse
Liver Fire Blazing	vertigo; headache; painful, red eyes; red face; quickness to anger; irritability; bitter taste and dry mouth; constipation; dark, scanty urine	red or scarlet material; yellow moss	wiry and full, or wiry and rapid
Turbid Mucus Obstructing Middle Burner (Spleen)	vertigo; head feels heavy, as if in a sack; poor appetite; nausea; chest and epigastrium feel pressure; numb limbs	thick, greasy moss	soggy or slippery
Arrogant Liver Yang Ascending	vertigo; tinnitus; blurred vision; palpitations; insomnia; bitter taste in mouth	reddish material; yellow moss	wiry

TABLE 55 *(cont.)*

Essential Hypertension

Pattern	Signs	Tongue	Pulse
Deficient Liver Yin and Deficient Kidney Yin	vertigo; headache; spots before eyes; tinnitus; palpitations; night sweats; irritability; afternoon fever; dry throat; sore lower back and knees	red material; little moss	sinking, wiry, thin, and rapid
Deficient Kidney Yang	vertigo; tinnitus; loss of hearing; bright white face; low Spirit; lower back and knees are sore and weak; fear of cold; watery stool; impotence	swollen, pale material	frail

TABLE 56

Hyperthyroidism

Pattern	Signs	Tongue	Pulse
Constrained Liver Qi	painful chest and flanks; anxiety; irritability; quickness to anger; menstrual irregularities; possible swelling in neck	thin white moss	wiry
Liver Fire Blazing and Heart Fire Ascending	protruding eyes; fear of light; red face; quickness to anger; irritability; tremors of tongue and hands; big appetite; dry mouth; palpitations	red material	wiry and rapid with strength
Deficient Heart Yin	insomnia; irritability; palpitations; night sweats; dry mouth	reddish material; thin moss	thin and rapid
Mucus Dampness Obstructing	soft, swelling neck; feeling of pressure in chest; nausea; vomiting; watery stool; (this pattern often merges with one of the above three)	thin, greasy moss	soggy or slippery

TABLE 57

Acute Pancreatitis

Pattern	Signs	Tongue	Pulse
Constrained Liver Qi	soreness in upper abdomen connects to chest and flanks; bitter taste and dry mouth; vomiting; sometimes heat flushes and then chills; frustration	thin white and yellow moss	wiry
Damp Heat in Spleen, Stomach, and Liver	left upper quadrant feels painful and full; no appetite; thirst but no desire to drink; jaundice; fever; pain that sometimes connects to back and shoulder; dark urine; constipation; pain resists touch	red material; greasy yellow moss	wiry, slippery, and rapid
Excess Fire in Liver and Gall Bladder	painful upper abdomen; pain that resists touch or stabbing pain that connects to back; nausea; vomiting; bitter taste in mouth; fever; irritability; thirst; constipation; scanty, dark urine	red material; yellow moss	floating, rapid, wiry, and full

TABLE 58

Infectious Hepatitis

Pattern	Signs	Tongue	Pulse
Damp Heat in Spleen and Gall Bladder	sore, painful flanks; jaundice; no appetite; fatigue; distended abdomen; patient is repelled by greasy food; scanty, dark urine; watery stool; possible fever	red material; greasy yellow moss	slippery and rapid
Heat Poison Collapsing into Ying and Blood stages of disease	acute, rapid onset; jaundice; high fever; irritability; delirium; bleeding; skin rashes	scarlet material; thick, greasy yellow or black moss	wiry and rapid
Constrained Liver Qi	distended, painful flanks; chest feels pressure; no appetite; nausea; belching	thin moss	wiry

TABLE 58 *(cont.)*

Infectious Hepatitis

Pattern	Signs	Tongue	Pulse
Constrained Liver Qi and Congealed Blood	piercing, fixed flank pain; palpable mass under ribs; darkish face; distended epigastrium and abdomen	darkish material or material with red or purple spots	wiry and choppy
Liver Invading Spleen	chest feels pressure; distention; belching; passing gas; little appetite; nausea; diarrhea; slight flank discomfort	thick moss	wiry and soggy
Deficient Liver Yin	slight flank pain; vertigo; irritability; fatigue; warm palms and soles; low fever	red material; little moss	wiry and thin
Deficient Spleen Qi	fatigue; bright white face; no appetite; distended abdomen; slight flank pain; watery stool	pale material; white moss	empty

TABLE 59

Liver Cancer

Pattern	Signs	Tongue	Pulse
Heat Poison in Liver and Gall Bladder	irregular fevers; jaundice; dark urine; bleeding from various places, e.g., nose or anus	red material; greasy yellow moss	wiry and rapid
Congealed Liver Blood	Liver quickly becomes large and painful; pain in fixed places; darkish face	darkish material	choppy
Liver Invading Spleen	distended and painful right flank; full epigastrium; distended abdomen; ascites; no appetite	greasy white moss	wiry
Deficient Spleen Yang and Deficient Kidney Yang	progressive emaciation; low Spirit; darkish face; day and night perspiration; no appetite; watery stool	pale material	frail

TABLE 60

Chronic Gastritis

Pattern	Signs	Tongue	Pulse
Liver Invading Spleen and Stomach	distended epigastrium and abdomen; no appetite; belching; soreness; stool passes uncomfortably	thin moss	wiry
Deficient Cold in Spleen and Stomach	Stomach discomfort relieved by cold and pressure; distention; no appetite; vomiting of clear liquid	pale material; thin white moss	slow and empty
Dampness Distressing Spleen	nausea; vomiting; no thirst; persistent distention; scanty urine	greasy white moss	soggy or moderate

TABLE 61

Cholecystitis

Pattern	Signs	Tongue	Pulse
Constrained Liver Qi	flank pain or twisting pain; bitter taste and dry mouth; no appetite; nausea; distended epigastrium and abdomen; constipation or diarrhea	normal	wiry
Liver Fire and Gall Bladder Fire	severe pain in flanks and epigastrium that connects to shoulder; intermittent fever and chills; dry mouth and throat; distention; nausea; constipation	cracked material; yellow moss	wiry and rapid
Damp Heat in Liver and Spleen	flank pain; distended epigastrium and abdomen; distention; heaviness; fatigue; fever; nausea; no appetite; thirst but no desire to drink; jaundice; constipation or diarrhea	red material; greasy yellow moss	slippery, rapid, and wiry

APPENDIX E

TABLE 62

Acute Glomerulonephritis

Pattern	Signs	Tongue	Pulse
Wind and Water in Conflict (Pernicious Influence Invading Lungs)	acute onset; at beginning, eyelids and face are swollen; headaches; fever; fear of drafts, or red, swollen, painful throat, or cough; urination is reduced; dark red urine; condition may progress to entire body with edema	thin white moss	floating, rapid
Damp Heat Collecting	whole body is swollen; skin is crystal-bright; scanty urine; sometimes blood in urine; frequent and urgent urination; headache; vertigo; bitter taste in mouth; constipation	greasy yellow moss	wiry, slippery, full
Deficient Spleen Yang and Deficient Kidney Yang	swollen body; bright white face; no appetite; tired Spirit; scanty urine; sometimes no urination; rapid breathing; vertigo; nausea; vomiting	pale material; white moss	soggy or frail
Dampness Distressing Spleen	yellow face; fatigue; no appetite; vomiting; whole body is swollen	greasy white moss	sinking, slippery

TABLE 63

Chronic Glomerulonephritis

Pattern	Signs	Tongue	Pulse
Deficient Spleen Yang	lower limbs are swollen; chronic intermittent edema; sallow face; fatigue; distended chest and abdomen; no appetite; watery stool	pale material; white moss	soggy or empty, or slow
Deficient Spleen Yang and Deficient Kidney Yang	chronic condition; reduced urination; swollen abdomen; edema in lower body; bright white face; fear of cold; cold limbs; no taste in mouth; sore lower back; watery stool	pale, swollen, moist material	frail

TABLE 63 *(cont.)*

Chronic Glomerulonephritis

Pattern	Signs	Tongue	Pulse
Deficient Liver Yin and Deficient Kidney Yin	headache; vertigo; afternoon fever; red cheeks; night sweats; tinnitus; dry throat; insomnia; lumbago; irritability; dark, scanty urine; slight or no edema	reddish material	thin and rapid

TABLE 64

Urinary Tract Infections

Pattern	Signs	Tongue	Pulse
Damp Heat Pouring into Bladder (Lower Burner Damp Heat)	frequent, urgent, and painful urination; dry mouth or thirst; or fever, backache, or blood in urine	red material; greasy moss	slippery and rapid
Deficient Kidney Yin with residual Damp Heat	frequent, urgent, painful urination; scanty urine; warm palms and soles; dizziness; dry mouth; low fever, sometimes intermittent	red material; greasy moss at root	thin and rapid
Deficient Qi and Deficient Yin with residual Damp Heat	fatigue; vertigo; white face; no appetite; frequent, urgent, and reduced urination; slight pain; some swelling; sore lower back	normal	empty
Deficient Spleen and Deficient Kidney	fatigue; no appetite; swollen limbs; cold back; frequent urination with slight discomfort	thin white moss	frail

TABLE 65

Arthritis

Pattern	Signs	Tongue	Pulse
Wind Obstructing Meridians	sore, painful joints; pain changes location; sometimes accompanied by fever; chills	white moss	floating
Cold Obstructing Meridians	painful joints; fixed pain; movement aggravates pain; heat relieves pain; cold weather aggravates pain	white moss	tight

TABLE 65 *(cont.)*

Arthritis

Pattern	Signs	Tongue	Pulse
Dampness Obstructing Meridians	joints are sore and feel heavy; discomfort; fixed pain; numb limbs; damp weather aggravates pain	greasy moss	soggy and moderate
Wind, Cold, and Dampness Obstructing Meridians	various combinations of the above		
Wind Heat Obstructing Meridians	sore joints; difficult movement; fever; thirst	red material; yellow moss	floating and rapid
Damp Heat Obstructing Meridians	fever; thirst; swollen and painful joints; or red eruptions on skin	red material; greasy yellow moss	rapid and slippery

TABLE 66

Cerebral Vascular Accident

Pattern	Signs	Tongue	Pulse
Wind Mucus Obstructing Meridians, Liver Yang Ascending	slow onset; mouth and eyes are askew; slurred speech; numb or trembling limbs; sometimes hemiplegia; vertigo; head is heavy and painful; excess saliva, or sudden loss of consciousness, or sudden collapsing	greasy white moss	wiry and slippery
Mucus Fire Suddenly Collapsing, Liver Fire Blazing	sudden collapse; unconsciousness; clenched teeth; clenched palms; tremors; hot body; red face; snoring; throat sounds phlegmy; headache; vomiting; scanty, dark urine; constipation	red material; greasy yellow moss	wiry, slippery, and full
Cold Mucus Obstructing	sudden collapse; tremors; slurred speech; headaches; vertigo; nausea; hemiplegia; pale face; purple lips	pale, puffy, darkish material	sinking and wiry
Yin and Yang Collapsing	open eyes and mouth; unconsciousness; pale face; slightly red cheeks; cold; sweat; open hands	variable	sinking, rapid, and thin, or hidden

TABLE 66 *(cont.)*

Cerebral Vascular Accident

Pattern	Signs	Tongue	Pulse
Deficient Qi, Congealed Blood	hemiplegia; slurred speech; numb limbs; sore body without strength; fatigue; sallow or pale face	pale material with darkness; white moss	sinking, thin, and choppy
Deficient Liver Yin and Deficient Kidney Yin	hemiplegia; emaciation; sore or numb body; vertigo; insomnia; red cheeks; dry mouth; night sweats; quickness to anger; scanty, dark urine; constipation	red material	wiry

TABLE 67

Anemia

Pattern	Signs	Tongue	Pulse
Deficient Qi and Deficient Blood of Heart and Spleen	pale or sallow face; pale lips and fingernails; vertigo; fatigue; palpitations; tinnitus; no appetite; watery stool; late menses with pale blood	pale material; white moss	empty or frail or thin
Dampness Distressing Spleen	sallow, yellow face; swollen body; vertigo; no appetite; no taste in mouth; nausea; distended abdomen; heavy, tired limbs; watery stool	pale material; greasy white moss	soggy or slippery or thin
Deficient Liver Yin and Deficient Kidney Yin	face lacks brightness; red cheeks, especially in afternoon; low fever; dry mouth; vertigo; tinnitus; bleeding gums	red or scarlet material	sinking, thin, and rapid
Deficient Spleen Yang and Deficient Kidney Yang	pale face; pale lips and fingernails; vertigo; spots before eyes; tired Spirit; tinnitus; lower limbs are weak; no appetite; no taste in mouth; watery stool; swollen lower limbs; sometimes amenorrhea	pale, swollen material; white moss	frail

TABLE 68

Diabetes

Pattern	Signs	Tongue	Pulse
Lung Fire, Upper Diabetes	great thirst; drinking of large quantities of water; dry mouth	red material; yellow moss	floating and rapid
Stomach Fire, Middle Diabetes	large appetite and excessive eating; thinness; constipation	red material; yellow moss	rapid
Kidney Fire, Lower Diabetes	frequent, copious urination; cloudy urine (as if greasy); progressive weight loss; dizziness; blurred vision; sore back; sometimes accompanied by ulceration on skin or itching; vaginal itching	red material	sinking, thin, and rapid

NOTE: There are two words in the Chinese language for diabetes: the traditional medical name, *xiao-ke*, which means "wasting and thirsting," and the modern term *tang-niao-bing*, which means "sugar urine illness." Discussion of diabetes by its traditional name appears in all the earliest texts, including the *Nei Jing*. Traditionally, it is divided into three types: upper, middle, and lower. Each type corresponds to a disproportionate emphasis on the three main symptoms—thirst, hunger, and excessive urination. Deficient Yin is usually associated with all three types. Also, a traditional diagnosis of "wasting and thirsting" may include illnesses besides the modern entity of diabetes. And the opposite is true—someone with *tang-niao-bing* would not necessarily have *xiao-ke*. See footnote on page 211.

TABLE 69

Pelvic Inflammatory Disease

Pattern	Signs	Tongue	Pulse
Fire Heat Poison Collecting in Lower Burner	acute onset; fever; painful lower abdomen; pain resists touch; yellow, thick, and foul-smelling leukorrhea; lower back pain; frequent or rough urination; no appetite; nausea; dry mouth; constipation	red material; yellow moss	wiry and rapid

TABLE 69 *(cont.)*

Pelvic Inflammatory Disease

Pattern	Signs	Tongue	Pulse
Stagnant Qi and Congealed Blood in Lower Burner	painful lower abdomen and hypogastrium; abdomen has falling feeling or stabbing pain; low back pain; leukorrhea; sometimes palpable mass in hypogastrium	pale, dark material; white moss or red dots	wiry and choppy
Deficient Spleen Qi and Deficient Kidney Qi	clear leukorrhea; sore lower back; distended lower abdomen that feels worse after exertion or intercourse; fatigue; swollen lower limbs; vertigo; fear of cold; no appetite; frequent urination; watery stool	pale, white material	frail and soggy

TABLE 70

Pneumonia

Pattern	Signs	Tongue	Pulse
Wind Heat Invading Lungs	sudden chills and fever; headache; sore throat; cough; chest pain; small amount of thick phlegm; dry mouth	thin white moss or thin yellow moss	floating and rapid
Heat Obstructing Lung Qi	high fever; red face; sweating but no reduction of fever, or little sweat; thirst and desire to drink; coughing of thick yellow phlegm, sometimes with blood; coarse respiration; asthma; chest pain	red material; yellow moss	rapid and slippery
Deficient Lung Qi and Deficient Lung Yin	usually occurs during recovery period after a high fever; dry cough; little phlegm; afternoon fever; tired Spirit; no desire to speak; irritability; quickness to anger; scanty urine; constipation	red or scarlet material; yellow or peeled moss	deep, thin, and rapid

TABLE 70 *(cont.)*

Pneumonia

Pattern	Signs	Tongue	Pulse
Heat Collapsing into Ying portion of four stages and Pericardium	high fever; cough; chest pain; coughing of phlegm with blood or foul mucus; dry throat; dry mouth but no desire to drink; Spirit is unclear; sometimes delirious speech; convulsions; red face; irritability; occasional coma	scarlet, dry material; grayish moss	sinking, wiry, thin, and rapid
Collapsed Qi	shallow respiration; cyanosis; gray-white face; no fever, or suddenly falling fever; cold limbs; cold sweat; muddled Spirit	pale material	frail

TABLE 71

Scarlet Fever

Pattern	Signs	Tongue	Pulse
Pernicious Influence in Wei portion of four stages	headache; fever; chills; red, swollen, painful throat; difficulty in swallowing; red eyes; nausea; scanty, dark urine	red eruptions on tip of tongue; greasy white moss	floating and rapid
Heat Pernicious Influence in Qi and Blood portions simultaneously	high fever; sweating; red, ulcerated sore throat; entire body has bright punctate eruptions; thirst; dry lips; constipation	red or scarlet material; yellow moss	floating and rapid
Qi and Blood both "Burnt"	eruptions close together; high fever; cough; rapid breathing; difficulty in breathing; gray or blue-green face; sweat; thirst	deep scarlet, cracked material with red dots	thin and rapid
Extreme Heat Generating Wind	high fever; irritability; delirium; Spirit is unclear; convulsions in all four limbs; eyes go up; clenched teeth; blue-green face; skin eruptions; coarse respiration; cyanosis	red, dry material	sinking, thin, and rapid
Deficient Lung Yin and Deficient Stomach Yin	scaly, dry skin that sheds (desquamation); tired Spirit; no appetite; dry lips; sore throat; this is a recovery stage	red, dry material	sinking and thin

TABLE 72

Common Cold

Pattern	Signs	Tongue	Pulse
Wind Cold Pernicious Influence	low fever; severe chills; no perspiration; sore limbs; stuffed or runny nose; itchy throat; cough with clear or white phlegm	thin white moss	floating and tight
Wind Heat Pernicious Influence	high fever; slight chills; headache; sweats; dry or sore throat; thirst; cough with thick yellow phlegm; dark urine	thin yellow moss	floating and rapid
Wind Cold with Dampness Pernicious Influence	Wind Cold signs; head feels swollen, as if in a sack; heavy, tired limbs; sore, heavy joints	greasy white moss	soggy
Summer Heat Dampness Pernicious Influence	Wind Heat signs; nausea; diarrhea; great thirst; irritability; great sweat; occurs in summertime	greasy yellow moss	soggy and rapid
Dryness Pernicious Influence	Wind Heat signs; dry nose; cracked lips; dry cough with no phlegm	red material; dry yellow moss	floating, thin, and rapid

Notes

1. Tables 53–72 were compiled from discussions appearing in the Chinese medical journals listed in the Bibliography and in the following texts: Chengdu Institute, Internal Medicine and Pediatrics [40]; Guangdong Provincial Institute, Traditional Chinese Internal Medicine [44]; Guangzhou Ministry, Essentials of Traditional Chinese Medicine [75]; Jiangsu Institute, Traditional Chinese Medicine Clinical Handbook of Common Illnesses [47]; Luoyang Regional Revolutionary Health Commission, Internal Medicine, vols. I and II [79]; Shanghai First Medical Hospital, Practical Internal Medicine [83]; Shanghai Second Medical Hospital, Handbook of Internal Medicine [88]; Zhejiang Provincial Committee, Clinical Study of Traditional Chinese Medicine [90].

APPENDIX F
The Curious Organs

The *Nei Jing* mentions six miscellaneous or Curious Organs and occasionally refers to one or another of them in passing. These Organs—the Brain, Marrow, Bones, Uterus, Blood Vessels, and Gall Bladder—are said to resemble the Yang Organs in form but the Yin Organs in function. They "store the Yin and imitate Earth; therefore, they store and do not disperse,"[1] whereas the Yang Organs "disperse and do not store."[2] These Curious Organs are actually of little importance, in both theory and practice; any distinct function they may have is subsumed under, and accessory to, the functions of the primary Organs. Treatment, therefore, is almost always aimed at one of the primary Organs or Meridians.

The Gall Bladder has been discussed earlier, with the Yang Organs (see Chapter 3).

The Brain, Marrow, and Bones are often indistinguishable from each other in the *Nei Jing* and are always inseparable from the Kidney, in both conception and function. Like the Kidneys, they are dependent on the combination of prenatal and postnatal Jing. "When an individual is created, first the Jing is formed; from the Jing comes the Brain and Marrow."[3] "The five-grain Jing [postnatal Jing] forms a cream, seeping into the empty spaces of the Bones to nourish the Brain and Marrow."[4]

The main function of the Marrow is to nourish the bones. It should be noted that the Chinese word here translated as "Marrow" refers not only to bone marrow but also to the spinal cord. If the Marrow is sufficient, the Bones are strong.[5] If the Marrow is insufficient, the Bones will be weak. Children with insufficient Marrow have problems with Bone growth.

The Brain is the "sea of Marrow."[6] It is responsible for the fluidity of movement in the body and for the sensitivity of the eyes and ears. The Brain, like the Bones, is nourished by the Marrow. When the Brain is not nourished, because the "Marrow is insufficient, the Brain lacks coordination and there is ringing in the ears, tremors, dizziness, poor vision, and languid idleness."[7]

The Bones are "ruled by the Kidneys" and give the body structural support.

Later in the medical tradition, there developed greater understanding of these Organs. Li Shi-zhen, for example, believed the Brain to be the sea of consciousness.[8] But however the Brain, Marrow, and Bones have been understood, their disorders have been treated with herbs or needles directed to the Kidneys or the Kidney Meridian.[9]

The Uterus is important to two major processes, menstruation and gestation. The Chinese believe, however, that both of these processes are governed, *functionally* if not anatomically, by other Organs and by the Meridians.

Menstrual periods cannot occur without a "communicating" Conception Meridian and a "full" Penetrating Meridian.[10] (The Penetrating Meridian is one of the extra Meridians and is known as the "sea of the Twelve Meridians.")[11] Both of these Meridians are said to "arise in the Uterus."[12] Menstruation also depends on the Kidney Jing and on the Blood functions of the Spleen and Liver. Therefore, although the Uterus is involved in the proper function of menstruation, treatment for menstrual disorders is generally directed toward the Liver, Spleen, or Kidneys and toward related Meridians.

Since the Uterus is also the place where the fetus resides during pregnancy, the word for Uterus in Chinese literally means "palace of the child." Most of the functions of pregnancy, however, are thought to be the province of the Conception and Penetrating Meridians and of the Spleen, Liver, and Kidneys. This is an example of Chinese medicine's emphasis on function and its relative indifference to structure.

The Blood Vessels are the "Yang Organ of the Blood"[13] and the means by which most Blood is transported through the body. The tradition states that Qi is associated with Blood in the Vessels[14] and that Qi and Blood are both in the Meridians, but the distinction between Blood Vessels and Meridians is not clearly stated. The implication is that Blood Vessels carry relatively more Blood and the Meridians relatively more Qi. Disorders of the Blood Vessels are treated through the other Organs; for instance, the Heart rules regularity of flow, the Liver rules evenness of distribution, and the Spleen rules the ability to keep the Blood within its pathways.[15]

Notes

1. *Su Wen* [1], sec. 3, chap. 11, p. 77.

2. Ibid.

3. *Ling Shu* [2], sec. 3, chap. 10, p. 104.

4. Ibid., sec. 6, chap. 36, p. 289.

5. *Su Wen*, sec. 24, chap. 81, p. 573.

6. *Ling Shu*, sec. 6, chap. 33, p. 275.

7. Ibid., p. 277.

8. Shanghai Institute, Foundations [53], p. 97.

9. One exception is found in the *Nan Jing*, in which the Bones and Marrow are thought to have their own "meeting point" that allows them to be treated not through the other Organs, but as distinct entities. The Bone point is Bladder 11 (*Da-zhu*) and the Marrow point is Gall Bladder 39 (*Jue-gu*, also called *Xuan-zhong*). *Nan Jing*, "Difficulty 45," p. 104.

10. *Su Wen*, sec. 1, chap. 1, p. 4.

11. *Ling Shu*, sec. 6, chap. 33, p. 275.

12. Ibid., sec. 10, chap. 65, p. 447.

13. *Su Wen*, sec. 5, chap. 17, p. 98.

14. *Ling Shu*, sec. 6, chap. 30, p. 267.

15. One exception, in which the Blood Vessels are treated as an entity independent of the other Organs, is in the discussion of "meeting points" in the *Nan Jing*. Acupuncture point Lung 9 (*tai-yuan*), the Blood Vessels' "meeting point," is said to treat the Blood Vessels directly. *Nan Jing* [3], "Difficulty 45," p. 104.

APPENDIX G
A Further Look at the
Looking Examination

This appendix is a brief summary of some basic traditional ideas concerning Looking Examination.

Head, Hair, and Face

The development of a child's head is a good indication of the state of the Jing, for Jing controls maturation. If a child's head is either too small or too large, and mental development is poor, it is a sign of Deficient Kidney Jing. A fontanel that collapses generally indicates a Deficiency condition; a raised fontanel is a sign of Excess.

The hair on the head is considered the "magnificence of the Kidney" and the "glory of the Blood." It is also called the "excess of the Blood." Thin hair (if it is not characteristic of the ethnic group or particular family), hair that easily falls out, dry, dull hair, or withered hair can be a sign of either Deficient Jing or Deficient Blood. Hair that falls out suddenly in big clumps is usually a sign of Deficient Blood Affected by Wind.

As in all traditional cultures, physiognomy flourished in China. The earliest medical texts mention it, but the mainstream medical tradition considered it arcane and paid it little attention. According to Chinese physiognomy, each area of the face corresponds to a particular Organ, so a disharmony in that Organ will affect the complexion, texture, or moisture of the corresponding facial area. Two such sets of correspondence are shown below in Figures 46 and 47. The first (Figure 46) is from the *Su Wen* section of the *Nei Jing*.[1] The second is from the *Ling Shu* section of the *Nei Jing*.[2] These illustrations are

FIGURE 46

Physiognomy in the *Su Wen*

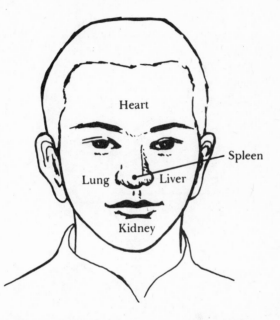

included for reference only and are marginal to Chinese medical practice.[3] They are also, incidentally, typical of the lack of internal consistency in the *Nei Jing*.

Eyes

Although it is the Liver that opens into the eyes, the state of all the Organs is reflected in them because the pure Jing Qi of all the Organs "pours through the eyes."[4] The general appearance of the eyes is especially important for perceiving the Shen. Lively eyes indicate that the Jing is uninjured. Stiff, "wooden," inflexible eyes show either a Wind or a Deficient condition. If the whites of the eyes are red, it is a sign of a Heat condition caused by either External Pernicious Influences or Excess Heat of an Organ. When the whites appear unclear or turbid, it is a sign of Dampness; a purple coloration indicates Liver Wind. Inordinate tears are usually a sign of Liver Fire. "Sand in the eyes," without redness, usually indicates Dampness or a weak Spleen. If the pupils are scattered and wide, it is a sign of Deficient Kidney Yin, or of poisoning, and is often a serious condition. Fear of bright light is usually a sign

FIGURE 47

Physiognomy in the *Ling Shu*

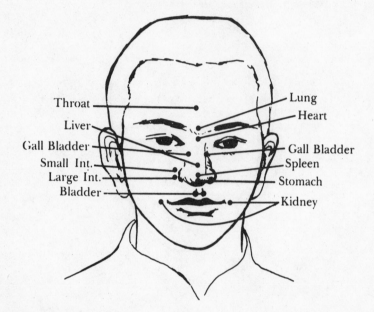

Throat — Liver — Gall Bladder — Small Int. — Large Int. — Bladder — Lung — Heart — Gall Bladder — Spleen — Stomach — Kidney

of Excess. When the eye sockets are gray and baggy, it often means Deficient Kidney Qi. Protruding eyes most often indicate Heat combined with Mucus.

Different areas of the eye are said to correspond to certain Organs. Blemishes, discoloration, eruptions, and other disorders of these areas are then thought to reflect the condition of the corresponding Organ. (See Figure 48.)[5] This correspondence is occasionally useful, but like all mechanical correspondences (see Appendix H), it is not very accurate.

Ears and Nose

The Kidneys open into the ears; the Triple Burner and Gall Bladder Meridians (Hand and Foot Shao-yang) pass through the ears and control them. The *Nei Jing* also states that all the Meridians connect to the ears,[6] and therefore the ears may reflect changes in many of the Organs.

Dry ears or contracted and gray-black ears, especially in chronic illnesses, are a sign of Kidney Jing becoming exhausted. Red ears signify Heat or Wind or both; purple ears indicate Cold and Deficiency; black ears show that Water is exhausted. Pus from the ears is usually a sign of Damp Heat in the Gall Bladder Meridian.

FIGURE 48

Areas of the Eye and Corresponding Organs

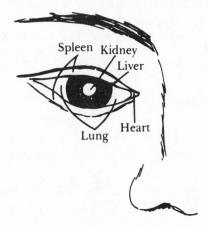

The Lungs open into the nose, and the Stomach and Large Intestine Meridians (Hand and Foot Yang-ming) pass through the nose and control it.

If the nose moves as though fanning itself, it is a sign of Heat in the Lungs. If the nostrils are dry, it is a sign of Heat or Dryness. Scorched black nostrils signify extreme Heat. A red nose indicates Heat. A drunkard's type of red, swollen nose indicates Stomach and Spleen Dampness, and Heat or Congealed Blood. A white nose signifies Deficient Qi; if it is also shiny, it often means there is Stagnant Food in the Intestines.

Lips, Mouth, Teeth, and Throat

The lips are the opening of the Spleen but can also reflect the states of other Organs. Pale white lips are a sign of Deficiency and Cold. Red Lips that are darker than normal signify Heat. Dry, scorched lips are a sign of Heat injuring the Fluids. Blue-green ("Qing" color) indicates Cold or pain; purplish blue-green is a sign that Cold is causing Congealed Blood. Cracking or chapping signifies Stomach and Spleen Heat. Trembling lips are usually a sign of Wind or of a weak Spleen that cannot hold the lips in place. Excessive salivation often indicates a weak Spleen distressed by Dampness or indicates Heat in the Stomach. If the mouth is askew (as in hemiplegia), Wind is indicated. Inability to close the mouth is a sign of great Deficiency.

The teeth are considered the "excess of the Bones." The Bones are ruled by the Kidneys, and therefore the teeth are closely related to the Kidneys. The Stomach Meridian (Foot Yang-ming) is connected to the gums. Dry teeth or gums are usually a sign of Stomach Heat. Gums that are red, swollen, or hot are usually a sign of Stomach Fire but can also be associated with Deficient Kidney Yin with Empty Fire Ascending. If the teeth look like dry bones, it generally indicates Deficient Kidney Yin. Grinding the teeth at night is said to be a sign of Heat, especially Empty Fire.

The throat is the "door of the Lungs," but all the Organs are said to be connected with it. If the throat or tonsils are red, swollen, or painful, it is a sign of Heat, especially in the Lungs or the Stomach (the Stomach Meridian passes through this area). If there are also ulcerations, it is a sign of extreme Heat. A chronic sore throat with little or no redness signifies Heat generated either by a pattern of Deficient Kidney Yin with Empty Fire Ascending or by a pattern of extremely Deficient Kidney Yang with Illusionary Yang Ascending. The sensation of a lump in the throat is often associated with stagnant Liver Qi.

Skin and Skin Eruptions

Withered skin is a sign that the Fluids are injured. Swollen skin that pits when pressed is a sign of edema and of Excess Fluids.

Rashes that can be felt with the hand are thought to be less serious than those that cannot be felt. If eruptions that are red and moist also appear darkish, they are a sign of severe illness. Eruptions that don't lose color when pressed and those with very clear edges are considered more serious than eruptions with less clear edges and those in which redness disappears with pressure.

When red eruptions occur during an External Pernicious Heat illness, they indicate that Heat has entered the Blood. The presence of such eruptions usually means that the normal Qi will be able to expel the Pernicious Influence. This is not so, however, in cases where there are an extraordinary number of eruptions or when the eruptions are clustered very close together. If eruptions do not occur during an illness in which they are typically a normal symptom, it indicates that the Pernicious Influence is obstructed in the Blood. This is considered a dangerous situation.

Red eruptions occurring in the absence of Pernicious Influences are usually signs of Interior Heat in the Blood. However, if the eruptions reoccur and there are no other signs of Heat, it often means that the Qi is too weak to hold the Blood in the Blood pathways.

Eruptions filled with fluid are a sign of Dampness.

Boils that are raised, swollen, red, hot, and painful are signs of "Fire Poison." Ulcerations that are not raised and do not affect the color of the skin are signs of Deficiency and are called Yin ulcerations.

Notes

1. *Su Wen* [1], sec. 9, chap. 32, p. 189.

2. *Ling Shu* [2], sec. 8, chap. 49, pp. 364–365.

3. The actual drawings are based on those in Guangdong Institute, Lecture Notes on Traditional Chinese Medical Diagnosis [43], pp. 30–31.

4. *Ling Shu*, sec. 12, chap. 80, p. 571.

5. Figure 48 is based on one that appears on page 2 of Sun Si-miao's Subtleties of the Silver Sea [18], a book that first appeared in 682 C.E., making it the first ophthalmology text in the Chinese medical tradition. Sun Si-miao's correspondence is based on his interpretation of a discussion in *Ling Shu*, sec. 12, chap. 80, p. 576.

6. *Ling Shu*, sec. 1, chap. 4, p. 39.

APPENDIX H
The Five Phases (Wu Xing)*

The theory of the Five Phases is an attempt to classify phenomena in terms of five quintessential processes, represented by the emblems Wood, Fire, Earth, Metal, and Water. Its place in Chinese medicine and other Chinese intellectual pursuits has been misunderstood ever since the first Occidentals tried to explain Chinese natural philosophy to the West over three hundred years ago. During this century, the academic world has made some advances toward a better appreciation of the Five Phases theory,[1] but true understanding is rare among people involved in the practice of Chinese medicine in the West. The aim of this appendix is to explain the Five Phases theory in the context of Chinese medicine and to shed some light on its clinical value.

The Five Phases are not in any way ultimate constituents of matter. This misconception has long been embodied in the common mistranslation "Five Elements" and exemplifies the problems that arise from looking at things Chinese with a Western frame of reference. The Chinese term that we translate as "Five Phases" is *wu xing*. *Wu* is the number five, and *xing* means "walk" or "move," and perhaps most pertinently, it implies a process. The *wu xing*, therefore, are five kinds of processes; hence the Five Phases, and not the Five Elements. The theory of Phases is a system of correspondences and patterns that subsume events and things, especially in relationship to their dynamics.

*This appendix was written in collaboration with Dan Bensky and the assistance of Kiiko Matsumoto.

More specifically, each Phase is an emblem that denotes a category of related functions and qualities. The Phase called Wood is associated with active functions that are in a growing phase. Fire designates functions that have reached a maximal state of activity and are about to begin a decline or a resting period. Metal represents functions in a declining state. Water represents functions that have reached a maximal state of rest and are about to change the direction of their activity. Finally, Earth designates balance or neutrality; in a sense, Earth is a buffer between the other Phases. In the sense that the Phases correlate observable phenomena of human life into images derived from the macrocosm, they serve a similar function as that of elements in other medical systems.

In more concrete terms, the Five Phases can be used to describe the annual cycle in terms of biological growth and development. Wood corresponds to spring, Fire to summer, Metal to autumn, and Water to winter. And what of Earth? Earth may represent the transition between each season (and it is commonly used to represent "Indian summer"). These correlations, as diagramed in Figure 49, are known as the Mutual Production order of the Five Phases. They represent the way in which the Five Phases interact and arise out of one another in the typical yearly cycle. There are thirty-six mathematically possible orders in which the Five Phases can be arranged, but only a few of them are actually used either in medicine or in other disciplines.

The application of the Five Phases to seasonable growth is only one exam-

FIGURE 49

Mutual Production Order of the Five Phases

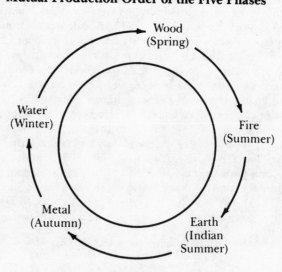

ple of how the system was used. In time, the five generic categories were used for classifying many more perceptions, from colors, sounds, odors, and taste sensations to emotions, animals, dynasties, the planets, and ultimately everything in the universe. (See Table 73.) Correlations were also made between the Phases and various Organs and anatomical regions, which is how the connection between the Phases and medicine came about.[2]

TABLE 73

Five Phases Correspondences

	Wood	Fire	Earth	Metal	Water
Direction	east	south	center	west	north
Color	blue green	red	yellow	white	black
Climate	windy	hot	damp	dry	cold
Human Sound	shouting	laughing	singing	weeping	groaning
Emotion	anger	joy	pensiveness	grief	fear
Taste	sour	bitter	sweet	pungent	salty
Yin Organ	Liver	Heart	Spleen	Lungs	Kidney
Yang Organ	Gall Bladder	Small Intestine	Stomach	Large Intestine	Bladder
Orifice	eyes	tongue	mouth	nose	ears
Tissue	tendons	blood vessels	flesh	skin	bones
Smell	goatish	burning	fragrant	rank	rotten

Before exploring the use of Five Phases theory in medicine, it is helpful to consider its history and relationship to Yin-Yang thinking. While Yin-Yang theory stretches back into China's remote antiquity, Five Phases theory was not documented until the fourth century B.C.E.[3] It is nevertheless reasonable to assume that a scheme as complex as the Five Phases theory did not emerge spontaneously. The framework must have been gestating for some time. Some intimation of the Five Phases can be found in many writings of the period from about 500 B.C.E. to 200 B.C.E., which was a time of great intellectual, political, and social ferment in China.[4] The Five Phases theory was first systematized by Zou Yen (approximately 350 B.C.E. to 270 B.C.E.) and his followers.[5] The original emphasis of the theory was as much political as it was scientific. The correct timing of rites and the succession of dynasties came largely to be interpreted through the dynamics of the Phases, which were then commonly called the Five Virtues or Powers. As Joseph Needham comments, "there were intense and anxious debates about the proper color, musical notes and instruments, sacrifices, etc. [according to Five Phases], appropriate to a particular dynasty or emperor."[6]

The number five was important in the numerology of the period, particularly for classifications of Earthly things. Various other numbers, such as six, four, and three, turn up in early classification schemes for things pertaining to Heaven.[7] It is difficult to determine whether the importance of the number five led to Five Phases theory or the popularity of the Five Phases theory led to things being classified in fives.

During the third and fourth centuries B.C.E., the Five Phases theory and the Yin-Yang theory existed simultaneously and independently of each other.[8] For example, Lao Tzu and Chuang Tzu refer extensively to Yin and Yang but do not mention the Five Phases. Unlike other traditional cultures with systems of elemental correspondences (e.g., the Greek Four Elements or the Hindu Three Doshas), the Chinese thus had two systems of referents. It was not until the Han dynasty, a period of great eclecticism and synthesis, that the two systems began to merge in Chinese medicine. "The five elements [Phases] [which] had not been part of the most ancient Chinese medical speculations" were incorporated into the clinical tradition that culminated in the *Nei Jing*.[9] Certain parts of the *Nei Jing* refer to the Five Phases, while others do not. Yet other texts, such as the Discussion of Cold-Induced Disorders and the biography of Bian Que in the *Shi Ji* or Historical Records,[10] make no mention whatsoever of Five Phases theory.[11] The Five Phases theory continued to undergo changes even after its incorporation into Chinese medicine. It is not until the Song dynasty (960–1279 C.E.) that the relationships between the Phases were commonly used to explain the etiology and processes of illness.[12]

Many attempts were made to fit the Five Phases neatly into the Yin-Yang structure. For example, Wood and Fire were considered the Yang Phases, being active in character, while Metal and Water, associated with quiescent functions, were the Yin Phases. Earth was the balance point between Yin and Yang. Yet, despite this apparently successful marriage between Five Phases and Yin-Yang theory, the two systems of correspondence frequently yielded different interpretations of health and disease.[13] For example, Five Phases theory might emphasize the following correspondences stated in the *Nei Jing*: The Liver opens into the eyes; the Kidney opens into the ears; the Heart opens into the tongue. Disorder in a particular orifice would necessarily be linked to its corresponding Organ. Yin-Yang theory, on the other hand, might emphasize the following quite different assertions of the *Nei Jing*: The pure Qi of all Organs is reflected in the eyes; all the Meridians meet in the ears; the tongue is connected to most of the Meridians. Yin-Yang theory would not necessarily see a link between a part and a part. Rather, all disharmonies of the eyes, ears, or tongue would be interpreted in terms of patterns. Thus, an eye disorder could be part of a Liver disharmony or perhaps a Lung, Kidney, or Spleen disharmony, depending on the configuration of other signs. The differences between these medical interpretations stem from the fact that Five Phases theory emphasizes one-to-one correspondences, while Yin-Yang theory emphasizes the need to understand the overall configuration upon which the part depends. And so, although Five Phases theory is ideologically more dynamic than, for instance, the Greek or Hindu systems, and is actually capable of being applied creatively to medical practice, it became a rigid system. Yin-Yang theory, on the other hand, with its emphasis on change and a Taoistic view of the importance of the whole, allowed for a great deal of flexibility. It was therefore easier to adapt to the needs of clinical practice.

Chinese medicine has had to take many liberties with the Five Phases theory in order to fit it to actual medical experience. The physiology that grew out of Five Phases theory, for example, is not identical with traditional Chinese medical physiology. The tradition is based on empirical observation and is intimately connected to Yin-Yang theory, concentrating on the functions of the Organs and extrapolating their interrelationships from their functions. The Organs are thus the key to the system. Five Phases theory does not always agree with this understanding, and in that case, it is simply ignored.[14] For example, in Five Phases physiology, the Heart corresponds to Fire. Traditional Chinese texts, however, consider the Kidneys (Life Gate Fire) to be the physiological basis for the Fire (Yang) of the other Organs. And so, the Five Phases theory's formal correspondence would be conveniently forgotten.

Use of the Five Phases in Medicine

Innumerable correspondences are associated with the Five Phases, some of which are useful and some not. Distinguishing between the two groups can be quite difficult, and every practitioner has his or her own view. Some practitioners are happy with such correspondence as those of plants and grains; others are not. Odors are excluded from many lists,[15] but a number of practitioners feel that they are clinically quite useful.[16] The correspondences that are in general use in medicine are listed in Table 73. The medically useful correspondences can be divided into two groups. There are those which make metaphysical sense in the Chinese mode of thought, or are construed to have associations outside the body (often forced associations). And there are correspondences derived not from metaphysical premises, but from the functions of the Organs or from empirical observation. The best example of the former is color: green for Wood (trees), red for Fire, yellow for Earth (the soil of northern China, where these correspondences originated, is yellow), white for Metal (silvery luster), and black for Water (the inky depths of the ocean). Similar explanations, however strained, are available for the seasons, climatic conditions, directions, tastes, and smells. An example of the latter type of correspondence is that between Metal and the nose. The nose has no actual relationship with Metal, and such a relationship was never posited by the ancient Chinese. The nose is, however, the opening most often affected by diseases of the Lungs, and in Chinese physiology the nasal tract is considered an extension of the Lungs. Because the Lungs are associated with Metal, the nose is also given that association. Similarly, the association of anger with the Liver is probably due to careful observation of people, rather than to any notion of the "woodenness" of becoming enraged. The distinctions between the two types of correspondence is important in explaining the dynamic behind the diagnostic use of the Five Phases theory, and also gives perspective on the whole system.

The Five Phases correspondence is at best a convenient way to organize significant clinical reality. Let us take facial color correspondence, delineated in Table 73, as an example. A yellow complexion often appears in a Spleen disharmony (yellow and Spleen are both associated with Earth), and a darkish complexion often appears in a Kidney disharmony (black and Kidneys are associated with water). A red face, however, although it can be part of a Heart pattern, is just as likely to be part of the Heat pattern of any Organ. A white face can appear with Lung disharmonies, but can also be part of the Cold pattern of any Organ. A blue-green complexion, while often part of a Liver disharmony, might as easily be part of a Congealed Heart Blood pattern. The correspondences of climate work much the same way. Although it is true that the Spleen is especially sensitive to Dampness, the Kidney to Cold, the Lungs to Dryness, and the Liver to Wind, Dryness does not necessarily imply a Lung disharmony, for it can easily affect the Stomach, Intestines, or Heart. Coldness does not necessarily imply the Kidneys, because the Spleen, Lungs, and Heart can also be affected by Cold. And so on. The Five Phases correspondence can be helpful as a guide to clinical tendencies, but the test of veracity in Chinese medicine remains the pattern. Yin-Yang theory is more applicable in the clinic because it focuses on the idea that the totality determines relationships, correspondences, and patterns. The flexibility of Yin-Yang theory resides in its insistence that all correspondences finally depend on the configuration of a unique whole.

The Five Phases are often used to describe clinical processes and relationships and to help in the conceptualization of proper treatments. It is an explanatory theory and is not meant as a binding doctrine. For example, as has been shown (see Figure 49), the Five Phases can be used to describe the general processes that take place during the annual cycle. That sequence—the Mutual Production order of Wood, Fire, Earth, Metal, Water—describes normal generative functions. In the sequence, the producer is called the Mother and the produced, the Child (an example of the tendency toward concreteness in traditional Chinese thought). Some patterns of disharmony can be explained by reference to the Mutual Production order, especially patterns of Deficiency. The Child of a Deficient Mother, for instance, becomes Deficient for want of proper nourishment. Conversely, when the Child is Deficient, it may "steal the Qi" of the Mother, making it Deficient as well. If an

Organ is Deficient, therefore, treatment can be affected by strengthening the Mother Organ. When there is an Excess in an Organ, the Child can be drained. This concept of treatment is important in acupuncture, but is seldom used in herbal medicine.[17]

Another sequence is known as the Mutual Checking or Mutual Control order. In this sequence, each Phase is said to check or control the succeeding Phase (see Figure 50). The Control order, like the Mutual Production order, describes naturally occurring phenomena, and it works to ensure that the Mutual Production order does not overgenerate and cause imbalances. A disharmony within the Control order might mean that an Organ is exerting Excess control over the Organ that it regulates. This would lead to a Deficiency in the regulated Organ. Or the Organ that should be regulated may become the regulator. Other situations can arise, but these two are the most likely. The former imbalance is known as an insulting cycle, and the latter as a humiliation cycle. Some common disharmonies of Five Phases patterns are summarized in Tables 74 and 75.[18] (Some of the examples may seem to contradict the presentation elsewhere in this book, or even to contradict Five Phases theory itself. This is because the schema underlying the Five Phases is often too rigid to describe physiological functions accurately. In other words, some fudging must be done by any practitioner determined to use Five Phases theory at all times.)

FIGURE 50

Mutual Control Order of the Five Phases

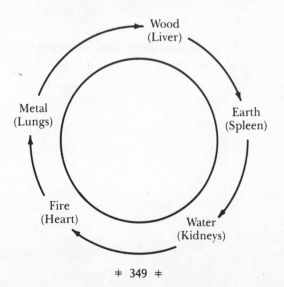

TABLE 74

Disharmonies of the Mutual Production Cycle

Disharmony	Description	Symptoms and Signs	Physiological Correlation
Wood not producing Fire	Liver (Wood) Blood not nourishing Heart (Fire)	weakness; timidity; palpitations; poor memory; insomnia; thin or choppy pulse	general Deficient Blood patterns
Fire not producing Earth	Heart (Fire) unable to warm Spleen (Earth)	aversion to cold; cold limbs; distended abdomen; diarrhea; edema	Kidney Yang unable to warm Spleen Yang
Earth not producing Metal	Spleen (Earth) unable to nourish Lungs (Metal)	phlegm; cough; fatigue; empty pulse	Deficient Spleen producing Excess Mucus in Lungs (actually the reverse of the classic Five Phases relationship)
Metal not producing Water	Lungs (Metal) not sending Water to Kidney (Water)	shortness of breath; thirst; scanty, dark urine; weak knees; sore lower back; other Deficient Yin signs	Deficient Kidney Yin
Water not producing Wood	Kidney (Water) not nourishing Liver (Wood)	tinnitus; low back pain; weak knees; vertigo; tremors; emaciation	Kidney Yin not nourishing Liver Jing

TABLE 75

Disharmonies of the Mutual Control Cycle

Disharmony	Description	Symptoms and Signs	Physiological Correlation
Wood insults Earth	Liver (Wood) Qi excessively Controls Spleen (Earth)	painful flanks; headache; distention; sore eyes; passing of gas (Excess Liver) with lack of appetite; diarrhea; lassitude (Deficient Spleen)	Liver Invading Spleen

TABLE 75 *(cont.)*

Disharmonies of the Mutual Control Cycle

Disharmony	Description	Symptoms and Signs	Physiological Correlation
Fire humiliated by Metal	Heart (Fire) Yang unable to control Lung (Metal) Fluids	frequent urination; palpitations; insomnia; shortness of breath	Deficient Heart Yang and Deficient Lung Qi
Earth's control of Water not adjusted	Spleen (Earth) insults Kidney (Water)	dry mouth and lips; thin, rapid pulse; constipation	Heat Pernicious Influence Injuring Yin (especially of Stomach)
	Spleen (Earth) humiliated by Kidney (Water)	edema and other Deficient Kidney signs	Deficient Spleen Yang and Deficient Kidney Yang
Metal humiliated by Wood	Lungs (Metal) unable to control Liver (Wood)	painful flanks; bitter taste in mouth; cough; irritability; wiry pulse	Liver Invading Lungs
Water humiliated by Fire	Kidney (Water) unable to control Heart (Fire) Yang	spermatorrhea; lumbago; irritability; insomnia; red tongue; thin and rapid pulse	Deficient Kidney Yin and Deficient Heart Yin (also called "Heart and Kidney Unable to Communicate")

Criticism of Five Phases Theory

The Five Phases theory has been the subject of criticism ever since its invention. The challenges to its veracity and practicality date as far back as Mohist contemporaries of Zou Yen (fourth century B.C.E.). For example, one comment on the Mutual Control order reads: "Quite apart (from any cycle) Fire naturally melts Metal, if there is enough Fire. Or Metal may pulverize a burning Fire to cinders, if there is enough Metal. Metal will store Water (but does not produce it). Fire attaches itself to Wood (but is not produced from it)."[19]

A few hundred years later, the great Han dynasty scientist and skeptic Wang Cong satirized the results of literal application of the Five Phases theory. Here are two short excerpts from his work:

The body of a man harbors the Qi of the Five Phases, and therefore (so it is said) he practices the Five Virtues, which are the Tao (Way) of the Phases. So long as he has the five inner Organs within his body, the Qi of the Five Phases are in order. Yet according to the theory, animals prey upon and destroy one another because they embody the several Qi of the Five Phases; therefore the body of a man with the five inner Organs within it ought to be the scene of internecine strife, and the heart of a man living a righteous life be lacerated with discord. But where is there any proof that the Phases do fight and harm each other, or that animals overcome one another in accordance with this?

The horse is connected with the sign *wu* (Fire); the rat with the sign *zi* (Water). If Water really controls Fire, (it would be more convincing if) rats normally attacked horses and drove them away.[20]

Despite such early criticism, the Five Phases theory became entrenched in Chinese medicine. One reason for this is that Chinese investigative study tends to be inductive only to a point and then proceeds with deductions based on the classics.[21] The Five Phases theory thus served as an orthodox reference for numerous speculative deductions. Most modern Chinese critics describe Five Phases theory as a rigid metaphysical overlay on the practical and flexible observations of Chinese medicine.

Another major criticism, and a primary difficulty in the application of the Five Phases theory to medicine, is its lack of consistency. To fit the theory to reality, the referents of the Phases and the relationships between them have continually been changed and corrupted. The results of such corruption can be seen in Tables 74 and 75 on the clinical use of the Five Phases.

Such a problem exists in all traditional systems of elemental correspondence.[22] The original classical Greek formulation by Empedocles of Agrigentum (c. 504–433 B.C.E.) is a system in which the basic elements of fire, earth, water, and air were considered the ultimate constituents of matter and were associated with various other categories of four such as the four fundamental qualities and the four humors. All varieties and changes in the world were associated with different mixtures of the four elements. Figure 51 is a schematic representation of this theory.[23]

When they tried to apply this theory to empirical observations, however, the Greek natural philosophers and physicians had to change an element or add one, or just ignore the theory. The Chinese, because their dependence on tradition would not allow them to abandon the Five Phases theory altogether, resorted to the use of two theories—one was the Five Phases theory, which became an "official theory" into which facts were sometimes made to fit, and the second was the earlier Yin-Yang theory. Yin-Yang always maintained its place as the principal guide to clinical practice because it had the flexibility to encompass change and unique situations.

FIGURE 51

Greek System of the Four Elements

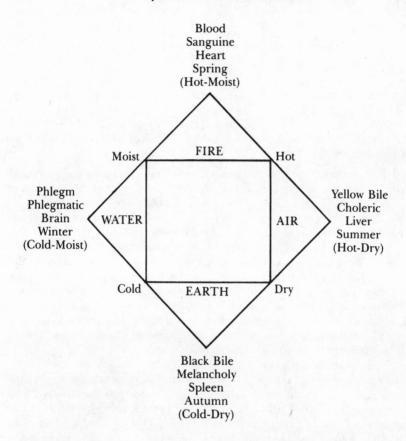

Western practitioners of acupuncture and Chinese medicine have special problems dealing with the Five Phases theory. The major difficulty is that much of the literature available in English describes diagnosis and treatment exclusively in terms of Five Phases theory. Writings that refer to the theory as the "Law of the Five Elements"[24] betray a misunderstanding of Chinese science—natural laws such as those promulgated by Aristotle and Newton simply were not developed in traditional China.[25] These writings also put undue emphasis on the importance of the Five Phases to the Chinese medical tradition; even respected defenders of the Five Phases theory readily admit that sometimes it is useful and sometimes it is not.[26] Even so, it is unfortunate that many practitioners simply consider Five Phases theory unscientific gibberish and do not try to understand it. It is actually an important secondary emblem system used to assess and discuss clinical reality.[27]

Notes

1. While their approaches are too academic for the purpose of understanding the Five Phases in relationship to clinical medicine, both Joseph Needham in *Science and Civilization*, vol. 2, pp. 243–268, and Manfred Porkert in *Theoretical Foundations*, pp. 43–54, do an excellent job of explaining Five Phases theory.

2. In the early periods of Chinese history there were many Five Phases correspondence schemes altogether different from the one predominantly used in the *Nei Jing* and reflected in Table 73. Masao Maruyama, in a fascinating essay written in Japanese, describes several of these alternative schemes. For example, there is a compilation of philosophical theories prepared for the Prince of Huai-nan (known as the *Huai-nan-zi*) in the second century B.C.E., in which correspondences of Wood to the Spleen, Fire to the Lungs, Earth to the Heart, Metal to the Liver, and Water to the Kidneys appeared. The other correspondences are also different. The fact that various systems existed confirms the impression that Five Phases theory is a somewhat arbitrary and mechanical network of correspondences. See Masao Maruyama, Studies of the Classics of Acupuncture Medicine (*Shinkyu igaku no koten to kenkyu* [Osaka: Sogen Publishers, 1952]), pp. 15–25.

Alternative and contradictory correspondences can be found even in the early medical texts. Perhaps they are remnants of prior schema or perhaps they recognize clinical realities. For example, in parts of the *Nei Jing*, fear corresponds to Deficient Liver Qi instead of to the Kidneys, and grief corresponds to Deficient Heart Qi instead of to the Lungs (*Su Wen*, sec. 2, chap. 8, p. 86). Another example is the three different correspondence schemas for the five tastes in *Su Wen*, chaps. 22 and 23, and *Ling Shu*, chap. 63.

Such discrepancy in the formative period of philosophic speculative medical systems is universal. For example, the Hippocratic corpus has several versions of the four humors. In the *Nature of Man*, the later orthodox version appears: phlegm, blood, yellow bile, and black bile. In *Diseases IV*, they are phlegm, blood, bile, and water; while *Ancient Medicine* assumes an unlimited number of humors.

3. Needham, *Science and Civilization*, vol. 2, p. 242.

4. Jia De-dao, Concise History [95], p. 29.

5. Needham, *Science and Civilization*, vol. 2, p. 232.

6. Needham, *Grand Titration*, p. 231.

7. Jia De-dao, Concise History, pp. 29–30. For example, Lü's Spring and Autumn Annals (246–237 B.C.E.) mentions Four Phases, omitting Earth.

8. Fung Yu-lan, *History of Chinese Philosophy*, vol. I, p. 8; Chan, *Chinese Philosophy*, p. 224; Hans Agren, "Patterns of Tradition and Modernization in Contemporary Chinese Medicine," in *Medicine in Chinese Cultures: Comparative Studies of Health Care in Chinese and other Societies*, ed. by Arthur Kleinman, et al. (Washington, D.C.: John E. Fogarty International Center, U.S. Dept. of HEW, NIH, 1975), p. 38.

9. Lu Gwei-djen and Joseph Needham, "Records of Diseases in Ancient China," *American Journal of Chinese Medicine* 4, no. 1 (1976):12.

10. Dan Bensky, "The Biography of Bian Que in the *Shi Ji*," unpublished manuscript, University of Michigan, 1978, p. 2.

11. Recent archeological discoveries of pre–*Nei Jing* texts confirm the impression that Yin-Yang was originally a much more important part of Chinese medicine than the Five Phases theory. See "A Simple Introduction to Four Ancient Lost Medical Texts Found at the Tomb of Ma-wang," Medical History Text Research Group of the Academy of Traditional Medicine, *Wen Wu*, no. 6 (1975), pp. 16–19. The Five Phases are not mentioned in these ancient medical writings. See Chapter 4, Note 3.

12. Jia De-dao, Concise History, pp. 165–166.

13. Porkert, *Theoretical Foundations*, p. 118. Traditional Chinese thought has a general tendency to reconcile and harmonize different or even mutually exclusive ideas in an arbitrary syncretism. Contrary doctrines—for instance, Taoism and Confucianism—are asserted to be mutually complementary. Nakamura's discussion of this Chinese characteristic states: "What stands out in this sort of reasoning is a certain sort of utilitarianism and early compromise, with cold logical considerations completely abandoned." Hajime Nakamura, *Ways of Thinking of Eastern Peoples* (Honolulu: East-West Center Press, 1969), p. 291.

14. Qin Bo-wei, Medical Lecture Notes [64], pp. 15–22.

15. Nanjing Institute, Introduction to Traditional Chinese Medicine [50], p. 19; Shanghai Institute, Foundations [53], p. 28.

16. Often patients will spontaneously smell a particular odor or exude a particular odor when the corresponding Organ is involved.

17. Acupuncture points are selected primarily because of their effect on patterns or symptoms. Five Phases theory plays an important role in point selection only in relation to the Five Transporting (*wu-shu*) points on the extremities. Originally, and throughout history, these crucial points (individually known as well, gushing, transporting, transversing, and uniting: *jing*, *rong, shu, jing, he*) were defined by their effect on patterns and symptoms (e.g., *Ling Shu*, sec. 1, chap. 1, p. 8; *Nan Jing*, "Difficulty 68," p. 148). The *Nei Jing* introduces a Five Phases connection with the Transporting points by mentioning that the well point of the Yang Meridians corresponds to Metal and the well point of the Yin Meridians corresponds to Wood (*Ling Shu*, sec. 1, chap. 2, pp. 14–28). No other point-Phase connection or therapeutic notion is mentioned in the *Nei Jing*. The *Nan Jing* completes a Five Phases connection with each of the Transporting points in "Difficulty 64" (p. 139), although no clear connection with point selection and therapeutics is made. (There are, however, some vague references in Difficulties 79 and 72.) Not until Gao Wu's famous text of 1529 C.E. is a precise connection made among Phase, Transporting point, and a therapeutic action of tonification or draining (Gao Wu, Gatherings from Eminent Acupuncturists [*Zhen-jiu Ju-ying*], [Shanghai: Shanghai Science and Technology Press, 1978], sec. 2, chap. 9, pp. 154–159). This particular method of Gao Wu's was only one of many he thought suitable for point selection, but nonetheless it became the basis of the rigid late-nineteenth-century Japanese *Nan Jing* school of acupuncture and therefore of the subsequent European emphasis on the Five Phases.

The *Nei Jing*, incidentally, mentions only one Transporting point (*fu-liu*, Kidney 7) as having a tonifying effect, and this mention is not in a Five Phases correspondence context (*Su Wen*, sec. 7, chap. 62, p. 338).

A second early source of this type of Five Phases usage in acupuncture is the famous "Song of Twelve Meridians, Mother-Child Points, and Tonification and Draining." This poem is later than Gao Wu's text and is reprinted in Selected Annotations of Acupuncture Songs and Odes (*Zhen-jiu Ge-fu Xuan-jie*) by Chen Bi-liu et al. (Hong Kong: China Medical Publishers, 1966 [reprint of 1959 Mainland edition]), pp. 213–226.

18. Tables 74 and 75 are based on Qin Bo-wei's discussion in Medical Lecture Notes, pp. 15–22. The chart includes examples of the Five Phases being used in sequences other than those described in the text. Such sequences result from the traditional attempt to make observable Organ disharmony fit into the Five Phases sequence, which is usually an attempt to make theory fit practice. There may also, however, be remnants of other Five Phases arrangements (see note 2). These different versions are explicit in early medical texts. For example, the Five Phase discussion in "Difficulty 75" of the *Nan Jing* indicates that to strengthen the Lungs it is necessary to strengthen the Kidneys instead of the Spleen. This reflects a version of the Five Phases that is different from the common one.

19. Quoted in Needham, *Science and Civilization*, vol. 2, pp. 259–260.

20. Ibid., pp. 265–266. Translation altered by author.

21. Nakamura, *Ways of Thinking of Eastern Peoples*, p. 190.

22. To get a sense of the cultural, psychological, scientific, ideological, religious, and intellectual factors that are involved in a correspondence system, it is worth examining the transition from the Aristotelian system of Four Elements to the Paracelsian Three Elements (*tria prima:* salt, sulfur, and mercury) in sixteenth-century Europe. An interesting discussion appears in Allen G. Dobus, "The Medico-Chemical World of the Paracelsians," in *Changing Perspectives in the History of Science*, ed. by Mikuluas Teich and Robert Young (Dordrecht, Holland, and Boston: D. Reidel Pub. Co., 1973), pp. 88–92.

23. Figure 51 is adapted from Elson J. Garner, *History of Biology* (Minneapolis: Burgess Pub. Co., 1960, 1972), p. 31.

24. An example is Denis and Joyce Lawson-Wood, *The Five Elements of Chinese Acupuncture and Massage* (Rustington, England: Health Science Press, 1965). The English overemphasis on the Five Phases is not derived from the Chinese tradition. Instead, the fascination of European acupuncturists with this method is due to the influence of the "Nan Jing traditional acupuncture movement" and to some of the Kei Raku Khi-Riyo (Meridian Treatment) schools, both of which developed around the turn of the twentieth century, in Japan. The European adoption of this method stems partly from a desire for an exotic schema and partly from lack of adequate information.

25. See Needham's discussion of Chinese thought and "law" in *Grand Titration*, pp. 299–330.

26. Qin Bo-wei, Medical Lecture Notes, p. 22.

27. An example is Frank Z. Warren, *Handbook of Medical Acupuncture* (New York: Van Nostrand Reinhold Co., 1976).

APPENDIX I
Historical Bibliography
Links in the Chain of Transmission
The Main Classical Texts of China

A complete list of Chinese medical writings can be found in Catalogue of China's Medical Books, Vols. I and II (*Zhong-guo Yi-xue Shu-mu*), edited by Gang and Hei [Taipei: Wenhai, 1971]. A much shorter version appears in Selected Explanations of Traditional Chinese Medical Terms [33], pp. 480–498. This annotated bibliography is a further condensation. Three versions of the *Nei Jing* are presented first; thereafter the titles are arranged in chronological order, by dynasty. Each entry includes an English translation or rendering of the Chinese title. The kind assistance of Dan Bensky in translating is gratefully acknowledged.

The Nei Jing

Inner Classic of the Yellow Emperor (*Huang-di Nei-jing* 黄 帝 内 经). Includes the Simple Questions (*Su Wen* 素 问) and the Spiritual Axis (*Ling Shu* 灵 枢). The earliest book on Chinese medical theory, known in the tradition, this was probably compiled around 100 B.C.E., but the present version contains material of a much later date (see below). Many sources put the compilation date much earlier, but such dating has more to do with Chinese legend than with history. The *Su Wen* or Simple Questions deals mostly with theoretical concepts and medical cosmology, while the *Ling Shu* or Spiritual Axis is primarily concerned with acupuncture and moxibustion.

Inner Classic of the Yellow Emperor: Great Simplicity (*Huang-di Nei-jing Tai-su* 黄 帝 内 经 太 素), 605–617 C.E., edited by Yang Shang-shan. Of the thirty original chapters, twenty-three are extant. This is the earliest available edition of the *Nei Jing*. It is similar to the *Su Wen* but is without the *Su Wen's* additions.

Revised and Annotated Inner Classic of the Yellow Emperor: Simple Questions (*Chong-guang Bu-zhu Huang-di Nei-jing Su-wen* 重 广 补 注 黄 帝 内 经 素 问), 762 C.E., edited by Wang Bing-ci. This and a further amended edition by the Song-dynasty physician Lin Yi are the standard versions of the work. Wang Bing-ci reorganized the entire work and added at least seven chapters of his own.

Han Dynasty (206 B.C.E.–220 C.E.)

Before the second century C.E. Pharmacopoeia Classic of the Divine Husbandman (*Shen-nong Ben-cao Jing* 神 农 本 草 经). The original is long lost. The present text was compiled at a much later date. Describes 365 medicines and divides them into upper, middle, and lower classes, the highest promoting longevity and the lowest treating disease.

Second century C.E. Classic of Difficulties (*Nan Jing* 难 经). Consists of eighty-one questions and answers dealing with difficult portions of the *Nei Jing*.

c. 220 C.E. Discussion of Cold-induced Disorders (*Shang-han Lun* 伤 寒 论), by Zhang Zhong-jing. Reorganized c. 300 by Wang Shu-he. Ten chapters, primarily concerned with the six stages of disease and diagnostic method in acute febrile diseases. This book is one of the clinical and practical foundations of traditional pharmaceutical medicine.

c. 220 C.E. Essential Prescriptions of the Golden Chest (*Jin-gui Yao-lue Fang Lun* 金 匮 要 略 方 论), by Zhang Zhong-jing. The standard edition was put together in the early Song dynasty by Lin Yi. The subjects include miscellaneous internal diseases, women's disorders, emergencies, and dietary restrictions. This was originally one book, together with Discussion of Cold-induced Disorders.

Jin Dynasty (265–420 C.E.)

280 C.E. Classic of the Pulse (*Mai Jing* 脉 经), by Wang Shu-he. Description of twenty-four pulses and a discussion of their meaning in terms of Organs, Meridians, diseases, management, and prognosis.

282 C.E. Systematic Classic of Acupuncture, sometimes translated as ABC of Acupuncture (*Zhen-jiu Jia-yi Jing* 针 灸 甲 乙 经), by Huang-fu Mi. Discusses physiology, pathology, the Meridians, diagnosis, the points, and acupuncture treatment. It is a systematic presentation of material from the *Ling Shu* and other early, but now lost, texts.

c. 341 C.E. Emergency Prescriptions to Keep Up One's Sleeve (*Zhou-hou Bei-ji Fang* 肘 后 备 急 方), by Ge Hong. Simple prescriptions using easily accessible drugs for emergencies. Extensively revised in later dynasties.

Southern and Northern Dynasties (420–581 C.E.)

c. 495 C.E. Prescriptions Left by the Ghost of Liu Juan-zi (*Liu Juan-zi Gui-yi Fang* 刘 涓 子 鬼 遗 方), Southern Qi dynasty, by Gong Qing-xuan. Earliest extant book on "external diseases." Primarily concerned with trauma, abscesses, rashes, and carbuncles. Includes discussion of antiseptic technique in minor surgery.

c. 536 C.E. Collection on Commentaries on the Pharmacopoeia Classic (*Ben-cao-jing Ji-zhu* 本 草 经 集 注), Liang dynasty, by Tao Hong-jing. The present text is actually a later compilation. The medicines are divided by type (mineral, plant, etc.).

Sui Dynasty (581–618 C.E.)

610 C.E. Discussion on the Origins of Symptoms in Illness (*Zhu-bing Yuan-hou Lun* 诸 病 源 候 论), by Chao Yuan-fang. Detailed descriptions of 1,720 illnesses under sixty-seven headings.

Tang Dynasty (618–907 C.E.)

652 C.E. Thousand Ducat Prescriptions (*Qian-jin Yao-fang* 千 金 要 方), by Sun Si-miao. A compilation of early Tang and previous works. Contents include important information on various specialties, acupuncture and moxibustion, and diet.

659 C.E. Newly Revised Pharmacopoeia (*Xin-xiu Ben-cao* 新 修 本 草), by Li Ji. All that is left of this book are fragments in Tang Shen-wei's Song-dynasty pharmacopoeia. (See Song-dynasty section.) Originally this was the National Pharmacopoeia with 844 entries detailing the type and flavor, area of origin, and use of the medicines. Illustrated.

682 C.E. Supplemental Wings to the Thousand Ducat Prescriptions (*Qian-jin Yi Fang* 千金翼方), by Sun Si-miao. Important additions to the earlier Thousand Ducat Prescriptions, including pharmacology concerns, acupuncture, Cold-induced disorders, gynecology, and pediatrics.

682 C.E. Subtleties of the Silver Sea (*Yin-hai Jing-wei* 银海精微), by Sun Si-miao. Full exploration of various eye disorders and their treatment.

847 C.E. The Treasure Produced with Cessation of Menstruation (*Jing-xiao Chan-bao* 经效产宝), by Zan Yin. Earliest extant book on obstetrics. Divided into three parts: pregnancy, labor and delivery, and postpartum.

Five Dynasties (907–960 C.E.)
752 C.E. Necessities of a Frontier Official (*Wai-tai Bi-yao* 外台秘要), by Wang Tao. An important collection of medical knowledge from this period. Includes more than 6,000 prescriptions.

946 C.E. Secret Methods of Understanding Trauma and Rejoining Fractures (*Li-shang Xu-duan Mi-fang* 理伤续断秘方), by Lin Dao-ren. Earliest extant work on bone setting that deals with the subject both from a diagnostic and treatment perspective in great detail.

Song Dynasty (960–1279 C.E.)
992 C.E. Sagelike Prescriptions from the Taiping Era (*Taiping Sheng-hui Fang* 太平圣惠方), by Wang Huai-yin. A compilation of 16,834 subjects dealing primarily with textual and folk prescriptions to its time.

1026 C.E. The Illustrated Classic of Acupuncture Points as Found on the Bronze Model (*Tong-ren Shu-xue Zhen-jiu Tu Jing* 銅人输穴针灸图经), by Wang Wei-yi. A description of the points listed in anatomical order on the Meridians.

1100 C.E. Discussion of Cold-induced and General Illnesses (*Shang-han Zong-bing Lun* 伤寒总病论), by Pang An-shi. An expansion of the Discussion of Cold-induced Disorders including such topics as summer diseases, epidemic diseases, pediatric and obstetrical Cold-induced diseases, and rashes.

1107 C.E. Book That Revives Those with Cold-induced or Similar Disorders (*Shang-han Lei-zheng Huo-ren Shu* 伤寒类证活人书), by Zhu Hong. Arranged in a question-and-answer format, with 101 questions. Explains the Discussion of Cold-induced Disorders and the meaning of each formula with references and prescriptions from many other important texts.

1108 C.E. Historical and Precise Pharmacopoeial Index Arranged According to Pattern Group (*Jing-shi Zheng-lei Bei-ji Ben-cao* 经史证类备急本草), by Tang Shen-wei. Description of 1,558 medicines including use, Meridian entered, and preparation. Also included are 3,000 prescriptions. The work served as the base for many subsequent texts.

1114 C.E. Formulary of Pediatric Patterns and Medicines (*Xiao-er Yao-zheng Zhi-jue* 小 儿 药 证 直 决), by Qian Yi. Discussion of patterns, case histories, and prescriptions for children.

1117 C.E. General Record of Sagelike Benefit (*Sheng-ji Zong-lü* 圣 济 总 录), compiled by Imperial Medical College. A relatively complete record of contemporary medical knowledge.

1132 C.E. Prescriptions of Universal Benefit from My Own Practice (*Pu-ji Ben-shi Fang* 普 济 本 事 方), by Xu Shu-wei. A description of prescriptions and diagnostics, including those developed by the author.

1150 C.E. New Book for Infants (*You-you Xin-shu* 幼 幼 新 书), by Liu Fang-ming. Includes discussion of etiology and diseases of the newborn.

1151 C.E. Professional and Popular Prescriptions from the Taiping Era (*Taiping Hui-min He-ji Ju-fang* 太 平 惠 民 和 剂 局 方), by Chen Shi-wen. A contemporary formulary, with most prescriptions in powder or pill form.

1174 C.E. Discussion of Illnesses, Patterns, and Prescriptions Related to the Unification of the Three Etiologies (*San-yin Ji-yi Bing Zheng Fang Lun* 三 因 极 一 病 证 方 论), by Chen Yen. An elaboration on the etiology scheme of the Essential Prescriptions of the Golden Chest. Deals with 180 illnesses.

1189 C.E. Formulary of the Pulse (*Mai Jue* 脉 决), by Cui Jia-yen. Description of the pulses based on the classification scheme of the *Nan Jing*. Written in verse form for easy memorization.

1220 C.E. Classic of Nourishing Life with Acupuncture and Moxibustion (*Zhen-jiu Zi-sheng Jing* 针 灸 资 生 经), by Wang Shu-chuan. Has section on the location and use of the points as well as acupuncture treatments for various diseases. Based on earlier works and the author's clinical experience.

1237 C.E. Complete Book of Good Prescriptions for Women (*Fu-ren Da-quan Liang-fang* 妇 人 大 全 良 方), by Chen Zi-ming. Discusses women's health problems under 260 headings. Appendices of prescriptions and case histories.

1241 C.E. Compass for Investigating Diseases (*Cha-bing Zhi-nan* 察 病 指 南), by Shi Fa. Begins with a discussion of twenty-four pulses and their meanings. Also includes a description of the pulses of twenty-one disorders and a list of common obstetrical, gynecological, and pediatric pulses.

1253 C.E. Prescriptions Beneficial to Life (*Ji-sheng Fang* 济 生 方), by Yan Yong-huo. Practical explanations of 400 prescriptions.

Jin Tartar Dynasty (1115–1234 C.E.)

1186 C.E. Collection of Writings on the Mechanisms of Illnesses, Suitability of Qi, and the Safeguarding of Life as Discussed in the *Su Wen* (*Su-wen Bing-ji Qi-*

yi Bao-ming Ji 素 问 病 机 气 宜 保 命 集), by Liu Wan-su. An exposition of many theoretical and practical medical issues.

1188 C.E. Standards of the Mysterious Inner Workings of the Origins of Illness as Discussed in the *Su Wen* (*Su-wen Xuan-ji Yuan-bing Shi* 素 问 玄 机 原 病 式*),* by Liu Wan-su. Discussions of the development of illness from the phase energetics section of the *Su Wen.* The use of cold treatments for Fire patterns is emphasized.

1228 C.E. Confucians' Duties to Their Parents (*Ru-men Shi-qin* 儒 门 事 亲), by Zhang Cong-zheng. Mainly promotes purgative treatment methods.

1231 C.E. Discussion of Dispelling Confusion between External and Internal Injuries (*Nei Wai Shang Bian-huo Lun* 内 外 伤 辨 惑 论), by Li Dong-yuan. A discussion of the differences between Externally and Internally generated disorders.

1249 C.E. Discussion of the Spleen and Stomach (*Pi-wei Lun* 脾 胃 论), by Li Dong-yuan. Based on his clinical experience, this book sets out Li's idea that the Spleen and Stomach are the most important Organs in health and disease. Many clinically useful concepts and prescriptions are included.

Yuan Dynasty (1271–1368 C.E.)

1335 C.E. Essential Meaning of External (Surgical) Diseases (*Wai-ke Jing-yi* 外 科 精 义), by Qi De-zhi. A compendium and commentary of earlier physicians' ideas on diagnosis and treatment of swellings and carbuncles. Includes use of internal prescriptions for a systemic approach.

1341 C.E. Ao's Golden Mirror Reflections of Cold-induced Disorders (*Ao-shi Shang-han Jin-jing Lu* 敖 氏 伤 寒 金 镜 录), by Dr. Ao. The first book devoted entirely to the tongue. An exhaustive description of thirty-six tongue types and their clinical significance. Illustrated.

1341 C.E. Elaboration of the Fourteen Meridians (*Shi-si Jing Fa-hui* 十 四 经 发 挥), by Hua Shou. Includes a discussion of Meridians, Extra Meridians, and special points.

1347 C.E. An Exhaustive Study of Excess (*Ge-zhi Yu Lun* 格 致 余 论), by Zhu Zhen-xiang. An elaboration of the notion that Yang is often in excess and Yin commonly insufficient.

1347 C.E. Secrets of the Cinnabar Creek Master (*Dan-xi Xin-fa* 丹 溪 心 法), by Zhu Zhen-xiang. The 100 topics in this book include Internally and Externally generated diseases, pediatrics, and obstetrics.

1361 C.E. The Meaning of the *Nan Jing* (*Nan-jing Ben-yi* 难 经 本 义), by Hua Shou. A collection of eleven commentaries on the *Nan Jing*, with corrections and emendations.

Ming Dynasty (1368–1644 C.E.)

1406 C.E. Prescriptions of Universal Benefit (*Pu-ji Fang* 普 济 方), by Zhu Xiao, et al. The book with greatest number of prescriptions: 61,739 in all. Also has 239 illustrations.

1505 C.E. Collected Commentaries on the *Nan Jing* (*Nan-jing Ji-zhu* 难 经 集 注). Commentaries by Wang Jiu-si, Yang Xuan-cao, Ding De-yong, Wu Shu, and Yang Kang-hou emphasizing pulse diagnosis, Organ theory, and acupuncture.

1528 C.E. Essentials of the Mouth and Teeth (*Kou-chi Lei-yao* 口 齿 类 要), by Bi Ji. First, a discussion of the mouth and teeth, throat, and tongue; second, a discussion of the treatment of choking, bugs, and miscellaneous topics.

1529 C.E. Gatherings from Eminent Acupuncturists (*Zhen-jiu Ju-ying* 针 灸 聚 英), by Gao Wu. Acupuncture theory and practice along with formularies for beginners. A general work on acupuncture and moxibustion.

1529 C.E. Essentials for Correcting the Body (*Zheng-ti Lei-yao* 正 体 类 要), by Bi Ji. A detailed description of the symptoms, treatment, techniques, prescriptions, and instruments dealing with trauma.

c. 1540 C.E. Profound Pearl of the Red Water (*Chi-shui Xuan-zhu*, 赤 水 玄 珠), by Sun Dong-su. Primarily a discussion of internal medicine.

1549 C.E. Ordered Case Histories of Famous Physicians (*Ming-yi Lei An* 名 医 类 案), by Jiang Quan. A collection of Ming and pre-Ming case histories.

1549 C.E. Elaboration of Pediatrics (*You-ke Fa-hui* 幼 科 发 挥), by Wan Quan. A discussion of fetal, neonatal, and childhood illnesses.

1549 C.E. Secret Methods for Poxes and Rashes (*Dou-zhen Xin-Fa* 痘 疹 心 法), by Wan Quan. Detailed descriptions of poxes and rashes including differential diagnosis of patterns.

1564 C.E. Pulse Studies of the Lakeside Master, also translated as the Pulse Studies of Li Shi-zhen (*Bin-hu Mai-xue* 濒 湖 脉 学), by Li Shi-zhen. A description of twenty-seven pulse types in verse.

1565 C.E. Outline of Medicine (*Yi-xue Gang-mu* 医 学 纲 目), by Lou Ying. A compilation of medical knowledge of the Jin Tartar–Yuan dynasty period.

1578 C.E. The Great Pharmacopoeia (*Ben-cao Gang-mu* 本 草 纲 目), by Li Shi-zhen. The product of thirty years of work, this book describes the nature, flavor, use, region, preparation, shape, methods of cultivating and/or harvesting, and formulae of 1,892 medicines. Over 1,000 pages of illustrations and 1,000 prescriptions.

1601 C.E. Great Compendium of Acupuncture and Moxibustion (*Zhen-jiu Da-cheng* 针 灸 大 成), by Yang Ji-zhou. A synthesis of the knowledge of acupuncture and moxibustion of the Ming and previous dynasties.

1617 C.E. Correct Lineage for External (Surgical) Diseases (*Wai-ke Zheng-zong* 外 科 正 宗), by Chen Shi-gong. A description of the pathology, symptoms, diagnosis, management, and successful and unsuccessful case histories of over 100 patterns. Emphasizes oral treatment along with early surgery.

1624 C.E. Classic of Categories (*Lei Jing* 类 经), by Zhang Jie-bing (Jing-yue). A reordering of the material in the *Nei Jing* by categories, along with commentary.

1624 C.E. Complete Works of Jing-yue (*Jing-yue Quan-shu* 景 岳 全 书), by Zhang Jie-bing. An important systematic presentation of theory, diagnosis, treatment methods, and discussion of various specialities.

1637 C.E. Essential Readings in Medicine (*Yi-zong Bi-du* 医 宗 必 读), by Li Zhong-zi. An introductory work including explanations of the pulses, pharmacopoeia, patterns, and medical theory with case histories.

1642 C.E. Discussion of Warm Epidemics (*Wen-yi Lun* 温 疫 论), by Wu You-xing. A preliminary discussion of Warm Diseases, their mode of infection, their progression in the body, and their differences from Cold-induced disorders.

1642 C.E. Important Knowledge from the *Nei Jing* (*Nei-jing Zhi-yao* 内 经 知 要), by Li Zhong-zi. Material from the *Nei Jing* is divided into eight categories (life style, Yin and Yang, various types of diagnoses, methodology of treatment, Meridians, etc.), and simple explanations are given.

Qing Dynasty (1644–1911 C.E.)

1658. Methods and Rules of Medicine (*Yi-men Fa-lu* 医 门 法 律), by Yu Chang. Presents miscellaneous disorders of the six Pernicious Influences from theoretical and practical perspectives.

1668. Mirror of the Tongue for Cold-induced Disorders (*Shang-han She Jian* 伤 寒 舌 鉴), by Zhang Deng. Discussion of the tongue in Cold-induced disorders, pregnancy, etc. With 120 illustrations.

1687. Medical Connection (*Yi Guan* 医 贯), by Zhao Xian-ke. Expounds the theory of the primary importance of the Kidney Yin and Yang.

1689. Discussion of Women's Disorders (*Nu-ke Jing Lun* 女 科 经 论), by Xiao Xun. A detailed description of women's disorders and their treatment.

1694. Concise Pharmacopoeia (*Ben-cao Bei-yao* 本 草 备 要), by Wang Ang. A clinical description of 460 commonly used medicines.

1723. The Four Examinations Pared Down to Their Essence (*Si-zhen Jue-wei* 四 诊 抉 微), by Lin Zhi-han. A compilation of previous works on examination techniques, with commentary.

1729. Collection of Pearls on Cold-induced Disorders (*Shang-han Guan-zhu Ji* 伤 寒 贯 珠 集), by You Yi. A reorganization by treatment method of Discussion of Cold-induced Disorders.

1742. Golden Mirror of Medicine (*Yi-zong Jin-jian* 医 宗 金 鉴), edited by Wu Qian. A complete compilation of all aspects of Chinese medicine, including the major classics. Written in easily understandable form.

1746. Case Histories That Act as Clinical Compasses (*Ling-zheng Zhi-nan Yi-an* 临 证 指 南 医 案), by Ye Tian-shi. Compilations and commentaries of the case histories of Ye Tian-shi.

c. 1746. Discussion of Warm Diseases (*Wen-re Lun* 温 热 论), by Ye Tian-shi. A discussion of the four stages of acute febrile diseases (*wei, qi, ying, xue*) by their developer.

1798. Refined Diagnosis of Warm Diseases (*Wen-bing Tiao-bian* 温 病 条 辨), by Wu Ju-tong. An expansion of the work of Ye Tian-shi, dividing disease into Upper, Middle, and Lower Burners. Description of patterns such as Wind Fever, Fever Poison, Summer Fever, and Damp Fever.

1801. Field of Epidemic Raspy Throat Rash (*Yi-sha-cao* 疫 痧 草), by Chen Geng-dao. Devoted exclusively to Epidemic Raspy Throat Rash (analogue of scarlet fever).

1839. Ordering of Patterns and Deciding Treatments (*Lei-zheng Zhi-cai* 类 证 治 裁), by Lin Pei-qin. A collection and systematic analysis of earlier concepts of pattern discernment and treatment methods.

1846. New Compilation of Tested Prescriptions (*Yan-fang Xin-bian* 验 方 新 编), by Bao Yun-shao. A selection of simple prescriptions, arranged according to subject.

1885. Discussion of Blood Patterns (*Xue-zheng Lun* 血 证 论), by Tang Zong-hai. Describes the relationship between Qi and Blood as well as the mechanism and treatment of Blood disorders.

1897. Refined Diagnoses of White Throat (*Bai-hou Tiao-bian* 白 喉 条 辨), by Chen Bao-shan. Discusses the etiology, diagnosis by Meridian and pulse, prognosis, treatment, and prohibition for white throat (analogue of diphtheria).

Selected Bibliography

Chinese Sources

As remarked in the Author's Note, this Chinese-language bibliography is divided into eight sections to indicate subject matter or type of publication. In most of the sections, book entries are arranged alphabetically by author or editor. English translations, or renderings, of the titles are given first, followed by the romanization and the Chinese characters. The numbered book entries are keyed to citations in the notes.

Nei Jing and Nan Jing and Commentaries

1. Inner Classic of the Yellow Emperor: Simple Questions (*Huang-di Nei-jing Su-wen* 黄帝内经素问). Beijing (Peking): People's Press, 1963. Cited as *Nei Jing* or *Su Wen*. This edition is the same as the revised and annotated one listed in Appendix I.

2. Classic of the Spiritual Axis with Vernacular Explanation (*Ling-shu-jing Bai-hua-jie* 灵枢经白话解). Edited by Chen Bi-liu and Cheng Zhou-ren. Beijing: People's Hygiene Press, 1963. Cited as *Nei Jing* or *Ling Shu* (it is the second part of the *Nei Jing*).

3. Classic of Difficulties with Annotations (*Nan-jing Jiao-shi* 难经校释). Edited by Nanjing Institute of Traditional Chinese Medicine. Beijing: People's Press, 1979. First appeared c. 200 C.E. Cited as *Nan Jing*.

4. Beijing Institute of Traditional Chinese Medicine, main ed. Explanations of the *Nei Jing* (*Nei-jing Shi-yi* 内经释义). Shanghai: Science and Technology Press, 1964.

5. Chen Bi-liu, ed. Classic of Difficulties with Explanation in Vernacular Language (*Nan-jing Bai-hua-jie* 难经白话解). Beijing: People's Health Press, 1963. First appeared c. 200 C.E.

6. Gao Shi-zong. Genuine Explanation of the Yellow Emperor: Simple Questions (*Huang-di Su-wen Zhen-jie* 黄帝素问真解). Beijing: Science and Technology Press, 1980. First appeared 1887 C.E.

7. Liu Wan-su. Standards of the Mysterious Inner Workings of the Origin of Illness as Discussed in the *Su Wen* (*Su-wen Xuan-ji Yuan-bing Shi* 素问玄机原病式). Beijing: People's Press, 1963. First appeared 1188 C.E.

8. Wang Jiu-si et al. Collected Commentaries on the *Nan Jing* (*Nan-jing Ji-*

zhu 难 经 集 注). Shanghai: Shanghai Commercial Press, 1955. First appeared 1505 C.E.

9. Yan Hong-chen and Gao Guang-zhen. Selections from the *Nei Jing* and *Nan Jing* with Elucidations (*Nei-nan-jing Xuan-shi* 内 难 经 选 释). Jilin (Kirin): People's Press, 1979.

10. Zhang Jie-bing. Classic of Categories (*Lei Jing* 类 经). Beijing: People's Health Press, 1957. First appeared 1624 C.E.

Other Classical Sources

11. Beijing Institute of Traditional Chinese Medicine, ed. Selected Readings in the Original Sources of Traditional Chinese Medicine (*Zhong-yi Yuanzhu Xuan-du* 中 医 原 著 选 读). Beijing: People's Press, 1978.

12. Beijing, Nanjing, Shanghai, Guangzhou (Canton), and Chengdu Institutes of Traditional Chinese Medicine, eds. Lecture Notes on Selected Ideas and Case Histories of Famous Physicians of the Song, Yuan, Ming, and Qing Dynasties (*Zhong-yi Ming-jia Xue-shuo Ji Yi-an Xuan Jiang-yi: Song, Yuan, Ming, Qing* 中 医 名 家 学 说 及 医 案 选 讲 义: 宋, 元, 明, 清). Beijing: People's Press, 1961.

13. Chao Yuan-fang. Discussion on the Origins of Symptoms in Illness (*Zhu-bing Yuan-hou Lun* 诸 病 源 候 论). Beijing: People's Health Press, 1955. First appeared 610 C.E.

14. Hua Shou. Elaboration of the Fourteen Meridians (*Shi-si Jing Fa-hui* 十 四 经 发 挥). Taipei: Whirlwind Press, 1980. First appeared 1341 C.E.

15. Huang-fu Mi. Systematic Classic of Acupuncture with Annotations (*Zhen-jiu Jia-yi Jing Jiao-shi* 针 灸 甲 乙 经 校 释). Annotations by Shandong Institute of Traditional Chinese Medicine. Beijing: People's Press, 1979. First appeared c. 282 C.E.

16. Li Shi-zhen. Pulse Studies of the Lakeside Master with Vernacular Explanation (*Bin-hu Mai-xue Bai-hua-jie* 濒 湖 脉 学 白 话 解). Edited and with commentary by Beijing Institute of Traditional Chinese Medicine, Fundamental Theory and Teaching Research Section. Beijing: People's Press, 1972. Text first appeared 1564 C.E. Cited as Pulse Studies.

17. Shanghai City Traditional Chinese Medical Archives Research Committee. Selections from Pulse Examination (*Mai-Zhen Xuan-yao* 脉 诊 选 要). Hong Kong: Commercial Press, 1970.

18. Sun Si-miao. Subtleties of the Silver Sea (*Yin-hai Jing-wei* 银 海 精 微). Beijing: People's Health Press, 1956. First appeared 682 C.E.

19. Sun Si-miao. Thousand Ducat Prescriptions (*Qian-jin Yao-fang* 千 金 要 方). Taipei: National Traditional Chinese Medical Research Bureau, 1965. First appeared 652 C.E.

20. Tang Zong-hai. Discussion of Blood Patterns (*Xue-zheng Lun* 血 证 论). Shanghai: People's Press, 1977. First appeared 1885 C.E.

21. Wang Shu-chuan. Classic of Nourishing Life with Acupuncture and Moxibustion (*Zhen-jiu Zi-sheng Jing* 针 灸 資 生 经). Taipei: Whirlwind Press, 1980. First appeared 1220 C.E.

22. Wang Shu-he. Classic of the Pulse (*Mai Jing* 脉 经). Hong Kong: Taiping Book Publishers, 1961. First appeared c. 280 C.E.

23. Wu Ju-tong. Refined Diagnoses of Warm Diseases with Vernacular Explanation (*Wen-bing Tiao-bian Bai-hua-jie* 温 病 條 辨 白 话 解). Commentary by Zhejiang Institute of Traditional Chinese Medicine. Beijing: People's Health Press, 1963. Text first appeared 1798 C.E.

24. Wu Qian, main ed. Golden Mirror of Medicine (*Yi-zong Jin-jian* 医 宗 金 鉴). 3 vols. Beijing: People's Health Press, 1972. First appeared 1742 C.E.

25. Wu You-xing. Discussion of Warm Epidemics with Notes and Commentary (*Wen-yi Lun Ping-zhu* 温 疫 论 评 注). Commentary by Zhejiang Province Traditional Medical Research Bureau. Beijing: People's Press, 1977. Text first appeared 1642 C.E.

26. Yang Ji-zhou. Great Compendium of Acupuncture and Moxibustion (*Zhen-jiu Da-cheng* 针 灸 大 成). Beijing: People's Press, 1973. First appeared 1601 C.E.

27. Zhang Zhong-jing. Discussion on Cold-induced Disorders with Clarifications (*Shang-han Lun Yu-yi* 伤 寒 论 语 译). Edited by Traditional Chinese Medical Research Institute. Beijing: People's Health Press, 1959, 1974. Text first appeared c. 220 C.E. Cited as Discussion.

28. Zhang Zhong-jing. Discussion on Cold-induced Disorders with New Commentary (*Shang-han Lun Xin-zhu* 伤 寒 论 新 注). Commentary by Cheng Tan-an. Hong Kong: Shaohua Cultural Service Society, 1955. Main text first appeared c. 220 C.E.

29. Zhang Zhong-jing. Essential Prescriptions of the Golden Chest with Simple Commentary (*Jin-gui Yao-lue Qian-zhu* 金 匱 要 略 浅 注). Hong Kong: Taiping Book Publishers, 1970. Commentary by Chen Xiu-yuan first appeared c. 1800 C.E. Text first appeared c. 200 C.E.

30. Zhang Jie-bing. Illustrated Wing to the Classic of Categories (*Lei-jing Tu-yi* 类 经 图 翼). Beijing: People's Health Press, 1965. First published 1624 C.E.

Reference Books

31. Gansu Hygiene School. Explanation of Common Traditional Chinese Medical Terms (*Zhong-yi-xue Chang-yong Ming-ci Jie-shi* 中 医 学 常 用 名 词 解 释). Gansu: People's Press, 1975.

32. Jiangsu New Medical Institute. Encyclopedia of the Traditional Chinese Pharmacopoeia (*Zhong-yao Da-ci-dian* 中 药 大 辞 典). Shanghai: People's Press, 1977.

33. Traditional Chinese Medical Research Institute and Guangdong Institute of Traditional Chinese Medicine, eds. Selected Explanations of Traditional Chinese Medical Terms (*Zhong-yi Ming-ci Shu-yu Xuan-shi* 中 医 名 词 术 语 选 释). Beijing: People's Press, 1973.

34. Traditional Chinese Medical Research Institute and Guangzhou (Canton) Institute of Traditional Chinese Medicine, main eds. Shanghai, Liaoning, Chengdu, Anhui, Hebei, Nanjing, Hunan, and Shanxi Institutes of Traditional Chinese Medicine, contributing eds. Concise Dictionary of Traditional Chinese Medicine (*Jian-ming Zhong-yi Ci-dian* 简 明 中 医 辞 典). Hong Kong: Joint Publishing Company, 1979.

35. Wu Ke-qian. Dictionary of Sources of Illness (*Bing-yuan Ci-dian* 病 源 辞 典). Hong Kong: Shiyong Publishers, 1965.

36. Xie Li-hang, ed. Traditional Chinese Medical Encyclopedia (*Zhong-guo Yi-xue Da-ci-dian* 中 国 医 学 大 辞 典), 4 vols. Hong Kong: Commercial Press, 1974. First published 1921.

Contemporary Introductory Texts Used to Train Traditional Physicians

37. Beijing Institute of Traditional Chinese Medicine. Foundations of Clinical Patterns in Traditional Chinese Medicine (*Zhong-yi Ling-zheng Ji-chu* 中 医 临 证 基 础). Beijing: People's Press, 1975.

38. Beijing Institute of Traditional Chinese Medicine, main ed. Foundations of Traditional Chinese Medicine (*Zhong-yi-xue Ji-chu* 中 医 学 基 础). Shanghai: Science and Technology Press, 1978.

39. Beijing Traditional Chinese Medical Hospital Revolutionary Committee. Essentials of Distinguishing Patterns and Dispensing Treatment (*Bian-zhen Shi-zhi Gang-yao* 辨 证 施 治 纲 要). Beijing: People's Press, 1974.

40. Chengdu Institute of Traditional Chinese Medicine. Internal Medicine and Pediatrics (*Nei-er-ke-xue* 内 儿 科 学). Sichuan (Szechuan): People's Press, 1975.

41. Chengdu Institute of Traditional Chinese Medicine. Practical Traditional Chinese Medicine (*Shi-yong Zhong-yi-xue* 实 用 中 医 学). Sichuan: People's Press, 1977.

42. Guangdong Institute of Traditional Chinese Medicine. Clinical Traditional Chinese Medicine: New Edition (*Zhong-yi Ling-chuang Xin-bian* 中 医 临 床 新 编). Guangdong: People's Press, 1972.

43. Guangdong Institute of Traditional Chinese Medicine. Lecture Notes on Traditional Chinese Medical Diagnosis (*Zhong-yi Zhen-duan-xue Jiang-yi* 中 医 诊 断 学 讲 义). Shanghai: Science and Technology Press, 1964.

44. Guangdong Institute of Traditional Chinese Medicine. Traditional Chinese Internal Medicine (*Zhong-yi Nei-ke* 中 医 内 科). Beijing: People's Press, 1976.

45. Hubei Institute of Traditional Chinese Medicine, main ed. Introduction to Traditional Chinese Medicine (*Zhong-yi-xue Gai-lun* 中 医 学 概 论). Shanghai: Science and Technology Press, 1978.

46. Jiangsu Institute of New Medicine. Traditional Chinese Medicine (*Zhong-yi-xue* 中 医 学). Jiangsu: People's Press, 1972.

47. Jiangsu Institute of New Medicine. Traditional Chinese Medicine Clinical Handbook of Common Illnesses (*Chang-jian Bing Zhong-yi Ling-chuang Shou-ce* 常 见 病 中 医 临 床 手 册). Beijing: People's Press, 1972.

48. Liaoning Institute of Traditional Chinese Medicine. Lecture Notes on Traditional Chinese Medicine (*Zhong-yi-xue Jiang-yi* 中 医 学 讲 义). Liaoning: People's Press, 1972.

49. Nanjing Institute of Traditional Chinese Medicine. Concise Traditional Chinese Internal Medicine (*Jian-ming Zhong-yi Nei-ke-xue* 简 明 中 医 内 科 学). Shanghai: Science and Technology Press, 1959.

50. Nanjing Institute of Traditional Chinese Medicine. Introduction to Traditional Chinese Medicine (*Zhong-yi-xue Gai-lun* 中 医 学 概 论). Beijing: People's Health Press, 1959.

51. Nanjing Institute of Traditional Chinese Medicine. Traditional Chinese Medical Ancillary Care (*Zhong-yi Hu-bing-xue* 中 医 护 病 学). Hong Kong: Shaohua Cultural Service Society, 1959.

52. Shanghai Institute of Traditional Chinese Medicine. Distinguishing Patterns and Dispensing Treatments (*Bian-zheng Shi-zhi* 辨 证 施 治). Shanghai: People's Press, 1972.

53. Shanghai Institute of Traditional Chinese Medicine. Foundations of Traditional Chinese Medicine (*Zhong-yi-xue Ji-chu* 中 医 学 基 础). Hong Kong: Commercial Press, 1975.

54. Shanghai Institute of Traditional Chinese Medicine. Lecture Notes on Traditional Chinese Internal Medicine (*Zhong-yi Nei-ke-xue Jiang-yi* 中 医 内 科 学 讲 义). Shanghai: Science and Technology Press, 1964.

55. Tianjin City Traditional Chinese Medical Hospital. Traditional Chinese Internal Medicine (*Zhong-yi Nei-ke* 中 医 内 科). Tianjin: People's Press, 1974.

56. Tianjin Institute of Traditional Chinese Medicine. Practical Clinical Handbook of Traditional Chinese Medicine (*Zhong-yi Shi-yong Ling-chuang Shou-ce* 中 医 实 用 临 床 手 册). Hong Kong: Commercial Press, 1970.

57. Wuhan People's Liberation Army Health Committee. Concise Traditional Chinese Medicine (*Jian-ming Zhong-yi-xue* 简 明 中 医 学). Hubei: People's Press, 1972.

Contemporary Writings
58. Chen Yu-ming. Essentials of Pathology, Diagnosis, and Treatment (*Bing-li Yu Zhen-duan Zhi-liao Gang-yao* 病 理 与 诊 断 治 疗 纲 要). Ningxi: People's Press, 1973.

59. Fang Yao-zhong. Seven Lectures on the Study of Distinguishing Patterns and Treatments (*Bian-zheng Lun-zhi Yan-jiu Qi-jiang* 辨 证 论 治 研 究 七 讲). Beijing: People's Press, 1979.

60. Li Tiao-hua. Patterns and Treatment of the Kidneys and Kidney Illnesses (*Shen Yu Shen-bing De Zheng-zhi* 肾 与 肾 病 的 证 治). Hebei: People's Press, 1979.

61. Liu Guan-jun. Pulse Examination (*Mai-zhen* 脉 诊). Shanghai: Science and Technology Press, 1979.

62. Ma Ruo-shui. Theoretical Foundations of Traditional Chinese Medicine (*Zhong-yi Ji-chu Li-lun Zhi-shi* 中 医 基 础 理 论 知 识). Guiyang: Guizhou People's Press, 1977.

63. Qin Bo-wei. Elementary Traditional Chinese Medicine (*Zhong-yi Ru-men* 中 医 入 门). Hong Kong: Taiping Book Publishers, 1971.

64. Qin Bo-wei. Medical Lecture Notes of Qian Zhai (*Qian Zhai Yi-xue Jianggao* 谦 斋 医 学 讲 稿). Shanghai: Science and Technology Press, 1964.

65. Qin Bo-wei et al. Traditional Chinese Medical References for Clinical Patterns (*Zhong-yi Ling-chuang Bei-yao* 中 医 临 证 备 要). Beijing: People's Press, 1973.

66. Ren Ying-qiu. Ten Lectures on the Study of Pulses in Traditional Chinese Medicine (*Zhong-yi Mai-xue Shi-jiang* 中 医 脉 学 十 讲). Hong Kong: Taiping Book Publishers, 1971.

67. Zhai Ming-yi. Clinical Foundations of Traditional Chinese Medicine (*Zhong-yi Ling-chuang Ji-chu* 中 医 临 床 基 础). Anyang: Henan People's Press, 1978.

Miscellaneous Sources
68. Anhui Institute of Traditional Chinese Medicine. Clinical Handbook of Traditional Chinese Medicine (*Zhong-yi Ling-chuang Shou-ce* 中 医 临 床 手 册). Anhui: People's Press, 1965.

69. Beijing Institute of Traditional Chinese Medicine, Diagnosis Research and Teaching Section. Traditional Chinese Tongue Examination (*Zhong-yi*

She-zhen 中 医 舌 诊). Hong Kong: Commercial Press, 1970, 1973. This text and the one following seem to be modified editions.

70. Beijing Institute of Traditional Chinese Medicine, Fundamental Theory and Teaching Research Section. Traditional Chinese Tongue Examination (*Zhong-yi She-zhen* 中 医 舌 诊). Beijing: People's Press, 1960, 1980.

71. Chen Xin-qian, main ed. Pharmacology: New Edition (*Xin-bian Yao-wu-xue* 新 编 药 物 学). Beijing: People's Health Press, 1951, 1974.

72. Eleventh People's Hospital of the Shanghai Institute of Traditional Chinese Medicine, Research Committee on Hypertension. Theory and Treatment of Hypertension by Traditional Chinese Medicine (*Gao-xue-ya-bing De Zhong-yi-li-lun He Zhi-liao* 高 血 压 病 的 中 医 理 论 和 治 疗). Hong Kong: Shiyong Publishers, 1971.

73. Guanganmen Hospital of the Traditional Chinese Medicine Research Institute. Collected Clinical Experiences of Zhu Ren-kang: Dermatology (*Zhu Ren-kang Ling-chuang Jing-yan-ji Pi-fu Wai-ke* 朱 仁 康 临 床 经 验 集 皮 肤 外 科). Beijing: People's Press, 1979.

74. Guangdong Provincial Traditional Chinese Medicine Hospital, Department of Ophthalmology. Traditional Chinese Ophthalmology (*Zhong-yi Yan-ke* 中 医 眼 科). Beijing: People's Press, 1975.

75. Guangzhou (Canton) Ministry of Health, Logistic Headquarters, Guangdong Dept. of Health, Hunan Province Dept. of Health, Guangxi Zhuang Autonomous Region Department of Health. Introduction to Traditional Chinese Medicine: New Edition (*Xin-bian Zhong-yi-xue Gai-yao* 新 编 中 医 学 概 要). Beijing: People's Press, 1974. Material for Western doctors to learn traditional Chinese medicine.

76. Hao Jin-kai, ed. Illustrative Charts of Extra Meridian Acupuncture Points (*Zhen-jiu Jing-wai-qi-xue Tu-pu* 针 灸 经 外 奇 穴 图 谱), 2 vols. Shanxi: People's Press, 1974.

77. Huzhou Institute of Traditional Chinese Medicine. Traditional Chinese Gynecology (*Zhong-yi Fu-ke* 中 医 妇 科). Beijing: People's Press, 1978.

78. Jinan City Health Dept. Revolutionary Committee, compilers and annotators. Clinical Cases of Wu Shao-huai (*Wu Shao-huai Yi-an* 吴 少 怀 医 案). Shandong: People's Press, 1978.

79. Luoyang Regional Revolutionary Health Commission, main ed. Internal Medicine: New Edition (*Xin-bian Nei-ke* 新 编 内 科). Vols. 1 and 2. Henan: People's Press, 1978.

80. Nanjing Institute of Traditional Chinese Medicine. Lecture Notes on Warm Illnesses (*Wen-bing-xue Jiang-yi* 温 病 学 讲 义). Shanghai: Science and Technology Press, 1964.

81. Nanjing Institute of Traditional Chinese Medicine. Study of Warm Illnesses (*Wen-bing-xue* 温 病 学). Shanghai: Science and Technology Press, 1978.

82. Shanghai First Medical Hospital. Clinical Handbook of Antimicrobial Medicines (*Ling-chuang Kang-jun Yao-wu Shou-ce* 临 床 抗 菌 药 物 手 册). Shanghai: People's Press, 1977.

83. Shanghai First Medical Hospital. Practical Internal Medicine (*Shi-yong Nei-ke-xue* 实 用 内 科 学). Beijing: People's Press, 1974.

84. Shanghai First Medical Hospital, Organ Research Committee. Studies on the Kidneys (*Shen De Yan-jiu* 肾 的 研 究). Hong Kong: Zhonghua Publishers, 1970.

85. Shanghai Institute of Traditional Chinese Medicine. Acupuncture (*Zhen-jiu Xue* 针 灸 学). Beijing: People's Health Press, 1974.

86. Shanghai Institute of Traditional Chinese Medicine. Study of Acupuncture Points (*Zhen-jiu Shu-xue Xue* 针 灸 腧 穴 学). Hong Kong: Shaohua Cultural Service Society, 1964.

87. Shanghai Institute of Traditional Chinese Medicine. Study of Prescriptions (*Fang-ji-xue* 方 剂 学). Hong Kong: Commercial Press, 1975.

88. Shanghai Second Medical Hospital. Handbook of Internal Medicine (*Nei-ke Shou-ce* 内 科 手 册). Beijing: People's Press, 1974.

89. Zhang Yao-qing and Chen Dao-long. Records of Clinical Patterns in Internal Medicine (*Nei-ke Ling-zheng Lü* 内 科 临 证 录). Shanghai: Science and Technology Press, Shanghai, 1978.

90. Zhejiang Provincial Committee for Trial Material for Western-style Doctors Learning Traditional Chinese Medicine. Clinical Studies of Traditional Chinese Medicine (*Zhong-yi Ling-chuang-xue* 中 医 临 床 学). Zhejiang: People's Press, 1978. Cited as Clinical Studies.

91. Zhejiang Provincial Committee for Trial Material for Western-style Doctors Learning Traditional Chinese Medicine. Foundations of Traditional Chinese Medicine (*Zhong-yi Ji-chu-xue* 中 医 基 础 学). Zhejiang: People's Press, 1972. Cited as Foundations.

92. Zhongshan Institute of Medicine. Clinical Use of Chinese Medicines (*Zhong-yao Ling-chuang Ying-yong* 中 药 临 床 应 用). Guangdong: People's Press, 1975.

Sources on the History of Chinese Medicine

93. Beijing Institute of Traditional Chinese Medicine. Lecture Notes on the History of China's Medicine (*Zhong-guo Yi-xue Shi Jiang-yi* 中 国 医 学 史 讲 义). Shanghai: Science and Technology Press, 1964.

94. Chen Bang-xian. History of China's Medicine (*Zhong-guo Yi-xue Shi* 中 国 医 学 史). Shanghai: Shanghai Commercial Press, 1957, 1937.

95. Jia De-dao. Concise History of China's Medicine (*Zhong-guo Yi-xue Shi-lüe* 中 国 医 学 史 略). Taiyuan: Shanxi People's Press, 1979.

Journals

Beijing Traditional Chinese Medicine (*Beijing Zhong-yi* 北 京 中 医).

Chinese Journal of Internal Medicine (*Zhong-hua Nei-ke Za-zhi* 中 华 内 科 杂 志). Cited as CJIM.

Fujian Traditional Chinese Medicine (*Fujian Zhong-yi-yao* 福 建 中 医 药).

Guangdong Traditional Chinese Medicine (*Guangdong Zhong-yi* 广 东 中 医).

Heilongjiang Traditional Chinese Medicine (*Heilongjiang Zhong-yi-yao* 黑 龙 江 中 医 药).

Harbin Traditional Chinese Medicine (*Ha-er-bin Zhong-yi* 哈 尔 滨 中 医).

Jiangsu Traditional Chinese Medicine (*Jiangsu Zhong-yi* 江 苏 中 医).

Journal of Traditional Chinese Medicine (*Zhong-yi Za-zhi* 中 医 杂 志). Cited as JTCM.

New Traditional Chinese Medicine (*Xin Zhong-yi* 新 中 医).

Shanghai Journal of Traditional Chinese Medicine (*Shanghai Zhong-yi-yao Za-zhi* 上 海 中 医 药 杂 志). Cited as SJTCM.

Wen Wu (Cultural Objects; 文 物). Beijing.

Zhejiang Journal of Traditional Chinese Medicine (*Zhejiang Zhong-yi Za-zhi* 浙 江 中 医 杂 志).

English-Language Sources

Chan, Wing-tsit, trans. and comp. *A Source Book in Chinese Philosophy*. Princeton, N.J.: Princeton University Press, Princeton Paperbacks, 1963. Cited as *Chinese Philosophy*.

Coulter, Harris L. *Divided Legacy: A History of the Schism in Medical Thought*, 3 vols. Washington, D.C.: Wehawken Book Co., 1975.

Dash, Vd. Bhagwan. *Ayurvedic Treatment for Common Diseases*. Delhi: Delhi Diary, 1979.

Department of Philosophy of Medicine and Science, comp. *Theories and Philosophies of Medicine*. New Delhi: Institute of History of Medicine and Medical Research, 1973.

Dwarkanath, C. *Introduction to Kayachikistsa*. Bombay: Popular Book Depot, 1959.

Fung, Yu-lan. *A History of Chinese Philosophy*. 2 vols. Translated by Derk Bodde. Princeton, N.J.: Princeton University Press, 1953, 1973.

Gruner, O. Cameron, ed. and trans. *The Canon of Medicine of Avicenna*. London: Luzac, 1930.

Huard, Pierre, and Wong, Ming. *Chinese Medicine*. New York, Toronto: World University Library, McGraw-Hill, 1968.

Jones, W. H. S., ed. and trans. *Hippocrates with an English Translation*. Vols. 1–4. Cambridge: Harvard University Press, 1931, 1952. Vol. 4 includes translations from *Heraceitis*. Cited as *Hippocrates*.

Kleinman, Arthur, et al., eds. *Medicine in Chinese Cultures: Comparative Studies of Health Care in Chinese and Other Societies*. Washington, D.C.: John E. Fogarty International Center, U.S. Dept. of HEW, NIH, 1975.

Leibowitz, J.O., and Shlomo Marcus, eds. *Moses Maimonides on the Causes of Symptoms*. Berkeley, Calif.: University of California Press, 1974.

Leslie, Charles, ed. *Asian Medical Systems*. Berkeley, Calif.: University of California Press, 1976.

May, Margaret Tallmadge, trans. *Galen on Usefulness of the Parts of the Body*. Ithaca, N.Y.: Cornell University Press, 1968.

McKeon, Richard, ed. *The Basic Works of Aristotle*. New York: Random House, 1941.

Nakamura, Hajime. *Ways of Thinking of Eastern Peoples*. Edited by Philip P. Wiener. Honolulu: University Press of Hawaii, 1964, 1978.

Needham, Joseph. *The Grand Titration: Science and Society in East and West*. London: George Allen & Unwin, 1969.

Needham, Joseph. *Science and Civilization in China*. Vol. 2. Cambridge: At the University Press, 1956.

Porkert, Manfred. *The Theoretical Foundations of Chinese Medicine*. M.I.T. East Asian Science Series, Vol. 3. Cambridge, Mass.: M.I.T. Press, 1974.

Quinn, Joseph R., ed. *Medicine and Public Health in the People's Republic of China*. Washington, D.C.: John E. Fogarty International Center, U.S. Dept. of HEW, NIH, 1973.

Rosner, F., and S. Muntner, eds. and trans. *The Medical Aphorisms of Moses Maimonides*, 2 vols. New York: Bloch Publishing, 1971.

SELECTED BIBLIOGRAPHY

Sigerist, Henry E. *A History of Medicine*, 2 vols. New York: Oxford University Press, 1951, 1961.

Temkin, Owsei, and C. Lilian Temkin, eds. *Ancient Medicine: Selected Papers of Ludwig Edelstein*. Translation by C. Lilian Temkin. Baltimore, Md.: Johns Hopkins Press, 1967.

Temkin, Owsei. *Galenism: Rise and Decline of a Medical Philosophy*. Ithaca, N.Y.: Cornell University Press, 1973.

INDEX

An italic *n* indicates a note number
(e.g., 31*n*32 refers to page 31, note 32).

relationship concept *(continued)*
  patterns vs. causation in, 15,
    141–142
  Yin-Yang five principles of, 8–12
research:
  assessment of traditional medicine
    in, 19–23, 28n20, 110–111n10,
    111–112n11, 112–113n12,
    113–114n15, 136n7, 136–137n11
  on correspondences between
    Chinese patterns and Western
    diseases, 321
respiration, in Listening
  Examination, 152
retinitis, 232
roots, outward manifestations vs., in
  treatment, 254–255n3

scarlet, in tongue examination, 148
scarlet fever, patterns corresponding
  to (table), 334
science, Western, 261–265
  causality in, *see* cause-and-effect
    concept
  dynamic revelation as basis of,
    263–265
  medical practices vs., 261
  philosophical roots of, 263–265
Science and Civilization in China
  (Needham), 27n18, 49n17,
  354n1
scrofula, 227
seasons, Pernicious Influences
  associated with, 119–120, 121,
  123, 124, 127
secretions, in Looking Examination,
  144, 151
sensations of cold or hot, in Asking
  Examination, 152, 153
sexual activity, excessive, as
  precipitating illness, 132–133
sexual dysfunction, 235
Shen, 45–46
  characteristics of, 45, 46
  disharmonies of, 46, 145–146, 202
  functions of, 45, 54
  Heat Pernicious Influence and,
    123

Shen *(continued)*
  hun aspect of, 49n17
  po aspect of, 49n17
  source of, 45
  as "Spirit," 45
  Taoist tradition and, 49n17
  as Yang Substance, 46
Shi Ji, 175n11
Sigerist, Henry E., 108–109n3
signs, 18
  art of interpretation of, 245–247,
    249–250
  in chief complaints (tables),
    279–299
  complaint vs., 143
  in Eight Principal Patterns,
    178–195
  in febrile diseases, 270–271
  in Four Examinations, 138–174
  other specific patterns related to,
    201–241
  relationships among, in complex
    patterns, 143, 229–231,
    249–250
  Western diseases correlated with,
    208–238, 278, 321–335
  see also diagnosis; patterns of
    disharmony
Six Pernicious Influences (six Evils),
  118–129
  climatic phenomena (six Evils) as,
    118–128
  clinical sketches relating to, 121,
    122, 124, 126
  see also Cold Pernicious Influence;
    Dampness Pernicious Influence;
    Dryness Pernicious Influence;
    Fire Pernicious Influence;
    Pernicious Influences; Summer
    Heat Pernicious Influence;
    Wind Pernicious Influence
Six Stages Pattern, in febrile
  diseases, 269–271
skin:
  in Looking Examination, 342
  Lungs and, 56
sleep, in Asking Examination, 152,
  157